THE POLITICAL ECON
OF INTEGRATION
IN THE EUROPEAN C

C000018552

To Nancy and Graeme, the new Europeans

The Political Economy of Integration in the European Community

Jeffrey Harrop

Second Edition

Edward Elgar

© Jeffrey Harrop, 1989, 1992

All rights reserved. No part of this publication may be reproduced, stored in a retrieval system, or transmitted in any form or by any means, electronic, mechanical, photocopying, recording, or otherwise without the prior permission of the publisher.

Published by
Edward Elgar Publishing Limited
Gower House
Croft Road
Aldershot
Hants. GU11 3HR
England

Edward Elgar Publishing Company
Old Post Road
Brookfield
Vermont 05036
USA

First published 1989
Paperback edition 1990
Reprinted 1991
Second edition 1992
Reprinted 1993

A CIP catalogue record for this book is available from the British Library.

Library of Congress Cataloging-in-Publication Data
Harrop, Jeffrey.
    The political economy of integration in the European Community/
Jeffrey Harrop. – 2nd ed.
        p.   cm.
    Includes bibliographical references and index.
    1. European Economic Community. 2. Europe–Economic
    integration.
    I. Title.
    HC241.2.H3935   1992
    337.1'42–dc20   91–28216
                                              CIP

ISBN   1 85278 590 X 2nd edition
        1 85278 589 6 2nd paperback edition
        (1 85278 008 8 1st edition)
        (1 85278 188 2 1st paperback edition)

Printed and bound in Great Britain by Athenaeum Press Ltd, Newcastle upon Tyne

Contents

v

Figures

Tables

Preface to the first edition

I have been fortunate over the years in visiting European institutions and have benefited from discussions at the European Community in Brussels with members of the Commission, the Council and the Economic and Social Committee; and also at the Parliament in Brussels, Luxembourg and Strasbourg. Other visits to the Council of Europe in Strasbourg and to NATO in Brussels have increased my awareness of the role of these other organizations.

I am grateful to many colleagues who have stimulated my interest in the European Community. These include Bill Robertson in my early days at the University of Liverpool; Professor Stuart Wilson at the University of Hull who was quick to recognize the need for a course on the European economy to complement – and eventually to replace – more established courses on the Commonwealth; Professor Stephen Holt, now at the University of Kent, who led me to specialize even more deeply in the field of European integration. His enthusiasm for the subject proved infectious, and his successor at the University of Bradford, Professor Kenneth Dyson, has been a fertile source of new ideas and encouragement.

Particular thanks are offered to those who have read sections of the book; for example, Professor Stephen Holt at the University of Kent; Tony Jones at Leeds University, who also took over some teaching when I was on study leave; also Rosemary Fennell in the Agricultural Economics Unit at Oxford University; and Michael Shackleton of the European Parliament in Luxembourg. In addition, my own colleagues in Bradford, Kevin Featherstone and Peter Wilson, have provided constructive comments on several chapters.

Finally, my indebtedness extends to my family who have had to take second place during the writing of this book, and particularly to my wife for preparing the manuscript for publication.

Preface to the second edition

I have retained the basic structure of the book with its ten chapters and three-part structure within each chapter. However, changes have been made to every chapter to incorporate the latest events. For example, there is a review of current defence organizations in Chapter 1. In particular there is a much fuller coverage of the single internal market in Chapter 3. Chapter 6 has been revised in its title and content to give greater emphasis to social policy accompanying regional policy, thus reflecting the proposals in the Social Charter. Chapter 7 has been updated on the progress of monetary integration to include the Delors proposals and UK membership of the ERM. The revolutionary changes in Eastern Europe are reflected in the revised section on Comecon in Chapter 9 and in a discussion of the movement of East Germany into the enlarged Community in Chapter 10. The latest statistics have been added to the tables and where appropriate there are completely new tables.

It is hoped that by incorporating recent developments readers will gain an even better understanding of the progress of the EC towards economic integration.

JEFFREY HARROP

Abbreviations

AASM	Associated African States and Malagasy (countries which participated under the Yaoundé Convention)
ACP	African, Caribbean and Pacific (countries which participate in the Lomé Convention)
ARION	Programme for study visits for education specialists
BRIDGE	Biotechnology Research for Innovation, Development and Growth in Europe
BRITE	Basic Research in Industrial Technologies for Europe
CADDIA	Co-operation in Automation of Data and Documentation for Imports, Exports and Agriculture
CAP	Common Agricultural Policy
CEDEFOP	European Centre for the Development of Vocational Training
CET	Common External Tariff
CFE	Conventional Forces in Europe
CFP	Common Fisheries Policy
CHIEF	Customs Handling of Import and Export Freight
CNC	Computer Numerical Control
COCOM	Co-ordinating Committee on Multilateral Export Controls
Comecon or CMEA	Council for Mutual Economic Assistance (grouping of East European countries)
COMETT	Community Programme for Education and Training in Technologies
COPA	Committee of Agricultural Organizations (Comité des Organisations Professionelles Agricoles des Pays de la Communauté Economique Européenne)
COREPER	Committee of Permanent Representatives

	(Comité des Répresentants Permanents de la CEE)
CPC	Community Patent Convention
CSCE	Conference on Security and Co-operation in Europe
CUBE	Concertation Unit for Biotechnology
DG	Directorate-General of the European Commission
EAGGF	European Agricultural Guidance and Guarantee Fund (FEOGA, Fonds Européen d'Orientation et Garantie Agricole)
EBN	European Business and Innovation Centre Network
EC	European Community
EC(6)	European Community: Belgium, France, Germany, Italy, Luxembourg and The Netherlands
EC(9)	The EC(6) plus Denmark, Ireland and the UK
EC(10)	The EC(9) plus Greece
EC(12)	The EC(10) plus Spain and Portugal
ECB	European Central Bank
ECE	United Nations Economic Commission for Europe
ECOWAS	Economic Community of West African States
ECs	European Communities (EEC, Euratom and ECSC)
ECSC	European Coal and Steel Community
ECU	European Currency Unit (a basket of European currencies)
EDC	European Defence Community
EDF	European Development Fund
EEC	European Economic Community
EEIG	European Economic Interest Group
EFA	European Fighter Aircraft
EFTA	European Free Trade Association
EIB	European Investment Bank
EMCF	European Monetary Co-operation Fund
EMF	European Monetary Fund

EMS	European Monetary System
EMU	Economic and Monetary Union
EP	European Parliament
EPU	European Payments Union
ERASMUS	European Action Scheme for the Mobility of University Students
ERDF	European Regional Development Fund (FEDER, Fonds Européen de Développement Régional)
ERM	Exchange Rate Mechanism
ESC	Economic and Social Committee
ESF	European Social Fund
ESPRIT	European Strategic Programme for Research and Development in Information Technology
ETUC	European Trade Union Confederation
EUA	European Unit of Account
EURAM	European Research in Advanced Materials
Euratom	European Atomic Energy Community
EUREKA	European Research Co-ordination Agency
EUROTECHNET	Programme for vocational training for technological change
EURYDICE	European educational information and exchange programme
EUT	European Union Treaty
EVCA	European Venture Capital Association
FAST	Forecasting and Assessment in Science and Technology
GATT	General Agreement on Tariffs and Trade
GDP	Gross Domestic Product
GEMU	German Economic and Monetary Union
GNP	Gross National Product
GSP	Generalized System of Preferences
IEA	International Energy Agency
IEPG	Independent European Programme Group (defence industry)
ILO	International Labour Organization
IMF	International Monetary Fund
IMPs	Integrated Mediterranean Programmes

IRIS	Programme to develop equal opportunities and vocational training for women
JESSI	Joint European Submicron Silicon Initiative
JET	Joint European Torus
LDC	Less-Developed Country
LEADER	Liaison Entre Actions de Développement de l'Economie Rurale
LEDA	Local Employment Development Action
LINGUA	Programme for the improvement of foreign language teaching
MCA	Monetary Compensatory Amount
MFA	Multi-Fibre Arrangement
MFN	Most Favoured Nation
NATO	North Atlantic Treaty Organization
NCE	Non-Compulsory Expenditure
NIC	Newly Industrializing Country
NICE	Nomenclature des Industries Établies dans les Communautés Européennes
NTB	Non-Tariff Barrier
OCA	Optimum Currency Area
OECD	Organization for Economic Co-operation and Development
OEEC	Organization for European Economic Co-operation
OPEC	Organization of Petroleum Exporting Countries
PEDIP	Portuguese Economic Development and Industrial Programme
PETRA	Programme for the vocational training of young people
PHARE	Poland and Hungary Aid for Reconstruction of the Economy
R&D	Research and Development
RACE	Research and Development in Advanced Communications Technologies for Europe
RETI	Régions Européennes de Tradition Industrielle
SAD	Single Administrative Document
SDR	Special Drawing Right

SEA	Single European Act
SEDOC	European system for the international clearance of vacancies and applications for employment
SMEs	Small and Medium-sized Enterprises
SPRINT	Strategic Programme for Innovation and Technology Transfer
STABEX	Export Revenue Stabilization Scheme
STAR	Special Telecommunications Action for Regions
STRIDE	Science and Technology for Regional Innovation and Development in Europe
SYSMIN	Scheme for Mineral Products (Système Minérais)
TARIC	Community Integrated Tariff
TEMPUS	Trans-European Mobility Programme for University Studies
UA	Unit of Account
UNCTAD	United Nations Conference on Trade and Development
UNICE	Industrial Confederation of the European Community (Union des Industries de la Communauté Européenne)
UNRRA	United Nations Relief and Rehabilitation Administration
VAT	Value Added Tax (TVA, Taxe sur valeur ajoutée)
VER	Voluntary Export Restraint
WEU	Western European Union

Introduction

This book on the European Community (EC) was written mainly for undergraduate students, in particular those studying within the context of an interdisciplinary European Studies degree and whose chief interest is in Economics. The increased provision of such courses at both undergraduate and post-graduate level partly reflects the greater European orientation in the United Kingdom, signalled by UK entry to the EC in 1973. At that time there was also an awakening of general public consciousness about the EC and since then there has been a growing demand for information about it. Some universities responded by providing adult education courses, and some of the material and ideas for this book were first collected for a diploma course in European Studies at the University of Hull and later for a similar course run jointly by the Universities of Bradford and Leeds.

The book has a common format to each chapter. Initially there is an outline of some of the basic issues; this is followed by the heart of each chapter which examines the progress of economic integration in the EC. Finally, the consequences of integration are examined from the perspective of the UK. The view from this angle is not intended to reflect any undue national preoccupation, but to meet the needs of most readers for an understanding of the extent to which the UK has become integrated in the EC and some of the difficulties which it has experienced.

Each chapter is self-contained and readers interested in a particular aspect of the Community need only turn to that chapter. However, I hope they will go on to read the rest of the book since one of the purposes in writing it has been to show the links between the different economic sectors which have provided the momentum to the process of integration.

The EC provides a natural interdisciplinary area for analysis, crossing the boundaries of many individual subjects. The two main disciplines considered here are Economics and to a lesser extent Politics. The book adopts a political economy approach covering both economic policies and institutions. It was felt that a wholly

1

theoretical positive economics book would fail to encapsulate fully the multi-dimensional elements of Community developments over the past 30 years or more. Interpretation of these developments is naturally influenced by value judgements, and from a UK economic perspective the writer's views of its relationship with the EC may appear somewhat critical at times.

Detailed knowledge and information about the Community has been generally low, reflected in the EC's decision recently to establish 187 European Information Centres. To aid understanding, this book contains as much up-to-date material as possible, while avoiding the mass of detailed, jargonized Euro-legislative material which students do not need to memorize. The main aim is to go beyond the descriptive level to a real understanding of the issues and principles which underlie the various sectors of economic integration in the EC.

I became conscious when gathering material over the years that it was accumulating faster than it could be digested. It became urgent to produce something concise and concrete, and the beginning of a new decade marks a very appropriate time to analyse past developments. Also, with the Mediterranean enlargement (entry of Greece, Portugal and Spain) and rejection of full Turkish membership, southern membership of the EC now appears to be complete. The next enlargement of the EC is most likely to incorporate former EFTA members such as Austria and Sweden, with the possibility of a reapplication by Norway. However, further widening of the Community in this direction may constrain a deepening of Community policies in some areas, such as political developments in foreign policy, security and defence. The Community re-examined its long-term political destination after the Single European Act in 1986 and an intergovernmental conference on political union in 1991. It has been decided by the Community that deepening should initially take precedence over widening until the single market is firmly in place. After that, in the longer term even applications from countries in eastern Europe, such as Hungary, may be placed on the agenda.

Evidently the book could not be wholly exhaustive in coverage and I decided to focus on the main developed sectors of economic integration. Some sectors are largely excluded, such as transport. While a common transport policy was seen in the Treaties as a vehicle for opening up trade, and was supposed to be achieved by 1970, progress has been slow – despite recent extensions from rail and road transport to shipping and air transport. Commission proposals to create more competition have often lacked political support but are now integral to 1992 and are discussed briefly in the context of the internal market in Chapter 3. Other areas such as energy are only touched upon briefly as part of the ECSC in Chapter 6 on regional policy. Environmental policy is likewise omitted, apart from a mention at the beginning of Chapter 5 on industrial policy. These areas are excluded not because they are unimportant – and indeed the completion of the internal market presupposes the implementation of many common policies in some of these areas – but to enable a sharper focus to be given in depth in other sectors: the customs union and internal market, agriculture, industry, regional and social policy, monetary and fiscal integration, external trade and enlargement. Agriculture is still perhaps the most important problem on the EC's agenda, with a mistaken pursuit of a higher share of the international market by a price-support policy covering less-efficient marginal producers. Agriculture is a stubborn problem because of its centrality and influence on other sectors; for example, regional policy, monetary integration and the use of Monetary Compensatory Amounts (MCAs), and because of its high budgetary costs. It is industrial policy which needs to be placed higher on the agenda so that the Community can raise its international market share in high technology products. The internal market programme represents an attempt to remedy this deficiency to allow the Community to compete more effectively with the USA and Japan.

For readers who wish to pursue areas excluded here, or to work even more deeply through the areas covered in the book, there are many sources available. The EC itself produces many publications – indeed, the mountain of printed papers can be compared with the agricultural surpluses! Nevertheless, some of these are valuable, and readers are encouraged to sift through some of the Community material which is housed in European Documentation Centres in many libraries. There is material emanating from the Commission – with reports from the various Directorates General, from the Parliament, the Council and the Court of Justice. Material from the latter and from other bodies such as the Economic and Social Committee (ESC) and the European Investment Bank (EIB) is somewhat less profuse.

There is plentiful documentation covering both primary legislation (relating to the founding of the ECSC in 1951 and the EEC and Euratom in 1957) and secondary legislation which is promulgated daily and published in the Official Journal. Community legislation is of four types:

1. *Regulations* which must be imposed and are directly applicable in the law of all member states;
2. *Directives* which are binding as to ends to be achieved, but leave to the national authorities the means of introducing them;
3. *Decisions* which are addressed to specific groups, which are binding in their entirety;
4. *Recommendations* and *opinions* which have no binding legal force.

Use of the term 'Community' is preferred to that of 'Common Market', even though the latter has tended to receive wide usage, particularly in the UK, and is being reinforced by the emphasis on the completion of the internal market by 1992. However, the EC's goal has been to move beyond the stage of a Common Market along a road leading not only to economic union but towards a real community. It is more appropriate to talk about a European Economic Community (EEC), or just to refer to the European Community (EC) which avoids neglecting the social and increasingly important political dimensions of the Community. The term EC is also favoured by its citizens; for example, Eurobarometer polls have indicated that a majority of the respondents favoured the EC, whereas a minority chose the term Common Market. Strictly speaking, one should refer to the European Communities since there are three of them: the European Coal and Steel Community, Euratom and the European Economic Community. However, a decision was taken formally to merge their separate institutions in 1965 and they are treated in the book in the singular under the abbreviated title EC.

The process of international integration is one of combining countries, leading towards a union between them in a regional bloc. The term integration has been chosen since in many respects it conveys more precisely the development of the EC than other words which are sometimes used: consultation, collaboration, concertation, co-ordination or unification. Progress towards integration has developed considerably in the postwar years between countries which consider that the elements they share are more important than those which divide them. Integration is not an end in itself, but more of an instrument to achieve certain goals more effectively than nation states can deliver themselves, such as economic prosperity.

The book is concerned with a very limited model of integration in western Europe, specifically that of the EC. While focus on its key features exemplifies many aspects of integration, readers should recognize the distinctiveness of the EC experience, bearing in mind that other examples of integration exist in the rest of the world (Robson 1980). For example, in the centrally planned economies in eastern Europe integration in Comecon has taken a different form. However, the disintegration in eastern Europe which began in 1989 reminds us that there is nothing permanent about the process of an imposed integration. Disintegration has also spread beyond Comecon to Yugoslavia which looks likely to fracture. Their economies are moving towards market systems, encouraged by the EC's experience, though we are unlikely to see a complete convergence of economic systems. Integration in the EC has been rooted firmly in market principles, whereby market signals determine the allocation of resources, and the Treaty of Rome reflected a liberal approach – mainly that of West German industry. Over the years the EC has developed some more interventionist policies, alongside those of individual member states with their more mixed economies. Some would favour going even further in this direction, arguing that otherwise the EC will remain an 'Uncommon Market' (Holland 1980).

1 Organizational stepping stones

Part I Disintegration and integration in Europe
A Pre-1945

During the nineteenth century the European economy became much more highly integrated, based initially on overlapping regional industrial developments and freer trade. The formation of the Zollverein in 1833 created a large free-trade area and enabled tariff concessions to be extracted from other countries. Italy was unified in 1860, creating a free-trade area. Other countries signed treaties to reduce tariffs, such as France with the UK. Numerous international organizations were established, relating to spheres such as communications (Pollard 1974). However, a setback was provided by depression in the late nineteenth century which encouraged greater protectionism; also national power caused international rivalry which was to result in the two catastrophic world wars in the first half of the twentieth century.

The First World War resulted in devastating losses of labour and capital, and for the first time even the victors had to conclude that war did not pay. It has been estimated that the War resulted in a slowdown of industrial production by approximately eight years; that is, the 1929 level of production, assuming pre-1914 trends, would have been achieved in 1921 (Svennilson 1954). The European economy disintegrated and the reshaping of national boundaries at the end of the War increased the number of separate customs unions in Europe from 20 to 27. Territorial realignments caused massive problems, creating dislocation in industrial links; for example, coal in the Ruhr and iron in Lorraine. Both Germany and the Austro–Hungarian Empire suffered substantial territorial losses. Massive reparation payments were imposed on Germany and these exceeded its capacity to repay them, contributing to instability in the 1920s (Aldcroft 1978, pp. 60–4). Inflationary finance and massive borrowings were undertaken. Unfortunately much of the borrowing was not used for productive investment; nearly half of it was short-term and eventually countries were borrowing just to pay back interest on the earlier borrowings. A collapse of the financial system resulted,

6

and in the late 1920s capital inflows into Germany were withdrawn, especially by the USA, resulting in enforced deflation.

Economic activity turned down after 1929 and the depression was aggravated by speculative activity. The Great Depression was international in scope and marked a deep collapse in industry, trade and finance. While there was some recovery after 1932, this was very weak in North America and also weak in some European countries such as France and Austria. The most successful economic recoveries took place in Sweden, the UK and Germany. In Sweden it was based on enlightened budgetary policies, unlike the UK where there was greater concern with balanced budgets. In the UK cheap finance for investment stimulated key sectors such as housing. Recovery was also helped by the growth of new industries, and sales to an expanding domestic market were assisted by protection. In Germany a great economic recovery occurred on a different basis with a massive growth in public spending, particularly on armaments. Germany's export trade was also well adjusted to the new trends in world demand, with a larger share being held by metal manufacture, machinery and chemicals. In its trade policy Germany sought to raise its level of self-sufficiency and the weaker European countries fell under its economic hegemony. German expansionist military ambitions plunged Europe and the rest of the world into yet another devastating war.

The adverse effects of the Second World War were similar to those of the First World War; there were massive losses of labour and capital and millions of people were killed and wounded while others found themselves refugees. Homes were in ruins and the transport system disrupted supplies, with shortages of essentials such as food and fuel. There was massive financial indebtedness to the USA which finally established itself as the major power in the world.

B Post-1945

Peace did not automatically result in an improved situation, and in the late 1940s there was continuing political and economic chaos. The division of Europe into two parts resulted in the Soviet Union consolidating its hold over eastern European states. The Soviet Union was seen as posing a threat to the West, turning the screw at sensitive points, such as Berlin. In some west European countries, for instance, France and Italy, the Communist parties scored major electoral gains.

Attempts to achieve integration in the past by military aggression had recently failed disastrously under Hitler, just as they had under Napoleon. Given the impermanence of European history there was a need to create an irreversible process of integration on a new basis. Most European countries were in such a dreadful condition that there was a greater receptiveness to integration.

It was not so much the ideas for integration that were new, but the conditions which were conducive for this to occur after 1945. Unlike the failure of Count Coudenhove-Kalergi's ideas to be applied after the First World War, the collapse of continental nations at the end of the Second World War left them with little choice but to integrate. The impetus for integration stemmed from a revulsion against nationalism; concern over the future of Germany; and a reaction against the adverse effects of protectionism. A peaceful process of integration on a voluntary basis was the only way to full recovery and to provide Europeans with a better future. Wartime resistance movements had gradually recognized this fact. The immediate practical problem was how to turn the dreams and aspirations of integration into reality. The driving force in this was provided by leading national figures who, through the force of personality and persuasion, were able to enlist the support of the political élite. Jean Monnet's role was crucial and his ideas were favourably received by politicians such as Robert Schuman in France, Konrad Adenauer in Germany and Alcide de Gasperi in Italy. These politicians came from the frontier areas which had been disputed areas ravaged by war.

Other support was forthcoming from political parties, with Catholic political parties, for instance, being more prepared to consider supranational instead of national solutions (Spinelli in Hodges ed. 1972). Spinelli himself perceived scope for tapping popular support of the general public for the process of integration (Pryce ed. 1987, p. 24). There was a high level of public support for European unification in the 1950s, even including the UK at that time.

The external influences on integration, in particular from the two superpowers – the USA and the USSR – created a constellation of new international circumstances. The USA was generally supportive of European integration, providing its own federal model as one which Europe could imitate. In contrast the USSR constituted a very threatening element, with fear of further extension of Soviet imperialism pushing European countries closer together for their own protection and security. Cold war pressures were especially acute in the early postwar years, but even in the mid-1950s there were constant reminders of vulnerability to Soviet power; for example, intervention in Hungary in 1956. That, along with other international events such as the Suez crisis, provided the background for renewed economic integration in the EEC.

Part II   European organizations
Although there were different views about the process of integration and the best ways of achieving it, there was much goodwill and idealism; these ideals were well-reflected in the Council of Europe.

A   The Council of Europe
This was established in 1949 and its founding members comprised: the United Kingdom, France, Belgium, The Netherlands, Luxembourg, Denmark, Norway, Sweden, Ireland and Italy, with other countries joining later. Its aim is expressed in Article 1 of the Statute: 'To achieve a greater unity between its members for the purpose of safeguarding and realizing the ideals and principles which are their common heritage and facilitating their economic and social progress . . . .' The phrase 'Council of Europe' was used by Winston Churchill in 1943 and its title reflected Britain's influence on the structure of the organization. It was an intergovernmental organization, based on unanimity in decision-taking and having a consultative assembly.

It was decided to locate the Council in Strasbourg on the ravaged Franco–German border. The Council has been concerned with all matters excluding defence, and its prime concern is to organize co-operation in social and human rights, public health, education, culture and sport, youth activities, the environment and planning, local and regional authorities and law. It has a large membership, though it is limited to European Parliamentary democracies which provide basic human rights. Its most tangible achievements are enshrined in the Council's Conventions and Agreements. A most important Convention is that for the Protection of Human Rights and Fundamental Freedoms to create a civilized society. After it came into force the European Commission of Human Rights was set up, and later the European Court of Human Rights. Although the Council failed to achieve political unity in western Europe, its initiatives in the field of human rights and meetings of its parliamentarians have represented useful achievements. The neutral countries have been keen on the Council of Europe, with countries such as

Austria, Sweden and Switzerland playing a prominent role. Since the recent momentous changes in eastern Europe and the concern to improve human rights there, countries such as Hungary have applied for full membership. Along with the USSR, Poland and Yugoslavia it has been given guest status in the Council.

B   Defence organizations

Other organizations have been established mainly to help states to tackle their many national problems more effectively in a co-operative framework; this is exemplified by the defence and security problems of western Europe. The division of Europe into two halves resulted in western European defence initiatives, notably in co-operation with the USA.

Various organizations were created, starting with the Dunkirk Treaty between Britain and France in 1947, followed by the Brussels Treaty in 1948. This agreement between Belgium, France, Luxembourg, The Netherlands and the UK provided for automatic mutual defence assistance in western Europe. It was concerned with the possibility of a revived German aggression, but the main preoccupation was with the Soviet Union. It established a military agency, the Western European Defence Organization. The French refused to agree to the rearmament of an independent Germany. France, along with other members of the European Coal and Steel Community (ECSC), agreed to set up a European Defence Community (EDC). Although a treaty to establish this was set up in 1952 it was not ratified by the French. France would not participate in a European army which included Germany unless Britain also took part, and the latter's support was lacking. The failure of the EDC and of Spaak's proposals to combine the institutions of the ECSC and the EDC into a European Political Community marked a failure for the federal approach to integration.

In 1954 the rejection of the EDC gave way to the extension of the Brussels Treaty Organization to include West Germany and Italy in the Western European Union (WEU). It enabled the rearmament of West Germany to occur in an acceptable form. WEU also facilitated political consultations between the EC and the UK (until the latter joined the Community). WEU was not a very effective organization, but difficulties in developing a security and defence profile for the EC, such as Ireland's neutrality, led in 1984 to attempts to reactivate the WEU. France decided that it wanted to contribute more fully to discussions on European security; hence 1984 marked the first ministerial meeting for eleven years. Both Spain and Portugal decided to apply to join the other seven members of the WEU in 1984.

WEU is an intergovernmental body and though militarily it is part of the North Atlantic Treaty Organization (NATO) defence system, it has the advantage of including France, which lies outside the integrated military structure of NATO. Since the WEU Treaty expires in 1998 there are proposals that its activities should be taken over eventually by the EC. This may pose difficulties for non-members of the WEU – especially Denmark and Ireland – though Greece has now become more disposed towards joining the WEU. A strengthening of the European pillar of NATO is thought by some to be desirable. Meanwhile the WEU has come to the fore even more since the Gulf crisis because, unlike NATO, its actions under Article 6 of the Treaty are not confined geographically. The Gulf crisis has shown the need for a common European position to match that of the USA, and to be capable of operating beyond the NATO area, such as in the Middle East, where the new military threats seem likely to occur in the future.

It is NATO, founded in 1949, which has constituted the main basis of Western defence. It linked ten European countries with the USA and Canada (Germany, Greece, Turkey and Spain joining later). Its treaty is brief and not set out in arcane language, the core of it being Article 5 which begins: 'The Parties agree that an armed attack against one or more of them in Europe or North America shall be considered an attack against all of them . . . .' NATO has been confronted by the Warsaw Pact, but despite the latter's Polish base whereby any countries leaving have to give notice to Poland, it has been under effective control by the Soviet Union – far more so than NATO has been controlled by the USA.

NATO is an intergovernmental organization and within its framework the Eurogroup, an informal association of European Defence Ministers, has promoted closer European co-operation in the alliance since 1968. In 1984 they created the Independent European Programme Group, which includes France. The IEPG is the principal forum for promoting equipment co-ordination and has been given the stimulus to create a European defence industry. This is the defence equivalent of 1992; the aim is to go beyond collaboration, creating a common market in military products in the same way as the EC has done in civil products. Perhaps, looking ahead, at some stage the IEPG may become part of the EC Commission.

As an alliance NATO has been a widely stretched defensive grouping whose strategy has been based upon détente and deterrence, and if the latter failed then its flexible response was to defend itself. Nations have faced many competing demands on their limited resources and quantitatively NATO has been worried about its inferiority in conventional forces to the Warsaw Pact. However, an aggressor would require a large enough quantitative superiority to be certain of success. The qualitative technical superiority of NATO has also lessened with recent improvements to equipment in eastern Europe. NATO has a triad of forces: conventional, non-strategic nuclear forces and strategic nuclear forces. NATO strategy was to hold any attack by the Warsaw Pact as far forward as possible with its conventional defence. The concern was that if this failed NATO would be forced to resort to the use of nuclear weapons at a very early stage. But the short-range nuclear flexible response was eliminated by the Intermediate Nuclear Forces Treaty signed at the end of 1987 which destroyed launchers and when for the first time the Soviets conceded on-site inspection. Agreements to eliminate intermediate nuclear forces were criticized strongly by NATO commanders such as General Rogers, the predecessor of the current commander General Galvin, on the grounds that it would significantly diminish the doctrine of flexible response.

NATO has stayed strong but has been prepared to negotiate since the Harmel Report of 1967. Mutually balanced force-reduction talks began in 1973 in Vienna. In 1990 the Conventional Forces in Europe (CFE) agreement finally put an end to the Cold War, mandating the physical destruction of arms and establishing rough equality between East and West. It has equalized numbers across a range of five weapon systems: tanks, armoured personnel carriers, artillery, fixed-wing combat aircraft and military attack helicopters. In addition, zones have been established in which to spread out the equipment, and no one country is to possess more than one-third of these armaments. The effect is to reduce the level of confrontation, removing the likelihood of a surprise attack. CFE provides added confidence since it is verifiable with various forms of inspection. In reducing the massive Soviet superiority in conventional weapons, the Treaty has run into problems. For example, the Soviet military has moved equipment east of the Urals and also switched some of their tanks to the navy, since the maritime area is excluded by the Treaty. Furthermore, the Treaty says nothing about troop numbers, nor quality of equipment, and obviously the oldest equipment is being destroyed first on both sides.

The ending of the Cold War, with the decline of the USSR and dissolution of its empire, has ushered in a more optimistic phase of co-operation. Three countries, Poland, Czechoslovakia and Hungary, are moving closer to the EC and to NATO. But the West must not rush economic integration for these countries because of difficult adjustment problems, nor seek to present a military challenge to the USSR. NATO still has to plan for a worst-case scenario of a threatening Soviet military dictatorship, plus new contingencies of ethnic minority unrest in Europe, plus problems in the rest of the world, such as in the Middle East. Thus NATO is revising its strategy since its forward-defence strategy has changed with the reunification of Germany and the abolition of the military component of the Warsaw Pact. New NATO strategy will rely on smaller, more mobile forces.

The Conference on Security and Co-operation in Europe (CSCE) which started at Helsinki in 1973 brings together 34 NATO, Warsaw Pact and neutral nations. It has provided greater confidence-building measures, such as notification of military force levels and manoeuvres, leading on to mandatory confidence- and security-building measures. Since the London declaration in mid-1990 on a transformed NATO alliance, the aim is to develop a strengthened institutionalized role for the CSCE. The CSCE is providing the outline of a new East/West order, with regular meetings; with a small semi-permanent secretariat in Prague, and with a conference centre in Vienna exchanging information.

C   Economic organizations

The United Nations Relief and Rehabilitation Administration (UNRRA) provided some relief and rehabilitation during the war and early postwar years. European governments created a few emergency organizations to complement UNRRA's activities and these were subsequently absorbed into an Economic Commission for Europe (ECE) to facilitate reconstruction throughout the whole of Europe. It was successful in bringing about all-European co-operation in research; in the exchange of technological and statistical information; and in the removal of many obstacles to East–West trade (Palmer and Lambert 1968).

The Organization for European Economic Co-operation (OEEC). The USA agreed to donate aid under the Marshall Plan if European countries would come together to frame their own recovery programme. It has been regretted by federalists that the aid was not made conditional on the creation of supranational political unity. Although assistance was offered throughout Europe it was refused by the Soviets who distrusted American intentions. Hence, rather than channel US aid through the ECE, a new body, the OEEC, was created in 1948. Sixteen west European countries, plus the commanders-in-chief of the western zones of Germany, signed the Convention establishing the organization. Canada and the USA became associate members of the OEEC in 1950; Spain and Yugoslavia also participated in the 1950s.

A major problem in all organizations has been whether to operate on an intergovernmental basis like the OEEC, or whether to operate at a more supranational level, as favoured by France at that time; though France has had to square this with its concerns relating to its own national independence. The decision-taking in the OEEC has been on the basis of unanimity to protect the interests of the smaller countries.

The basic international problem in the early postwar years was recognized as one of restoring freer trade and payments, since if industry were to recover and expand it would need access to a large international market. Freer international payments were helped by the European Payments Union (EPU) which was set up in 1950 to assist countries which faced balance-of-payments deficits.

By the beginning of the 1960s over 90 per cent of trade was free from quotas. After this, attention focused mainly on the other impediments to both visible and invisible trade. Unfortunately, a lack of consensus on the approach to reducing tariffs was to lead to the fragmentation of the OEEC. This led it to concentrate more on other international issues, symbolized by its change of name to the Organization for Economic Co-operation and Development (OECD). The Convention establishing the OECD was signed by 20 countries in 1961 and it has subsequently increased its membership to 24 full members: 19 European countries, USA, Canada, Australia, New Zealand and Japan.

The European Coal and Steel Community (ECSC), the European Atomic Energy Community (Euratom), and the European Economic Community (EEC). The organizations discussed so far have been intergovernmental ones, in which decisions are the responsibility of a Council of Ministers and in which unanimity is the normal voting procedure. The Secretariat usually has little scope for initiative, whereas in the European Community the Commission has far more weight than a Secretariat. Both the ECSC and the EEC were designed to be more supranational in character, in particular the former.

The Schuman Declaration in 1950 had proposed the pooling of French and German coal and steel in an organization open to all European countries. In 1951 Belgium, France, Germany, Italy, The Netherlands and Luxembourg (the Six) accepted the Schuman Plan and signed the ECSC Treaty. It allotted strong supranational powers to its High Authority and the Council did not appear in the original plans of Schuman and Monnet. In the EEC greater weight was given to the Council since countries were reluctant to relinquish sovereignty over many other sectors of their economy. The ECSC offered France some control of these key strategic and heavy industrial resources to prevent any potential renewed German aggression. For West Germany it offered better prospects than the system of Allied control. Tariffs and quotas were removed to create a single market for coal, coke, iron ore, scrap iron, pig iron and steel among the Six, with some initial exemptions for Italian coke and steel products and Belgian coal. Generally the creation of the ECSC worked out easier than expected, resulting in increased trade.

A limitation of the ECSC was its confinement to two main sectors and the recognition that to enjoy greater success, integration had to be widened to include other sectors. For example, although trade restrictions in the ECSC were removed by 1953, it was not until 1957, with the introduction of the international through-rates for transport, that competition took place on a fairer basis. In transport, countries tended to have lower freight charges for domestic products and subsidies for exports. Imports often had to face terminal charges for reloading at frontiers. Hence, there was a need to develop a common transport policy, and also to go further with energy policy beyond coal and cover other energy sources.

The creation of the EEC in 1957 with the signing of the Treaty of Rome included oil, natural gas and electricity. Meanwhile, research on atomic energy came under Euratom which seemed to offer considerable potential for co-operation. Indeed, in some quarters there was greater optimism about Euratom than the EEC. For instance, France was very keen to form Euratom, whereas West Germany and the Benelux countries showed greater interest in achieving an EEC customs union. Unfortunately, the desire by national governments to control their own nuclear programmes has hampered the progress of Euratom. In addition, expectations of the role of nuclear power were too high, and only after 1973 did the need for such a supplementary energy source become vital.

The Benelux countries had already experimented with their own customs union. They agreed to form one during the later stages of the war and from the beginning of 1948 they removed all intra-tariffs, establishing a common external tariff (CET) to outsiders, plus some attempt to harmonize economic policies. Benelux sought to go further, and it was Paul-Henri Spaak, a Belgian closely involved with the process of postwar integration, who was chosen to chair an intergovernmental committee which produced the important report bearing his name in 1955–6; this laid the foundation stone for the Treaty of Rome.

The smaller European countries, not being major powers, have had less to lose through integration, though they recognized that there would have to be a satisfactory voting system to ensure that their views would not be overridden by larger European partners. The smaller members have been able to exercise international influence via the EEC, in particular when occupying the Presidency of the Council of Ministers. Both Belgium and Luxembourg house European institutions, with Brussels being acknowledged as the capital of the Community; these institutions are an important source of revenue and Luxembourg has fought hard to try to retain its position. These smaller countries are all highly dependent on trade and access to an open trading system is crucial to them.

The EEC is the most important of the three Communities and economic spill-over has occurred with the interdependence of different sectors. The starting point was the customs union in which a precise and detailed timetable was laid down for removing intra-bloc trading barriers. Individual national tariffs were replaced by a common external tariff which was applied on imports from outside countries – this, the CET, was the visible symbol of the EC's presence to the rest of the world. The EC has become most integrated in the free flow of goods, but a free flow of factors of production has also taken place. These intra-EC factor flows are less than those for goods and the EC has not reached the same common external policy on factor flows (Molle 1990). Nevertheless, this first phase of integration created a Common Market in which the internal barriers which had been erected were steadily removed.

Another phase of integration has consisted of positive policies in new fields leading towards economic union, and this has proved difficult and contentious, since whereas negative integration was underpinned by Treaty provisions, positive integration has depended more upon new agreements. Its economic justification has been to create conditions of fair competition and to avoid a situation of 'second best'. The latter arises if countries are importing from their partners not because of natural comparative advantage, but because of different national policies subsidizing particular sectors of the economy. For example, those countries with cheaper food, lower taxes and lower charges for transport and energy, and so on, would have an unfair trading advantage; hence the rationale for a high degree of economic integration. This has been carried out more extensively in some sectors, such as agriculture, than in others.

Apart from natural economic spill-over, political pressures have also underscored the process of integration. The EC has shown a bureaucratic appetite for expansion into new areas, sometimes impinging upon the work of more specific organizations. Nevertheless, progress has not been as automatic as expected since countries have fought obdurately to defend particular national interests. The process of bargaining has often produced 'package deals', whereby countries have only been willing to make concessions in return for some *quid pro quo* in an ancillary area. Indeed, the actual formation of the EEC along with Euratom exemplified the linking of interests in its inception, but over the years the process has become more pronounced, such as the linking of the internal market to institutional changes of greater majority voting by the Council, and additional powers for the European Parliament; likewise the two intergovernmental conferences on political union and on EMU in 1991. In some respects it is paradoxical that at times inability to reach agreement on one issue has resulted in more widespread integration in other fields in which some countries perceive prospective gains. This process of integration may be a source of potential problems, and has on occasions invoked strong national interests which resulted in complete deadlock; for example, the Community seized up in the mid-1960s after the French boycott and its opposition to moving towards majority voting.

New goals were established for integration during the 1970s to move it towards a real Community. On the eve of EC enlargement in 1973, the widening of EC membership from six to nine was also to be accompanied by deeper integration in an attempt to create the ambitious goal of European union by 1980. In some respects Community enlargement actually seems to be incompatible with a deeper and faster process of integration. Nevertheless the EC has sought to progress from microeconomic policies of integration in particular sectors towards macroeconomic integration. The progression towards monetary union became necessary because free trade and common pricing in a sector such as agriculture is undermined when national exchange rates are highly unstable. Monetary union in turn has reinforced the case for strengthening the Community's regional policy. Monetary integration itself can only be sustained by the adoption of convergent economic policies, in particular to avoid disparities in national rates of inflation. In the long run, if macroeconomic policy-making becomes more centrally controlled, with a larger budget, then political institutions at a supranational level may develop more fully towards a political union – provided these are not frustrated by continuing national interests.

Unfortunately, a setback to macroeconomic integration was provided by the steep rise in oil prices after 1973. Since then the Community has resembled more closely a zero-sum game in which gains are made in one country increasingly at the expense of another country. Progress is much easier where a variable-sum game exists, since all countries expect to gain real benefits from EC membership. The minimum condition that needs to be fulfilled is laid down by Paretian social welfare in stating that 'changes are desirable if it is possible to compensate losers so that no one is worse off and at least some people are better off' (Dosser *et al.* 1982, p. 5); hence some countries need to be better off and to compensate losers so that the latter are no worse off.

During the 1980s EC integration recovered its dynamism as the Community decided to reinforce its original basic theme of completing the Common Market via its internal market initiatives. It has had to couple this with enhanced structural funding to help weaker member states, particularly those in southern Europe; otherwise the latter would lose out if the focus were solely on the internal market, the central feature of the Single European Act which came into force on 1 July 1987. The single market is likely to be accompanied in the 1990s by a single currency rather than by a common currency preferred by the British. The EC is an organization growing in importance, moving towards an integrated foreign policy, towards a common security policy, and towards a common defence policy.

European Free Trade Association (EFTA). The OEEC split created a Europe of 'Sixes and Sevens' in which seven countries opted for a looser free-trade area instead of joining the six in a customs union. Seven countries signed the Stockholm Convention in 1960: Austria, Denmark, Norway, Portugal, Sweden, Switzerland and the UK; they were joined later by Finland and Iceland.

The departure of the UK and Denmark from EFTA in 1973 – along with the later withdrawal of Portugal – and their entry into the EC has led to the conclusion in some quarters that EFTA was a failure and that it has now disintegrated. That would be not only a premature but a mistaken conclusion. EFTA continues to exist, providing an interesting comparison, particularly for the three members mentioned which have belonged to both organizations. In 1973 the bridge-building between the enlarged EC and EFTA led to the establishment of much closer economic relations between the two organizations; this was decisively reinforced after the Ministerial Declaration of Luxembourg in 1984.

A primary and distinctive difference between EFTA and the EC is that the former has been concerned solely with economic integration. It never sought political integration as its goal, unlike the EC, and this has deterred most EFTA countries from joining the EC. For example, Austria and Finland were constrained by Soviet pressure, while Switzerland has been concerned with preserving its long-standing neutrality. Finland was only an associate member of EFTA, but decided to become a full EFTA member – after the departure of Portugal into the EC.

EFTA is an intergovernmental organization; its key institution is the Council which consists of occasional meetings attended by representatives of its member governments, while the Heads of the Permanent Delegations meet more frequently. EFTA has made little use of voting and has generally proceeded on the basis of unanimity. It lacks a body such as the Commission of the EC to provide initiatives for federal integration and it has only a very small Secretariat of under a hundred employees. The official language continues to be English, even though German might seem to be more appropriate, given the membership of countries such as Austria and Switzerland. EFTA reflects pragmatic traditions, with its absence of supranational institutions. Unlike the growing workload of the Court of Justice in the EC, relationships in EFTA have been relatively harmonious with only a few disputes arising and those were referred to the Council. The operating costs of EFTA have been low, not only because of its limited economic scope and its falling membership, but also because of its low institutional overheads. For example, EFTA budgetary expenditure was only 7.0 million Swiss francs in 1967–8 and 9.4 million Swiss francs in 1978–9.

EFTA has been concerned with industrial free trade and each country retains its own tariff to outsiders. This necessitated rules of origin to prevent imports creeping in through the country with the lowest tariff. EFTA also failed to develop the range of common policies which characterize the EC. Nevertheless, EFTA has shown a high degree of success for its members in terms of macroeconomic performance. The growth of trade led to low rates of unemployment in all EFTA countries and the problem countries – the UK and Portugal – have transferred their problems to the EC.

EFTA now constitutes a more homogeneous group and some of its members would be better candidates for progress towards full economic integration than some of the new members which have enlarged the European Community. Many EFTA countries have gained economic benefits from free-trade access into the Community market, via the Common Economic Space, without paying the full price of membership. The EC's developments of the internal market by 1992 are now testing EFTA's ultimate intentions and if it wishes to maintain its preferential position with the EC then it may have to fall into line, perhaps ultimately applying the EC's CET and approximating taxes.

EFTA has steadily declined in economic significance and its members have a limited range of options. The least attractive is to cling to the existing arrangements, since the internal market will make EC businesses more efficient with lower costs and multinational investment more attractive in the EC than in EFTA. Hence EFTA countries are likely to apply the internal market measures and have held joint discussions with the EC to create a European

Economic Area. Difficult stumbling blocks to be resolved include agriculture, and in particular fisheries; the role of the Court of Justice; and EFTA's participation in decision-making. Meanwhile Austria has applied for full membership of the EC, followed by Sweden whose relative economic position has declined and role as 'model' for others diminished. The benefits from neutrality appear increasingly less convincing in the 1990s, with the ending of the Cold War divisions in Europe.

Part III   The United Kingdom
The UK's ambivalent postwar relationship with the EC has something of a tragic farce about it. Various phases can be distinguished and in the 1950s when the ECSC and the EEC were being formed and UK participation would have been welcomed, the UK aloofly remained outside. In the 1960s when the UK sought to join, the boot was on the other foot and British overtures were rejected. Finally, after eventually joining the EC in 1973, the UK has since agonized over whether it took the right decision, with the trauma of the referendum in 1975 followed by perpetual disputes over agricultural and budgetary issues.

The mistake of standing aside in the 1950s
The pressures underlying European integration were much greater on the continent than in the UK, which had held firm during the war. Although at that time Churchill had proposed a union between France and Britain, in the early postwar years the UK was reluctant to participate in any continental integration which went beyond intergovernmental organizations. The UK was unwilling to join the ECSC at its inception since the British coal and steel industries had been nationalized by the Labour government and there was opposition to placing these key industries under a higher supranational authority. At that time the UK produced about half the coal and about a third of the steel output of Europe so that its absence from the ECSC was significant, as was its later failure to join Euratom – in a field where the UK again held a strong position. The UK stood apart since it had very real doubts as to whether European integration could be successfully achieved in a durable way. With its glorious history, why should it choose to take the risky jump into the unknown when it could continue with its more certain, reliable and traditional partners such as the USA and the Commonwealth? The

UK had sufficient political power in the 1950s and hoped that EFTA would provide a sufficient additional economic stop-gap. The UK was able to mould EFTA so that it could play a similar pivotal role in it to that which it exercised in the Commonwealth. EFTA was a complementary organization enabling the continuance of traditional Commonwealth trading links such as those for the import of cheap food. Unfortunately the UK failed to maximize its opportunities in EFTA, partly because it was always seen as a temporary creation, and British business had to make special marketing arrangements for the different Scandinavian and Alpine markets.

The case for joining the Six was so much less compelling at the time than it was for its continental neighbours who appreciated the political and economic benefits from reconciliation. Whereas they opted for change, the UK chose continuity. It saw its past and its future as an outward-looking maritime power which did not wish to be drawn into an inward-looking continental bloc. In retrospect the UK made a crucial and major miscalculation in the 1950s. It took the safe decision, and the one that most people would probably have taken in the circumstances at that time. But with the benefit of hindsight it was a fundamental error – given that later the UK was to withdraw from EFTA and join the EC, which had been moulded and developed to suit different continental interests. The UK joined in an even weaker position with poorer terms.

Courtship of the Community from the 1960s
In the early 1960s the UK decided that it wanted to join the EC and its change in position can be attributed to both political and economic factors. The political arguments for joining increased because of the weakening links with the Commonwealth, whilst those with the USA also deteriorated, notably after the Suez crisis. Unfortunately, in 1963 entry negotiations were called off after President de Gaulle stated that the time was not ripe for British membership of the Community. De Gaulle still harboured some resentment towards the UK; whereas Britain felt that it had treated France well during the war, de Gaulle was less than flattered by his wartime relationship with Churchill. In the 1960s de Gaulle was also very concerned about the dangers of increased American influence creeping into the Community via UK entry. In suggesting that Britain was not ready for membership one can detect a recognition of the competitive threat posed by British industry that was greater at that

time than later. France would hardly accept such competition unless the UK accepted the key aspects of integration, particularly the Common Agricultural Policy. Negotiations became bogged down not only over agriculture and the Commonwealth, but over a multiplicity of other items.

The EC doubted whether the UK was prepared to play a constructive role in the Community. The United States, which had pursued an equal Atlantic partnership with Europe based upon the UK in the EC, found its strategy rebuffed. Instead of enlarging the Community, France and Germany reinforced their partnership, signing a Treaty of Co-operation which was ratified in 1963. West Germany added a preamble to the Treaty to reduce criticism from outside, such as that from the USA, though de Gaulle considered that it diminished the value of the Treaty (Groeben 1985).

The Labour government in 1966 decided to pursue British membership of the Community. This arose partly from some disillusionment with the Commonwealth and problems in particular countries such as the illegal Unilateral Declaration of Independence (UDI) in Rhodesia. The Prime Minister and Foreign Secretary made a tour of capital cities in the Community, pointing out, amongst other things, the technological advantages which Britain could bring to the Community. In 1967 de Gaulle said '*non*' yet again.

De Gaulle may have been right in thinking that the British would not turn out to be '*communautaire*', though France itself had often been unco-operative when it suited national interests. For example, while de Gaulle was prepared to use the EC to pursue French economic interests, politically he believed that only national governments could deal with the high policy areas. In the EC France withdrew from its institutions in the latter half of 1965 since it was concerned to perpetuate a national veto on decisions of major importance. Similarly in 1966 France decided to withdraw from the integrated command structure of NATO. The French preferred their own '*force de frappe*', objecting to American dominance of NATO and being less certain of the US nuclear guarantee to Europe.

After the resignation of de Gaulle in 1969 the UK made better progress since France was prepared to recognize that the UK could provide some counterweight to the growing power of West Germany. France also saw that enlargement could be linked to the completion of the Community's budgetary system of own resources. The Hague Summit in 1969 cleared the way for a round of new and successful negotiations. The UK was worried about particular issues such as agriculture, fisheries, the Budget, and so on. In 1971 Heath and Pompidou compromised, with the UK accepting the own-resources budgetary system, and France giving ground over its concern about the overhanging sterling balances.

The first enlargement, 1973
The UK agreed to accept the existing treaties, but negotiated a period of transitional adjustment for five years in which it aligned itself to the EC system. The UK would have preferred a shorter transitional period for its industry and a longer one for agriculture. The interests of the Commonwealth were accommodated for imports of dairy produce from New Zealand and sugar cane from important Commonwealth producers. The attempt to meet specific Commonwealth interests has aggravated subsequent agricultural problems in the Community, adding to its embarrassing surplus of farm products. The entry terms for the UK were approved by the House of Commons with a vote of 356 to 244 in favour of joining the Community. Ireland and Denmark also entered the EC.

It was inevitable that Ireland would be drawn towards the EC because of the UK's application. In some ways Irish membership was less contested than that of the UK since Ireland had not incurred the strength of French opposition. Ireland also stood to benefit strongly from the Community's agricultural policy and indeed the absence of agricultural concern in EFTA was one reason why Ireland was a non-member of that organization. A referendum produced overwhelming support in Ireland with an 83 per cent 'yes' vote for EC membership. Ireland has generally fared quite well, though the recent restraints on agricultural spending have proved unpopular. In addition, closer co-operation on issues such as European security, as part of the Single European Act, led to Irish delay in ratifying this. In May 1987 the Irish government arranged a referendum on the SEA, with a majority of 70 per cent in favour.

Denmark saw the UK as one of its major export markets agriculturally which had to be retained. In the EC efficient Danish farmers have been able to improve further on their already adequate incomes. The economic benefits have cemented Denmark in the Community, despite considerable opposition and in 1986 a further referendum was necessary so that Denmark could sign the Single European Act.

A Nordic Council had been created in 1954 and Denmark co-operated closely with other Scandinavian countries. In joining the Community Denmark also expected Norwegian entry but unfortunately, whereas Denmark voted 63.5 per cent in favour of entry, the Norwegian referendum rejected membership with 53.5 per cent voting 'no'. The major sources of opposition in Norway were the primary and peripheral sectors comprising agriculture and fisheries, although it also included other fringe protest groups. These were confronted by industry, commerce, shipping and consumers, but in the end the more urban groups were defeated (Allen 1979). Norway negotiated a trade agreement with the Community, after hard bargaining over several sensitive industrial products and the level of fishing tariffs. At some stage in the future Norway may still reapply for full membership of the EC.

A referendum to resolve the issue of UK membership
The UK was relieved to finally obtain its objective of membership of the Community, but it soon seemed to forget why it had joined and pressure resurfaced for a withdrawal. Although the UK had committed itself firmly to the EC for an unlimited time period, this was not necessarily considered to be binding since Westminster was in a position to revoke membership. The Labour government which was returned to office in 1974 was highly dissatisfied by the terms of entry achieved under Prime Minister Heath. There is little doubt that the gradual weakening in the UK's bargaining position and its determination to join the EC almost at any cost had not resulted in the negotiation of the best terms. Community policies had moved on in areas such as agriculture, fishing and budgetary matters and these were to prove contentious for the UK. The Labour government sought a review of particular items and was determined to secure better terms. In June 1975 the UK underwent the innovation of a referendum – whereas greater use is made of referenda in other European countries.

The old issues were reopened and the major political parties were divided. Consequently, the campaign was between two groups: Britain in Europe, which was pro-market, and the National Referendum Campaign, which was anti-market. The major political figures supporting Britain in Europe made important pleas. Edward Heath asked: 'Are we going to stay on the centre of the stage where we belong, or are we going to shuffle off into the dusty wings of history?'

Roy Jenkins, who was President of the Britain in Europe Organizing Committee, argued that 'not to have gone into Europe would have been a misfortune, but to come out would be an altogether greater scale of self-inflicted injury'. In the pamphlet urging a 'yes' vote for Britain in Europe, some of the following points were made: traditions would be safe; jobs would be retained; food secured at fair prices; and ultimately no better alternatives were foreseen. The financial weight of this group was stronger than that of the National Referendum Campaign which urged a 'no' vote. The latter was concerned with the UK's right to rule itself, and with the adverse effects on food prices, jobs and the trade deficit. It also recognized the favourable alternatives available to EFTA countries.

The decisive factor was the government's own position and its pamphlet entitled 'Britain's New Deal in Europe'. The Prime Minister, Harold Wilson, claimed that the renegotiation objectives had been substantially achieved. Therefore the government 'decided to recommend to the British people to vote for staying in the Community'. The voters were naturally inclined to trust the government's advice and certainly holding a referendum on whether to withdraw from the EC was a different matter from the decision not to hold a referendum on whether to join in the first place.

The referendum was a way of helping to heal the intra-party divisions which were most intense in the Labour Party. The turnout in the UK was 64.5 per cent and some 17 million people voted 'yes' to stay in the EC and about 8 million people voted 'no', although the result concealed wide regional and local variations. In the north less support was recorded, but only Shetland and the Western Isles voted against remaining in the Community.

The electorate has had considerable difficulty in understanding the complex subject of the EC and public opinion on the issue has been extremely volatile. Unfortunately, in the EC there tended to be an over-optimistic interpretation of the referendum result in deducing an apparently new-found enthusiasm by the UK for the Community. This was largely mistaken, but at least the main virtue of the referendum was that it settled the issue, confirming that the UK's future role and destiny lay in the EC. Withdrawal would have been a setback, although Greenland withdrew from the Community in February 1985. Obviously a UK decision to withdraw would have had far more devastating consequences.

2 The structure and operation of Community institutions

Part I   The decision-making process

It is important to understand the institutions which engage in decision-making and exercise power in the Community, and to consider the changes which have taken place in the interplay between them. It has been suggested that the EC's achievements have been constrained by failings in its decision-making and also that these need to become more democratic. The five institutions examined in the chapter are the Commission, the Council of Ministers, the European Parliament (EP), the Economic and Social Committee (ESC) and the Court of Justice. It should be borne in mind when discussing the European Communities that there have been differences between the ECSC, the EEC and Euratom, since each had separate Commissions and Councils, but with a common Parliament and Court. A Treaty to merge the three was signed in April 1965 and entered into force in July 1967. Since that time there has been a single Commission and Council. The whole structure institutionally will be referred to as the EC, notwithstanding a few differences in the way in which the ECSC and Euratom operate on the basis of their original Treaties.

While the main concern of economists is with policy outputs, as shown in subsequent chapters of the book, it is important to understand the inputs which go into the decision-making process. This is crucial not only for political scientists but for all those seeking to influence and participate in decision-making. It is true that there has still not been the decisive transfer of identity and power towards the Community which was hoped for and the key actors are still the nation states. Also, the political spill-over brought about by European interest groups has so far not kept pace with the economic spill-over of integration. Nevertheless, over time more and more crucial decisions are being taken at the Community level, with far-reaching implications both for business and for citizens in the Community.

The decisions which are taken are not imposed secretively by the bureaucracy in Brussels, as perhaps the media might imply, but represent the articulation of many different views in a very open, participative and consensual system. This framework results in a very slow process of decision-making – on average a period of three years before proposals are turned into law, with difficult issues often taking very much longer. Thus there are considerable opportunities to influence policy-making, but to do this effectively it is necessary to identify the role of the institutions and to exercise timely and appropriate lobbying. It is preferable to do so at as early a stage as possible, starting when the Commission is formulating new legislative proposals and these are being considered by experts and working parties.

Further channels to reshape policies occur when the proposals are being considered by the Economic and Social Committee and by the European Parliament, and since the latter now has enhanced powers to amend legislation it is likely to be lobbied far more in the future. Another opportunity to influence policy arises when the revised draft is being reworked by the Commission and discussed by the Committee of Permanent Representatives (COREPER), before being submitted to the Council of Ministers. Since policies evolve and are moulded to suit the different national interests of the twelve member states, there is considerable scope to modify legislation. While influence is best brought to bear at the European level, it should not be neglected at national level both in the House of Commons and in the House of Lords, since the latter scrutinizes Community legislation closely.

It will be shown that power has shifted over time from the Commission – which is now just one among several other bodies – to the Council, and in particular the European Council. Furthermore, since direct elections in 1979 to the EP, the latter has increased its influence, tending to diminish that of the ESC. In addition, there has been a growing demand by the EP to enhance its powers further and some concessions have been made to it in the Single European Act; for example, the co-operation procedure between the three main institutions in certain areas, such as the internal market. Previously, the Council only had to approve the Commission's proposals or to amend them by unanimous vote. Now, in areas where the Single European Act (SEA) provides for majority voting, the EP has been given strong powers to approve, reject or amend legislation.

Since the SEA only came into force in 1987 it is still early to predict and assess all the implications of this major and systematic revision of the Treaties. Nevertheless, there have been some early indications that the Council is not sticking to the basic rules of the co-operation procedure in some instances; for example, it has systematically rejected the EP's amendments on public procurements. In addition, a snag arose over the freedom of financial services in 1988 relating to insurance (excluding life assurance), since the Council's proposals do not bear much resemblance to the EC's opinions first expressed in the late 1970s, and the EP feels it should be re-consulted and the process started afresh. It is clear that the Council of Ministers and the European Council still remain the ultimate decision-makers, though the Community has once again set out on a new course continuing its 'journey to an unknown destination' (Shonfield 1973).

Part II   EC institutions
A The Commission
Structure. The Commission is a small and open bureaucracy whose maximum authorized staff in 1989 was 16,309 employees. Nearly two-thirds of the staff are based in Brussels with other significant numbers mainly in Luxembourg and at its research centres, such as Ispra. Around a quarter of the graduate staff is engaged in linguistic work, made necessary by the use of nine working languages. The Commission is the Community's Civil Service and is able to minimize its staffing towards the comparable modest level of the Lord Chancellor's Department in the British Civil Service. This is possible since the Commission depends heavily upon national civil servants for implementing its policies, such as the Common Agricultural Policy (CAP). The Commission has also sought to improve its internal management and working practices, along with a desire to devolve some of its tasks to specific agencies.

   A distinction has to be drawn between the Commissioners and their staff. The Commissioners are appointed for a period of four years, with the President being appointed for two years on the assumption that this will be renewable. The first President, Walter Hallstein of West Germany, served for longer, and it has also been difficult to match the excellent spirit of co-operation in the first Commission (Groeben 1985, p. 47). The President has to mould the team together and has usually been an important national figure. The Frenchman, Jacques Delors, succeeded Gaston Thorn from Luxembourg as President in 1985.

The President is assisted in his task by six Vice-Presidents. The Commission consists of two Commissioners from the larger countries and one Commissioner from the smaller countries. There has been some concern about it becoming unwieldy as a consequence of enlargement, but proposals to appoint only one Commissioner from each country have been turned down. In the allocation of portfolios between the Commissioners, some are thought to be more significant and rewarding than others; hence, some haggling occurs over the initial distribution of posts. Commissioners exercise influence according to their portfolios and their personal characteristics of charisma and drive. Some strong personalities, including those from smaller countries, such as Viscount Davignon, have often wielded considerable power (Butler 1986, p. 18).

Despite different political views, the national appointees have to work together effectively, transferring their allegiance to the Community. While naturally they retain close links back home, they are definitely not delegates following national instructions. They have to act impartially in the Community interest and occasionally in doing this they have incurred national criticism. For example, in 1987 the two German Commissioners came under attack from a few national Ministers for failing to defend German agricultural interests and also its beer purity laws. However, Commissioners cannot be dismissed during their term of appointment either by their national governments or by the President of the Commission. Although the Commission as a whole is directly responsible to the Parliament – which can dismiss it by a two-thirds majority – the Parliament cannot take formal action against individual Commissioners.

The Commission is organized into 23 Directorates-General (D-Gs) and they are usually identified by number, ranging from DG I on External Relations to DG XXIII on Enterprises, Distributive Trades, Tourism and Social Economy. Some are of greater importance than others; for example, DG III on the Internal Market and Industrial Affairs, and DG VI on Agriculture. The main organizational links are vertical, with very weak horizontal links between the D-Gs.

The Commission takes several decisions routinely and other straightforward matters follow a written procedure; if no reservations are entered then the proposals are adopted. For more important issues, majority voting is used. Where a vote is taken the

Commission operates like a College and the minority abide by the collective decision.

Each Commissioner is supported by the French form of private office or Cabinet, which helps to keep the Commissioner well-informed and is usually filled with his own personal choice of staff. The Chef de Cabinet will deputize for an absent Commissioner. The power of the Chefs de Cabinet may have reduced some of the authority of the Directors-General. Each of the Directorates-General cover broad policy areas and are divided into sections dealing with various aspects, presided over by Directors, beneath whom are the Heads of Division.

The allocation of posts in the D-Gs are distributed to secure a balance between the twelve members of the Community. To enable this balance to be maintained after enlargement, some existing staff took early retirement on generous terms. The blending together of different nationalities has generally worked well, avoiding a splintering into rival national factions. The main dissatisfaction arises from career-minded staff who, although well paid, may feel that their promotion is restricted because of national quotas on staff in different grades and areas. However, in the lower-grade posts the quota is disregarded and a disproportionate number of staff are nationals of the countries in which the institutions are situated (Henig 1980, pp. 45–6).

Functions of the Commission. The Commission embodies the ideals of the Community and carries out a range of political and administrative functions which can be classified in five main ways. In the first instance, the Commission proposes new policies, since the Treaty establishing the EC was more of an outline sketch than that of the ECSC or Euratom. Hence the Commission has filled in the detail of existing policies and initiated new policies. It is the master of both the form and the timing of new proposals, without which the Council cannot act. The Commission often has to modify these proposals, but tries to act as the powerhouse of closer integration. Commission power is strongest where it has clear Treaty provisions supporting its actions.

Secondly, the Commission carries out executive powers to implement the policies in the Treaties. It prepares decisions and regulations to implement the provisions of the Treaty, such as on trade, and enactments of the Council; for example, a mass of regulations is passed each year relating to the CAP. The Commission also administers Community Funds and research programmes. The Commission works closely with member countries to operate policies effectively, often by means of management committees, such as those for agriculture. While national administrators may lack the Commission's commitment to integration, they have been helpful in monitoring proposals and in reducing the administrative burden.

Thirdly, the Commission acts as guardian of the Treaties; it fulfils a watchdog role and investigates any action which it considers infringes the Treaties. It demands explanations for actions which may arise from a misinterpretation of the Treaties. If the Commission is still dissatisfied with the explanations given, then it issues a reasoned opinion with which the state must comply. If the state does not do this the matter is referred to the Court of Justice, although in the case of competition and cartels the Commission has direct powers itself to fine offending companies.

Fourthly, the Commission has the formal right to attend Council meetings where it presents its views vigorously in order to pilot its legislation through. Likewise, the President of the Commission attends meetings of the European Council ('summit meetings'). The Commission seeks to steer through its own proposals, being the centre of bargaining and the thirteenth member of the Council, and even though the Commission has no vote it possesses the expertise. It mediates and strives to secure agreement between the differences of the member states – as does the President of the Council. The Commission is also the hinge between the Parliament and the Council at the second stage under Article 149. Often the overall policy outcome is simply one of establishing the lowest common denominator, far removed from the initial Commission proposal based on a strong, adventurous initiative for integration.

In addition to the functions outlined, a final responsibility of the Commission is to represent the EC in various international organizations and also in the Community's external relations with non-member countries. The Commission in conducting its activities has developed over time into a more bureaucratic organization. It has been suggested that such a highly structured and mechanistic role is less consistent with its activities of initiating policies and engaging in mediation (Coombes 1970).

B   The Council of Ministers

Structure. The Council was given only a minor role in the ECSC but has had a very important position to play in the EC and its power has grown in significance. Ministerial representatives from the member states along with their officials make up the Council. Its meetings are usually in Brussels but also in Luxembourg, and the latter, having suffered from the decision of the Parliament not to hold meetings there, is keen to retain some Council meetings.

Unlike the other EC institutions, the Ministers' mandate is to represent their own country. The most frequent visitors to Council meetings are the Ministers of Foreign Affairs and of Agriculture. Ministers of Finance also meet on a regular basis, whereas other Ministers meet less frequently. Sometimes Ministers even from the same country may adopt contradictory positions; for example, Ministers of Agriculture have supported farming interests, whereas Ministers of Finance have been concerned to limit the financial expenditure on agriculture. The Foreign Ministers have the most important responsibility since they are also expected to provide the general role of supervision and co-ordination.

The Presidency of the Council is held by each member state on a rotating basis, and is held for a period of six months. The President has an important job in exercising political weight of mediation to try to secure agreement – with the Commission's role being to produce the technical solutions to the problems.

The establishment of the Council's own Secretariat has altered the Commission's role in servicing the Council. The Council's Secretariat has over 2000 employees and it is organized, like the Commission, into a small number of Directorates-General. The major administrative task of the Secretariat is to organize and administer the Council's decision-making; it makes EC legislation available in different languages and many of its staff are translators and legal linguists.

The Council of Ministers has extended vertically over the years, spreading downwards to include the Committee of Permanent Representatives (COREPER). This comprises both the Permanent Representatives and their Deputies, with the former (COREPER 2) dealing with external questions, significant political questions and highly contentious issues. Meanwhile the Deputies (COREPER 1) focus more on internal issues such as the internal market, transport, social affairs and the environment. Note that agriculture has its own

Special Committee, staffed by senior officials either from the Permanent Representatives or from national Ministries of Agriculture. COREPER resolves many issues, providing the groundwork for the Ministers themselves to approve agreements (as 'A points') on their agenda, and to enable them to make greater progress on more important and difficult matters ('B points').

The vertical links of the Council have also extended upwards, reflected in the activities of the European Council; this consists of regular meetings of Heads of Governments. These summit meetings were not provided for in the Treaty of Rome, but it was agreed to establish them in 1974 and they are now written into the Single European Act under Article 2. Although they have limited the supranational characteristics of the Community in favour of inter-governmentalism, they have been vital in breaking the log-jam of business and in propelling the Community forward. The European Council has met three times a year and now meets twice a year; the meetings are held in the capital cities of the countries which hold the Presidency during the year.

Membership of the European Council is restricted to Heads of Government (or Heads of State), Ministers for Foreign Affairs, and two representatives from the Commission. The relatively small group of 26 people, operating in a fairly informal way with a flexible agenda, are able to focus on current Community and international issues and can resolve immediate problems. Often a package deal emerges as the easiest resolution, sewing up several problems together; for example, the Fontainebleau Summit in 1984, tackling Britain's agricultural and budgetary problems. At other Summits new direction has been provided, such as in 1985 on the internal market programme, or in 1990 at the Rome Summit with the Italians getting further progress on dates for EMU.

Although Heads of Government interact less frequently than Foreign Ministers, when they have enjoyed amicable personal relationships these have been most helpful to the Community's progress. For example, Franco-German links are crucial and the meeting of minds between Schmidt and Giscard d'Estaing provided the Community with leadership in fields such as the European Monetary System. Sometimes relations have been strained and meetings unsuccessful as Heads of Government have become bogged down with too many details which they have been incapable of comprehending, and an over-lengthy agenda. Problems have been compounded by some indecisive national Ministers who might have settled some of the issues themselves in the Council instead of leaving these to be shifted upwards to the European Council. Perhaps with greater use of majority voting in the Council of Ministers the European Council will be able to focus on fewer major problems; it is the one body which can set a clear agenda of objectives (Tugendhat 1986).

Functions of the Council. Power resides in the Council of Ministers since it takes the decisions, but being the least supranational of the Community bodies it has provided a brake on developments. There has been some concern about the way in which decisions are taken; voting can be by unanimous vote or by absolute or qualified majority vote (Commission of the European Communities 1987b, p. 29). Unanimity is generally needed for the initiation of new policies (or if an existing policy framework is to be modified or developed further), and when the Council is seeking to amend a Commission proposal against the Commission's wishes. Majority voting usually applies where proposals are concerned with the operation of existing policies; and has applied to such matters as internal staffing and budgetary procedure (Nugent 1989, p. 105).

The Treaty of Rome laid down a voting procedure which, in the earlier years, required a unanimous vote for most of the decisions. But in other areas, such as agriculture, a qualified majority vote was sufficient. France raised objections to Commission proposals in 1965 for a package deal to develop agricultural policies more completely and to move towards decision-making by majority voting. France not only opposed the substance of the latter, but objected to the way in which the Commission's proposals were first delivered to the EP before being forwarded officially to the Council of Ministers. The paralysis of the Community was resolved by an extraordinary meeting of the Council of Ministers, which was held in Luxembourg rather than Brussels, and the outcome was the so-called Luxembourg Compromise. De Gaulle was not prepared to see France outvoted where very important national issues were at stake. It was agreed, therefore, that countries would continue to negotiate with each other until unanimous agreement was reached. After the enlargement of the EC, most new members supported this national right of veto. However, in 1982, when the UK invoked the Luxembourg Compromise to veto a proposed increase in agricultural prices for which the usual price-fixing package had not been agreed satisfactorily, it was voted down. Nevertheless, the Luxembourg Compromise can still be invoked where important national interests are involved.

A general reluctance to make wide use of majority voting slowed down the decision-making in a search for compromise and consensus. It became obvious after the southern enlargement of the EC in the 1980s that changes were needed to bring about greater use of majority voting, otherwise the Community was likely to grind to a halt in many fields. The SEA has made an important breakthrough by introducing majority voting for most aspects in the creation of the internal market. It thus embodies a significant step forward in improving the Community's decision-making process. The Council's Rules of Procedure were formally amended in July 1987 in order to allow not just the President but any national representative and the Commission to have the right to call for a vote, and a vote must be held if the majority agree. But it is important for the EC to progress as far as possible in a united and consensual way to ensure that legislation is implemented. For example, at the end of 1990 whilst technically the qualified majority voting system could have been applied to farm reform in GATT, Italy did not wish to expose Franco-German opposition to this (but with only 20 votes between them they could have been outvoted on this issue).

Under the qualified majority voting system, the votes are distributed so that the 'big four' – France, West Germany, Italy and the UK – have ten votes each; Spain has eight votes; Belgium, Greece, The Netherlands and Portugal have five votes each; Denmark and Ireland have three votes each, and Luxembourg has two votes. From this total of 76 votes a qualified majority consists of 54 votes, though when the Council is not acting on a proposal from the Commission an additional condition is that the votes should be cast by eight members (Mathijsen 1985, p. 30). The Mediterranean votes of Italy, Spain and Greece together are in a position to block some decisions with their 23 votes. With less scope for an individual national veto, countries need support for a blocking minority; hence Italy has a crucial role in southern Europe, since the other southern countries just fall short of a blocking minority. In northern Europe, the UK and Germany, along with one small country (Denmark or The Netherlands or Belgium) can likewise block measures in the areas which they feel strongly about – perhaps budgetary expenditure. In fact there is the dangerous prospect of an *impasse* over the cohesiveness of the Community between its northern and southern member states, with the former holding the purse strings over tackling issues such as Mediterranean regional imbalance.

C   The European Parliament

Structure. The European Parliament used to be called the Assembly. Its structure can be examined in two ways: the members of the European Parliament (MEPs) can be divided either by their national membership or by their party political distribution. There were 410 MEPs after the first direct elections in 1979 and since the southern enlargement of the EC the total number of MEPs has risen to 518. The 'big four' – Germany, France, the UK and Italy – each have 81 MEPs; Spain has 60, The Netherlands 25, and there are 24 MEPs each from Belgium, Greece and Portugal, plus 16 from Denmark, 15 from Ireland and 6 from Luxembourg.

The MEPs, drawn from some 70 national political parties, have come together into a small number of political groups. These transnational groups seek a common approach to issues and ultimately they may grow into real political parties. The strength of the groups and their national membership in the EP in 1990 is shown in Table 2.1.

The largest transnational group is that of the Socialists, with MEPs belonging to it from every country including one from Ireland in the current Parliament. Nevertheless, Socialist MEPs differ in their approach, with one cleavage, among others, being whether they represent urban or rural areas. There are also often differences in their links with the national party; for example, the Spanish Socialists have closer links with their national party at home than do others, such as their Danish colleagues.

The second largest group is the European People's Party, with MEPs from all states belonging to it – including one representative from the UK in the current Parliament. The Christian Democrats in this group have most representation from Germany and Italy, reflecting business interests, including agriculture, and they have strongly supported the progress of European integration. The Liberal Democratic and Reformist group has members from all countries, except Greece and the UK. This group is perhaps least coherent ideologically since there are wide interpretations of the word 'liberal', but it has shown concern for a liberal economy based

Table 2.1 Political groups in the European Parliament, 9 October 1990

	B	Dk	G	Gr	S	F	Irl	I	L	N	P	UK	12
Soc	8	4	31	9	27	22	1	14	2	8	8	46	180
EPP	7	2	32	10	17	6	4	27	3	10	3	1	122
LDR	4	3	4	–	6	13	2	3	1	4	9	–	49
ED	–	2	–	–	–	–	–	–	–	–	–	32	34
Greens	3	–	7	–	1	8	–	7	–	2	1	–	29
EUL	–	1	–	1	4	–	–	22	–	–	–	–	28
EDA	–	–	–	1	2	13	6	–	–	–	–	–	22
ER	1	–	6	–	–	10	–	–	–	–	–	–	17
LU	–	–	–	3	–	7	1	–	–	–	3	–	14
RBW	1	4	1	–	2	1	1	3	–	–	–	–	14
Ind	–	–	–	–	1	1	–	5	–	1	–	1	9
Totals	24	16	81	24	60	81	15	81	6	25	24	81	518

Notes:

Soc	Socialist Group
EPP	Group of the European People's Party (Christian Democratic Group)
LDR	Liberal Democratic and Reformist Group
ED	European Democratic Group
Greens	Group of the Greens in the European Parliament
EUL	Group of the European Unitarian Left
EDA	Group of the European Democratic Alliance
ER	Technical Group of the European Right
LU	Left Unity
RBW	Rainbow Group
Ind	Non-attached

B: Belgium; Dk: Denmark; F: France; G: Germany; Gr: Greece; I: Italy; Irl: Ireland; L: Luxembourg; N: Netherlands; P: Portugal; S: Spain; UK: United Kingdom

Source: European Parliament 1990

upon private enterprise and democratic institutions to guarantee human civil rights.

British MEPs have formed a more restrictive and largely national party group, the European Democrats. This fourth group is tightly knit and most coherent in its voting with very few dissidents. It has also been able to co-operate closely with other groups, especially the Christian Democrats, though the trade union wing of the latter has been a barrier to the Conservatives joining the European Peoples' Party. The centre-right have an overall majority in the Parliament, though this has been less clear-cut since Mediterranean enlargement.

The Greens have become a larger group in the EP, its members reflecting concern for environmental interests, especially in West Germany (though the Greens fared badly in the all-German national elections at the end of 1990). The Rainbow group has a broader base and also includes Regionalists from Italy and Spain seeking stronger regional independence.

The Left is divided between the Group of European Unitarian Left, dominated by Italians, and Left Unity, with half its membership comprising French MEPs. The Group of the European Democratic Alliance likewise has sizeable French membership and, along with significant Irish members, they have strongly supported agricultural interests. Meanwhile the Technical Group of the European Right consists of seventeen members, with ten from France, six from Germany and one from Belgium.

The parliamentary groups receive financial assistance and Parliament has laid down that if a group contains representatives from three countries or more, then twelve MEPs constitute the minimum group size. Where MEPs are drawn from fewer member states, then eighteen MEPs are needed from only two states, and if they all come from one member state, then 23 MEPs are necessary to constitute a political group. The speaking time in the Parliament is in relation to the strength of the groups. There are only a few MEPs who are independent of party groups – such are the perceived advantages of group assistance.

The political groups do much work, not just in Parliament itself, but in the eighteen Permanent Committees: these comprise the engine-room of the Parliament. Each group's membership of the Committees is proportional to its size, while the independent members have the right to membership of one Committee only. Some Committees have much more importance than others; for example, Agriculture, Budgets, Economic and Monetary Affairs, and the Political Committee. By increasing the number of its Committees, Parliament has shown that it is concerned to be a working Parliament (Bourguignon-Wittke *et al.* 1985, p. 42). The political groups have the right to fill the Chairmanships of the various Committees. The Committees appoint a rapporteur, following French tradition, who draws up a draft report for discussion, modification, and redrafting and revision into a final draft resolution for adoption. The Committees' reports then go to a plenary session.

Parliament has been peripatetic; its Committee meetings and party group meetings are held regularly in Brussels and there is little doubt that it would have been more efficient and economic to site the Parliament itself in Brussels – beside the Commission and the Council. Unfortunately, the location of the Parliament's activities has been very much a tug-of-war between Strasbourg and Luxembourg, with the Parliament's Secretariat based in Luxembourg beside EC institutions such as the European Court of Justice and the European Investment Bank. The wish of France to consolidate Strasbourg as the seat of the Parliament has been achieved by considerable financial expenditure to facilitate EP operations there.

Functions of the EP. The EP's role has been mainly consultative and advisory in non-budgetary matters, but since direct elections in 1979 it has tried to increase its powers based upon the strength of its democratic electoral support. With regard to the latter, in the Community as a whole voting turnout in EP elections has fallen slightly: 62.5 per cent in 1979; 59.0 per cent in 1984; and 57.2 per cent in 1989. The range of turnout varied widely between the member states, there being a particularly high turnout, around 90 per cent, in Belgium.

The normal functions of any parliament, apart from expressing views, are to legislate, to exercise financial responsibilities and to control government. It has been argued that the EP does not properly fulfil the traditional powers of a national parliament – even the latter's powers are receding (Lodge and Herman 1978, and Lodge ed. 1989). This is partly because some of the traditional parliamentary powers lie with the Commission and the Council. Parliament has sought to influence both these bodies, but in general has done so more effectively in the case of the Commission, since any accretion of the EP's powers is regarded as a direct challenge by the Council. The proposals from the Commission go to the EP for its opinion and often the Commission has made changes to incorporate its suggestions. The EP is also able to make its own initiatives, trying to encourage the Commission to legislate in particular fields.

Parliament has had considerable scope for questions, especially to the Commission. For example, in 1986 3023 written questions were tabled: 2671 to the Commission, 195 to the Council and 157 to the Conference of Ministers for Foreign Affairs (Political Co-operation). There were also in the same year 1277 oral questions, of which 800 were to the Commission, 290 to the Council and 187 to the Conference of Ministers for Foreign Affairs (Commission 1987b, p. 39).

The EP's budgetary powers have also been limited and confined mainly to small non-compulsory expenditure; it would like the last word on the vast amount of compulsory expenditure which takes place mainly in financing the CAP (these distinctions in the Community Budget are discussed more fully in Chapter 8). The conciliation procedure between the Parliament and the Council has been used extensively for the Budget.

It is the institutional weaknesses of the Parliament in relation to the Council which have most concerned the MEPs. The Council has a changing composition, and some of its activities have occurred outside the EC framework in the past; for example, European Political Co-operation (POCO), but this will become more integrated into the EC and conducted by it. However, the Council is reluctant to accede to European accountability superseding national accountability. It is true that national Ministers themselves have been appointed from elected MPs, but the operation of national officials in COREPER has been criticized, especially for not being accountable to the EP. The Ministers are held to account by attending the different Committee meetings. It has been suggested that Parliament should go further and use Congressional-type Committee hearings to interrogate Ministers (Tugendhat 1986).

The EP has been locked into a vicious circle in which it has failed to command popular support because it has lacked powers to match those of national parliaments. This has resulted in citizens focusing their main allegiance and expectations on the latter. One attempt to tackle the EP's remoteness from Community citizens has been to encourage those with grievances to appeal to its Committee on Petitions, and these public petitions rose in number from 57 in 1979 to 279 in 1986–7. Further institutional changes have been made to raise the EP's profile under the SEA (some of these are discussed more fully later). They provide greater consultative powers for the EP, and a new system of co-operation for particular activities, such as the internal market, and so on. In addition, the Council has to obtain the approval and assent of the EP – by an absolute majority of its component members – for applications for membership of the Community, and for its association agreements. Early in 1988 the EP started to use the latter powers; for example, to block three protocol agreements to the Community's trade agreement with Israel to show its condemnation of Israeli behaviour towards the Palestinians on the West Bank.

D   The Economic and Social Committee

The Economic and Social Committee (ESC) is marginal to the main decision-making process, though it has an influence on some policy details. The ESC consists of 189 representatives of interest groups in the twelve member states. It parallels the national systems for institutionalizing interest-group participation – these have had a long history going back to the 1920s in Germany and France.

The ESC under the Treaties has to be consulted compulsorily on many issues: agriculture, freedom of movement of workers, right of establishment, transport, approximation of laws, social policy and funding, and vocational training; also, under the Euratom Treaty it has had to be consulted on various nuclear areas. The ESC has also had to be consulted on other areas where this has been appropriate; for example, regional, environmental and consumer policy, and so on. Since 1974 the ESC has had the rights of initiative on questions affecting the EC; the high level of unemployment since that date has been one of the issues raised frequently.

The ESC consists of three groups: employers (group 1); workers (group 2); and various other interest groups (group 3) – representatives of agriculture, transport, trade, small enterprises, the professions and consumers. The trade unions in group 2 feel that on some issues the group 3 members tend to vote with the group 1 employers. The ESC's functions are consultative and its influence has tended to be eroded by the elected EP. It has been criticized further for being a 'quango' (in its appointments), and in its procedures, since it has been consulted only at a late stage (Taylor 1983). Its influence has also been diluted by the growth of the independent interest groups themselves – even though not organized as powerfully transnationally as neo-functionalists expected. For farmers there is the Comité des Organisations Professionelles Agricoles (COPA); for employers, the Confederation of Industries of the European Community (UNICE); and for trade unions, the European Trade Union Confederation (ETUC).

If the ESC is to be of influence it has to have well-produced recommendations, but on some economic and social affairs each group has used the Committee as a platform for its own views, though on other issues such as safety standards (for example, cars) the three sides have been much more in agreement. The Committee is an unelected body like the Commission and it has seen the latter as its ally, needing to prevent the overlap and duplication of the ESC with the stronger elected EP. The latter often waits for ESC deliberation, but also deals more directly with other pressure groups. The ESC sends its opinions to the Commission and Council before the latter takes its decisions.

A consensus among the 189 members is difficult, so the ESC is divided into nine sections representing key areas. If the Commission asks for an opinion it is sent to one of these sections. Each member of the ESC sits on two or three sections. A small study group is then set up, representative, as far as possible, of the three interest groups and member states. The study group elects a rapporteur and listens to the members, and where a very technical issue is concerned, such as that of nuclear power stations, then there is also a resort to outside expertise. In 1989 the ESC issued 154 opinions, including thirteen on its own initiative, and four information reports.

E   *The Court of Justice*

The Court of Justice has no connection with the Council of Europe Court on Human Rights in Strasbourg. The Court of Justice sits in Luxembourg and its structure comprises thirteen judges who are appointed for a period of six years, with provision for reappointment. While the judges come from member states they are expected to be independent of the pressure of national governments. This is facilitated by judgments emanating from the Court instead of from individual judges; hence governments do not know if any particular judge has supported its views or not (Henig 1980, p. 87).

The judges are assisted by six advocates-general, appointed from the member states. The office of advocate-general is based on the French system and they prepare the ground for the Court by giving a reasoned opinion. There is an advocate-general for each case.

The Court is supranational and its main function has been to ensure that in the member states Community law is applied, with the Treaties being understood and implemented correctly. Where a citizen goes to the national court and the latter is in doubt about matters, it can refer to the European Court for clarification. Given that the EC's prime concern is with economic integration, the Court has been occupied very much in ensuring that key economic objectives are carried out; for example, free trade, where the Court has ruled against different types of protectionist measures; the CAP has also resulted in numerous Court cases. In addition, the Court has been active in tackling practices by businesses which are contrary to its Competition Policy.

The Court has resolved cases of infringement of the Treaty which have been referred to it. Member states have preferred not to bring proceedings against other member states, leaving it to the Commission to do so. The Court has also, among other things, ruled both on the actions and on the failures to act properly of Community institutions. Even the EP has gone to the Court claiming that the Council had breached its obligations under the Treaty to introduce a common transport policy.

The Court is sovereign, overruling national courts, but the latter apply the law. The European Court itself has no EC army or police force for this purpose! The Court of Justice is very active and has dealt with over 5000 cases since first taking up its duties in 1953. It has a growing workload and to relieve this the SEA has provided for the establishment of an additional European Court of First Instance.

F   The changing relationship between the institutions and the impact of the Single European Act

What was the initial relationship established between Community institutions and how has this changed over the years? In the first instance, the Commission wielded great power, its strength providing the driving force for integration. However, after the Luxembourg Compromise of 1966 to maintain a national veto, the Commission became somewhat subdued, lacking the leadership which was necessary to ensure the progress neo-functionalists sought. The Commission has tried to create greater backing for its proposals, but it has had to be flexible and compromise, for example, with the EP and particularly with the Council. Its main limitation, which has to be emphasized, is that it is no longer the dominant institution and is just one among several. Nevertheless, it remains the most central and permanent of the Community institutions, with some potential since the SEA to restore part of its role. For example, the SEA recognizes that implementation of EC legislation should be left more to the Commission. Furthermore, its powers in some fields, such as Competition Policy under Articles 85 and 86, are highly developed already, more than its potential power in other areas such as state aids, in which the Commission has shown greater sensitivity to the wish of national governments to pursue their own industrial policies.

There have been many proposals for institutional change; for example, in 1979 the Spierenburg Report focused on the Commission's decline and made various proposals. These included recommendations to strengthen the role of the Commission President and to reduce both the number of Directorates and the number of Commissioners. Although some countries, such as the UK, are prepared to go along with proposals for one Commissioner, the enlargement of the EC has actually resulted in a further increase in the number of Commissioners.

Over the years the power of the Council increased, especially after the Luxembourg agreement in 1966. Countries have been able to block developments; to alleviate this problem 'package deals' have been resorted to increasingly to offer compensatory gains to countries in some areas, in an attempt to offset losses elsewhere and to secure agreement. But the pursuit by countries of their own national interests and their attempt to claim domestic victories has created slow, inefficient decision-making. With enlargement of the Community, complete paralysis would probably have occurred. Greater use of majority voting was recommended by the Committee of Three (Biesheuvel, Dell and Marjolin) in its Report in 1979. Certainly, the wider application of majority voting under the SEA represents a valuable step forward in cutting through the vast growth of Community business to ensure that this is executed more effectively.

The elected EP has been concerned to increase its power in relation to the Commission and especially *vis-à-vis* the Council. Under the influence of Altiero Spinelli it took the lead in bringing about institutional reform by drafting a Treaty to establish European Union (EUT). There was strong support for this, particularly from Italian and German MEPs, in keeping with the earlier Genscher-Colombo Plan. There was a Solemn Declaration on European Union in 1983 and the EUT was adopted by the EP in February 1984 by 237 votes to 31, with 43 abstentions (Lodge 1986, pp. 35–6). It led the European Council at the Fontainebleau Summit in 1984 –

having dealt with the UK budgetary issue – to establish two Committees on European Union. These were the Dooge Committee on Institutional Affairs (along the lines of the earlier Spaak Committee which provided the basis for the Treaty of Rome), and the Adonnino Committee, which was concerned with improving the EC to create a so-called People's Europe. This included, among other things, aspects such as a Community flag, emblem and anthem; introduction of common postage stamps and minting of the ECU as European coinage. The European Council Meeting in 1985 proposed an intergovernmental conference in Luxembourg in autumn 1985 which led to agreement to amend the Treaty of Rome and to sign the SEA in 1986. Although this was a far-reaching development, especially for countries such as Ireland and Denmark which had difficulty in ratifying it, it fell short of the radical proposals by the EP for European Union.

Some of the speeches and statements at the signing of the SEA reflected these disappointments. Andreotti, the Italian Minister for Foreign Affairs, felt that the SEA did not reach the joint decision-making which had been sought both by the Italian Parliament and by the European Parliament. The Vice-President of the EP, Alber, also expressed the view that not enough had been done to give the EP more democratic control. However, various amendments have been made in the Treaties so that the EP is now recognized in the SEA by its preferred description as a Parliament and not as an Assembly.

The new system of co-operation, laid down in Articles 6 and 7 of the SEA, provides for very intensive consultation with the EP. Whereas under the existing Treaties the EP's opinion was only sought once, now it has another opportunity at the next-to-last stage. The EP first provides an opinion and later it may, by an absolute majority of its component members (260 votes), propose precise amendments to the Council's position or may by the same majority reject the Council's position. If the EP has rejected the Council's common position, unanimity is then required for the Council to act on a second reading. Thus the EP's powers are much enhanced if it rejects the legislation, because the Council is likely to be mindful of the EP's vote and it seems possible that some of the member governments will go along with the EP's position preventing unanimity. With regard to amendments, the situation is more complicated and the EP's powers are weaker unless it can enlist the support of the Commission for its amendments. If the Commission's new version is acceptable, then the Council can enact a law by a qualified majority, whereas for the EP's position alone, unanimity in the Council is necessary. While the EP now has a say on two occasions – its opinion beforehand and amendment afterwards – this still falls short of allowing the EP to take over the legislative powers of the Council. Furthermore, the EP is constrained by the time provision at the final stage which provides that if the Council fails to act within three months, proposals shall be deemed not to have been adopted.

Both the Commission and the Council are having to pay greater attention to the Parliament. The co-operation procedure for key areas, such as the internal market, is leading the EP into the legislative area, more like a national parliament. The EP is also monitoring what happens to its amendments, and ultimately a failure to accept its views could lead to a threat to reject legislation outright or a vote of no confidence by the Parliament in the Commission and the latter's dismissal. Procedures in the SEA, while seeking to maximize close inter-institutional co-operation and dialogue, are still not without their problems. These could unfortunately lead to even more likelihood of deadlock – as seen in the past when the EP has exercised its budgetary powers.

An intergovernmental conference in Rome began in December 1990 to discuss institutional reform and political union. Italy, Germany and some of the smaller countries such as Belgium have favoured additional enhancement of the EP's powers. However, other countries, such as France, wish power to revolve mainly round the Council rather than the Commission and the EP. Also, small countries such as Luxembourg have far more influence in the Council than in the EP. The UK in particular is concerned about any new political constitution for the EC.

Part III   UK adjustment to the institutions
The UK has had to adjust to different styles of legal and political systems. Its national voting system, based on the 'first past the post' system – rather than the system of proportional representation in other EC states – has distorted the representation from the UK political parties to the European Parliament. For example, it has denied representation to the UK Liberals who might have strengthened Liberal forces in the EP. Both Labour and, particularly, Conservative MEPs have fitted uneasily into the EP's political par-

ties. Although Labour MEPs are part of the Socialist group, the anti-market views of some Labour MEPs have reduced the cohesiveness of the group. Furthermore, the Conservative Party was unable to fit into existing party groups and hence formed the European Democrats; this is virtually a national party group though it has included a sprinkling of Danish and sometimes Spanish MEPs. But at the Rome Summit in December 1990 Helmut Kohl suggested to John Major that a bargain could be struck which might allow the Tories to join the Christian Democratic grouping as equal partners. The European Democrats have tried to introduce a whipping system, though this has been much less effective than at Westminster (Daltrop 1982, p. 68).

The European Parliament has not had the impact which was hoped for, failing to receive anything like the degree of media coverage given to Westminster. Most of the major political personalities are still attracted to Westminster, with some MEPs from the UK using the EP either at the beginning or at the end of their political careers. National parliaments have been reluctant to see any overwhelming transfer in powers to the EP with a major difference in views, as in the past between Mrs Thatcher in Westminster and Lord Henry Plumb in the EP. Nevertheless, national parliaments have lost some of their influence over the economic areas covered by the Community. Scrutiny of EC affairs is often limited and retrospective, with the scrutiny committee of the House of Commons, and the more effective one in the House of Lords, sifting through material, trying to highlight important issues.

Lack of enthusiasm for the EC in the UK has been shown by low electoral turnout and by Eurobarometer national opinion polls in which most people consider that they have not benefited from EC membership. Indeed, at times there may have actually been some weakening of the mass commitment to European integration (Pridham 1986). Various polls of public opinion have shown that the percentage of people who believe that the UK has benefited from the EC is much lower than in most other EC countries. The lack of popular support for the EC has been brought about by the conflictual approach of the UK government over issues such as the costs of the CAP, the inequity of the Budget and the stages of monetary integration. Hence the UK has been less positive about the Community than have other countries such as France or Italy (Hewstone 1986).

The UK has despatched some distinguished political figures to the Commission, whose own self-image is one of a political bureaucracy. One of the most significant was Roy Jenkins who in his capacity as President of the Commission was successful in launching the EMS – unfortunately he failed to carry the UK into its crucial exchange rate mechanism (ERM). Other senior figures appointed have included Christopher Soames, Arthur Cockfield and Leon Brittan. The second Commissioner appointed has reflected a bipartisan political approach, being a member of the opposition party.

In the Council, governments have defended their own national interests tenaciously and the British have proved no exception, with vigorous defence of crucial issues such as agriculture and the Budget. The pattern has tended to be one in which northern European countries have fought very strongly in the Council and created more difficulties than southern European countries. Nevertheless, the former have a good record in implementing the law, with relatively few cases against them, whereas the latter have raised problems of implementation. After the Fontainebleau Summit in 1984, which marked significant progress in tackling the outstanding Budgetary problem, there was expectation of a better phase in the UK's membership of the Community. Thus the UK's acceptance of the Community was reflected in the absence of the EC as an issue in the 1987 national election campaign.

However, the UK has natural problems with the EC, and divisions brought about by the approach to Europe contributed to splits in the Labour Party, though this is now more in harmony with various aspects of the Community's interventionist policies; for example, the Labour Party is prepared to accept majority voting in areas like social and environmental policies. Meanwhile, in the 1980s the issues of the EC opened up significant divisions within the Conservative Party. Mrs Thatcher's vision of Europe, and one which is supported by the Bruges group, was based upon a limited co-operation of independent states, being opposed to the creation of any federal and bureaucratic European superstate. After the departure of pro-European members of the Cabinet, such as Heseltine, Brittan, Lawson and Howe, a backlash followed with the resignations in 1990 of the Euro-sceptics, Ridley and finally Mrs Thatcher herself. She will be remembered for her conflictual policy style, although it was under her government that the UK signed the SEA and entered the ERM of the EMS – albeit reluctantly. The substance of British policy reflects more continuity than change, since there is always a natural tendency both by politicians and the media to use the Community as a scapegoat for the UK's own problems. The UK has been quite keen to expand into new co-operation in industry and technology and also in the political sphere.

Although the UK may not be wholly '*communautaire*', it appears more committed to the Community when compared with other new entrants which have had to contend with some difficult problems of their own and have contested Community competence; for example, Denmark, Greece and Ireland. The signing of the SEA shows how firmly embedded the UK has become in the European Community. Its reservations were less than those of the other countries mentioned, though naturally there was some concern by anti-market-eers, which was shared initially by the British government (especially over the extension of powers of the EP and the extension of majority voting). But the outcome of the SEA was a pale shadow of the draft European Treaty, and the compromise disappointed the federalists since it omitted the word 'union' in its title. Yet the anti-marketeers consider that the SEA has gone too far in further eroding British sovereignty through the primacy of Community law – even though this has arisen mainly from the Treaty of Rome rather than additional provisions in the SEA. In both the House of Commons and the House of Lords there was a large majority for the government. It was recognized, quite sensibly, that having joined the EC then the SEA offered an opportunity to exploit its potential further, in particular in the internal market in which majority voting suits the UK. Under the UK Presidency of the Council in the second half of 1986, many measures were pushed through to create an internal market since it was recognized that these would occur anyway once the SEA was in force.

The UK has also played an enthusiastic role in the development of foreign policy and European political co-operation has been intergovernmental, based on consensus, with plenty of declarations being made. Consultation on foreign policy has taken place since the Davignon Report in 1969; but this was kept at an informal intergovernmental level separate from the Community, which France was prepared to accept since it lacked any legal supranational element. There are regular meetings of Foreign Ministers; the EC has reached common views on key international issues, and its members tend to vote together at the United Nations. The SEA now carries foreign policy a stage further by recognizing that the Community 'shall endeavour to formulate and implement a European foreign policy'. The UK imprint in the SEA is shown clearly in foreign policy co-operation and the internal market. In other areas the UK has provided a brake on more rapid progress; for example, towards giving the EP the even greater powers to which it ultimately aspires of full co-decision-making with the Council.

An Intergovernmental Conference on political union which began work at the end of 1990 is aiming to bring about institutional reform through correcting the Community's democratic deficit. The Conference is also likely to bring EC and European political co-operation even closer together in decision-making. The Gulf crisis, while successful in trade sanctions, reflected weaknesses in foreign policy and there was no joint Community military effort. The EC is trying to press forward in the high-politics area in which it failed in the mid-1950s. Furthermore, even with a common foreign policy which can 'bark', it needs defence for a forceful 'bite', and this will depend on a willingness by the UK to accept greater integration in these areas.

3   Free trade, the customs union and internal market

Part I   GATT's efforts to maintain a free trade system

The signing of the General Agreement on Tariffs and Trade (GATT) in 1947, originally by 23 countries, was a crucial step forward in ensuring that a freer trade system would predominate in the postwar years. It has provided the best defence for the international economy, minimizing the re-emergence of a paralysing protectionism. It is founded on basic principles, such as that of non-discrimination. Advantages in trade conferred on one party have had to be extended to all, which then receive Most Favoured Nation treatment (MFN). Since exceptions already existed for preferential agreements, such as those in the British Commonwealth, further advantage was taken of the exceptions which were made for customs unions.

Both the ECSC and the EEC took advantage of the concessions which were permissible, but have failed in some respects to comply fully with the conditions for creating customs unions: these were to cover virtually all the trade between member countries, whereas the ECSC covered only iron and steel. Yet when the ECSC required a waiver from GATT, the only opposition came from Czechoslovakia. The Common External Tariff (CET) was not to be fixed at a higher or more restrictive level than that which the member countries themselves applied before the formation of the customs union. While the CET in the EEC was set below the tariff rates of some individual members, it initially involved the raising of tariffs in countries such as West Germany. The development of the EC since the 1970s has also manifested several restrictive tendencies; for example, the free-trade area between the EC and EFTA excludes agricultural products. In addition, there has been concern over whether the extension of the customs union between the EC and certain Mediterranean countries can be completed within a reasonable time period (Hine 1985).

The EC has taken over from the individual member states which were the contracting parties to GATT, and has participated in many rounds of trade negotiations. These reduced the EC's CET from 12.5

per cent in 1958 to about 6 per cent after the Tokyo round of negotiations. The main achievement of the Tokyo round, which ended in 1979 after six years, was to reduce nominal industrial tariffs in the developed world by nearly a third on average. Unfortunately, however, some countries, including those in the EC, have begun to infringe the general principles of GATT far more – partly as a consequence of recession. Whilst agriculture, textiles and clothing were to a large degree exempt from GATT rules and discipline, trade in several other products has now become distorted by the use of quotas and by Voluntary Export Restraints (VERs).

Community countries still retain national quotas on many imports which often predate the Treaty of Rome. These national quantitative restrictions are likely to be phased out with the removal of internal frontier controls in the single European market by 1992. Any controls will then have to be imposed on a Community-wide basis. While VERs have become more widespread, they are not really voluntary, but countries recognize that if they refuse to accept them they will be likely to experience a universal non-negotiable reduction in their exports. VERs have been accepted since they enable sellers to obtain higher prices in compensation for their goods than if other forms of trade restriction were used (Hine 1985). In the mid-1980s the EC had around 50 VERs, and over a third of Japanese exports to the EC were thought to be covered by these.

In an attempt to salvage GATT some 105 countries met at Punte del Este in Uruguay for an eighth round of negotiations beginning in September 1986. Beforehand, suggestions had been made for a GATT-Plus (or Super-GATT) paralleling the kind of *à la carte* or variable geometry in EC integration in which the leaders move on more quickly (Tsoukalis ed. 1986). Differences have arisen between developed countries and LDCs, with the latter being sceptical about opening up trade in sectors such as services. In addition, the Code on Subsidies and Countervailing Duties negotiated during the Tokyo round has failed to tackle export subsidies effectively, particularly in agriculture, though there are even greater difficulties in doing much about agricultural production subsidies in which the EC is an obstacle to progress. This manifested itself clearly in the suspension of GATT talks in Brussels in December 1990, with acrimony between the USA and the EC over agriculture. Subsequently negotiations resumed in 1991 and it is important that the EC shows more flexibility on agriculture. The USA also needs to continue its commitment to the multilateral system of GATT instead of using its strength independently to extract separate trading concessions. Finally, Japan, which has come to the fore as a major beneficiary of GATT, should accept its new-found responsibilities by adopting a higher profile. This will involve difficult concessions by all participants, be it the EC on agriculture or Japan in areas such as rice protectionism. Unless the Uruguay negotiations reach a successful conclusion, the dangers are that the international economy will fragment into blocs, with the USA following the EC pattern of more continental-based trade and engaging in even closer trading relations with North, Central and South America.

Part II   The EC customs union and internal market
A   Key concepts of a customs union: trade creation and trade diversion
The most important characteristic of a customs union is a complete removal of tariffs between member countries. This constitutes a movement toward free trade, at least within the regional bloc. However, a customs union is also characterized by the imposition of a Common External Tariff (CET) on imports from the rest of the world, and the higher its level the more adverse is its impact on outsiders.

Whether a customs union is beneficial depends, amongst other things, upon the two concepts of trade creation and trade diversion. Trade creation occurs when a country in the customs union finds it cheaper to import from a partner country. Instead of producing a good domestically, it switches its supply to the partner, which has a lower price since the intra-tariff is removed. Let us assume there are three countries: 1, 2 and 3. Assume further that initially the price of a good, x, is £4 in country 1, £3 in country 2 and £2.80 in country 3. If country 1 imposed a 50 per cent tariff against imports, then it would produce the product domestically, since it would cost £4.50 to import it from country 2 (£3 plus 50 per cent tariff) and £4.20 (£2.80 plus 50 per cent tariff) to import it from country 3.

If countries 1 and 2 form a customs union (and country 3 remains outside, facing a 50 per cent CET), then country 1 imports the product from country 2 at the price of £3. Figure 3.1 helps to clarify these production gains, assuming for simplicity elastic supply schedules (quantity supplied at constant costs); also, for the present, any demand effects are ignored, with a completely inelastic demand schedule being shown in country 1.

The total cost to country 1 of producing the good domestically is

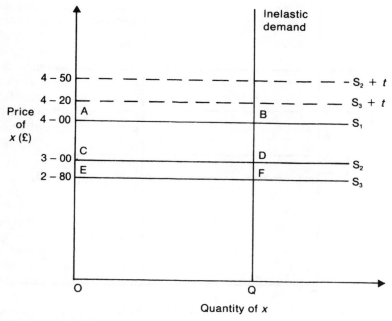

Figure 3.1   Trade creation

the area under its supply schedule OABQ. The total cost of importing the same quantity OQ from country 2 is OCDQ. The difference
between the two rectangles constitutes a resource saving of ABCD.
It is apparent that there would be greater consumer gains by enlarging the customs union to include country 3, since this would provide
additional resource savings of rectangle CDEF.

A paradox exists as to why country 3 is excluded from the customs
union. What are some of the implications for outside countries? The
concept of trade diversion shows the consequences for outside
country 3 which in the pre-customs union situation was the lowest-
cost supplier to country 1, but was excluded by 1's tariff; that is, the
tariff of 50 per cent resulted in country 3 being priced out of the
market. Let us assume, therefore, that a pre-customs union tariff of
only 10 per cent was originally in force. Then country 1 imported
from country 3, since the cost of importing from country 3 was £3.08
(£2.80 plus 10 per cent tariff), while the cost of importing from
country 2 was £3.30 (£3 plus 10 per cent tariff). When a customs

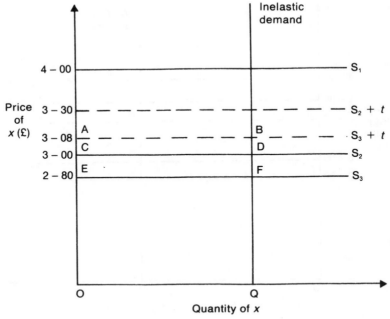

Figure 3.2   Trade diversion

union is formed between countries 1 and 2, with country 3 excluded, trade is now diverted completely from a lower-cost supplier outside the union to a higher-cost member, since country 1 can save 8p by importing tariff-free from country 2 instead of from country 3 (which still faces the CET of 10 per cent).

Although in Figure 3.2 country 1 enjoys a consumer saving of rectangle ABCD by importing from country 2, it sacrifices welfare as shown by the rectangle CDEF, since country 3 has production costs of only OEFQ. The diversion of trade in this instance has clearly had adverse trading consequences for outside countries.

Jacob Viner was the pioneer of customs-union theory, using partial equilibrium analysis to examine the effects on a single product. He was influenced by classical economists in thinking about production changes – even though consumption changes had already been introduced into the international trade literature. It is necessary therefore to modify the earlier analysis by adding changes in consumption. When prices are reduced (by removing tariffs),

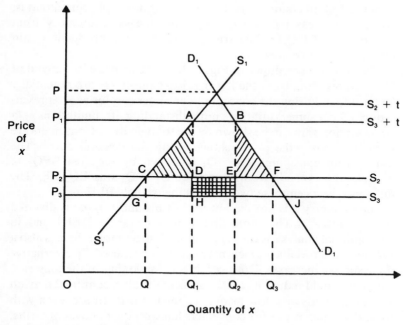

Figure 3.3   Trade creation and diversion

demands tends to increase and trade expansion takes place. Figure 3.3 shows the normal downward sloping demand curve, plus a more normal upward sloping supply curve for the home producer.

The demand and supply curves in country 1 intersect at price OP. By importing good *x* consumers can enjoy a lower price than OP. With a tariff imposed by country 1 on imports from countries 2 and 3, country 1 produces domestically along its supply schedule up to OA and it imports quantity AB from country 3. What changes occur if a customs union is formed between countries 1 and 2 in which the lowest cost producer, country 3, is excluded? Since the EC is open to full membership by European countries, then many low-cost world producers are excluded.

The welfare effects are that in a customs union, country 1 reduces its own domestic supply to OQ and switches all of its imports to country 2 and imports CF. In the trade-creating effects of the customs union there is the supply-side effect discussed earlier; this is now shown by a triangular area ACD. The costs of producing quantity QQ_1 in country 1 is the area under its supply curve; that is, AQ_1QC, whereas the cost of importing the same quantity from country 2 is CQQ_1D. The triangle ACD is the production gain between these two areas.

The new element shown in Figure 3.3 is the increase in demand of $Q_2 - Q_3$ resulting from the lower price. Consumers are potentially better off, and using the concept of consumer surplus as a representation of consumer utility – notwithstanding its limitations – a consumption gain can be shown by the triangle BEF. Consumers are prepared to pay the prices shown along the demand curve. The utility from consuming $Q_2 - Q_3$ is shown by the area BFQ_3Q_2, whereas the expenditure incurred for $Q_2 - Q_3$ was EQ_2Q_3F. The difference between these two areas is the triangle BEF.

Since country 2 is not the lowest-cost producer, trade is diverted from country 3. The trade diversion is rectangle DEIH and in conventional analysis is clearly harmful. Furthermore, there is also a loss of tariff revenue, which may have to be raised by alternative domestic tax increases. However, it is possible that in the long run, country 2 could reduce its costs significantly; also, country 2 may on welfare grounds be a low income country. Furthermore, even with trade diversion, prices for consumers fall with the removal of tariffs. It has been argued that trade diversion empirically is not widespread and a general presumption in favour of customs unions should be retained (Bracewell-Milnes 1976). In addition, where customs unions have contributed to rising internal incomes and outside countries have been supplying complementary products, the latter have been able to derive benefits – this has been true particularly where the CET has been set at a low level. Customs unions which are bigger in membership are likely to be better since they reduce the likelihood of the lowest-cost producer being excluded. Where the customs union partners have a high proportion of intra-trade and only a low CET to outsiders then the degree of trade diversion is likely to be small.

However, with completely free trade there would be no trade diversion at all and in Figure 3.3 there would only be gains: higher production gains AHG and higher consumption gains BIJ. Thus it has been argued (Cooper and Massell 1965) that a non-preferential trade policy which reduces protection will always be superior to the formation of a customs union. Yet if the traditional consumer gains for importing countries can be obtained by unilateral tariff reductions, why do countries rarely reduce tariffs unilaterally but instead favour the formation of customs unions? They are prepared to accept a second-best solution partly because pursuit of consumer interests has to be modified and related in reality to the costs of industrial adjustment which are imposed. The reallocation of resources even in a Common Market is not painless but is accompanied by some unemployment.

B   The rationale behind customs unions

The initial reasons for forming customs unions were not wholly economic, including both strategic and political considerations. However, it is helpful where an economic explanation is given, to focus not only on consumer gains but also on the gains to producers in a customs union.

In Figure 3.4, a low-cost supplier in one EC country – where Di is domestic demand, Si is domestic supply and a low equilibrium price OPi prevails – is able to export quantity QQ_1 to the rest of the EC. Although its own consumers face higher prices (since supply is imperfectly elastic) its producers' export gain is the large shaded triangle in Figure 3.4(a). Thus industry is able to expand along its domestic supply curve (Si) supplying the rest of the EC – with subscript r in the figure referring to the rest of the Community. A common price OPc, which equals the EC price, then exists throughout the Community, with its consumers benefiting from lower prices.

The concern with expanding production *per se* has led to perhaps the most cogent explanation for the formation of customs unions. It is argued that a country has some collective preference for domestic industrial and agricultural production which yields social benefits (Johnson 1973). In a predominantly trade-diverting customs union, a country which has a strong preference for such production, but with only a weak comparative advantage internationally, can achieve its preferences. But why do countries not achieve this by measures such as domestic subsidies and taxes? To achieve a sufficiently high level of production and exports countries would need to resort to export subsidies, and these have been used widely in agriculture. But industrially they infringe international trading agreements, whereas customs unions have been able to develop within the GATT framework. Therefore the constraints on the use of first-best domestic policies and constraints on trade policies help to explain the formation of customs unions (Jones in El-Agraa ed. 1985).

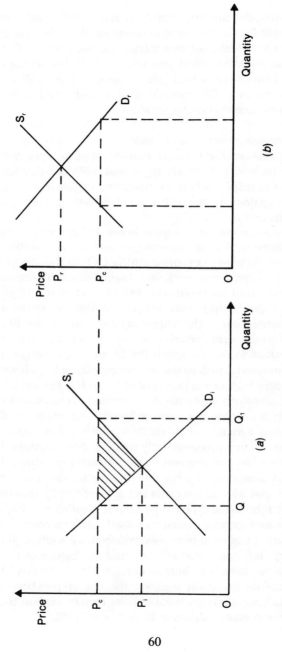

Figure 3.4 (a) The market in an individual EC country (b) The market in the rest of the EC

Producer gains have been significant for another reason and this is that much of the trade expansion has been of an intra-industry type; that is, countries simultaneously export and import similar or even homogeneous products in the same industry. Freer trade has enabled countries to concentrate production in fewer, larger plants. While intra-industry trade has always existed, it has increased significantly within the EC (Grubel and Lloyd 1975; Greenaway 1987; Millington 1988). In 1980 intra-industry trade ranged from 50 per cent for Italy to 65 per cent for both France and Belgium–Luxembourg. It exists particularly in differentiated products in which multinational companies are active, with a significant growth of intra-firm trade in, for example, passenger cars.

Countries in a customs union are able to derive other advantages. For example, by acting collectively rather than separately they are able to increase their bargaining power and their terms of trade may improve relative to outside countries. If the latter are producing competitive goods whose output is inelastic, then to avoid displacement of their exports the price falls. EC countries have been able to get much better prices for their own exports relative to their import prices. Terms of trade gains of up to 1 per cent of GNP have been estimated (Petith 1977). However, later studies have been less optimistic about the size of these terms-of-trade gains, though they have confirmed that the larger the economic area, the more substantial is the improvement likely to be in the terms of trade (Marques Mendes 1987, p. 106).

Finally, the customs union is important as the basic starting point along the road to more extensive integration in other sectors. A customs union, then, is part and parcel of the whole process of integration in a regional bloc.

C Dynamic gains in a customs union
Modern industry is characterized by the growth of giant firms which are able to reap static and dynamic economies of scale within a large market such as that in the EC. These economies of scale enable firms to meet greater market demand by moving down their long-run average cost curves. Economies of scale are significant in the formation of all customs unions, not only the EC but also the customs unions which have been formed in other parts of the world between less-developed countries (LDCs).

In the case of key industries such as the motor industry, a customs union between LDCs helps to make the actual production of cars viable, whereas in developed countries it enables cars which are already being produced to be made at an even lower cost. Optimum economies of scale in the EC car industry would occur with a company output of up to 2 million cars annually, every doubling of output up to this level reducing unit costs by about 10 per cent – no European manufacturer has yet reached this level of output. It indicates that the European market can accommodate only a few large firms. The more successful producers have been able to benefit from export opportunities and French car producers have significantly increased their net sales to other markets in the Community. West Germany has also been very successful in penetrating other EC markets, especially in a sector such as commercial vehicles. In the latter, economies of scale are lower, though the 100,000 unit producer had a cost advantage of about 16 per cent over the 20,000 unit producer (Owen 1983). In other sectors, for instance, white goods, it is Italy which has shown the way forward. Economies of scale in products such as refrigerators and washing-machines have enabled Italy to sell with great success in other markets within the Community. Some economists have placed particular emphasis on the role of economies of scale in lowering unit costs in such industries (Owen 1983), and these have been given central prominence in delivering a significant proportion of the predicted gains from the internal market programme.

The scope for exploiting economies of scale naturally varies from one industry to another. In some industries the level of concentration which has been reached may well be above that which is justified by the need for economies of scale alone. Furthermore, large firms operating in oligopolistic markets and lacking sufficient competition are often prone to some X-inefficiency. Nevertheless, the aim of the EC has been to provide a market size to try to match the economies of scale, standardization and productivity levels of the USA. There the market has been large enough to support a sufficient number of optimally sized plants without resulting in the danger of monopoly exploitation which was a problem in national European markets.

While multinational companies can only develop on the basis of a large market, historically some of the world's major multinationals have actually grown up in small national markets such as Switzerland and Sweden. But they have been able to grow mainly by selling to the international market rather than to the domestic one alone. Membership of EFTA and the latter's free industrial trade agreement with the EC have further facilitated the growth of such multinationals, even if they did not cause it initially. The smaller EFTA countries have also been able to co-operate with the EC in some industrial sectors in which scale is crucial to success. Not being full members of the EC has not precluded co-operation by outside countries in sectors such as aerospace. Even before 1973 the UK, for example, was an active participant in European aerospace projects.

Apart from economies of scale, another mechanism of dynamic gain is provided by increased competition which can stimulate a higher level of efficiency. In a more competitive environment less-efficient producers are undercut, being forced either to improve their production methods or be driven out of business. Monopolies in domestic markets find their position undermined by exposure to highly competitive imports. But for gains to be actually realized, these firms have to compete effectively by altering their existing pricing policies (Hine 1985, p. 28).

A further benefit is that a large expanding market is conducive to a greater level of both indigenous and inward investment – a key factor in raising the rate of economic growth. In the heyday of EC expansion businesses feared the consequences of not investing aggressively in new plant and equipment, but in the recession since 1974 investment has slackened. Although the EC has contributed to an increase in the aggregate rate of economic growth, some individual countries such as West Germany actually achieved a higher growth rate before joining the Community; also, the UK economic growth rate since joining the EC has not accelerated. While dynamic factors as a whole are important, they may not be sufficient to outweigh any losses which show up in a static analysis of customs unions (Lundgren in Denton ed. 1969).

D   *Empirical measurement*

There have been many studies which have tried to measure the growth in trade which can be attributed to the formation of a customs union *per se*. The two basic approaches are either *ex ante* or *ex post*. The former is a system of simulating the effect of tariff changes on the pattern of trade, with results depending on demand

and supply elasticities. The *ex post* method involves looking at the changes in trade patterns which have taken place as a result of a customs union. Balassa (1975), for example, used *ex post* income elasticities of demand (assuming that they would have been unchanged in the absence of the EC). He confirmed the predominance of trade-creating effects and these were strongest in the early stages of the EC. However, to avoid overstating trade creation it is generally useful to try to normalize the expected trade shares more realistically by examining how income elasticities have changed in other countries outside the EC, such as the USA. Even with such downward adjustments they showed trade creation exceeding trade diversion by at least four times.

There are great variations in both the empirical results and also in the welfare analysis of the implications of trade creation and trade diversion (Jones in El-Agraa ed. 1985). Nevertheless, some sensible orders of magnitude of static effects are possible and in several studies trade creation has been around $10 billion and trade diversion around $1 billion (Swann 1984, pp. 118–19). There are, though, one or two studies which show significantly lower aggregate trade creation and more trade diversion, such as those by Truman and by Kreinin (Kreinin 1974). Overall static customs union gains are limited to 1 or 2 per cent of GNP, since not all goods and services are traded.

A particular dissatisfaction with traditional customs-union analysis has been expressed by some economists. For example, Millington (1988) found little support for the explanatory power of traditional customs union theory. Meanwhile, Marques Mendes (1987) went further than the basic problems of trade creation and trade diversion and the unreliability of their results, pointing out the neglect in measuring the important dynamic effects, let alone all the other features of the Community. He has questioned the underlying theoretical assumptions, such as the automatic adjustment in the balance of payments. He adopted a different approach, using the foreign-trade multiplier to capture trade effects, relating those to output growth. His results showed strong trade effects and he concluded that in the EC, integration resulted in 1981 in a GDP that was 5.9 per cent higher than in the non-integration situation (Marques Mendes 1987, p. 104). This is a much higher result than earlier estimates by other economists, and the role of trade, the CAP, factor movements and so on, are all included in his analysis.

E   Intra-EC trade and the internal market

The removal of tariffs between countries in the EC was much easier
than anticipated since the countries were in a fairly similar competitive position (apart from the south of Italy). Also, at a time of
general economic growth in the 1960s, firms were able to expand and
any factors of production which became redundant could be
absorbed with relative ease into other sectors. Just over half of the
EC's trade now consists of intra-trade (Eurostat 1986); this growth
has been assisted not only by the removal of tariff barriers but also
by other developments such as the emergence of greater similarity in
the pattern of consumer preferences. Once manufacturers have
developed a competitive product, they look for exports in other
markets which have similarity in both income per head and in the
pattern of demand for those products. Thus more horizontal trade,
at least in modern consumer durables, has developed between countries with similar factor proportions and not, as the Heckscher-
Ohlin theory predicted, between countries with different factor proportions. Many products are the result of innovation and the most
developed EC countries with high R&D expenditure tend to dominate trade in new technological sectors. Export of such products
enables both dynamic and static economies of scale to be reaped.

With the onset of economic recession since the early 1970s,
member states in the Community have sought to exploit Article 36
of the Treaty of Rome far more – this allows justified exemptions to
free trade. EC countries have started to make greater use of Non-
Tariff Barriers (NTBs) to defend their products. These NTBs can,
for example, take the form of different technical standards to protect
national health, safety and the welfare of citizens. This lack of a
complete common market still constitutes a significant obstacle to
increasing the competitiveness of European industry. In exporting
products, firms complain that the Community is an 'uncommon
market' and that they have to make modifications to meet the
separate national requirements of each European market.

It is to rectify these problems of continuing market obstacles that
the Community is now pursuing vigorously the completion of the
internal market for which plans were first published in a White
Paper in June 1985. It will provide a catalyst for the Community's
regeneration and agreement on this has proved possible since the
lack of a single internal market is much more costly than the CAP,
and tackling the former seems less intractable than the latter. The

distinctive features are that it is a complete programme and set within the time period for completion by 1992, though there may be some slippage since it is not legally binding. The internal market, according to Article 13 of the SEA and the new Article 8a of the EEC Treaty, 'shall comprise an area without internal frontiers in which the free movement of goods, persons, services and capital is ensured'. Article 14 of the SEA and the new Article 8b of the EEC Treaty is concerned with a balanced implementation of measures, with the Commission to report to the Council on the progress made, with decisions taken on the basis of qualified majority voting. Article 15 of the SEA and Article 8c in the EEC Treaty recognize the heterogeneous nature of the Community since its enlargement, with provisions for temporary derogations.

The single internal market is one which is going to dominate all others over the next few years. The focus in this section is on border controls, technical barriers and preferential public purchasing impeding the flow of goods and services in the customs union. Different aspects of the internal market are included in other chapters, such as taxation in Chapter 8, but it should be recognized that this is mainly the consequence of removing frontier controls, rather than any new macroeconomic preoccupation with fiscal integration *per se*. Indeed, the single European market indicates a re-commitment to microeconomics to reap the benefits accruing from the free play of market forces, running in parallel with more liberal policies in many member states.

The stimulus towards the internal market programme has come from a combination of external and internal pressures. The external threat has provided urgency to greater EC integration in the 1980s in the form of the economic challenge from American and Japanese industrial power. This has highlighted the EC's acute deficiency in the new rapidly growing high-tech sectors. Internally the EC found it relatively easier to agree on the single market programme than on other more contentious avenues which might have been chosen for integration. The single internal market is in many respects completing the negative phase of economic integration, rather than tackling additional new and more controversial elements of positive integration.

The single market, in addition to completing fully the creation of the Common Market, has largely refocused its profile away from the agricultural concerns of the 1950s towards policies for new growth sectors of the 1980s and 1990s. These embrace the high-tech sectors, and the rapidly growing service sector which has been more pronounced domestically and in terms of employment than its growth in intra-EC trade. Although the emphasis on transport is not new, the attempt to liberalize financial services is a major new development, as is the attempt to open up trade and competition in the purchasing policy of the large public sector in member economies. Above all, what is crucial is the psychological recognition that there can be no turning back in the process of economic integration, thus providing a valuable stimulus to business confidence and new business strategies for the larger market which in future will be seen as a large home market.

The barriers to be removed. The Kangaroo Group, a European Parliamentary pressure group, has drawn attention to the multiplicity of barriers which still exist and campaigned for their abolition, exemplified by issues of the *Kangaroo News*. A major source of market fragmentation has been the continuation of physical border controls. Despite the absence of intra-EC tariffs, controls have provided a national safeguard by controlling the flow of particular imported goods to maintain health and safety; also, there has been the need to prevent drug smuggling. Border controls also fulfilled the necessary functions to collect trade statistics; to deal with VAT on imports; and the administration of the complex system of monetary compensatory amounts for agricultural products. Frontier controls have also been used to limit the undesirable movement of particular individuals, like terrorists, with some countries such as Spain and the UK having particular concerns to prevent the movement of terrorists across uncontrolled borders.

Some steps have already been taken to reduce various irksome form-filling for traders. Although the customs union was completed in July 1968, checks at frontiers have continued. To simplify these, procedures were agreed on a package of customs changes from January 1988. The Single Administrative Document (SAD) has replaced about a hundred export and import forms and Community transit documents (T-forms) used in the EC and for trade with EFTA. Nevertheless, most firms consider that this has not helped them significantly, and only its abolition within the single market will make trading much easier after 1992. Some forms have had to be retained, though revised and aligned to the SAD, in order to provide proof that certain goods, such as those covered by the CAP, are used or disposed of in a particular way.

Since 'Customs 88' there has also been a reclassification of tariff codes to a new Harmonized Commodity Description and Coding System. This consists of six digits recognized world-wide; seven and eight digits for EC sub-divisions and nine for the UK; for imports from outside the EC and especially for agricultural products, an additional digit tariff is used. While the change in code has changed some duties, the overall effect is neutral. A new computer system for Customs Handling of Import and Export Freight (CHIEF) has been introduced to accommodate changes brought about by the SAD and the Community Integrated Tariff (TARIC). Automation of customs data will speed up administration and cut costs for industry and commerce: the programme for Co-operation in Automation of Data and Documentation for Imports, Exports and Agriculture (CAD-DIA) is currently proving very successful.

The EC Commission sponsored various studies to estimate the cost of different impediments to trade including border-related controls. Ernst and Whinney for the Commission (1988) have divided the costs on a six-country basis into three components which include: the costs to firms of meeting customs formalities (ECU 7.5 billion); the costs to governments of administering the controls (ECU 500–1000 million) and some 15,000–30,000 staff; and the opportunity cost or potential business forgone by firms (ECU 4.5–5.0 billion). The study was based on six countries and the costs were highest for Italy and lowest for Benelux. The greatest burden was also imposed on smaller firms.

A further calculation has been made for the Commission of the costs imposed by transport delays. This is based upon road transport and, like other studies, is dependent upon the response by firms, some of which were reluctant to provide full disclosure of confidential information. The maximum cost of transport delays was estimated at ECU 830 million, and in order to avoid overstating cost savings, it may be better to take the range upwards from half of this figure; that is, ECU 415 million. This is because otherwise one would be assuming that replacement work would always be available for the driver and vehicle to fill the time saved. Another aim in transport policy is to remove the quantitative quota controls which require hauliers to apply for permits to transport goods across borders. In addition, the objective is to change 'cabotage'; that is, the restrictions on non-resident hauliers carrying and delivering goods within a member state. These have contributed to extra costs in the form of lorries having to make return journeys empty.

However, the costs of delays at frontiers are less than those which have arisen from the operation of different national technical standards. Firms engaged in exporting products have faced the extra burden of having to modify their exports to meet the national standards imposed. While the intentions in setting high standards are often very laudable, such as those to ensure health and safety, in some instances they have provided hidden forms of national industrial protection. Those industries most adversely affected have included engineering, chemicals, foodstuffs, and precision and medical equipment, though many other industries have been affected to a lesser degree (European Economy 1988, p. 51). For example, in foodstuffs intra-EC trade has tended to stagnate and major companies, apart from Unilever and Nestlé, tend to be American. Trade has been restricted and national prices kept higher than necessary for products such as pasta in some European countries and especially in Italy.

The European Court has decided that restrictions can only be justified if they conform to three criteria. These are, first, that of causality and a direct cause-and-effect relation between the measure and the objective or essential requirement being pursued. Secondly, the criterion of proportionality whereby the measure should not be disproportionate to the objective. Finally, the criterion of substitution: if an alternative way that does not impede trade is available to reach the objective, then it should be used. In the case of the 1967 Italian pasta law, which laid down that pasta should consist exclusively of durum wheat and not less expensive soft wheat, the law failed on all three criteria. It fell at the first hurdle since mixed pasta is just as healthy; there was a disproportionate impact with negligible imports; and finally there are alternative ways of dealing with this, such as labelling, without adverse effects on trade. With the removal of the pasta law imports should rise and prices be reduced.

A test case of considerable significance was that of Cassis de Dijon 1979 in which a French liqueur made from blackcurrants was deemed to have too low an alcoholic content for the West German market. The European Court of Justice decided otherwise and laid down that if a product had satisfied the standard requirements in one country then its import should in principle be allowed into another member country. The ruling has since provided precedent for other cases, such as that concerning beer imports into West Germany and Greece. In Germany the *Reinheitsgebot* insisted that beer could contain nothing more than malted barley, yeast, hops and water. Germany claimed that their law was not discriminatory since if national manufacturers made beer in this way they could sell to the German market. This claim was successfully contested by the European Court of Justice. However, Denmark, which has generally been progressive in opening up markets, has also banned imports of beer from other member states, unless it is in reusable beer bottles. While this may be a useful conservation measure, it again reduces imports of foreign beer because of the distances involved in comparison with the more convenient locations of Denmark's own breweries.

Standards have varied and in West Germany the Standards Institute has imposed very high standards, whereas most French and British standards have not been compulsory. When every product has to be submitted for approval by each country, this has led to delays and often to imported products being subjected to a more thorough process of testing. The process of harmonizing standards has also been slow, often taking years to adopt, whereas technology may have moved on in the meantime. Since 1983 member states have had to notify the Commission in advance of any new standards they intend to introduce. A stand-still period has been imposed to allow time for the Commission to examine them, initially for three months, which can be extended up to twelve months. In addition, the procedure for complaints is being improved for those industries adversely affected by such barriers.

The EC has achieved agreement by issuing European standards for many products. It has abandoned the idea of trying to harmonize every detail of a particular product, and it has tried instead to establish minimum standards for health and safety, exemplified by a mass of items ranging from pressure vessels to toys, with many further proposals of essential requirements for items such as construction products and machine safety. Likewise, to remove technical barriers for foodstuffs, instead of complicated specifications on their composition, the EC's food harmonization is based on 'framework' directives for food labelling, additives, food for certain nutritional uses, and materials and articles in contact with food. Common standards will be of great benefit to European producers, but they will have to operate on the basis that the whole Community market is in fact their home market. Unless this happens, the major beneficiaries may well be outside suppliers such as Japan and the USA since they much prefer to work to one standard rather than to twelve different national standards in the Community.

There has been a new attempt to reduce national preferences for public contracts, since public purchasing accounts for up to 15 per cent of the EC's GDP. The contractual part of public purchasing, that is, public procurement, accounted for between 6.8 and 9.8 per cent of GDP and in the short term it is this which will be opened up, but in the long term the majority of public purchasing will be open to non-national suppliers (European Economy 1988). The reluctance to buy from outside suppliers has been aided by lack of proper advertising and by the complexity of tendering procedures. The bias in favour of national suppliers has continued, despite the adoption by the Council of directives on public works contracting as long ago as 1971, and further directives in 1977 on public supply contracts. Directives apply to contracts above particular threshold levels; for example, ECU 200,000 for supply contracts for regional and local authorities which are subject only to EC rules, and ECU 1 million for public works contracts.

The exclusion of important sectors, such as transport, water, gas and electricity, and telecommunications, is being rectified to prevent the national industrial champion from preserving a monopoly of orders for power stations and telecommunications. This has resulted in excess capacity and higher costs of European firms in these sectors. Significant savings have been estimated (ranging from ECU 8–19 billion) via three mechanisms. First, the static trade effect yields cost savings by buying from the cheapest supplier (ECU 3–8 billion). Secondly, the competition effect will reduce the prices charged by national producers in the face of foreign competition (saving ECU 1–3 billion). Finally, the restructuring as firms benefit from shared R&D costs (saving ECU 4–8 billion). These total gains are equivalent to 2–5 per cent of public purchasing, and exclude all the gains for private sector purchases. They also exclude dynamic effects on innovation and growth and the relative strengthening of EC industry *vis-à-vis* the rest of the world.

In several technological sectors, discriminatory public purchasing coincides and reinforces separate national standards, such as telecommunications. For example, in telephone exchange switching equipment the Commission has estimated that open procurement will reduce the price per phone line to about £80 (compared with £53 a line in the US), resulting in only two Community suppliers. Open procurement will limit single tendering and lengthen the time-period for bids. Also, better policing has been proposed to tackle non-compliance so that action can be instigated against offending purchasers. An attempt is being made to use European standards to define the technical specifications for contracts. For example, IT systems have been incompatible but Open Systems Interconnection (OSI) standards are being developed and in 1987 the EC adopted a decision requiring public purchasers to specify these standards when buying IT systems.

In opening up public procurement internally, the EC has been divided over whether this should apply equally to public sector purchases from outside the Community. The more protectionist-minded countries such as France and Italy would prefer continued discrimination against others. Some compromise is likely whereby public sector purchases will occur mainly from internal EC sources if there are only small differences between external and internal prices; for example, up to 3 per cent cheaper than the best Community tender – though the European Industry Ministers failed to agree on this proposal in December 1989.

Microeconomic and macroeconomic effects. The lack of a single internal market was estimated on average to have added some 15 per cent to total costs (Booz Allen and Hamilton Inc. 1986). The removal of unnecessary restrictions will result in microeconomic gains arising initially from the removal of the costly barriers affecting trade and production. The consequence is a significant reduction in costs; for example, removing barriers at frontiers could result in cost savings of ECU 8–9 billion and public-purchasing savings of ECU 20 billion could accrue. Studies of individual sectors have identified significant cost reductions and one of the few wholly Community-wide surveys resulted in an estimated fall in costs of 1.7 per cent for manufacturing industry. Further market-integration benefits accrue significantly from economies of scale (likely to reduce average cost by some 1.5 per cent). These economies of scale provide the largest single source of economic benefit and they arise very much as restructuring takes place. A further effect of increased competition is in reducing X-inefficiency and monopoly rents. Gains in economic welfare for seven countries have been recalculated upwards for the EC(12) and estimated at between ECU 174–258 billion. Taking the midpoint would yield gains of ECU 216 billion, equivalent to some 5.3 per cent of GDP (Cecchini 1988). The magnitude of these gains is shown in Table 3.1

The sources of the gains in economic welfare were illustrated earlier in the customs union (Figures 3.3 and 3.4). Producers will gain since they will be able to lower costs through taking advantage of cheaper sources of EC component supplies and lower costs of financial services and distribution. The greatest benefits will arise when business reorganization permits greater concentration on major product lines, reaping economies of scale and often rationalization of a firm's operations on one site. However, consumers will gain more than producers since intense competition will drive down prices.

There has been a continuing wide dispersion of prices between national markets and this has tended to increase slightly in those least open to competition. Whilst up to a quarter of the price differential may be attributed to different taxes, and recognizing the difficulty of comparing products because of qualitative differences, there still remains a large residual price differential. One measure of market fragmentation has been the continued practice by firms – for example, in the motor industry – of charging different prices between national markets; car prices have varied by up to 50 per cent, being cheapest in Belgium and dearest in Denmark. There have been even wider price variations for many other products, and in pharmaceutical products, for example, the widest dispersion was as high as ten to one. In an integrated market with resale arbitrage, firms would be forced by competition to charge similar and lower prices. Prices would tend to converge downwards towards the lowest price so that in the long run a common single price would prevail. A more conservative hypothesis would be one in which only prices above the Community average converge downwards to that average. Estimates of potential gains for the latter convergence for the EC(9) were 2.1 per cent of GDP for goods and services, compared with 8.3 per cent for the extremely optimistic hypothesis that prices would converge on the minimum price (*European Economy* 1988, p. 123).

The price gains will vary, being limited in those sectors and countries which are already competitive and close to being a single market. For example, in the textiles and clothing industry most internal barriers have been dismantled and there have been massive

Table 3.1   *Potential gains in economic welfare for the EC resulting from completion of the internal market*

	Billions ECU	% GDP
Step 1 Gains from removal of barriers affecting trade	8–9	0.2–0.3
Step 2 Gains from removal of barriers affecting overall production	57–71	2.0–2.4
Gains from removing barriers (sub-total)	65–80	2.2–2.7
Step 3 Gains from exploiting economies of scale more fully	61	2.1
Step 4 Gains from intensified competition reducing business inefficiencies and monopoly profits	46	1.6
Gains from market integration (sub-total)	62*–107	2.1*–3.7
Totals For 7 member states at 1985 prices	127–187	4.3–6.4
For 12 member states at 1988 prices	174–258	4.3–6.4
Mid-point of above	216	5.3

Notes:
*This alternative estimate for the sum of steps 3 and 4 cannot be broken down between the two steps.
   The ranges for certain lines represent the results of using alternative sources of information and methodologies. The 7 member states (Germany, France, Italy, United Kingdom, Benelux) account for 88% of the GDP of the EC(12). Extrapolation of the results in terms of the same share of GDP for the 7 and 12 member states is not likely to overestimate the total for the 12. The detailed figures in the table relate only to the 7 member states because the underlying studies mainly covered those countries.

Source: Commission of EC, study of Directorate-General for Economic and Financial Affairs, in Cecchini (1988, p. 84)

imports. Hence prices of textiles and clothing may only fall by a further 0.5–1.5 per cent. In other sectors the scope for price reductions is far higher; for example, in financial services great gains will occur for consumers in southern Europe. In pharmaceutical products, prices already tend to be low in southern Europe, and therefore prices are likely to fall in other countries where prices have been controlled at higher levels to support domestic production and research. Besides lower prices, the range of consumer choice will also continue to widen.

At the macroeconomic level countries have found the attainment of their basic economic objectives increasingly elusive. The attempt to squeeze out inflationary pressures tends to slow down economic growth, resulting in higher unemployment. The attraction of the single market is that it offers the opportunity to attain a better overall macroeconomic performance. Macroeconomic gains have been modelled, deriving from the primary microeconomic effects outlined earlier, and the secondary effects resulting from econometric models have been simulated for four areas. These are: the removal of customs barriers; public procurement; liberalization of financial services and capital markets; and finally the supply-side effects based upon the strategic reactions of companies to their more competitive environment. These results are shown in Table 3.2.

For GDP the effects under each of the four headings have been aggregated, with particularly significant medium-term benefits in financial services and overall supply effects. The overall effect would be to raise GDP on average by 4.5 per cent, with a beneficial effect in creating 1.8 million new jobs. What is remarkable is that this would not be inflationary and there would be downward inflationary pressure. This would derive from the more favourable budgetary and trading balances. The general governmental budgetary position would improve, for example, through lower expenditure in public purchasing; whilst the Community's external balance would improve as its internal market measures make it more competitive *vis-à-vis* the rest of the world. In addition there may well be some marginal trading benefits at the expense of outsiders and these have given rise to fear by outsiders of a Fortress Europe problem. Some of the industrial consequences of inward overseas investment to minimize any displacement of imports is discussed in Chapter 5.

Some initial job losses may occur, such as the loss of jobs of customs collectors, and redundancies created through company restructuring and loss of market share by less competitive firms. Given that governments are likely to achieve a more favourable macroeconomic trade-off between their conflicting policy objectives, they

*Table 3.2 Macroeconomic consequences of completion of the internal market:
Community as a whole in the medium term*

	Frontier controls	Public procurement	Financial services	Supply effects[1]	Total Average	Total Range
Relative change (%)						
As % of GDP	0.4	0.5	1.5	2.1	4.5	3.2 to 5.7
Consumer prices	−1.0	−1.4	−1.4	−2.3	−6.1	−4.5 to −7.7
Absolute change						
Employment (thousands)	200	350	400	850	1800	1300 to 2300
General government borrowing requirement as a % of GDP	0.2	0.3	1.1	0.6	2.2	1.5 to 3.0
External balance as a % of GDP	0.2	0.1	0.3	0.4	1.0	0.7 to 1.3

Note:
[1]Scenario including the supply effects estimated by the consultants, the economies-of-scale phenomena (industry) and the competition effects (monopoly rents, X-inefficiency).

Source: European Economy, no. 35, March 1988, p. 159

could use their better budgetary and trade position to reflate their economies. The effect of using some of this additional flexibility to expand their economies further could result in the creation of some 5 million new jobs, depending upon the amount of accompanying expansion. For example, to maintain external balance, some 4.4 million new jobs could be created, but with some deterioration in the external balance as many as 5.7 million jobs could result. These are shown in Table 3.3, though no spatial distribution of these jobs is shown (the regional dimension of the EC is discussed further in Chapter 6).

In addition, one must recognize that the Commission studies of internal market gains are merely forecasts, based upon the programme being realized in full, and having built-in margins of error of ± 30 per cent. Such forecasts could turn out to be over-optimistic if there is any slippage in implementing the proposals. Also, using slightly different assumptions, the gains in employment may be significantly reduced. For example, altering the Cecchini assumption that two-thirds of productivity gains are transmitted into real wage increases to an assumption that all the productivity gains are transmitted into real wage increases removes the large job-creation effects from the single market. In addition, the sequence of interlinking steps from microeconomic benefits to macroeconomic employment gains rests upon a reflationary choice of action actually being taken. This will depend very much upon German economic policy decisions and the new framework of EC monetary and fiscal integration which is being developed (see Chapters 7 and 8).

Part III   UK trade in the EC

The removal of tariffs on trade between the UK and the EC has led to a reorientation in the pattern of trade. In 1958 21.8 per cent of UK imports and 21.7 per cent of UK exports were with the EC; in 1973 32.8 per cent of UK imports and 32.3 per cent of UK exports were conducted with the EC (Holmes in Cohen ed. 1983, p. 23). By 1989 53.0 per cent of UK imports and 54.6 per cent of UK exports were with the EC (*European Economy*, December 1990, p. 264). The main problem has been that imports from the EC have tended to rise faster than UK exports to the Community. This was to be expected to some extent, given the diversion in UK imports of agricultural products towards Community suppliers. Although North Sea oil has developed as a valuable export to the EC, in some respects, by

Table 3.3 Macroeconomic consequences of completion of the internal market accompanied by economic policy measures (medium-term estimates for EUR12)

Nature of economic policy	Room for manoeuvre used	Economic consequences				
		GDP as %	Consumer prices as %	Employment (in millions)	Public deficit as % point of GDP	External balance as % point of GDP
Without accompanying economic policy measures (from Table 3.2)		4.5	-6.1	1.8	2.2	1.0
With accompanying economic policy measures	Public finance	7.5	-4.3	5.7	0	-0.5
	External position	6.5	-4.9	4.4	0.7	0
	Disinflation	7.0	-4.5	5.0	0.4	-0.2

Margin of error: ± 30%

Notes:
The accompanying economic policy (public investment and reduction in direct taxation) is such that the room for manoeuvre created by completion of the internal market in respect of the public finance position (or in respect of the external balance or prices) is fully exploited.

It has been assumed, in this case, that the accompanying economic policy is so arranged as to exploit 30% of the room for manoeuvre created by the fall in consumer prices. Full use of that room for manoeuvre would give unrealistic results (sharp deterioration in the external balance in particular).

Source: European Economy, no. 35, March 1988, p. 165

pushing up the UK's exchange rate, this made it harder for the UK to export manufactured products.

A summary of UK transactions with the EC since 1973 has shown the UK generally to be in balance of payments deficit, and in relatively few years, such as 1980 and 1981, was the UK in small surplus in its current account transactions with the Community. In 1986 the deficit on all current account transactions had widened to £9165 million (Central Statistical Office 1987, p. 63). The general imbalance can be attributed mainly to the deficit on visible trade, but the UK has also been in small deficit on invisible trade with the EC, apart from a few years, such as 1981 to 1984. In 1986 the UK's deficit on invisibles was £783 million and this can be attributed mainly to government transfers associated largely with the Community budget which has offset the surplus on items such as private sector financial services.

Of major concern has been the growing imbalance on UK trade in manufactures. In 1973 the EC took 31 per cent of the UK's total export of manufactures and provided 39 per cent of its imports of manufactures. By 1984, although the EC received 39 per cent of UK exports of manufactures, it supplied 50 per cent of UK imports of manufactured products. Over half the UK trade deficit with the EC in manufactured goods has been accounted for by the UK's trade with West Germany (Dearden 1986). Unlike the UK, West Germany has enjoyed a massive trade surplus, especially in its trade with the Community. West Germany's exports as a percentage of its GDP are not significantly different from the UK's, but the latter's imports as a percentage of GDP are far higher. Key sectors such as information technology, consumer electronics and motor vehicles have accounted for a large part of the UK current account trade deficit. For example, by the mid-1980s over half of UK motor vehicles originating in the EC came from West Germany. The total UK trading imbalance in motor industry products deteriorated in the 1980s and by 1989 motor vehicles accounted for just over one-third of the total deficit in manufactured goods. For the first time, trade in parts and accessories moved into a deficit in 1986 of £346 million. UK demand has exceeded its supply capabilities, and although foreign investment in the UK motor industry will help to close the trade gap in motor vehicles, the latter will still remain too high unless the vehicles produced contain a greater domestic content.

The export–import ratio of the UK in its trade has been in deficit in most manufactured sectors. Apart from road vehicles, there have been deficits in, for example, machinery, iron and steel, and textiles, though the UK did have a surplus in a few sectors such as clothing and chemical products (Holmes in Cohen ed. 1983). The UK performance has been disappointing, given the promising position from which many of its industries started in their trade with the EC (Han and Liesner 1971). The UK, perhaps surprisingly, performed relatively badly in those sectors in which it was quite strong in the selected pre-entry year 1970–1 up to 1978–9 (Millington 1988, p. 71).

It would be wrong, however, to attribute all of the UK's trading problems solely to its membership of the EC. The UK's basic problem has been the low world income elasticity of demand for its exports and a high UK income elasticity of demand for world imports. Indeed, the UK's dilemma has been that it has not only been in deficit in its manufactured trade with the Community, but also with other developed countries. Furthermore, the export–import ratio for UK trade in manufactures with both Japan and North America has deteriorated far more than that with the EC. The pattern for the UK has been one of tending to sustain trading deficits in manufactures with major developed competitors, and to offset these partially by running a trading surplus on manufactures with less-developed countries. The UK would therefore suffer badly from any Fortress Europe consequences of the single market. Its trading imbalance in manufactures has resulted from ongoing microeconomic deficiencies, exacerbated by macroeconomic problems, such as a periodic overvalued exchange rate.

While UK industry has obtained export benefits in EC markets, the UK trade balance has not benefited sufficiently because of rising imports – though precise estimates of the trade balance vary according to the sources used (Morgan in Wallace ed. 1980). In the light of the massive decline in the UK's domestic manufacturing output, one conservative estimate is that it reduced this by at least £3 billion, about 1.5 per cent of GNP, and the effect could easily be twice as high (Winters 1987, p. 328). Despite the adverse effects on domestic unemployment, Winters has taken the optimistic view that the welfare benefits to users and consumers of manufactured products could be high enough to outweigh the losses to home producers.

Apart from the lack of competitiveness in manufactured trade, the UK has also suffered from insufficient integration in sectors in which it is more competitively placed, such as financial services and air transport. Hence the extension of integration in these sectors is welcome and during the UK Presidency of the EC Council in 1986 it sought to consolidate integration in these sectors of the internal market where the UK can benefit from its comparative advantage. Financial services account for some 7 per cent of the EC's GDP, and the aim of the internal market is to go beyond the rights of establishment in other member states to the direct provision of these services. For example, an EC non-life insurance services directive will provide cover irrespective of where the insurer is established (though transitional arrangements in Greece, Ireland, Portugal and Spain will delay its application until after the end of 1992). Nevertheless, in opening up the market in financial services it will be important for the UK to ensure that this does not have an adverse effect on those non-Community financial institutions which are already active in the 'City'. The UK will also have to compete with other countries which will begin to enjoy a more liberal and less regulated financial framework. But overall the UK clearly enjoys a comparative advantage in particular sectors, such as insurance and Stock Exchange dealings.

London's position as the leading European financial centre has been confirmed by its choice as the location for the new European Bank for Reconstruction and Development to channel financial aid to eastern Europe. The next key decision will be whether the base for any new European Central Bank is to be in London or elsewhere, such as Frankfurt.

The single internal market is a source of new opportunities, but not without risks, and some manufacturing sectors may suffer from greater import penetration without these being outweighed by extra export sales. Some industries, such as textiles, have already reorganized after long exposure to stiff international competition, and other industries now face similar rationalization. If British business fails to involve itself more actively in European Standards bodies problems will arise in working to new foreign technical standards. Once a harmonized standard has been agreed by a majority vote in the Community, then conflicting national standards have to be removed. Recently the UK has held the Secretariat of far fewer technical committees of the European Standardization Committee than either West Germany or France.

The view that the internal market is attractive since it is largely costless in budgetary terms neglects other costs, such as those imposed on depressed areas. Many local authorities have made use of public purchasing to stimulate development by favouring local suppliers. They have also exercised a social influence over the employment practices of their suppliers. The opening up of public procurement policies is likely to be a further source of imports and to dilute local economic development policies.

The UK has introduced a more active internal market publicity campaign than West Germany – the latter has done well already in industrial exports and is hesitant about opening up its protected service sector. Other countries, such as France, have been quick to publicize *'quatre-vingt-douze'* (1992). In addition, Italian businessmen, in particular Carlo de Benedetti, the head of Olivetti, has begun to exploit the EC as a natural base for industrial growth. This was illustrated by his attempts to gain control of Belgium's Société Générale early in 1988. Parts of UK industry will similarly become even more vulnerable to foreign takeovers, whereas many continental countries are better protected against such incursions.

The single internal market will generate aggregate economic gains for the EC, and also for parts of the UK economy, such as high-tech industries and much of the service sector. (The importance of the service sector in terms of employment is shown in a 3-variable graph in Chapter 4.) Nevertheless, in the short term some of the changes will be uncomfortable and result in further job displacement in weaker industrial sectors.

Dynamic effects on the UK economy. It was always hoped that there would be strong dynamic effects on British industry in the EC, arising primarily from the opportunities for greater economies of scale, a sharper competitive climate and faster growth; these will be further reinforced in the single internal market. There are some distinct examples of industries in which static and dynamic economies of scale have been reaped, but often the greatest gains have been made by continental producers in industries such as passenger cars, commercial vehicles and white goods (Owen 1983). Given the UK's relative decline in manufacturing industry, the truth about the dynamic effects may be closer to some of the early gloomy predictions (Kaldor 1971).

The benefits for consumers of lower prices from a process of 'Darwinian destruction' have to be set against some of the adverse effects on UK producers. Although some firms have been jolted into greater efficiency as a result of more competition, others have been unable to survive, resulting in a substantial loss of domestic capacity. Furthermore, excessive competition by lowering profits can inhibit some much-needed long-term investment. Nevertheless, it does appear that the heightened competitiveness in the Community may have helped to tackle the 'British disease', whereas only a few years ago pessimists concluded that the main hope lay in spreading the disease to others (Einzig 1971)!

The assumption that membership of the Community would automatically shift the UK on to a higher plateau of economic growth was over-optimistic. Certainly the UK has become a more attractive location for inward investment and its growth rate was good in 1973 – the year of entry into the Community – but the subsequent economic recession reduced economic growth rates. Between 1960 and 1972 the UK rate was only 2.9 per cent per annum, compared with 5.1 per cent in the EC. Since 1973, while there has been a convergence of the UK growth rate towards that of the EC, this has been at a much reduced level of aggregate economic growth. Between 1973 and 1986 the UK rate of economic growth was 1.9 per cent per annum compared with 2.2 per cent per annum in the EC. UK growth as a percentage of that in the EC rose from 57 per cent in 1960–72 to 82 per cent in 1973–86. If one assumes that outside the Community the UK had continued to grow at its pre-entry rate (57 per cent of that in the EC), then UK economic growth would have been only 1.3 per cent from 1973 to 1986, closing even further in the late 1980s (C. Johnson 1987). For example, in 1983–8, the total UK growth rate per annum was 3.6 per cent (compared with the EC average of 2.8 per cent), and growth per head of population was 3.4 per cent per annum in the UK (and 2.5 per cent per annum for the EC). Another result in line with this has shown that the EC accounted for about 30 per cent of the UK's economic growth rate from 1974 to 1981 (Marques Mendes 1987). Since the early 1980s the UK's comparative growth-rate internationally has been much improved and it is hoped that the internal market will reinforce its vibrant economy.

It is always difficult to disentangle the effects of the EC from other major changes taking place over the same period, of which perhaps the major one has been the production of North Sea oil. Although this has helped to loosen the overall balance of payments constraint for the UK, its effect in pushing up the exchange rate has aggravated the trading competitiveness of manufacturing industry. Hence the expansion in sectors such as oil has been partly offset by further deindustrialization. This has limited some of the projected dynamic gains from belonging to the Community.

The faster growth of manufacturing imports from the EC and elsewhere has clearly contributed to rising unemployment in the UK. Between 1980 and 1986 UK unemployment averaged 10.6 per cent, compared with 9.9 per cent in the EC. Weaker economies, such as the UK with its structural problems in particular regions, have tended to suffer unduly from freer trade. Furthermore, Community membership may have added 0.75 per cent to the UK inflation rate since 1973. Between 1960 and 1972 its inflation averaged 4.5 per cent, compared with 4 per cent in the EC. Between 1973 and 1986, UK inflation averaged 11.3 per cent, as against 9.6 per cent in the EC; hence UK inflation was 113 per cent that of the Community from 1960 to 1972 and 119 per cent that of the Community from 1973 to 1986 (Johnson 1987). The main inflationary bias has been given to food prices, since the removal of tariffs actually reduced the relative prices of industrial products.

4 Agriculture and fisheries

Part I   The economic characteristics of agriculture

Agriculture possesses distinctive characteristics: these result in short-run fluctuations in price, while in the long run agricultural prices tend to decline in real terms. The latter have necessitated movement of resources out of agriculture and into other sectors of the economy.

A free agricultural market, at the mercy of weather and climatic conditions, is likely to veer from good harvests to bad ones. The marked fluctuation in price is shown in Figure 4.1.

Reading along the supply curve: with a poor harvest, quantity OQ_1, shortages result in a high price OP_1. Quantity OQ_2 and price

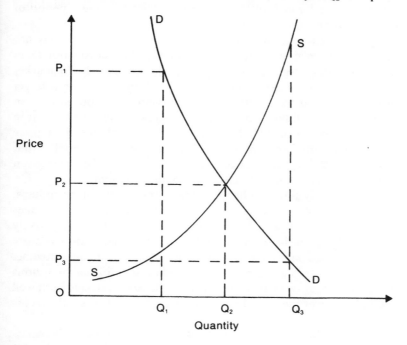

Figure 4.1   Agricultural market

85

OP$_2$ provide the market equilibrium. A golden bumper harvest, quantity OQ$_3$, results in the low price OP$_3$. A difference between agriculture and many other markets is the relatively inelastic short-run supply and relatively inelastic demand. The steep slopes of these curves magnify the range of price fluctuations.

Why is agricultural supply so unstable and unpredictable? It takes a long period of time to adjust output, and the production of many joint products means that increasing output of one product in high demand may result in the surplus of another product. Agriculture, unlike many industrial sectors, is still characterized by smaller units, though farm size has risen and some sectors of agriculture approximate to factory production, as in poultry. Resources are often trapped in farming with investment in product-specific equipment. In the short run, farmers continue to produce as long as they can cover their low variable costs; for example, labour costs, in which there has been a much reduced labour force to remunerate. However, relative immobility has been intensified by an ageing farm population and a lack of better alternative jobs during a period of much slower economic growth.

Agriculture is still highly competitive, but some farmers may not be solely maximizing profits, but maximizing their satisfaction from family farming. Agriculture may respond less closely to market signals than economists would like. Some farmers choose a target income level and to maintain this they continue to produce in an attempt to offset falling prices. Past experience has borne this out in various sectors (Capstick 1970, ch. 4). Even with the right price signals, policy-makers find it difficult to achieve the required output level; but with the wrong price signals, which have often been given in the EC, overproduction has been a major problem.

On the supply side, equilibrium is not achieved in some products. In the stable cobweb cycle a convergence towards equilibrium does not occur where supply and demand curves both have a relatively inelastic slope. In the divergent cobweb cycle, when supply is more elastic than demand, there is an explosively divergent outcome. While these lagged adjustments are based on simplified assumptions and assume that farmers never learn, the basic cycles have been well exemplified over the years in various sectors; for example, the recurrent pig cycle.

The other determinant of prices, demand, is also relatively inelastic. Both price and income elasticities are well below unity for agricultural foodstuffs; that is, a 1 per cent fall in price or rise in income results in a less than 1 per cent rise in demand. Since the 1950s food consumption has risen only slowly in most EC countries. The population increase in the EC(12) rose only 0.7 per cent per annum 1950–75, with a projected increase of only 0.3 per cent per annum 1975–2000. Total food consumption in Western Europe was expected to rise by only about 0.6 per cent per annum 1975–2000 (Duchêne *et al.* 1985, p. 81). The EC's agricultural consumption, especially since the recession in the 1970s, has failed to keep pace with rising supply. Agriculture is inevitably a declining industry in terms of demand in mature, advanced economies, but paradoxically has been expanding in supply, with a sustained rate of productivity growth based on technological and biological change.

It is generally recognized that there is a need to shield agriculture from the completely free operation of market forces, though there are policy disagreements on the most appropriate measures to adopt. There is a danger that a search for stability and cushioning in the short term can aggravate the need for long-term adjustments. The EC is now confronted by this fundamental problem of major agricultural adjustment.

Part II The Common Agricultural Policy (CAP)

A *National historical traditions*

Historically, agriculture in the major continental countries has manifested widespread protectionism. In the nineteenth century, farmers in Germany, France and Italy resorted to protectionism and resisted change, whereas their counterparts in the UK, Denmark, The Netherlands and Belgium modernized and reorganized their farming systems. Cheap imports of grain from the new world were impeded by high tariffs in countries such as France and Germany. In The Netherlands and Denmark imports of cheap grain were used to adapt their agriculture and they began to specialize in the production and export of high-value dairy produce and meat.

Between the First and Second World Wars, especially in the 1930s, agricultural policies became highly protectionist as a result of the collapse of international markets due to the depression. Germany and Italy became concerned even more with promoting self-sufficiency. Germany realized the importance of this in reducing import dependency, since war disrupted outside agricultural supplies.

In the 1940s feeding the population became the major agricultural priority. After the Second World War, with scarce foreign currency reserves in Europe, countries continued to support domestic agriculture in order to improve their balance-of-payments position.

B   The evolution of the CAP

Essentially, the evolution of the CAP represented some continuity of the national agricultural policies by the major continental countries, particularly German policy, based on high prices. Because of a new Franco-German *rapprochement* at the heart of postwar integration, a balance had to be struck between the interests of the two countries. It was decided to adopt common policies for both the industrial and agricultural sectors. West German industry recovered strongly after 1945, based upon a liberal market approach with low tariff protection; it looked forward to increasing its share of industrial trade within the customs union and has become the dominant European industrial power. France as a large agricultural producer sought reciprocal benefits for its agriculture in the EC. The major food exporters, France, The Netherlands and Italy, sought to capture the German market, partly at the expense of non-European suppliers.

A decision to include agriculture was taken during the preliminary conference in 1955, since the removal of barriers to trade and industrial products *per se* would be insufficient, unworkable and incomplete. The Commission examined various agricultural systems before coming round to more interventionist policies; this reflected national political expediency. While efficient agricultural producers like the Dutch could have prospered with a less regulated CAP, their producers, especially of dairy products, gained substantially from higher prices.

The less-efficient and high-cost countries – Germany, Belgium and Luxembourg – which were net importers, would only open up their markets if prices were set at a level sufficient to support their own farmers. To accommodate them, a range of product prices was agreed, with the first crucial prices being set for grain in 1964. Once a high price had been fixed for cereals it became necessary to set the prices of other products at comparable levels to maintain the right inter-product relationship. One of the important products was milk; its price was raised substantially to cover higher-cost producers. During the 1960s the CAP was extended to cover almost all agricultural products, with the few gaps being filled during the 1970s (see the final section of this chapter on the Common Fisheries Policy).

C   Grand objectives

The objectives of the CAP were laid down in Article 39 of the Treaty of Rome. The five aims were: to raise agricultural productivity; thereby to ensure a fair standard of living for the agricultural community; to stabilize markets; to assure availability of supplies; to ensure that supplies reached consumers at reasonable prices. This was an ambitious list of highly desirable but sometimes conflicting principles. The consequence has been a failure to achieve some of these objectives, particularly reasonable prices; for example, many products can be purchased at much lower prices on the world markets.

Policy has been most successful in achieving the objective of secure supplies, indicated by a growing self-sufficiency in many products. However, full security of all supplies is neither desirable nor feasible, given the growing dependence on energy. It is of great importance to produce those products for which there are no close substitutes available on world markets. For other products it is prudent to buy them cheaply from the world markets, rather than to become over-conscious about security and build up massive surpluses. These surpluses have made price stabilization very difficult and though the Community has had some success in stabilizing markets, this has been at the expense of creating even more instability on world markets.

The EC has been far more concerned with raising production than productivity (Fennell 1985), but labour productivity has increased through large-scale drift from the land and mainly through greater inputs of capital. Environmentalists have become concerned about the excessive use of inputs such as fertilizers; they are also concerned about the destruction of hedgerows to create larger fields and the adverse effects on wildlife. Since the CAP was designed to benefit farmers, their incomes have risen, though the ratio of agricultural income per head to that of the economy as a whole has remained relatively constant (Van den Noort in Coffey ed. 1983). There are problems in comparing agricultural incomes closely with incomes earned in other parts of the economy since farmers' incomes consist not only of a return on labour but also on capital and land which yield capital gains; farmers also consume some of their own output.

Finally, farmers do not incur the high costs of travelling to work as do many industrial workers.

Apart from an uneven distribution of income, many farmers are dissatisfied on other counts; they complain that too many of the benefits are siphoned off by suppliers of farm inputs and the processors of their raw materials. Where the farmer has himself gained, the capital value of his farm has been driven up, making it more difficult for new entrants to agriculture. The relatively low pay of many farm workers has led to part-time working becoming the norm in some areas. Many part-time farmers work evenings and weekends on the farm, relying on wives and elderly parents to do the real work. In West Germany, for example, the majority of farmers are part-timers, supplementing their income substantially from other jobs.

D   The system of common prices

While the system of common prices differs from one product to another, a general account will provide a basic picture and understanding of the main elements in the CAP pricing policy. There are four key prices: target, threshold, intervention and world prices; these are shown in Figure 4.2. The target price (*prix indicatif*), Px, is the internal wholesale price which should generally be obtainable, and it is important in determining other prices. This price is set for the main cereals and is based on the area which produces the lowest proportion of its own grain requirements and is the highest-cost area – this is Duisburg in the heavily industrialized Rhine–Ruhr area. For some other products slightly different price terminology is used, such as guide prices, basic prices and norm prices, though these correspond to the highest price shown in the diagram.

The next price in the diagram, the threshold price (*prix de seuil*) Pt, is important in relation to extra-EC trade, and more will be said about this later in relation to the world price. Other terminology analogous to the threshold price is also used, such as sluice-gate prices, reference prices and so on. The difference between the target price, Px, and the threshold price, Pt, is accounted for by handling charges and transport costs; for example, for grains, the costs between Rotterdam and Duisburg.

The intervention price (*prix d'intervention*), Pi, is the important support price below which prices are not allowed to fall. The EC Farm Fund (EAGGF) buys up supplies as the price falls to this level; it is obliged to buy everything offered to it at the intervention price,

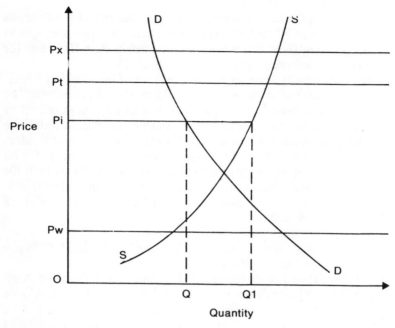

Figure 4.2   Key agricultural prices

providing the commodity meets the quality and quantity criteria laid down; for example, quantity Q–Q1 in the diagram. The intervention price for cereals has been based at Ormes, a city in the Paris basin, which has the maximum cereal surplus, and for rice the intervention centre is Vercelli in northern Italy. The intervention storage is carried out either directly by intervention agencies or by contracts with merchants to undertake the storage, with the merchants owning the cereals. Intervention prices have resulted in very effective and high-price support for key products such as cereals and milk. In other products, such as fruit and vegetables, the price support is at a much lower level, while some products – eggs and poultry – have lacked internal support.

The world price, Pw, represents the price at which EC consumers would purchase their imports in a completely free market. The imposition of variable levies on imports raises the import price to the threshold level; this ensures that importers cannot undercut Community suppliers on price. For some products customs duties are levied and for others in which the Community lacks indigenous supplies, such as oil and oil seeds, then a deficiency payment system is in operation (how this works is discussed in Part III, while for more details on specific products see Fennell 1988).

The Community, with its growing surplus of intervention stocks, has had to dispose of these on the world market at price OPw. The export subsidy used is generally described as an export refund or restitution: in the diagram, Pi–Pw = export restitution. A wide price gap has long existed between some Community and world product prices. In October 1986 EC intervention prices, compared with estimated representative world prices, were over twice as high for wheat, over three times as high for sugar and butter and over nine times as high for skimmed milk powder (*Financial Times* 18 December 1986, p. 25).

E   Agricultural expenditure: the European Agricultural Guidance and Guarantee Fund (EAGGF)
The EAGGF or Fonds Européen d'Orientation et Garantie Agricole (FEOGA) comprises two financial sections. The Guarantee section is concerned with support prices (as outlined earlier), and the Guidance section seeks to improve the structure of agriculture. Until 1966 the Guidance section expenditure could amount to one-third of the Guarantee section; but with Guarantee sums rising rapidly a ceiling was imposed. Financial support to the farmers in the EC has escalated, and for the total of the four years 1986–9 total transfers associated with agricultural policies were $425 billion, whereas the USA over the same period spent $310 billion to support fewer farmers. Transfers comprise those for both consumers and taxpayers and the former were far higher in the EC. In 1990 state subsidies to EC farmers were around $49 billion, with consumer subsidies of $85 billion in higher food prices (above prevailing world levels), compared with $47 billion federal subsidies to farmers in the USA, and only $28 billion as a subsidy to American consumers (*Financial Times* 2 November 1990). EAGGF expenditure is shown in Table 4.1.

Guarantee spending has swamped the tiny Guidance payments. While net expenditure has been reduced by the receipt of ordinary levies and sugar levies, these small sources of revenue have lacked buoyancy and the early ideas of a self-financing agricultural policy soon had to be abandoned.

Table 4.1   EAGGF expenditure, 1986–90

1	Unit 2	1986 3	1987 4	1988 5	1989[3] 6	1990[4] 7
EC budget	million ECU	34,863.2[1]	35,469.2[1]	41,120.9[2]	44,840.6	46,850.7
EAGGF	million ECU	22,910.9	23,876.4	28,866.8	29,681.3	30,111.5
Guarantee	million ECU	22,137.4	22,967.7[7]	27,687.3[8]	28,247.3	28,360.0
Titles 1 and 2[5]	million ECU	22,137.4	22,967.7	26,447.3	26,778.3	26,820.0
Set aside of arable land (Item 3,900)	million ECU	–	–	–	20.0	70.0
Depreciation of stocks and disposal of butter	million ECU	–	–	1,240.0	1,449.0	1,470.0
Guidance[6]	million ECU	773.5	908.7	1,179.5	1,434.0	1,751.5
Charges under the common agricultural policy:	million ECU	2,287.0	3,097.9	2,895.3	2,736.1	2,537.0
ordinary levies	million ECU	1,175.5	1,626.1	1,504.6	1,419.2	1,152.4
sugar levies	million ECU	1,111.5	1,471.8	1,390.7	1,316.9	1,384.6
Community GDP	thousand million ECU	3,535.7	3,721.2	4,018.3	4,361.7	4,689.1
Gross EAGGF guarantee expenditure	million ECU	22,137.4	22,967.7	27,687.3	28,247.3	28,360.0
% of GDP	%	0.63	0.62	0.69	0.65	0.60
Net EAGGF guarantee expenditure	million ECU	19,850.4	19,869.8	24,792.0	25,511.2	25,823.0
% of GDP	%	0.56	0.53	0.62	0.58	0.55

Source: EC Commission, Directorate-General for Agriculture.
[1]Reports of the Court of Auditors.
[2]Financial Report of the European Communities.
[3]1989 budget & supplementary and amending budget No. 1/89.
[4]1990 preliminary draft budget.
[5]Including the common organization of the market in fishery products.
[6]Including the EAGGF Guidance Section's share of expenditure on fisheries and set-aside.
[7]Expenditure charged against the 1987 budget (1 January 1987/end of October/beginning of November 1987).
[8]Expenditure charged against the 1988 budget (beginning of November 1987/15 October 1988).

The high level of expenditure in supporting prices can be attributed to the high prices set and to the fact that EC expenditure has replaced national expenditure on price support. For Guidance expenditure the EAGGF pays only a proportion, with the remainder coming from national governments and, where relevant, the individual beneficiary. It would make more sense to raise expenditure on Guidance, but while there have been movements towards this, it can only be done prudently by reining back the level of price support. If the semblance of a common policy is to be maintained, it would be better for the Community to take over more of this Guidance expenditure and to limit the tendency of national governments to frustrate a '*communautaire*' policy by excessive aids to their own farmers – this is on the likely assumption that the EC wishes to continue with the basic principles of a common policy instead of shifting its financial costs to national exchequers.

Guidance expenditure takes place for a wide variety of schemes and projects and like Guarantee expenditure it has a direct regional impact (Moussis 1982, p. 215). Assistance should go mainly to those in need and it is important to ensure that Guidance expenditure does not add to existing farm surpluses. The Commission proposed in 1986 to pension off workers over 55 years of age, rejuvenating the workforce and adopting less capital-intensive production methods. However, elderly farmers do not have as much energy to produce surpluses as younger farmers with heavy borrowing who may produce even greater quantities of unwanted food.

F   Political pressures

The political pressure exercised by the agricultural lobby – which means that more than a third of farmers' incomes is derived from subsidies – is totally disproportionate to the numbers employed in farming and to its share of GDP. National agricultural interest groups have been influential in France, seeking to exploit the full potential of its large land area, with French farm ministers continuing the passionate defence of French farming interests. Similarly, in Germany farming has tremendous political weight and the German Minister of Agriculture, Ertl, in power from 1969 to 1983, drew considerable support from farmers. Meanwhile, Helmut Kohl's reluctance to lose Christian Democrat support from farmers before the first postwar all-German elections late in 1990 partly explained the failure to produce agricultural concessions in the GATT round, contr.buting to the breakdown of negotiations. In the smaller countries with fewer farmers, but with significant upstream and downstream linkages, agricultural organization is often even stronger and more effective.

Since the EC represents aggregate national interests, interest group activities have also moved upwards to the Community levels. The Federation of EC farming interests is the Comité des Organisations Professionelles Agricoles des Pays de la Communauté Economique Européenne (COPA). This has lobbied strongly in the various Community institutions and its influence has far exceeded that of consumer interests.

In setting farmers' incomes each year the annual price review has generally raised prices to try to keep incomes on modern farms in line with average incomes in other sectors. Commission proposals, and particularly agreements by the Council of Ministers, have tended to concede to agricultural pressures. In the highly politicized decision-making process agriculture ministers are expected to defend their own farming interests vigorously, since they do not wish to be criticized for selling their own farmers short. Package deals have been stitched together and trade-offs made, but invariably a final agreement has only been possible by trading-up the settlement. It is only financial constraints which have restored a sense of realism to agricultural policy-making by the Council, along with recent disquiet voiced by the European Parliament.

G   Agricultural problems

1. Low farm incomes. The CAP includes a diversity of countries with differing levels of dependence on agriculture and a wide range of farm incomes. The percentage of the labour force employed in agriculture relative to that employed in the industrial and service sectors can be illustrated, as in Figure 4.3, on a 3-variable graph.

Reading across the left-hand axis, Greece had 27 per cent of its labour force employed in agriculture; reading down the right-hand axis, 28 per cent of its labour force in industry; and reading up the horizontal axis, 45 per cent of its labour force in the service sector. These graphs are useful in illustrating any 3-variable distribution which sums to 100 per cent. Southern European countries are shown as having relatively high dependence on agriculture when measured in terms of employment. If this had been illustrated differently in

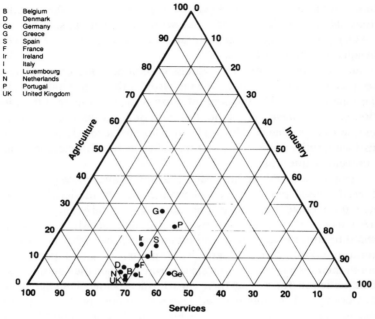

B	Belgium
D	Denmark
Ge	Germany
G	Greece
S	Spain
F	France
Ir	Ireland
I	Italy
L	Luxembourg
N	Netherlands
P	Portugal
UK	United Kingdom

Source: Eurostat (1990)

Figure 4.3   Percentage distribution of employment in agriculture, industry and services, 1988

terms of agriculture's contribution to GNP, it would tend to be lower; for example, comprising 17 per cent of Greek GNP, reflecting lower productivity.

Farm incomes are lowest in Southern Europe, which has suffered from generations of poor soil-conservation policies and lack of irrigation. Farmers in Southern Europe have received less generous support for their produce than have their counterparts in Northern Europe. In Northern Europe some specialization has occurred, raising incomes for cereal growers in areas such as central France and eastern England, and also for pig and poultry producers in close proximity to ports in The Netherlands through which animal feeding-stuffs can be imported cheaply. Perhaps in the future Spain will begin to specialize – more successfully than Italy has done – in supplying fruit and vegetables to Northern European markets. This is far more sensible than maintaining expensive glasshouse production in countries like The Netherlands by subsidies on heating oils.

The policy of trying to raise farm incomes has had paradoxical results, since the large number of small farmers which are most in need of welfare support have tended to receive least, whereas the smaller number of large and highly productive farms in least need of any such support have benefited the most. The attempt to raise farm incomes by increasing farm output prices has distorted the allocation of resources and failed to tackle the problem of low income farmers effectively. More appropriate policies would be by direct supplements to labour income.

Structural policies would help to create more viable and efficient farms. Though much progress has been made in increasing the average size of farm and in better production methods, many farms are still sub-optimal. More than half of the farms in the EC are less than ten hectares (a hectare is equal to 2.4711 acres). By the end of the century there is still likely to be a third of EC farms of this modest size, even though total numbers employed in farming will continue to decline. Land fragmentation and scattered strips of land have restricted mechanization and the scope for economies of scale. Nevertheless, the optimum size of farm is still lower than the optimum unit in manufacturing industry, and well below the size of the large collective farms created in Eastern Europe. But there is a danger that larger units with greater capital investment will tend to intensify production with accompanying problems of surpluses and greater environmental damage. The alternative is one of persisting with the structure of many small farms, often on a part-time basis, and perhaps seeing as a positive rather than a negative virtue that they do not optimize output.

2. Farm surpluses. Agricultural output is far more variable and unpredictable than industrial output. Clearly underproduction as a result of a bad harvest would be catastrophic, particularly where countries were unable to purchase supplies on the world market. Overproduction, while less of a crisis than underproduction, has generated embarrassing surpluses which have tended to recur in some products. The main problem is not so much that of natural seasonal surpluses but of structural surpluses; these are the consequence of fixing prices artificially above their equilibrium level.

Technological progress has added further to the capacity of agriculture to produce in excess of demand. By the use of fertilizers and other techniques, farm yields have risen, because farmers have found that it costs almost as much to cultivate a field to produce one tonne an acre as to produce three tonnes. These have been stimulated by high prices, though real prices for many products have actually fallen (Duchêne *et al.* 1985, p.14). Indeed, for some years now agriculture has been subject to quite a strong cost/price squeeze which likewise has resulted in the need to raise yields. Expansionary technological forces are making the problem of surpluses a permanent feature of the agricultural landscape.

Overproduction has led to massive stocks, and the value of products in public storage rose to ECU 12.3 billion in 1987. The most costly stocks are of butter and skimmed milk powder. Since it is inconvenient to store fresh milk, surpluses are manifested in mountains of butter and skimmed milk powder. The actual worth of some of the stocks was only about one-third of their book-value since many of them had deteriorated with age (Commission 1987, p. 7). In disposing of them one needs to think less in terms of the sunk costs of acquiring them and more in terms of their opportunity costs (Chalkley 1986).

The EC(6) moved from a situation of 91 per cent self-sufficiency at its inception to one of overall self-sufficiency for the EC(10) after Greek enlargement. Furthermore, this actually understates the full rise in self-sufficiency, since UK entry into the EC depressed the Community's ratio of self-sufficiency. The EC(12) has now generated further overproduction of some products such as wine, though it is still in marginal deficit in products such as fresh fruit, citrus fruit, and oils and fats. The agricultural land area utilized in Spain is second only to that in France and its potential productive capacity is substantial, as agricultural prices for Spanish producers rise to the higher levels in the EC. While the newer states may complement the northern members of the Community in some respects by importing more cereals and meat from them, in the long run the Iberian peninsula could become self-sufficient in grains. If additional surpluses do not arise, then it can only be due to the mixed blessing of inefficient farming, which is the case in Portugal.

Meanwhile, the incorporation of East Germany into the Community adds further agricultural problems. Its farms, larger than in West Germany, have none the less been inefficient because of overmanning and old unreliable machinery. Although EC farm prices are lower than those which existed before in East Germany, over time its agricultural efficiency is likely to rise, contributing to overproduction in some sectors. In sugar, for example, East Germany has received a generous quota, adding to the EC's existing surplus. Furthermore, if other countries, such as Hungary, were to join the EC, agricultural support costs would rise still more. Even outside the EC, any future agricultural growth in Eastern Europe is likely to drive down world prices, increasing the cost of EC export subsidies.

The EC has adopted a combination of internal and external measures to alleviate the problem of surpluses. Internally, it has destroyed products such as fruit and vegetables; in addition, some denaturing of products occurred in the past, rendering them unsuitable for human consumption and fit only for animal feed. Consumers prefer the surpluses to be sold domestically, and specific products, for example, butter and beef, have been subsidized for consumption by pensioners and families on low incomes.

The Community's external policies have consisted partly of selling off the surpluses cheaply to other countries. This has aroused almost as much emotional concern in the UK as the destruction of the surpluses, particularly when they have been exported to the Soviet Union. It is paradoxical that Soviet agriculture's main problem has been one of underproduction, whereas that of the EC has been that of overproduction. Other external policies are also controversial, especially the use of export subsidies to make products saleable on world markets. The only policy with any popular support, certainly on humanitarian grounds, is helping the needy people in the Third World. Yet even food aid in the long term may encourage a taste for different imported products and actually reduce the recipient's own agricultural output as prices are lowered. Compared with butter, products such as milk powder have higher nutritional value and are fairly cheap to store. The EC's aid policies have been motivated by a desire to remove its food surpluses, and critics of aid believe that a policy of assisting agricultural developments *per se* may be a more effective approach in less-developed countries (LDCs).

3. Distortion of international trade. The CAP has led to some alteration in the pattern of international trade. The EC's agricultural trade has gone through two phases. The first phase consisted of a massive growth of intra-trade in foodstuffs which rose more rapidly than extra-EC food imports. France and The Netherlands, more so than Italy, have increased their exports, largely to the main import markets of West Germany and the UK. But the Community market has become satiated as West Germany and the UK have increased their own levels of agricultural self-sufficiency.

In the second phase the Community, though still a major world importer, was transformed into a major world exporter of food second only to the USA. In a few products the EC actually became the world's number one exporter (Duchêne *et al.* 1985, p. 55). However, since international trade in agricultural products represents only a small proportion of world production, major changes in the league table can occur based on rather marginal quantities. Expanding import markets for agricultural sales have opened up only slowly in Japan, the newly industrializing countries (NICs), the Organization of Petroleum Exporting Countries (OPEC) and in Eastern Europe (Comecon). Both India and China have become net exporters of wheat, and many LDCs in great need of food have unfortunately lacked the foreign exchange to translate this into effective demand. World food consumption is failing to increase at a pace necessary to absorb the surpluses of temperate developed countries.

The EC's sales in international markets are only competitive by using large export subsidies, though other countries like the USA also maintain exports in other ways. In 1985 a third of EC appropriations were for export refunds since as a single transaction in many cases it is cheaper than storage. Efficient international suppliers in the rest of the world naturally resent any displacement of their own sales by the EC. They have seen the loss of many of their exports to the EC itself and this has then been compounded by displacement from other world import markets. EC exports of agricultural products to the rest of the world rose from an index of 100 in 1973 to 295 in 1986, whereas its imports from the rest of the world rose from an index of 100 in 1973 to 166 in 1986. EC policy runs counter to the whole purpose of free trade which is to create beneficial international specialization on the basis of comparative advantage. EC policy has created a further adverse effect of greater instability in world market prices.

Temperate food producers, such as Australia and New Zealand, have been badly affected, despite some continuing special arrangements to mitigate the worst effects on the latter. The rules of GATT for agricultural trade have been inadequate; for example, the code obliging countries to avoid export subsidies which would lead to an inequitable share of world markets has been too imprecise. The challenge by the more fair-minded exporters will hopefully lead to a more effective GATT. At meetings of the GATT International Dairy Agreement Australia has accused the EC of using secret subsidies. New Zealand has greatly cut back its own subsidies since 1984, with its milk producers, for example, surviving on a price only one-fifth of the level in the EC.

Both Canada and the USA have made complaints about EC exports eroding their sales of products such as wheat. The EC's world market share of wheat rose from 12 per cent in 1979–80 to 17 per cent in 1984–5. The Iberian enlargement led to further American concern about a possible loss of its traditional exports of wheat, corn and oil seeds. It demanded compensation and at the beginning of 1987 threatened to introduce a 200 per cent tariff on a range of European goods, including gin, brandy, white wine, blue cheese and endives. A compromise was reached, averting an open trade war between the two blocs. Nevertheless, it will be difficult to reconcile the EC's concern with a managed market with the American preference for a freer market, even though the latter does not operate a policy based on a completely open market (Josling in Tsoukalis ed. 1986).

The CAP has had adverse global effects on poorer countries in an even more vulnerable position; for example, in South America, Argentina derives approximately three-quarters of its export revenue from agriculture and is a major producer of maize and beef. The EC took temporary measures against Argentina during the Falklands crisis, but the long-term effects of the CAP have had a much more significant impact on the displacement of Argentinian products from the EC market.

Similarly, Brazil has failed to develop its export potential sufficiently to prevent a growing problem of financial indebtedness. The EC's sugar policy has been an additional factor in Brazil seeking to convert sugar surpluses into fuel to reduce its import bill for energy. Despite favourable treatment of sugar imports from the Lomé countries, the EC's own high price, and dumping of sugar on world markets, has created major difficulties for producers like Cuba, the Philippines, the Dominican Republic and Thailand – the latter also having a different complaint relating to the Community's policy on cereal substitutes. Despite sugar quotas for the EC's own producers, the CAP has shifted the price adjustment on to the residual world market. LDCs have tended to become net importers of food, not only because of the EC, but mainly because of their own inadequate agricultural policies which result in low agricultural investment, with low domestic food prices being set in the interests of urban consumers.

H   Reforms to the CAP

Proposals for the reform of the CAP abound, but their application, though reducing the share of agricultural spending in the EC Budget, have often been cosmetic; they have fallen short of the fundamental root-and-branch changes which are necessary. The CAP has gradually become outmoded as underproduction has given way to overproduction. Reliance largely upon one policy instrument of high prices has had to be modified by a more rigorous approach, whereby prices are reduced and accompanying policies, such as income supplements, adopted. The latter is more effective, especially in improving distributional equity (Tarditi 1984). The Commission's Green Paper in 1985 recognized that a policy of continuing to lower farm prices would have to be supplemented by some income support for small farmers. In 1987 the Commission proposed that direct income aids should be applied to help 'intermediate' farms; that is, potentially viable farms. However, the EC Farm Fund was not prepared to co-finance income for the 'social problem' farm, but to encourage the use of other EC regional funds, and the EC has seen the importance of setting a framework for strict limits on national aids. The proposals by the EC's Farm Commissioner, MacSharry, in 1990 would go further, moving the EC towards direct income aids for smaller farmers. For example, in cereals it was proposed to direct aid to cereal farms of less than 30 acres to counterbalance a reduction by some 40 per cent in the intervention price.

A policy of continuing price-cuts is vital for products in surplus, and though prices could be raised for products in deficit, unfortunately more and more products are in surplus. The key product is cereals, where price reductions provide immense benefit to livestock producers who have switched to cheaper imported substitutes to feed their animals. The Commission proposed for 1988–9 a guaranteed maximum of 155 million tonnes of cereals for the EC, after which prices would be reduced. At the emergency summit meeting of Heads of Government in Brussels in February 1988 agreement could only be reached on a slightly larger output of 160 million tonnes, after which cumulative price cuts of 3 per cent a year would be imposed for four years. Community policy has to make clear that price reductions will be imposed cumulatively so that farmers will recognize the new signals over the coming years. Certainly the EC has recognized that unlimited guarantees of prices and intervention cannot continue and the return of intervention buying towards its original safety-net function to deal with short-term fluctuations is welcome. The stabilizers now reduce intervention price when production exceeds certain ceilings.

The reluctance in the past to apply the most direct and effective policy of price-cuts often resulted in weaker alternatives. Co-responsibility levies, for example, have been applied to milk since 1977, but have generally been too low to be effective. They have operated on supply, to reduce price, and on demand, with the levy being used in an attempt to stimulate the falling sales of milk.

Quotas have also been introduced since they seem to cause least disturbance to the existing situation but manage to reduce surpluses, dumping and budgetary costs. They have long been used for sugar beet and in 1984 were introduced for milk, but have been set at too high a level and production has continued to outrun consumption. In 1986 the Commission agreed on a further substantial reduction in milk quotas over a three-year period. It sought to make farmers individually responsible for keeping within their milk quotas to prevent those who were overproducing from incurring the penalties of the super levy. Quotas can be applied most easily in the case of the products mentioned where there are a limited number of factories and dairies: their disadvantage is that when rigidly set they tend to freeze the existing pattern of production inefficiently. There is a danger of being forced to extend quotas elsewhere and ending up with an even more controlled and managed system. The Commission proposed in 1987 that the sugar quota for 1988–9 should be unchanged and the milk quota seems likely to be renewed in 1992.

Other suggestions floated have been to go beyond quotas on output and to impose them on inputs such as nitrogenous fertilizers also. Quotas on the latter would hit the operations of the larger and more efficient farms; but they would fit in with a policy of cutting output without driving the small farmer out of existence. There is certainly less scorn being shown now for a return to low-input organic farming.

The most significant proposal for important structural reform was contained in the *Memorandum sur la réforme de l'agriculture dans la Communauté Economique Européenne*, more popularly referred to as the Mansholt Plan of 1968. Unfortunately, neither sufficient movement of labour from the land nor the significant reduction in the agricultural land area which it proposed have taken place. The latter may now be rectified by the Commission placing a new emphasis on setting land aside to take it out of cultivation for a minimum of five years. This could result in at least 20 per cent of arable land being retired from use by the late 1990s and used for other purposes. However, its effects in cutting output may still be negated if farmers leave their poorest land fallow and simply produce more intensively on their existing land. Furthermore, if the land is used for grass and fodder crops, this will simply transfer the arable problem to the livestock sector.

The consequences of technical change and agricultural surpluses are that less land will be needed for agriculture, releasing land for other purposes. These include additional land for building in areas of population pressure, plus its use for tourism, reafforestation, for example, or the designation of parts of it as environmentally sensitive areas (ESAs). The latter may help to preserve the much diminished wetland areas with their variety of wildlife; and by growing suitable trees such as willows, traditional rural crafts such as basketmaking can be revitalized. Transfer of income to farmers will be switched away from the production of unwanted quantities towards better-quality food and towards compensating farmers for the maintenance of particular landscapes and amenities. Unfortunately in relatively few of these, other than tourism, for example, are farmers able to receive their income from the market, so continuing farming subsidies will be necessary. It remains to be seen whether these changes will prove any more desirable to society in the future than the transfers to produce food.

Rising agricultural expenditure threatens budgetary bankruptcy with the falling value of the dollar further increasing the cost of EC export subsidies. The EC seems determined to maintain the principle of common financing, although this has resulted in the major agricultural importing countries contributing a disproportionate share. Any return to national financing is opposed by the major agricultural producing countries who argue that it would undermine the CAP. Furthermore, it is likely that richer member states would still choose to subsidize their agriculture heavily, but at least the support cost would be nationally apparent. The countries most affected would be those in Southern Europe which lack the national financial resources necessary to support their farmers.

I Green currencies and monetary compensatory amounts (MCAs)

Why did green currencies arise? The CAP was constructed on the basis of common prices, but unfortunately the international monetary system of fixed exchange rates began to collapse in the late 1960s. In August 1969 the French government decided to devalue the franc and this was followed in October 1969 by a revaluation of the Deutschmark. Both countries wished to retain the common price system of the CAP. France was not prepared to accept the inflationary effects of devaluation on its consumers, while Germany was concerned about the adverse effects of revaluation on its farmers and their loss of exports. Therefore it was decided to retain agricultural prices at their original levels by instituting a special new system.

The system adopted is known as 'green currencies'. It might be questioned why a special procedure should apply to agricultural exchange rates and not to other products; for example, there is no 'black currency' for trading coal. The reason is that the Community has not tried to stabilize common prices for coal with an intervention system, nor has coal in recent years assumed the overriding importance of agriculture. It was decided that temporarily the difference between the new market rates of exchange and their original level (that is, green rates for agriculture) would be bridged by the use of Monetary Compensatory Amounts (MCAs). This meant that in the case of France a negative MCA was applied, and a positive MCA for Germany.

MCAs apply to agricultural products subject to the intervention mechanism and which would otherwise suffer from currency fluctuations. Initially the MCAs were financed by national governments, but in July 1972 – for trade with non-EC countries – and in January 1973 – for intra-EC trade – compulsory MCAs were introduced and financed by the EC. While the joint float of EC currencies in 1973 made the system more manageable, the first enlargement of the Community brought in new countries with representative (green) rates; also, there were still problems with EC countries not able to operate in the joint float.

Any assessment of the consequences of green currencies depends upon the extent to which one considers that agriculture should be insulated from exchange rate changes. Is there something distinctive about agriculture *per se*? Whereas industrialists in trading products can choose to trade at the new exchange rates or to adjust domestic prices accordingly, farmers (without MCAs) face an immediate change in farm prices and in trading patterns. MCAs, by trying to freeze the original situation, have led to some misallocation of resources; for example, Germany's positive MCA system has enabled its farmers to sell more products abroad, reducing inroads of inherently more efficient imports from other Community countries. West German producers, benefiting from lower imported input costs, have raised agricultural self-sufficiency, much to the chagrin of countries such as France.

The MCA system was extremely complex, varying between products. It mainly covered those heavily traded products for which intervention prices existed (though there were exceptions to this, with poultry and eggs being included, despite absence of intervention prices, mainly because of their dependence on cereals for which there are very significant intervention prices). The existence of MCAs added to the risks involved in trade since buyers preferred to purchase at fixed prices instead of having to carry the risk involved with an MCA; for example, the Community lost some long-term export contracts overseas by refusing to quote fixed prices.

Despite these criticisms of green currencies, they did offer some advantages, especially in the short term, in maintaining price stability which would have been wrecked by floating currencies. MCAs helped to maintain a veneer of common prices, whilst at the same time conferring some freedom of manoeuvre on national governments – via devaluation or revaluation of their green currencies – to set prices to suit their own interests. The use of MCA adjustments has sometimes facilitated agreements at meetings of agriculture ministers; this was because any prudent price increases could be varied by national governments for their own farmers by MCA adjustments. Nevertheless, it has been accepted that on balance MCAs should be phased out in the long term.

Part III   The UK and the CAP
Historically, Britain imported foodstuffs freely from the rest of the world, but during and after the Second World War steps were taken to raise the level of domestic self-sufficiency. A distinctive system of

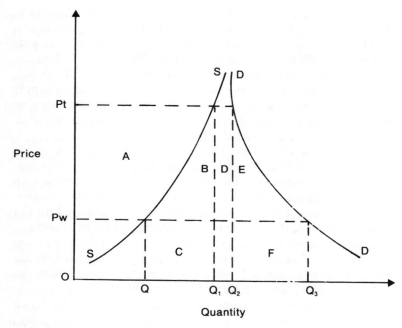

Figure 4.4   Effects of the CAP

deficiency payments to farmers was introduced to cover the difference between the realized market price which the farmer obtained on the open market and the higher guaranteed price. This system increased domestic production whilst at the same time enabling imports to continue relatively freely, giving consumers the benefit of low food prices. The system was financed out of general taxation, but rising budgetary costs led the government to introduce more selective policies, including guaranteed prices only for standard quantities of various products.

The UK has switched over to the Community system of farm support, though in some products, like the sheep meat regime, the UK has been allowed to operate a variant of the original deficiency payments system. But the Commission proposed in 1987 that this should be phased out as part and parcel of Community agricultural reform to limit costs.

Under the CAP, the main difference for the UK has been the fixing of a high target price as shown in Figure 4.4. The effect of setting a high price, OPt, induces more resources into agriculture, BC, and enables a larger surplus to be reaped by existing producers, A. Whereas under the deficiency payments system consumers purchased foodstuffs at the world price, OPw, under the CAP there is a loss of consumer satisfaction, EF, since demand has fallen from OQ_3 to OQ_2. High prices have the unfortunate effects of raising supply and cutting demand with resultant surpluses. While the levies on imports, D, are a source of revenue they have been insufficient to finance the massive agricultural expenditure.

From the viewpoint of the UK, the import levies do not accrue directly to the British government, but form part of the Community's 'own resources'. Since the UK is still very dependent on imports of foodstuffs from outside the EC, it contributes disproportionately in levies. Likewise, substantial levies are collected by The Netherlands, since Rotterdam is the single biggest point of entry.

Many Community countries are net exporters of foodstuffs and the total cost of subsidizing export surpluses is illustrated by the shaded area in Figure 4.5. Whereas in any national system the exporting country would have to bear the cost of this itself, in the Community it is financed from the 'own resources' provided by all EC members. This may be logical if one believes in a 'Community', but its consequence is that the UK contributes to financing the surpluses of other EC countries – the latter having less incentive to reduce such surpluses when they are not financing the full cost themselves.

Various estimates have been made of the budgetary costs to the UK arising from the CAP (Buckwell *et al.* 1982). In addition to the focus on budgetary costs, total costs to the UK are even higher when one adds the trade costs of buying at EC rather than world prices. Higher agricultural prices have led to a redistribution of benefits from consumers to producers and in the UK the losses have outweighed the benefits. Various studies have indicated a range of substantial costs to the UK (Whitby 1979; Buckwell *et al.* 1982; Hill 1984; El-Agraa 1985).

Much depends upon assumptions about what the scenario would be if the UK were not part of the Community. Would world prices still be lower than EC prices, and would any increase in UK demand on the world market be matched by increased supply? EC surpluses would be available on the world market, carrying export subsidies, and other world producers could probably ensure sufficiently abun-

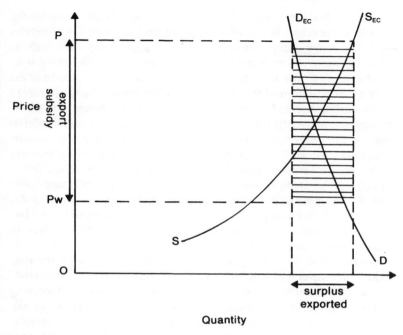

Figure 4.5   The CAP and export surpluses

dant supplies. The UK economy would gain most in welfare from free trade (Buckwell *et al.* 1982). This would not be attractive to UK farmers and in reality such a policy seems less feasible than choosing between the CAP and some alternative system of farm support.

The CAP has had a negative effect on the UK growth rate (Marques Mendes 1987, p. 100). It has also had an inflationary effect on the UK economy and has added to the balance-of-payments costs by paying higher prices for food imports. Although the higher price of food has tended to dampen demand, this has again been at the expense of consumers.

The green currency system for sterling has been operated inconsistently, but in its early years was operated in the interests of British consumers. The pound floated downwards so that it fell substantially below its 1973 representative 'green' rate. Negative MCAs were applied and a widening gap opened up between the market and the green rate for the pound. Other Community countries objected to making budgetary contributions to subsidize British consumers. This in some respects was absurd, given that some of the countries with budgetary complaints about excessive contributions, such as West Germany, were benefiting in their trade from higher agricultural exports to the British market. A combination of pressures led to some devaluation of the green pound. The major change occurred when sterling became a petro-currency and the exchange rate of the pound rose above the green rate. After that time, consumers suffered but, on the other hand, British farmers have welcomed the opportunity to raise output with positive MCAs. However, by the late 1980s British farmers again felt disadvantaged as the pound fell in value, but the green currency system held UK support prices down and pushed up MCA levies on British exports. A 10 per cent devaluation of the green pound would raise consumer prices but by less than 1 per cent, and at the same time increase UK commodity support prices by £600 million.

Overall, UK farm output has grown at a faster rate than its industrial output and British farmers have helped to bridge the trade gap left by the continuing poor performance of the manufacturing sector in the wake of deindustrialization. A higher level of agricultural investment has been undertaken, raising farm incomes, despite the squeeze of high costs, price restraints and the imposition of quotas. The UK has raised its self-sufficiency, supplying more than 80 per cent of its temperate food needs, compared with just over 60 per cent in 1973. Instead of being a sizeable importer of grain, by the mid-1980s the UK had become the sixth largest exporter of cereals in the world. Cereal farmers, located largely in eastern England, have benefited substantially, more so than livestock and dairy farmers in the poorer western upland areas of the UK.

On the whole the CAP has been much criticized, particularly in the UK, for its adverse effects on consumers, and some consider the policy to be a comprehensive failure (Hill 1984, p. 117). It has certainly distorted resource allocation, but its central importance in the process of integration means that policy changes are likely to be marginal rather than substantial. Yet without radical reform disintegration may occur and the UK has to make up its mind whether it should approve price cuts towards world levels, if the *quid pro quo* is enhanced direct income aid to smaller farmers, of which the main beneficiaries are likely to be the more numerous smaller continental farms.

The Common Fisheries Policy (CFP)

Fisheries are included in the definition of agricultural products, and the market regime for the CAP included some market support for fish prices. France was the main proponent of such market support, being worried about the impact of free imports on its own fishing industry. The introduction of the CFP before the first enlargement negotiations with other important fishing countries resulted in major problems. Norway objected to proposals for a CFP and opted out of the EC, pointing out that the four prospective applicants had a fishing catch nearly three times as high as that in the EC(6) (Nicholson and East 1987, p. 122). For the UK, the agreement incorporated in the Act of Accession to the EC reduced its inshore fishing limit.

The Law of the Sea Conference in 1975 resulted in coastal states having resource zones extending out to 200 miles or the median line. The EC extended its own fishing limits out to that distance at the beginning of 1977. Both the UK and Ireland argued that the principle of equal access conflicted with their demands for domestic preference. But the UK was only successful in retrieving the twelve mile limit which had existed under the 1964 Fisheries Convention. Negotiations to reach an acceptable CFP have been difficult and protracted, despite the agreement in 1977 and the revised CFP introduced in January 1983.

The concern of the CFP is to conserve and manage stocks, setting total allowable catches for species threatened by overfishing and then dividing them into national quotas. Each nation has to declare its catch and be open to inspection, but difficulties have arisen over proper verification and its enforcement in all Community countries. There are worries about too much industrial fishing by countries such as Denmark and its adverse effects on fish stocks. Market organization has tried to provide an adequate level of income for fishermen and, in addition, finance has been provided to restructure the industry.

For the UK, whereas the CAP generally yielded a golden harvest for British farmers – at least until quotas – under the CFP its fishing industry has declined. For example, between 1971 and 1980 its nominal catch of marine fish and shellfish fell, whereas that of the EC(10) rose over the same period (Macsween 1987). While the decline of the British fishing industry and its overcapacity may be attributable to factors other than the CFP, the latter's principle of free access has added to its problems.

The origins of its difficulties lay in the loss of distant fishing rights after the Icelandic victory in the cod war. International sympathies were with little Iceland which was so dependent on fishing, and it could also call upon American goodwill because of the important NATO base located there. The UK lost the valuable white demersal fish (caught near the ocean floor) which were the traditional purchase of the British consumer. The UK started to land lower-priced pelagic fish (caught near the surface), greatly reducing the value of domestic fish landings. Iceland's declaration of its own 200-mile limit led to a laying-up of British trawlers, with devastating effects in fishing areas like the Humber ports where much of the fish processing industry is based. Frozen-fish processors began to meet the UK's traditional taste for white fish much more from imports.

In the revised CFP, which was based on the historic pattern of fishing for each stock, the UK had to settle for less than its percentage share of Community fishing waters. Another difficulty for the UK has been that the EC makes agreements with outside countries, so that it is all Community fishing countries which obtain reciprocal concessions. The EC has signed fishery agreements with non-EC countries, whereas national agreements made by the UK before it joined the EC would probably have led to greater national benefits on a *quid pro quo* basis. Agreements have been signed with countries such as Norway which share joint stocks with the Community; also with Canada in return for reduced import duties on Canadian fish. The EC has also purchased fishing concessions from less-developed countries, particularly in Africa.

The fishing industry has been whittled down in size, particularly in England, and its plight is a testimony to mismanagement when an island economy becomes a net importer of fish. Some of its problems have been common to all industries, such as rising fuel costs, high interest rates and overvaluation of sterling. Fishermen have been squeezed by these elements, accompanying quotas and new measures agreed in December 1990 to tie up boats for a given number of days each month. Dwindling fish stocks have arisen from overfishing, and despite limits on Spanish fishing rights in the Community pond for its first ten years of membership, disputes with France and the UK soon arose; for example, over the registration of Spanish vessels in the UK which thereby ate into the British fishing quota.

5 Industrial and technological policies

Part I Industrial problems and policies

What kind of progress has been made by the Community in developing a common industrial policy, and what form has this taken? Why is industry in the EC in general not as strong technologically, nor as efficient, as that in the USA and Japan? What can, and is, being done to remedy this? These are just a few of the questions to be examined in this chapter. It will become evident that even if the EC had not existed, it would have been necessary eventually to establish something like it, in order that European industry could enjoy the benefits of a larger market to reap economies of scale and collaborate to reduce the costs of research and development.

Industrial policy creates the conditions in which industry can flourish, and its main concern has been to create a competitive and efficient industrial structure. Government intervention has sought to improve industrial performance. In addition, it has been concerned with the regional implications of industrial change and the social costs arising from this (Chapter 6 provides a fuller account). There are also social costs to the environment which are associated with industrial activities.

A Community environmental policy began only in 1973 but since that time a much greater concern has emerged about ecological issues. It is agreed that the environment needs to be safeguarded and improved, and that the principle that the 'polluter pays' should be used as much as possible. However, such a guide has some limitations since firms may have to close down if they cannot meet pollution costs. Some countries have sought to avoid giving the Community too much leeway to impose rigorous standards on them. Hence, in the Single European Act it was agreed that the EC would only take action where the objectives could be achieved more effectively at Community rather than national level.

It is not intended here to focus on environmental issues, but rather to examine the more traditional concerns of industrial policy-makers. These have been concerned with controlling monopolies, restrictive practices and mergers. But they have had to be tempered by a recognition that large firms are necessary in some sectors to compete technologically and efficiently with American and Japanese firms. Unfortunately, European policies have often tended to support national champions, failing to recognize that the Community has opened up opportunities to develop firms on a continental scale and to co-operate more closely.

Traditionally, monopoly has been condemned since it results in a misallocation of resources. Furthermore, because of the absence of competition, a high degree of 'X-inefficiency' may exist under the operation of monopoly. *Prima facie*, a strong legal anti-monopoly policy can be implemented on the basis of a highly concentrated industrial structure: the USA has favoured such an approach. However, the case against monopoly is not always wholly conclusive, for various reasons. First, in practice oligopoly tends to prevail in most sectors rather than outright monopoly. In oligopoly, firms may either collude or compete, and both the number of firms and the kind of products being produced are influential in determining the behaviour of such firms. Secondly, large firms are able to benefit from economies of scale and are able to spend more on research and development. The EC requires companies to be of a sufficient size to compete with large international corporations. Therefore, in Europe there has been a less dogmatic policy towards large firms than in the USA. Instead of an outright condemnation of firms on the structural grounds of high concentration ratios, there has been a preference to use this as a guide, but then to go further by examining other aspects of behaviour such as conduct and performance.

Part II EC industrial competitiveness and policies to promote technology

A Concentration and competition policy

Concentration. Industrial concentration is reflected by the growth of large firms which have come to dominate particular industries and national economies. Absolute industrial concentration is measured from the percentage share of indicators such as employment, output, sales and so on, held by the few largest firms. Somewhat different results emerge when these indicators are used; for example, in 1989 Europe's three largest firms in terms of number of employees were Siemens, Daimler-Benz and BAT Industries, each with over 300,000 employees. When the ranking was based on sales, the top three firms were Royal Dutch–Shell, IRI and British Petroleum; and when based on stock market capitalization, the top three firms were Royal Dutch–Shell, British Petroleum and BT (*Financial Times* 19 December 1989). Since the behaviour of giant firms is likely to be influenced by, amongst other things, the total number of firms in the industry, then other measures, such as relative concentration, can take this into account. Often it is the same industries internationally which tend to be much more highly concentrated; for example, plotting industrial concentration ratios for West Germany, France and Italy has shown certain industrial similarities.

Although the extent of industrial concentration has increased in the national economies of member states, there are some factors restraining this. One of these has been the diversification of large companies into different sectors; for example, one of many firms involved in an extensive process of diversification in the late 1980s was Daimler-Benz, and the West German government overruled objection by its Cartel Office to its takeover of the Messerschmitt-Bölkow-Blohm (MBB) aerospace group. Giant companies have become much more significant in national economies, establishing themselves as conglomerates. However, their dominant share of specific industries has often been diluted by new entrants: these have either been other giant companies or – where entry barriers are sufficiently low – from the start-up of new small companies.

When measuring the level of industrial concentration the most crucial determinant is the size of market. The EC's *nomenclature des industries établies dans les Communautés Européennes*' (NICE) adopted a three-digit classification – compared with the more detailed classification used in the United States (Jacquemin and Jong 1977, p. 45). The degree of concentration is greater where the market is defined more narrowly; for example, a local market for a particular kind of product like a bottle or container is more concentrated than if one uses the whole container market at a Community level. The creation of the Community and the steps towards a single internal market provide a major constraint on local or national monopoly power. Although firms have expanded the scale of their operations in the larger market – recently in particular by mergers and acquisitions – overall the problem of monopoly is less intense at Community level. For example, in the motor industry Fiat is just one of many companies to complete virtually a national monopoly by swallowing such firms as Alfa Romeo and Ferrari, and taking effective control of Maserati and Innocenti. But the car market is highly competitive, with Volkswagen having overtaken Fiat as Europe's largest car producer.

Competition policy

1. Restrictive agreements   Competition policy is covered by Treaty Articles 85–94. This first section will focus mainly on Article 85 which relates to agreements or concerted practices between two or more enterprises. It will be followed by attention to Article 86 which refers to abusive behaviour by monopolies or firms with market dominance.

The Community has favoured free competition, through the interplay of demand and supply, since this provides the basic ingredient for efficiency. Competition policy has provided the means whereby the Community has achieved and maintained its object of free internal trade. It has tried to prevent the erection of new trading barriers, and competition policy has applied not only when trade with other member states is actually affected but also where there has been an adverse potential effect. In addition to free trade, the other pillar of the Community has been to maintain open competition, based upon consumer sovereignty. Anything which appreciably distorts open competition in member states is prohibited. The *de minimis* rule applies to agreements of minor importance where firms together have no more than 5 per cent of the market and their aggregate turnover does not exceed ECU 200 million. Only minor exceptions have been made to the open competition policy; for example, where restrictive agreements are of minor importance and are encouraging co-operation between small- and medium-sized enterprises, such as that in R&D. Likewise, some exceptions have been made in the public sector with the application of state aids being permissible for particular depressed regions and industries. However, the aim is to ensure that the aid is on a selective and transparent basis so that state aids do not distort competition, for example, under Treaty Articles 92–94.

The Community in forming such a strong competition policy, particularly against restrictive practices, has been influenced by West German practice, since the latter legislated against restrictive practices itself in 1957 (Bayliss in El-Agraa ed. 1985). The Commission has received firm support from the Court of Justice. Firms have to notify the Commission about any agreements and arrangements that they have made with other firms, and these are generally considered invalid unless the firms concerned account for only a small part of the market or there are some benefits available; for example, in improving the production or distribution of goods, or promoting technical and economic progress; in ensuring that a fair share of the benefits go to consumers, and so on. EC competition policy has been very tough and has allowed fewer exemptions than the UK's range of gateways (George and Joll 1978). But subsequently it has introduced several block exemptions for various agreements where the harmful effects are sufficiently counterbalanced by beneficial features; for example, relating to specialization between SMEs, R&D joint exploitation, exclusive distribution, exclusive purchasing, patent licensing, distributive agreements for automobiles, and more recently new ones for franchising and know-how licensing.

Generally, horizontal and vertical agreements between firms have violated Article 85 – though this does not include non-binding agreements unless such concertation is followed by prohibitive practices (Mathijsen 1985, p. 170). Often, collusion is difficult to prove, like that of parallel price movements which may be quite coincidental, and have to be shown to arise from concertation, which will be manifested by their repetitive occurrence. Apart from price agreements, cartels have often been established to share out markets; for example, the Dutch cement market was shared out for many years between Dutch, German and Belgian producers, leaving only a small part of the market for free competition (Swann 1984, p. 129). The EC is opposed to such territorial market-sharing and has tackled other examples of this, such as that in detergents in which Dutch and Belgian producers had agreed not to sell in each other's territory. In other practices, such as exclusive dealing agreements, these have been prohibited once geographical restrictions have been created (Mathijsen 1985, p. 178). Joint purchasing and joint selling agreements have also tended to be prohibited under Article 85.

The temptation for firms to collude during recession has been enhanced in oligopolistic markets; for example, in 1986 Shell, ICI, Hoechst and Montedipe held 65 per cent of polypropylene sales (a key product used in the manufacture of a wide range of plastics). The companies argued that between 1975 and 1983 they had lost £1000 million, but the EC showed that they were in fact operating a cartel and fixing prices. Competition policy restrains companies from getting together, though one consequence of this has perhaps been a slower downward adjustment of surplus capacity than in Japan.

2. Dominant-firm abuse   Concern about dominant firms goes back to the days of the ECSC when France was fearful of any renewed concentration of the German coal and steel industries. In the EC Article 86 has tackled different types of abuse by dominant firms; for example, firms such as Commercial Solvents, which controlled materials and refused to supply them freely to other firms. Other cases of some significance have included that of Hoffmann-La Roche, which was drawn to the Commission's attention by Stanley Adams who subsequently was badly let down by the Commission. Hoffmann-La Roche dominated the market for vitamins, charging different prices in various markets and also giving fidelity rebates which were aggregated across all products.

The concept of dominance depends upon how the product and the market are defined. One important case in this respect was that of Continental Can, a large American multinational manufacturer of containers. It obtained a dominant position in the German market through a takeover, followed by a takeover of a large Dutch producer. This was likely to suppress competition in both markets. The German firm had a dominant position in the market for preserved meat and fish and for metal caps for preservative jars. There was clearly more of a monopoly when the market was defined narrowly (as touched upon earlier). The Court's judgment came out against the Commission's view about Continental Can creating a dominant position, but it did provide a precedent in enabling the Commission to move into the field of scrutinizing mergers.

The Commission's powers to control mergers were generally limited, allowing them to be challenged only after they had taken place. Recent Competition Commissioners, such as Peter Sutherland and Leon Brittan, have pressed for greater controls on anti-competitive mergers. This led in 1990 to the Commission being empowered to examine large mergers between companies whose combined sales world-wide total ECU 5 billion (£3.5 billion) or more, and where at least two of the companies each have EC sales of ECU 250 million or more. Thus the Commission has to be notified by the companies involved where these thresholds apply, and failure to do so, or providing wrong information, may result in a fine of up to ECU 50,000 (£35,000). Should the companies press on with the merger, they can be fined up to 10 per cent of their aggregate turnover. The Commission is mainly concerned to prevent any adverse effect of mergers in reducing competition. Where the combined market share of the companies involved is less than 25 per cent, it is likely to be compatible with the common market, but above this (and especially above 40 per cent) it is likely to be incompatible. Between these levels a dominant market position is judged by reference to criteria such as market structure, actual or potential competition from inside or outside the EC, supply and demand and barriers to market entry (*Financial Times* 21 September 1990, p. 4).

There is concern in some countries, especially those with well-developed policies of their own, about ceding powers to a relatively slow-moving Commission. If the Commission fails to reach a decision in time, the merger goes ahead automatically. On the other hand, other critics favour giving the EC greater powers to examine mergers with a lower turnover figure of ECU 1 billion (instead of the new rule of ECU 5 billion) to ensure that countries with few or no merger rules (such as Greece, Denmark and Italy) are constrained from leniently supporting domestic mergers to create national champions. It is felt in some quarters that it would be best to establish a completely independent agency, modelled perhaps on the West German Kartellamt, seeing the Commission, despite its theoretical independence, as being open to national political pressures. Some past mergers may have been allowed to go through because of such pressures; for example, a merger in 1988 between two Dutch coffee companies, Douwe Egberts and Van Nelle, created a near monopoly in the Benelux market.

In its competition policy the Commission under Articles 85 and 86 goes through various stages in its approach. These may include negative clearance (making sure agreements are not prohibited); where agreements do exist it obliges firms to put an end to infringements; it can issue a declaration granting an exemption. When making investigations, the Commission has wide-ranging powers to enter premises and to examine records. For example, in early 1987 the Commission took legal and financial action against the West German government for not forcing Hoechst to admit anti-cartel investigators into one of its plants. Finally, extensive penalties or fines may be imposed and in some cases may even be extended to firms outside the EC, such as in Switzerland, since the EC has claimed extra-territorial jurisdiction.

B   American and Japanese industrial challenge: inward investment
Some of the companies that have taken fullest advantage of the large EC market have been overseas multinationals. The large market and the common external tariff to outsiders have encouraged the growth of inward investment, mainly from the USA but also more recently from Japan. J. J. Servan-Schreiber in *The American Challenge* (1968) expressed concern, but by the mid-1970s the American Challenge was being rebuffed (Heller and Willat 1975). The threat of American industrial hegemony has been reduced by the growth of large European companies, some of which in recent years have begun to invest on a large scale in the USA itself. This trend has been stimulated by the fall in the value of the American dollar against European currencies such as the D-mark. For example, companies like Thyssen, Renault, Hoechst, ICI, Rhône-Poulenc, BASF, Elf and so on, were all involved in takeovers in the USA in the late 1980s.

Countries recognize they are in keen competition with each other, but if there is to be inward investment in Europe, they may as well provide the location for it instead of importing products from another country in which the new investment has been based. In the longer term there is worry about adding to the danger of overcapacity in some sectors and of indigenous industry being weakened from within rather than from without. Furthermore, new inward investment has received generous subsidies in many instances; from the Community viewpoint it would be better if these were scrapped and the money redirected instead to European industry.

The main source of inward investment into the Community has come from the USA. Cumulative American investment in the EC(9) (excluding Denmark, Portugal and Greece) reached $93.15 billion by the end of 1985. In comparison, cumulative investment from Japan in the EC(9) was only $9.9 billion by the end of 1985. From 1951 to 1985 only 11.9 per cent of total Japanese direct investment took place in the EC, partly because Japanese investment was drawn rather to the large and more homogeneous American market and to investment closer to home in South East Asia (*Financial Times* 13 November 1986). Nevertheless, the recent pace of Japanese investment in the Community has accelerated, stimulated by the rising value of the yen and protectionist pressures in the Community which have threatened to cut back on Japanese exports. Japan's effect in particular sectors is now significant and inroads are being made into new sectors such as financial services. Most Japanese investment has consisted of setting up overseas subsidiaries. In the few instances of collaborative deals, the Japanese have been criticized for stripping away the technical capabilities of their partners.

The Japanese challenge has caught some of Europe's major companies off balance. For example, Philips compared with Hitachi had far too many factories; in 1984 it had 450 factories, whereas if it had been organized on a Japanese basis it would have had about 30 (Turner 1986). This led to new strategies at Philips of rationalization and focusing on its ten product divisions rather than the many national organizations, and of spending more on R&D and spreading the costs of this by means of joint ventures. Nevertheless, in 1990 Philips fell into a state of financial crisis, necessitating further rationalization and cutbacks. Despite its strong record in R&D, for example in VCRs and compact discs, it is the Japanese who have been most successful in turning VCRs into a mass market. Unless Philips is successful, the gradual dismantling of Dutch anti-takeover barriers could result in a takeover of some of its activities. It would be a tragedy for Philips, the standard-bearer of the European electronics industry, to return to its basic roots making light bulbs.

The Japanese move into the production of goods in the EC such as VCRs, electronic typewriters, photocopiers and microwave ovens has been influenced by the EC's concern about the dumping of those products and its consequent imposition of controls and anti-dumping duties. For example, early in 1987 the Commission raised its anti-dumping duty on photocopiers from 15.8 per cent to 20.0 per cent. By the end of 1989 there were 529 Japanese factories in Western Europe, the most popular location for Japanese overseas investment in the Community being the UK with 132 factories, while France had 95, Germany 89, and Spain 55. France started to adopt a very pragmatic policy in this respect during the 1980s, with the Japanese being shaken by the Poitiers affair in 1982 when France insisted that all Japanese VCRs had to be routed through this customs post. Japan's initial preference to create new businesses on greenfield sites has now given way to acquiring companies with established brand names. There is a need to ensure that Japanese production in the EC does not consist simply of screwdriver factories but that there is sufficient input of national products. The EC has a ruling of 60 per cent local content measured by ex-factory prices. In the UK, for example, Nissan aimed to achieve the 60 per cent mark by 1988 and up to 80 per cent by 1991.

C   EC industrial policy

Whereas the EC has a strong competition policy based upon treaty requirements, it has lacked the same legal basis for the development of an industrial policy (Butt Philip 1983). The initial approach was market orientated and generally non-interventionist. It was only in 1970 that the Community published the Colonna Report on Industrial Policy which mainly reflected a non-interventionist approach, trying to create a unified market. It was concerned with tackling various issues which included: the elimination of technical barriers to trade; the harmonization of the legal, fiscal and financial frameworks; the encouragement of transnational mergers; the adaptation of industry; greater technical collaboration; and the control of multinationals (Arbuthnott and Edwards 1979, p. 92).

During the 1960s there had been a big increase in merger activity, most of which occurred within national boundaries; where there were transfrontier mergers, far more of these were with foreign firms than with firms in member states of the Community. European mergers have been hampered by fiscal difficulties; for example, a true merger involves a legal liquidation in one country, and some countries imposed liquidation taxes and capital gains taxes. Although fiscal concessions were often made, the authorities were less willing to do so when this involved the disappearance of national companies. Legal difficulties also existed, with Dutch law not providing for company mergers and German law precluding mergers between German and foreign companies.

National mergers, however, have tended to create national monopolies, whilst mergers with American or Japanese companies lead to a fragmentation of European co-operation. A few major European cross-frontier links are of long duration; for example, between the UK and The Netherlands with Royal Dutch–Shell (since 1907) and Unilever (since 1927). More recent successors to such mergers have included Agfa-Gevaert (formed in 1964); this was not a true European company but only consisted of 'Siamese twins' (Layton 1969). Some later European mergers have proved even less successful, such as the Dunlop–Pirelli merger in 1971, even though this seemed to offer some complementarity in markets. Dunlop's strength lay in the

Commonwealth and North American markets, whilst Pirelli's strength lay in Europe and Latin America. Their marriage was dissolved in 1981, and in 1990 Pirelli launched an almost unheard-of contested bid in Germany to take over the Continental company. Unidata, the French-German-Dutch computer group which was set up in 1973 to challenge IBM, sank quickly. The eleven-year marriage of the aircraft firms VFW of West Germany and Fokker of Holland has also been dissolved. Difficulties have arisen in blending together different styles of management, for example CMB Packaging.

Nevertheless, pressures on companies to combine have continued in the run-up to the single market in order to obtain economies of scale and to finance the costs of R&D. The more recent internationalization of stock markets and the lowering of barriers to capital movements have stimulated further cross-national takeovers. These span the gamut of industries, even including agriculture where close Italian–French business links have been established. Policymakers need to ensure that mergers are underpinned by efficiency gains rather than by the search for market power, since the latter would reduce competition. Contestable markets are most desirable where large existing firms are threatened by potential new entrants.

A landmark in the EC's development of industrial policy was the Spinelli Report in 1973. It proposed new measures for industrial and technological policy, although these were still couched within the framework of a competition-orientated industrial policy. Among new measures were those for harmonization; freeing tenders; encouraging transnational enterprises; and help to small- and medium-sized firms to co-operate or merge. Co-operation between such firms, especially on R&D, does not fall foul of the anti-restrictive practices policy. A Business Co-operation Centre was created to help small firms to find partners.

European Economic Interest Groups (EEIGs) were first proposed in the Colonna Report, though a regulation was not finally adopted until 1985. These are aimed mainly at co-operation between small- and medium-sized enterprises; for example, in R&D. Their main characteristic is that they are non-profit-seeking.

The recession during the 1970s provided a turning point towards more interventionist policies. National governments came under pressure to help industries, and to avoid trading distortions many of these policies were taken over, though sometimes reluctantly, by the Community in order to co-ordinate them and to make the assistance transparent. This is well exemplified in industries such as steel and shipbuilding. In the former, the Davignon system has operated with price and production quotas. During the 1980s European steel-makers removed millions of tonnes of excess capacity in their re-adjustment of productive capacity to lower demand. But those criti-cal of such intervention led the Competition Commissioner, Sir Leon Brittan, to consider repeal of the Paris Treaty which gave the EC its special powers to intervene in the steel industry. In the shipbuilding industry national subsidies led to an agreement by the EC in 1986 to limit direct subsidies to a common standard per cent of cost on contracts. Overcapacity has manifested itself in many other sectors, such as the car industry in which the EC market is close to saturation. Its two biggest producers, Volkswagen and Fiat, have turned increasingly towards Eastern Europe for sales. Fiat has established links with car producers in the Soviet Union, Poland and Yugoslavia, and Volkswagen has links in the eastern part of Ger-many and in Czechoslovakia through a joint venture with Skoda. Volkswagen beat off the challenge of Renault for Skoda in 1990, so that Renault is likely to increase its ties with Volvo of Sweden.

Although the Commission has executive authority on state aids, these have proliferated. The number of cases of state aids referred to the European Court of Justice rose from 6 in 1970 to 61 by 1981, and by 1986–8 EC(12) state aids were about ECU 82 billion per annum. The Commission has to be notified of state aids, but at times has been ambivalent about taking national governments to task over all their state aids. This is partly because such aids were recognized after the Copenhagen Summit in 1978 as measures enabling adaptation to competition from the NICs, albeit interim measures. The White Paper on the Internal Market 1985 proposed much tighter surveil-lance of aids to make member states aware of the damaging effect of their national policies in other member states. Nationalized indus-tries, though compatible with the EC Treaty, tend to conflict at the margin with progress towards the single market. For example, a few state companies in France, with subsidized access to finance and immune from takeover, have started to make incursions to buy out private firms abroad.

A problem for the EC has been that national governments have often possessed stronger industrial instruments, such as those of finance, and the Community has tried to strengthen its own instru-ments. The fifth Medium-Term Economic Policy Programme 1981–5 proposed the introduction of 'Community preference' to help EC firms in areas like R&D. Other developments have included the founding of the European Venture Capital Association (EVCA); a European Business and Innovation Centre Network (EBN); and the Commission's own Small and Medium Enterprise (SME) Task Force. They are concerned to help small- and medium-sized enterprises in particular, and these have found favourable support in the UK where all new Community regulatory proposals have to be assessed for their impact on business.

D   The EC's lag in technology

The pace of structural change has highlighted the need to replace the declining or sunset industries by new sunrise sectors. The future lies with new high-tech sectors in which EC countries can utilize their high educational skills. Over time, the traditional down-market industries are likely to become the mainstay of the NICs. If the EC is to remain at the forefront of major industrial powers, then policies to promote technology, comparable with those of the USA and Japan, are imperative.

New technology is a mainspring of growth and lower inflation, even though its employment-creating effects are less clear-cut. Employment is most likely to increase when technology is devoted to creating and marketing successful new products, rather than to developing process technology which reduces the input of labour. Despite microeconomic readjustment and displacement of labour, historically the long-run impact of technology in aggregate has been to increase demand and employment opportunities. Japan in recent years has enjoyed much lower unemployment than the EC and those countries which lag in new technology gradually become less competitive and lose jobs. Therefore the EC has little alternative – despite the adverse short-term effects of new technology – but to encourage the transition from declining industries to expanding new high-technology industries.

The EC does not manifest a general technological lag across all industries. Indeed, in some industries the Community is strong; for example, in chemicals and nuclear power. In addition, individual countries such as West Germany are strong in specific areas like industrial machinery, while the UK shows potential in the new area of biotechnology. The main problem for the EC is not so much technology *per se* but the managerial gap in applying this technology commercially (Sharp 1985, p. 291). The Community has lost market share in high-technology products and has a particular lag in electronics and information technology. This is serious because it affects performance in the various sectors that use electronics, currently experiencing phenomenal growth. European firms have been confined largely to national markets failing to achieve adequate economies of scale, R&D and effective innovation. The merger in 1990 between Siemens, with its strength in computer hardware, and Nixdorf, with its strength in software, may mark the trend towards Europe eventually having only one European-owned computer manufacturer. The EC has shown a poor performance in computers, consumer electronics, industrial automation, integrated circuits and office equipment. Its trade in telecommunications equipment has only been held in balance by some restrictions on imports. Western Europe has too few companies which are internationally competitive in information technology.

In robotics, European countries have lagged far behind Japan, and a high proportion of robots in the EC are imported. Estimated numbers of robots in Japan were approximately four times the aggregate in West Germany, France, Italy and the UK (Harrop 1985).

Those countries which are most progressive in terms of innovation capture a larger share of world markets. They are able to keep one step ahead of the NICs, which use more outdated technology. What has been worrying the EC is that it has not been moving up-market at a sufficient pace, nor providing sufficient diffusion of innovation quickly enough within the economy. Apart from the pressure by the NICs in the more down-market areas, the EC has also been outpaced by Japan and it has failed to cut back on the existing technological gap with the USA.

An index of technological specialization has been constructed, defined as the share of each bloc in world trade in high-technology products divided by its share of world trade in manufactured products. The EC figure fell from 1.02 in 1963 to 0.88 in 1980, whereas Japan's rose from 0.56 in 1963 to 1.41 in 1980, surpassing the USA figure of 1.20 in 1980 (Heertje 1983, p. 102). The Community has a deficit on its trade in high-technology products with both the USA and Japan.

European companies have experienced an inadequate scale of operation in some sectors because of fragmented national markets, due to such practices as national purchasing policies. Yet economies of scale are important in many sectors, not only in terms of static efficiency and reducing costs of production, but also in terms of dynamic efficiency given the high threshold costs of financing R&D. For example, in telecommunications the major American companies – AT&T, Northern Telecom and ITT – plus Japanese suppliers NEC and Fujitsu, have developed built-in advantages in digital exchanges, resulting in lower costs per line.

European firms have been at a disadvantage compared with their American counterparts in fields such as patents and trade marks. In order to avoid the costly procedure of applying for separate patent protection in each country, in 1978 the European Patent Convention provided for European patent protection through a single application. This also extended to Austria, Switzerland and Sweden, though unfortunately it excluded Denmark, Ireland and Portugal. An additional defect is that litigation has to be conducted separately in each country. Instead of a collection of national patents, the EC has proposed a Community Patent Convention (CPC) under which a single Community patent would exist and the judgment in a Community Patent Court in one member state would be effective throughout the Community. Although Denmark and Ireland have failed to ratify the CPC, it is part and parcel of creating the internal market by 1992.

Trade marks are important in denoting the origin and quality of goods, but firms have had to protect them by making separate applications in each member state. In 1980 two proposals were presented by the EC Commission to harmonize the legislation on granting trade marks, and it is planning a Community Trade Mark. National systems will still continue, but a Community Trade Mark covering the whole EC will result from a single application to a European Trade Marks Office. Various sites have been short-listed for this office, with strong competition between London and Madrid, since the latter is pressing for some institutional placement there to reflect its commitment to Southern Europe.

E   Technological co-operation

Co-operation helps to avoid wasteful duplication and is appropriate in the following conditions: where high-risk capital is involved; where the partners are of fairly equal size; where some standardization of the product is acceptable; and when R&D costs are high.

But project assessment needs to be an on-going process to avoid becoming locked into non-viable commercial ventures. Some examples are given in the next section on the aerospace industry.

Since the early 1980s it has become imperative to widen Community funding of collaborative R&D efforts beyond industries such as coal, steel and nuclear power towards other key sectors. This has been done in various Framework Programmes: the first one ran from 1984–7; the second from 1987–91 (with a budget of ECU 5.4 billion) and was underpinned by the SEA which accords greater status to R&D policy and enables specific programmes to be decided by qualified majority voting. The Third Framework Programme 1990–4 has a budget of ECU 5.7 billion and by overlapping the second programme by two years provides an added ECU 3.1 billion, giving a total budget of ECU 8.8 billion. The distribution of finance in the Third Framework Programme 1990–4 is: 38.9 per cent to information and communications technologies; 15.6 per cent to industrial and materials technologies; 9.1 per cent to the environment; 13 per cent to life sciences and technologies; 14.3 per cent to energy; and 9.1 per cent to intellectual resources. Advisory committees help to establish priorities, with new priorities in the Third Framework Programme, such as environmental research, biotechnology, and so on, whilst information technology continues to be a major focal area. Less emphasis is now being given to energy research.

The finance is to support high-quality collaborative research and is not allocated on the basis of quotas, unlike regional funding. It supports basic research which is mainly pre-competitive (at the stage before products are developed for the marketplace) in order not to conflict with EC competition policy. The major form of research support is contracted research in which the Community normally reimburses up to half of the project costs, the participants raising the rest themselves. In other instances, such as medical research, the EC merely reimburses the co-ordination costs but not the research costs. Finally, the Community carries out its own research in the Joint Research Centre.

The launching of the European Strategic Programme for Research and Development in Information Technology (ESPRIT) in 1983 was a major development. It is centred on five main areas: advanced microelectronics, software technology, advanced information processing, office systems and computer integrated manufacture. It has been concerned with joint pre-competitive research, with the EC covering up to half the costs of the exercise and industry providing the remainder. Participants have included some leading European electronics companies which have been able to increase their linkages. In the late 1980s ESPRIT was the Community's most costly project, followed by the large JET project (Butler 1986, pp. 56–7). The Commission sought a further ECU 2 billion for a second phase of ESPRIT to run from 1987–91; it was considered likely that there would be some movement forward from pre-competitive research to the production of saleable products. Nevertheless ESPRIT and the JESSI (Joint European Submicron Silicon Initiative) in advanced microchips have not yet succeeded in creating a more competitive and strong European electronics industry. The EC's market share for chips and electronic products has fallen, its trade deficit has widened and in 1990 most of the leading European electronics companies were in financial difficulties.

The Community has several other significant R&D programmes which include Research and Development in Advanced Communications Technologies for Europe (RACE) – this is complementary to ESPRIT and is trying to lay the basis for Europe-wide broadband communications networks in the 1990s. Other R&D programmes for industrial technologies include Basic Research in Industrial Technologies for Europe (BRITE), launched in 1985, which seeks to encourage advanced technology in traditional industries; and European Research in Advanced Materials (EURAM). There are many other acronyms gaining currency in the new technological Community (for a full list, see Commission 1990). For example, Forecasting and Assessment in Science and Technology (FAST); Community Programme for Education and Training in Technologies (COMETT); Biotechnology Research for Innovation, Development and Growth in Europe (BRIDGE); and also the Strategic Programme for Innovation and Technology Transfer (SPRINT).

Another major European research programme of a slightly different kind has been the French inspired EUREKA. This covers all twelve EC countries plus seven EFTA countries and Turkey. It was established in July 1985 to give Europe research resources on the same scale as the Strategic Defense Initiative in the USA. It was given no central Community financing but has drawn upon support from national governments. By the end of 1987 there were some 165 EUREKA projects with a total value of £2.8 billion, with the UK taking part in nearly a third of these (*Midland Bank Review*, Winter 1987). The funding for EUREKA projects has now reached around ECU 1 billion annually. Projects are concerned with commercial products that have clear market applications, but with each country favouring particular projects; for example, West Germany chose several which were of environmental interest. Now small- and medium-sized companies are playing a more significant role in EUREKA. Although EUREKA is separate from the Community, a small secretariat has been set up in Brussels. Essentially the co-operation is between companies to avoid a highly bureaucratic framework, and has no joint funding or even automatic state funding. EUREKA covers many high-tech projects in an exclusively civilian sector, close to the marketplace. While many of the larger companies would probably co-operate anyway, EUREKA has induced smaller companies to co-operate much more with each other. The company-level approach, with mainly privately financed schemes, provides a marked contrast with other Community-level projects like BRITE, RACE and ESPRIT in which the EC meets 50 per cent of the cost of projects (Dinkelspiel 1987).

The Community's R&D programme is far too small since in the 1980s it still accounted for only about 2.5 per cent of the EC's budget, and only about 2 per cent of total public and private expenditure on R&D by the member states (Albert and Ball 1983). The Commission proposed a substantial increase for the period 1987–91 to enhance the EC's innovative and competitive capabilities, but this was trimmed down. By the end of the century one would like to see EC R&D funding closer to half the Community budget and half of member states' national public spending on R&D. Since the late 1980s there has been some scaling-down of the R&D devoted to the energy sector so that other costly programmes such as electronics, advanced microchips and high-definition television (HDTV) can take up a larger share of R&D spending. But there are criticisms that EC financial support has been spread too thinly; that companies become too dependent on financial support and trade protection (with the latter bringing greater competition by location within the EC). A policy of supporting indigenous EC firms thereby becomes more difficult, and the latter are turning increasingly towards non-EC links; for example, Siemens with IBM and Toshiba in memory chips; and Daimler-Benz with Mitsubishi of Japan in electronics and aerospace. The major European countries with independent R&D strength, and which are making large contributions to the Community budget, have become cautious about the amount and direction of R&D spending, stressing the need for it to be cost-effective. For example, the UK has sought to restrict expenditure, especially on non-commercially orientated projects – not only in the EC but also in the European Space Agency – yet these are among the few areas of technological collaboration from which the UK derives a net benefit.

F   Case study of the aerospace industry

Nature of the problem. EC co-operation in aerospace was not called for in the Treaty of Rome; the only indirect reference was related to a common transport policy (deemed to extend to air transport). Military affairs are not the preserve of the Community, since these are dealt with by NATO. Why, then, has the EC regarded it as imperative to foster co-operation in aerospace projects? These are an essential ingredient of its common industrial and technological policy.

National aircraft industries in Europe are too small to compete effectively on their own against the United States. The dominance of the USA has applied both to military aircraft, stimulated by massive defence expenditure, and to civil aircraft, based upon a large domestic market. Consequently, it has benefited from economies of scale with long production runs and high productivity, offsetting the higher real wages in the USA (*vis-à-vis* the Europeans). The American labour market is very flexible, tending to fluctuate in accordance with demand in terms of 'hire and fire' policies.

The USA accounted for 86 per cent of world aerospace output in 1960 and its share was still 62 per cent in 1987 (with Europe's share having risen from nearly 11 per cent to 27 per cent over the same period). Large scale of production is crucial, with the number of manufacturers diminishing as the size and development costs of aircraft increase. The three American giants in the aerospace industry were Boeing, McDonnell-Douglas and Lockheed. Some American aeroplanes have enjoyed outstanding success and profitability, such as the Boeing 727, and up to 1984 when production ended 1831 were ordered. Similarly, 1732 McDonnell-Douglas DC9s were ordered up to 1986. The production run of European planes has been lower, but the successful Fokker F-27 had 786 sales, and since 1969, 421 F-28s have been sold.

American firms are dominant throughout the aerospace industry from airframes to engines and from space rocketry to the simpler production of helicopters. In aero-engines economies of scale are greater than in the production of airframes; hence the market is dominated by even fewer firms, with the American firms Pratt & Whitney and General Electric being world leaders, followed by Rolls-Royce in the UK. R&D costs are enormous, with the result that co-operation is very much the key word in the industry, and an increasing amount of investment is now going into bigger engines to power the new generation of wide-bodied aircraft. The commercial payback on engines is nearly twice as long as that for airframe manufacturers. To share out cost, lessen risks and tap new national markets, the big three have all developed international link-ups. For example, General Electric with SNECMA in France, Pratt & Whitney with Daimler-Benz, and Rolls-Royce with BMW in Germany; also, Japanese companies have become minor participants.

In helicopters American firms are again dominant: Bell, Boeing-Vertol, Sikorsky and McDonnell-Douglas. The European firms challenging them are Westland in the UK, Augusta in Italy, Aérospatiale in France and Messerschmitt-Bölkow-Blohm (MBB) in West Germany. Aérospatiale is strong in helicopters and in 1990 established a holding company with MBB, making it the world's second-largest helicopter concern behind Sikorsky. Not only is there a large military market but a growing civil market, as exemplified by their use in North Sea oil development.

Policy options: independence or co-operation. One example of an independent company approach has been that of Dassault in France: it created the very successful Mirage range of military aircraft. However, even this company has been forced to modify its policy in recent years. Its failure to agree on the European Fighter Aircraft (EFA) left the company to develop its own fighter aircraft, the Rafale, and it has sought to interest European countries, such as Belgium and Spain, in this project.

An independent policy can prove costly where the market is small and where costs rise excessively, hence co-operation has become a byword in all parts of the industry. Nevertheless, there have been notorious examples of commercial failures of co-operative projects. One example of this was the bilateral Anglo-French Concorde project, which had both economic and political origins. The UK government also hoped that the project might be helpful in its initial application to join the European Community.

No cost-benefit analysis was ever published for Concorde, though it was shown subsequently that the costs exceeded the benefits (Henderson 1977). The main benefits have been derived from technical 'spin-off' and from the prestige attached to the technical achievement *per se*. If some of these technical advances had never taken place – even if funds had been devoted to such research – then this 'X' element of aerospace co-operation is invaluable. Many alleged economic benefits both to employment and to the balance of payments did not materialize and there were also some significant social costs. While all investment decisions are risky, particularly in industries such as aerospace, cost-benefit analysis is essential before decisions are taken; otherwise there is a tendency for some political interest groups to push particular projects vigorously. Unfortunately, once under way they tend to acquire a momentum of their own for fear of incurring cancellation charges. The escalation of costs and the small number of planes built means that Concorde was a major commercial mistake – though there have been others in other industries, such as the British advanced gas-cooled reactor (Henderson 1977).

Other types of co-operation have been multilateral in nature, including not only members of the EC but also other European countries, the USA and more recently Japan. Those who support a European solution wish Europe to possess indigenous technology, seeking to exclude outsiders such as the USA. Whatever the type of co-operation, it is vital to secure a long production run to reap economies of scale. The learning curve means that the first aircraft in a series can cost four times as much as the 250th plane produced (see Figure 5.1).

Assume that production is at a limited national output OQ_n on the long-run cost curve LAC_1; then average cost is OC_n. If output increased to OQ_m then average cost on LAC_1 would fall to OC_1. The small national European markets preclude production at such a low cost, though co-operation does enable the production of a higher combined output, OQ_m. Unfortunately, the long-run average cost curves are likely to be pushed to the right, because of the costs involved in drawing suitable partners together. They have to decide on a project that matches their different needs, and often the outcome is an over-elaborate and expensive compromise. In addition,

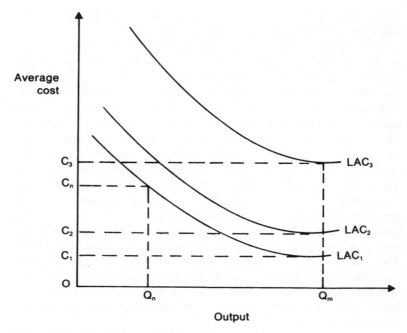

Figure 5.1   Economies of scale in the aircraft industry

the allocation of the work may not be based on comparative advantage but on an equitable distribution between the partners.

Figure 5.1 shows two different scenarios for long-run average cost: in the first of these, on LAC_2 co-operation is successful in reducing average costs to OC_2. This shows the expected reduction in average costs compared with national production. However, if political and bureaucratic influences result in an escalation of expenditure and partners duplicate production, then a suitable scenario is shown on LAC_3. In this situation average costs are even higher than in the original national markets! Furthermore, it is possible that the counterfactual is not domestic production but the purchase of aircraft at even lower cost from the USA. Some comparative estimates of alternative costs have been made for the Tornado project relative to the F-14, F-15 and F-16 (Hartley 1982, p. 180).

Additional orders for the Tornado have pushed up its production to 933 planes, assuring production for Panavia until at least 1992. As Tornado production turns down, the gap will be filled by the new

European Fighter Aircraft: the plan is for nearly 800 aircraft in total – about 260 each for the UK and West Germany, 160 for Italy and 100 for Spain. It is Europe's largest defence programme worth around £30 billion – though there have been doubts about Germany's real commitment to it – with a search for additional participants to share the costs. The initial participation agreed was 33 per cent each for the UK and Germany, 21 per cent for Italy and 13 per cent for Spain. The company set up to manage the venture is jointly owned by British Aerospace, MBB, Aeritalia and CASA of Spain.

The success of the Airbus. Airbus Industrie was set up in 1970 after the signing of a Franco-German agreement in 1969 and an earlier agreement of 1967 which had also included the UK. The latter's ambivalence about the project resulted in only Hawker-Siddeley retaining a toehold, but subsequently the UK rejoined the project. Airbus is owned 37.9 per cent by Aérospatiale, 37.9 per cent by MBB (now Daimler-Benz), 20 per cent by British Aerospace and 4.2 per cent by CASA of Spain. Specialization in production occurs with, for example, BAC producing the wings, Daimler-Benz the fuselage and Aérospatiale the final assembly. Germany has mounted a challenge for the latter work, successfully gaining assembly in Hamburg for the new A321 aircraft. Overemphasis by Airbus on *juste retour* restricted the attainment of full efficiency, and the loosely knit organization with weak central management failed to control costs effectively. Partners haggle for their share of the production, trying to charge the consortium as much as possible for their work, thereby adding to its costs. But Airbus was established as a grouping of mutual economic interests, and in taking that form under French law it maximized co-operation and minimized the amount of disclosure and tax payment. The structure adopted concealed subsidies received, much to the displeasure of the USA. The latter argued that they infringed the rules of GATT, keeping down the price of Airbuses and incurring massive losses. Airbus Industrie defied the USA over this, pointing to Federal Defense contracts which have helped to underpin American plane-makers. However, Airbus has agreed to remove production subsidies and to cut R&D subsidies radically. By the early 1990s Airbus was moving into profitability through revised accounting methods and successful sales, and was considering establishing a more normal company structure. But recession hit orders, and pricing and payment for planes in dollars hit Airbus profits when the dollar was low in value.

In 1970 aircraft manufacturers in the EC had less than a 4 per cent share of the world civil market and only a 15 per cent share of the European market itself. By 1982 sales of the A-300 and A-310, as a proportion of total world commercial twin-aisle jet sales, were 52 per cent. By the end of 1990 the A-320 had over 600 firm orders and appears to be a commercial success, since it will make a return on invested funds once 600 aircraft have been delivered and paid for in the 1990s. Airbus Industrie optimistically forecasts its share of new aircraft sales 1988–2006 at $147 billion for the narrow-body A-320, accounting for 41 per cent of the market; at $216 billion for the wide-body, 3–4 engine, with the A-340 taking 18 per cent of the market; and for the wide-body, twin-engine, total sales of $147 billion, with the A-300, A-310 and A-330 taking 53 per cent of the market.

Success in aircraft production stems from producing a family of planes, and Airbus have plans for extending this with the A-330, a twin-engined short- to medium-range aircraft with 330 seats, and the A-340, a four-engined long-range aircraft with between 250 and 350 seats. Airbus have succeeded in outselling Boeing on some planes; with the A-330 and the A-340, by incorporating commonality of many parts, it will provide stronger competition across the product range for its American rivals. Sales of the A-330 show more market potential than the A-340 and it was suggested that Airbus should co-operate on the latter with McDonnell-Douglas to reduce costs and widen markets. Meanwhile, being behind Europe's A-330 has prompted Boeing to commit itself to the 777, defraying part of the cost by the participation of Japanese producers in building 15–20 per cent of the airframe.

Overall, Airbus has been successful in denting American dominance, albeit via a heavily subsidized approach. The key to its continuing development lies in successful co-operation between European partners across a growing family of planes which currently comprises six models in production or under development. Members of the consortium are not allowed to develop an aircraft which competes directly with an existing Airbus. However, internal tensions exist, such as the plans by Deutsche Aerospace to expand in aircraft production, including a smaller plane of 130 seats (compared with the smallest Airbus A320 of 150 seats), outside the consortium in partnership with Alenia in Italy.

Part III The UK's industrial dilemma

The UK's relative industrial decline has given way to absolute decline in many sectors. It has concentrated too much on traditional down-market, low-skill and low-technology sectors of production, retaining a higher market share of these than of the up-market areas. For example, in man-made fibres the UK retains a higher share of international rayon production than synthetic fibre production, and whereas in the former its plant size in the mid-1980s was similar to that of the USA, its plant size for synthetic fibres was only about a third of that of the USA and lower than that of Japan, West Germany or Italy. The European man-made fibres industry has sought to cut back its massive overcapacity, concentrating on higher value fibres. The UK has lost ground in textiles to West Germany, with the latter's high productivity, efficient machinery and use of outward processing. Italy is a bigger textile producer than West Germany and has a large, successful and expanding woollen industry based on a flair for design, state enterprise and small firms operating on the fringe of the black economy (Department of Industry 1981).

It is the same story in other industries such as machine tools, in which product innovation in the UK has been lower than that of its major competitors. The UK has lost ground not only to Japan but also to Italy, which has been prominent in developing low-cost machining centres, and to West Germany. The latter's strength lies in its highly trained and adaptable labour force (Sharp 1985, p. 287). The UK's main deficiency lies in too little investment in education and training, with insufficient engineering graduates and too little provision of vocational training. Although the UK was in the forefront of the early application of numerical control in the aircraft industry, it has failed to develop as strongly in computer numerical control (CNC) because of weak upstream links with electronics suppliers and weak downstream links with the firms using machine tools.

UK industrial strategy seems to be one of depending increasingly upon inward investment and the 20 per cent of manufacturing capital now foreign-owned could rise to 40 per cent by 1995 (Foley 1990). Whilst the ideal would be indigenous industrial resurgence, this dependence on inward investment may offer the only alternative and realistic way for the UK to recover its industrial dynamism, transforming its trade performance in key sectors such as the motor industry. For example, this has taken place already in televisions, with the UK now having a trade surplus in that sector even though there are no indigenous producers since Ferguson was sold to the French firm of Thomson. In a very open economy UK companies have been taken over more freely than those in continental Europe. However, there are dangers from particular types of overseas investment. Thus the sale by STC of ICL to Fujitsu in 1990 marked the strategic loss of Britain's last mainframe computer firm. This has threatened its right to participate on joint European research projects and ruled out any European solution, enabling Japan to gain another firm foothold in the internal market. It left the British electronics industry in decline, with its main strength being in the lower added-value software sector. Meanwhile, it also contrasts markedly with the French policy of state support both for its own ailing computer-maker, Bull, and for Thomson, the struggling defence and consumer electronics group. The latter is pinning part of its hopes for the future on beating the Japanese in high-definition television.

An influx of continental investment by state companies concerned the British government so much in 1990 that it decided the Monopolies Commission should subsequently consider this ownership in their investigations. British monopoly policy in the past was too concerned with avoiding domestic national monopolies; hence, for example, allowing the important firm in the confectionery industry, Rowntree, with its attractive brands, to fall to the Swiss firm of Nestlé. Although the UK succeeded in retaining indigenous ownership of Rover in British Aerospace, undisclosed governmental subsidies were subsequently clawed back by the EC Commission.

Technologically the UK has fared favourably compared with other countries in terms of indicators such as the balance between patent receipts and payments, and R&D spending; but its performance has declined relatively, and the British stock market forces companies to pursue short-term profitability at the expense of longer-term growth. Meanwhile there has been a maldistribution of technological effort, reflected in an overcommitment to military expenditure, including industries such as aerospace. Other industries have been starved of technological manpower, while new technology which might have been transferred to them has been locked away in defence establishments. This weakness has been recognized by government emphasis on new technology transfer, and in 1985

Defence Technology Enterprises was established in an attempt to use commercially some of the technology located in the Ministry of Defence. Private industrial R&D in the UK has been low in comparison with its major competitors, such as West Germany. While research is important, the UK has often been less successful in the crucial development of the marketplace. One example of this is carbon fibre technology, which was developed by the UK aerospace industry, yet Japan now dominates its production.

Since the end of the Second World War, total British government outlay on aircraft launch aid has been well over £2 billion. Less than 10 per cent of that expenditure has been recovered, despite the success in Rolls-Royce engines and in aircraft such as the Vickers Viscount, with 440 being sold. The colossal expenditure involved has brought successive British governments around to the view that co-operation is essential. The dilemma is what form the participation should take and whether it is to be predominantly with other countries in Western Europe or with the USA. For example, the Westland Helicopters affair reflected the continuing pull of American producers such as Sikorsky compared with British participation in European programmes like the NH-90.

The UK recognizes that international co-operation reduces the costs of R&D, but it has learnt from past experience, such as the expensive commercial flop of Concorde. The multilateral Airbus project is more successful, though British government finance has been limited, despite new launch aid for participation in the A-330 and A-340 Airbuses. The UK has also favoured other forms of wider European-based co-operation such as EUREKA, since it is focused towards more privately funded activities and applied technology. The conditions for participation in co-operative projects have to meet stringent criteria. These now include regular evaluation; efficient administration; and an *à la carte* menu from which the UK can choose projects in which to participate.

6 Regional and social problems and policies

Part I

A Economic characteristics of regions

The uneven pace of economic development and changing comparative advantage have resulted in spatial imbalance. Staple industries drawn in the past to locations on or near the coalfields have declined. Industrial areas with over-specialization and over-concentration on traditional industries (that is, with specialization and concentration location quotients greater than 1, where 1 is the national average) have declined, leading to regional and urban decay. Nevertheless, the central core area of Northern Europe still possesses important attributes such as converging transport networks which are favourable to industrial development.

The periphery of the European Community is less industrialized and more rural, with a lower level of economic development. Agricultural problem areas comprise both underdeveloped areas and also developed agricultural areas in which employment has declined inexorably. There are also border areas which have experienced problems resulting from their peripheral situation, though some of these have been lessened by the creation and enlargement of the EC. France in particular has been able to open up its eastern border areas. Even its peripheral coastal regions, such as Brittany, benefited from Community enlargement, with the development of the deep-water port at Roscoff providing a link to the south-west of England (Ardagh 1982, p. 138). Both the EC and the Council of Europe have encouraged border area co-operation, in which a better transport network has been the key to linking up regions. In 1986 France, together with Belgium and Luxembourg, put forward a proposal for border restructuring of the Longwy–Rodange–Aubange area. Furthermore, West German border problems with East Germany have now been removed, but the five new small Länder there with low incomes will require considerable financial support.

To what extent are free market forces able to reduce regional divergence? Neo-classical economists have argued that there is a tendency towards the equalization of factor incomes spatially, given certain assumptions such as free mobility of capital and labour, equal technology and so on. Yet factors are not perfectly mobile, and even on the assumption that they are, labour would have to emigrate from declining regions, and capital to flow into those declining regions. In a dynamic world, as neo-Keynesians have shown, capital has often been drawn towards regions which are already prosperous since they offer higher rates of return. Capital cities have provided a magnetic attraction, since economic advantages have been consolidated by being at the heart of cultural and political influences. Multinational companies have favoured proximity to such centres for their headquarters and decision-making. Firms have obtained external economies of scale from location in large urban areas. However, there has been a tendency in recent years for pleasant medium-sized towns located on the outer fringe of such areas to attract new firms.

While dynamic growth effects may 'spill over' to benefit the less developed regions, the latter are more likely to experience adverse 'backwash' effects, resulting in cumulative relative decline (Myrdal 1957). A polarization of resources occurs in which less-developed regions experience high rates of unemployment, deindustrialization, emigration of labour – often younger and enterprising people – and a run-down, shabby infrastructure. Therefore the free market fails to create convergence and any desirable balanced equilibrium between regions.

B   Objectives of regional policy

Countries are concerned to reduce economic and social disparities which arise from the wide differences in rates of regional unemployment. Unfortunately, however, regional policy is likely to be less effective when the overall level of unemployment is high, since this is a reflection of low demand and there are few firms wishing to expand and to relocate their activities. The absolute numbers unemployed are also high, even in the more prosperous city regions, though their percentage rate of unemployment is relatively low, with much of the unemployment being frictional and not of long duration like that in the declining areas.

A higher rate of economic growth is a precondition for reducing unemployment and raising activity rates in the depressed regions.

While the automatic link between growth and numbers employed may have weakened – with capital substituted for labour – it is vital to raise the level of demand, particularly where labour supply is increasing rapidly. While aggregate economic expansion creates inflationary pressures, balanced regional development helps to alleviate this, since demand can be channelled into areas with idle capital and redundant labour. This is less inflationary than pumping demand into regions of high demand which are already running up against supply bottlenecks.

Firms are concerned in their decision-taking with maximizing their private profits, but in so doing they fail to consider the social costs or social benefits which would accrue to society from a more even distribution of economic activity. The preference of firms to locate in already congested cities imposes additional social costs. By relocating in the depressed and less-developed areas, social benefits could be increased. Furthermore, since many firms are 'footloose' this can be done without adversely affecting their economic performance.

Regional problems have sometimes coincided with demands for regional autonomy to meet different cultural and linguistic interests. Politically countries have had to show a sensitive awareness to regional differences to maintain national unity. For example, in Belgium the government has tried to contain the tendency towards fragmentation between the French-speaking and declining Walloon area in the south and the more prosperous area of Flanders to the north.

Part II   EC regional policy and the structural funds
A   The case for EC regional policy
While the case for national regional policies is well accepted and established, is there also a case for a strong regional policy at Community level? If so, should the policy supplement national policies or replace them? The latter is what has happened with regard to the Guarantee section of the CAP. The case for an EC regional policy stems largely from the way a large free market tends to exacerbate regional problems (Holland 1976; Vanhove and Klassen 1980, pp. 227–53).

The removal of trading barriers in the customs union has led to the contraction of less-efficient industries and although new industries have emerged, these have often been attracted elsewhere to the 'core' areas. Newer industries perceive the advantages of maximizing sales, lowering transport costs and gaining external economies of scale by locating at the heart of the EC market. The free mobility of factors of production in the common market have tended to flow from the periphery to the core, particularly labour, though recently there has been some encouraging evidence that capital has started to flow back towards the periphery. However, weaker regions encounter difficulties in selling their products competitively, particularly when workers receive nationally based wage rates or expect to receive rates of pay comparable to similar work being done in the prosperous areas of the Community. National collective bargaining, rather than regional or local bargaining, and also Community-wide pay comparability tends to make regional labour markets rather inflexible. In addition, the operation of national and multinational companies in charging uniform prices wherever they are located is a further source of disequilibrating activity.

Further progress towards closer integration is likely to reinforce regional problems; for example, the creation of the single internal market by 1992 will not only accelerate existing flows of trade and factors but will also open up the Community market for services; these tend to be concentrated in the developed regions of the Community. In its external trading policy, pressure for easier access to Community markets, especially to accommodate imports from LDCs which produce more basic products, will result in an even faster contraction of traditional industries in many weaker regions.

Enlargement of the Community has brought in the peripheral European economies. This has widened regional divergencies, since these are greater in countries with low levels of national income and with a high dependence on agriculture. In the EC(12) regional disparities are now twice as high as in the USA in the case of GDP and three times as high in terms of unemployment. Meanwhile, further progress towards monetary union is likely to reduce the leeway for national authorities to increase their industrial competitiveness by exchange rate depreciation. The less competitive industries, which suffer most, tend to be those located in remote regions with high transport costs. Since the European Monetary System (EMS) confers desirable monetary advantages, a concomitant of this is to tackle some of its disadvantageous regional effects by stronger EC regional policy.

B   Regional policies

Different types of regional policy can be pursued, either by improving the working of market forces or by intervening with positive policies of incentives to encourage relocation by private firms and active relocation of some public-sector activities in the weaker regions. In addition, to try to force development towards such regions, restrictions may be imposed to curb expansion in the over-developed and congested areas.

Labour mobility. Unemployment and low wages result in outward migration which is pulled into other areas where jobs are plentiful and wages are higher. Up to 1973 massive labour migration occurred inter-regionally and internationally during the economic boom in the European Community. Labour emigrated from the Mezzogiorno to the north of Italy and also to the rapidly growing economies of West Germany and France. The EC became a highly integrated labour market with free labour mobility becoming a reality after 1968. Demand for labour became so high that the main inflow was sucked in from Southern Europe where there was an even stronger 'push' element. Some of these countries – Greece, Spain and Portugal – in the 1980s became full members of the EC, hoping to concentrate on exporting more goods to the Community instead of labour.

Some proponents of labour mobility have argued that it leads towards economic convergence between regions and countries. Areas receiving labour are able to meet their high labour demand, while areas losing labour may gain through the removal of surplus labour which was either unemployed or underemployed. In the host regions and countries much hinges upon whether the immigrant labour supply matches the demand, or whether it leads to a dynamic growth in which demand continues to expand faster than supply, with continuing inflationary consequences. Migrant labour is exploited by low wage rates and long hours of work, since it is often weakly unionized (Castles and Kosack 1973). Businesses make higher profits from which they can finance a greater level of investment: the latter leads to the employment of both capital and labour as output rises, although some firms may prefer to continue with cheaper labour-intensive production methods.

The emigration of labour is not the panacea for regional imbalance in areas which lose labour on such a large scale that they become depopulated and continue to decline. A policy of marginal labour movement is more appropriate where this creams off an overpopulated area. The reduction in outward migration since 1973 is not really a good indicator of any marked improvement in regional performance, since it tends to reflect the lower demand in the core of the Community. The number of migrants living in the Community has fallen back as a consequence of repatriation, and by 1984 there were estimated to be some 3.3 million migrants living in the EC(6) and about 4.3 million in the EC(10).

Positive regional policy. Instead of reducing excess labour supply by labour mobility, a positive regional policy aims to raise the level of demand for workers. In private enterprise economies, inducements are given mainly through subsidies and tax concessions on capital, to encourage firms to expand and to relocate in unemployment black-spots. A policy of subsidizing capital has encouraged a substitution of capital for labour, tending to swamp any additional output effect on the employment of labour. Often taxpayers' money has been given to multinational companies which have used their bargaining power to extract maximum subsidy.

Where new firms have been attracted, these have often been branch factories of large multinational companies and in recession these have tended to be the first to face cutbacks. A lower propensity to invest during recession has resulted in a refocusing of regional policy towards greater indigenous expansion by small- and medium-sized firms with technological potential within less-developed regions. This has been consolidated by attempts to link Community R&D programmes to such regions. But these policies are constrained by an existing overconcentration of R&D and innovation in the prosperous regions; also, it is difficult to develop 'leading edge' technologies in weaker regions, even though these can be applied not only to new industries but to revitalize traditional ones as well. To help weaker regions the Community has launched programmes such as Special Telecommunications Action for Regions (STAR) – with about £50 million over five years – and more recently Science and Technology for Regional Innovation and Development in Europe (STRIDE).

Proponents of really interventionist planning-style regional policies advocate greater state expenditure in less-developed areas; this consists of spending more on infrastructure and also of laying down specific guidelines to increase the level of nationalized industry spending in such regions. Countries in the EC have differed in their regional policy emphasis, with Italy providing one of the best examples of state enterprise (Holland ed. 1972). In contrast, West Germany with fewer regional problems has tended to place greater reliance on market forces of labour mobility and inducements to private enterprise.

Italian regional policy has gone through several different phases in trying to tackle its problem of regional dualism, with the underdevelopment of the Mezzogiorno. The Cassa per il Mezzogiorno was founded in 1950 but was finally wound up in 1986 with its successor to be the Agenzia per la Promozione dello Sviluppo del Mezzogiorno. The Cassa sought to improve agriculture and infrastructure and then tried to force the pace of industrialization by laying down specific targets for investment by state enterprises. State firms were instructed to make 60 per cent of their total investment and 80 per cent of their new investment in the Mezzogiorno. Italy has made positive use of its large state holding companies as a catalyst to encourage private-sector development. It succeeded in raising the percentage of national industrial investment in the Mezzogiorno from only about 15 per cent of total investment in the early 1950s to around 30 per cent in the 1970s. But too much of this investment has been in highly capital-intensive sectors yielding relatively few immediate jobs. The Mezzogiorno's private consumption per head (at just under three-quarters of the Italian national average) and its share of Italian GDP (at just under a quarter) showed little change from 1951 to 1978 (Klassen and Molle 1983).

Italy has found it difficult to narrow the gap between the so-called 'two Italies'. The research institute Svimez noted that in 1986 GNP in the north rose by 3.1 per cent, but by only 1.5 per cent in the south. Productivity per worker in southern industry was only 73 per cent of that in the north, and in southern agriculture 63 per cent of that in the north. For example, in April 1989 average unemployment in Italy was 10.9 per cent but ranged from 4.1 per cent in Lombardy to over 20 per cent in southern areas such as Basilicata, Calabria, Sicily and so on. Nevertheless, there is little doubt that without a regional policy divergencies would have been even greater, and faster emigration would have had to occur from the south. A real base has now been laid in the Mezzogiorno, despite criticisms of its industrialization without real development and an over-reliance on loss-making activities by state enterprises. Southern Italy now compares favourably with other Mediterranean countries and the changing focus of the Community towards Southern Europe means that southern Italy is better placed for future development. The Mezzogiorno has been a priority for both the Italian government and also for EC aid-giving institutions.

Negative regional policy. Negative regional policy refers to measures to limit overexpansion in prosperous and congested areas. Such measures have been used by several countries, including France and the UK. At a time of economic expansion they could be justified, although generally it is better to attract firms positively to depressed regions instead of preventing them locating at their chosen site. Since the more depressed economic conditions of the early 1970s such restrictions have had little rationale. This is because investment has fallen, and preventing firms investing in particular areas is likely to have two effects: either the firm may postpone its investment completely, or it may decide to locate in some other region to avoid the controls – this could be in other EC countries or even in some other part of the world. A reluctance nationally to apply negative measures so strongly during recession left a gap in Community policy to control areas of overconcentration (Vanhove and Klassen 1980, p. 452).

C   The funding of EC policies

National regional policies are still more significant in many respects than EC regional policies; for example, total regional expenditure by national governments greatly exceeds that by Community aid-giving bodies. In addition, the range of regional policy measures at national level exceed those at Community level. Furthermore, Community-level funding by regional bodies has actually tended to operate via national governments. The optimum assignment of regional powers between different levels of authority is difficult to determine and the process has been likened to that of providing public goods (Armstrong 1983). It may well be that the role of national governments both in formulating and implementing regional policy represents the most appropriate division between the federal and the national level. It is national governments that are most knowledgeable about their own specific regional problems, and they have sought to retain their power in the Community. Even in those countries where regional power is decentralized, such as West Germany and Italy, EC regional policy has tended to strengthen national control (Keating and Jones 1985).

The rationale of Community regional policy is to ensure that regional assistance is channelled to those regions which have the most acute problems. However, the prosperous areas are reluctant to see income transferred to weaker regions. For example, in West Germany the Finanzausgleich which provides financial compensation was challenged at the beginning of 1986 in the West German constitutional court by six German regions which thought they were either contributing too much or not receiving enough. Since regions are reluctant to accept national transfers where one might expect citizens to have some regard for the plight of their fellow citizens, there is likely to be even less willingness to support transfers for weaker regions in other Community countries. Nevertheless, on equity grounds such transfers are justified since even the poorest areas in West Germany are still better off than the richest areas of Portugal and Greece.

A Community regional policy has had to be pursued to limit the excessive degree of support granted by countries at a national level to support their own weaker regions when such regions actually lie above the EC average on basic indicators such as employment, income per head and so on. Therefore the Community has had to control carefully the degree of support given by countries like West Germany to assist regions which are prosperous by European standards. For example, in 1986 the EC Commission asked the West German government for an explanation of its alleged subsidy to Daimler-Benz to build a new plant in Baden-Württemberg in an area not eligible for special regional assistance. The local authorities there replied that it was merely general aid to improve the region's industrial infrastructure.

The Belgian government, which was lavishing regional assistance widely to avoid cultural divisions, has similarly had to curtail the breadth of its regional assistance. Both the number of regions designated for regional aid and the level of aid have had to be reworked in such a way as to prevent non-needy areas from attracting an undue share of regional aid. EC regional policy has both co-ordinated national policies and also offered structural aid in sectors such as iron and steel and agriculture. It then moved on, after the first enlargement, to the establishment of a specific Regional Development Fund.

D Regional funds: an appraisal

This section examines the following EC aid-giving bodies: the European Coal and Steel Community (ECSC); the European Agricultural Guidance and Guarantee Fund (EAGGF); the European Investment Bank (EIB); and the European Regional Development Fund (ERDF). The European Social Fund (ESF) and its role in social policy is covered separately in Section E. It should be borne in mind that some schemes have been financed jointly; for example, ERDF subsidies on EIB loans. Together EIB loans plus ERDF grants have covered up to 80 per cent of the total costs of some local developments.

Any appraisal of the structural funds is determined by their size and composition, and receipts by member states from the EAGGF, Regional Fund and Social Fund are shown in Table 6.1. Judgement about the effectiveness of expenditure is influenced by the level at which intervention occurs, in particular at a Community level; also, the extent to which policies contribute to economic objectives or simply provide a social 'hand-out'. In addition, regional priorities may differ between agricultural and industrial areas. Some of the traditional industrial regions have formed an association for Régions Européennes de Tradition Industrielle (RETI) to resist any further erosion of their regional assistance towards less-developed areas, such as those in the Mediterranean. Over the years the operation of the various funds has been modified and improved with the establishment of clearer priorities. Furthermore, under the Single European Act (Article 23) a new title has been included in the Treaty on Economic and Social Cohesion.

In 1987 the Commission proposed that budgetary resources for the structural funds should be doubled in real terms, rising from about ECU 7 billion in 1987 to around ECU 14 billion in 1992. It also proposed to concentrate the activities of the funds on five specific objectives. These are to be achieved by supplementing existing activities with ERDF programmes determined on the basis of Community support frameworks. The first objective was to help less-developed regions to catch up (that is, those with per capita GDP less than 75 per cent of the Community average); these regions cover some 20 per cent of the EC's population. It was proposed that

*Table 6.1   Receipts by member states from EC agricultural,
regional and social funds: total for the four years
1986–9 (in ECU million)*

	EAGGF		Regional	Social
	Guarantee	Guidance	Fund	Fund
Belgium	3,060.7	77.5	122.7	194.2
Denmark	4,267.7	57.2	60.4	165.8
France	21,716.1	882.9	1,250.7	1,354.3
Germany	16,600.6	488.1	426.6	565.0
Greece	5,746.5	506.9	1,334.0	624.4
Ireland	4,230.4	332.4	542.2	819.6
Italy	15,588.4	793.2	2,660.3	1,788.1
Luxembourg	8.2	12.8	12.5	5.9
Netherlands	12,242.8	57.6	74.9	206.0
Portugal	508.0	279.0	1,139.1	717.8
Spain	4,502.8	277.2	2,183.1	1,363.3
UK	7,372.3	316.7	2,223.6	2,207.1
Allocation not available	19.9	–	1.6	–
EC(12)	95,864.4	4,081.5	12,031.7	10,011.5

Source: Calculated from the *Official Journal of the European Communities*, December 1990

ERDF appropriations to these regions would rise from 70 per cent to 80 per cent, as happened for commitments in 1989. While the second objective is to assist conversion in declining industrial regions, the Commission proposed that ERDF aid for industry was to be cut back from 30 per cent to 20 per cent of ERDF appropriations. The third aim is to combat long-term unemployment and the fourth is to facilitate the occupational integration of young people. The final objective is to speed up the adjustment of agricultural structures and to promote the development of rural areas. The EAGGF will be used for this, as well as contributing to the first objective of helping less-developed regions. The ERDF will also contribute to these two objectives, plus that of assisting conversion in declining industrial regions. The European Social Fund is expected to contribute to the achievement of all five objectives. The Commission's approach is based on complementing national measures, consultative partnership, and in particular even greater use of programming (with a gradual disappearance of EC help to small projects). Procedures are to be simplified with better co-ordination and a re-use of dormant commitments (Commission July 1987(f)).

The European Coal and Steel Community. The coal industry's fortunes have fluctuated very much in the postwar period, with initial expansion to fuel Europe's industrial recovery giving way to contraction as greater energy choice emerged between different fuels in a competitive multi-fuel situation. The EC has pursued a low-cost energy policy – unlike that in agriculture. In the 1960s as the Community enjoyed super-economic growth it imported cheap oil on a large scale and also found it cheaper to purchase coal from some low-cost world suppliers. The EC recognized that it had to be as competitive as possible with other countries which were using cheap oil, such as Japan. While the energy policy chosen appeared judicious at that time from a macroeconomic perspective, at the microeconomic level it resulted in massive regional and structural decline in coal-mining areas. Whereas coal accounted for nearly two-thirds of primary energy consumption in 1960, between 1973 and 1985 its share fell to just under a quarter. While this contraction could be tackled satisfactorily when there was buoyant growth in the economy by reabsorbing displaced workers into new industries, the decline became far more difficult to cushion during the 1970s and 1980s. During the 1990s this decline in employment will continue because of rising productivity displacing workers; environmental policy to reduce sulphur emission in coal-fired power stations; and in the case of the UK, electricity privatization ending the contracts to purchase British coal by 1993.

At the macroeconomic level, the decision taken to rely on the import of oil led to problems as oil prices were raised by the OPEC cartel and balance-of-payments positions deteriorated in EC countries. The rather insecure and now high-cost oil imports moved the Community to a greater recognition of the benefits of indigenous energy supplies. Meanwhile, a slowing down in the rate of economic growth created by the energy crisis has reduced the overall demands for energy inputs. Oil prices have been volatile and, with the weakening of the OPEC cartel, prices have again become more competitive

– this is desirable at the macro level for oil importers, but is detrimental to the future of the coal industry in the Community.

The ECSC has made loans to both the coal and the iron and steel industry to finance investment projects, and for schemes for conversion and housing modernization and improvement (at a very low rate of interest); also grants have been made to assist the redeployment of workers. The ECSC has been able to finance its expenditure partly from a levy imposed on sales of its products. Cheap and large loans are also available to firms prepared to move into coal and steel regions.

Unlike the coal industry, the steel industry experienced a longer period of economic expansion until the early 1970s when it was hit very badly by the depression. Traditional steel-making areas operating old-fashioned small-scale plants and in close proximity to local sources of ore have been closed down. New giant plants have been constructed, many at coastal sites, since competitors such as Japan led the way with tremendous cost advantages accruing from economies of scale. Conversion has become very important to try to create and transform undertakings capable of reabsorbing redundant workers. To redeploy workers emphasis has been given to resettlement allowances and to financing the acquisition of vocational training skills. Under the Davignon Plan the EC steel industry has been greatly restructured and slimmed-down to enhance its competitive efficiency. For example, in 1986 just under 63,000 workers in the ECSC were affected by restructuring.

The European Agricultural Guidance and Guarantee Fund. This Fund was developed to administer the CAP and because of the high price support most of the expenditure has consisted of guaranteeing prices, with only a small proportion being concerned with guidance expenditure. CAP expenditure helps all farmers, not only smaller farmers in very peripheral regions. It is therefore neither an efficient agricultural policy nor an effective regional policy. However, efforts have been made to link the EAGGF more closely to regional policy and one indication of this was in 1974 when 150 million EUA were transferred from the Guidance section of the EAGGF to the European Regional Development Fund (Vanhove and Klassen 1980, p. 422). The larger farms in the EC operating in regions with favourable conditions have gained most, especially those involved in grain and dairy production which have received very high price support.

Although structural measures have been developed very much to favour those in Southern Europe, expenditure on this has had to be curtailed because of the undue weight given to the Guarantee section of the Fund.

Structural measures have generally given farmers a minimum of 25 per cent of the total cost of projects for modernization of farms, rationalization, improvement of processing and marketing; help with movement of workers from the land, plus help to mountain and hill farming in less-favoured areas (the latter scheme was strengthened further in March 1987). Also restructuring aid has been extended to the fishing industry. The Commission has proposed a focus on particular priorities in order to avoid spreading resources too thinly (Commission August 1987(j)).

While policies to assist declining sectors like agriculture are vital, they can only cushion its decline. They cannot maintain, let alone increase, agricultural employment in the future. Hence there is a need to develop related ancillary activities, such as tourism, food processing, marketing of local products and the establishment and development of small firms, especially in conjunction with part-time employment. The EC has also moved forward with Integrated Development Programmes, particularly in the Mediterranean. This is sensible since reliance on the CAP price-support policy has little effect on some Mediterranean areas, such as Andalucía in Spain, with its landless labourers and many unemployed workers (Duchêne *et al.* 1985, p. 184). The EC's latest initiative has been to provide ECU 400 million up to the end of 1993 to implement programmes for the development of rural communities. The programme will be known as LEADER, a French acronym (Liaison Entre Actions de Développement de l'Economie Rurale).

The European Investment Bank (EIB). The EIB has been empowered to provide loans for projects which fall into the following categories: for developing less-developed regions; for modernizing or converting undertakings, or for developing fresh activities; and for projects of common interest to member states.

The Bank's subscribed capital was doubled to ECU 28,800 million from 1 January 1986. Italy's subscription was raised from that date to 19.127 per cent – the level each subscribed by Germany, France and the UK. However, most of the Bank's funds are raised on international capital markets at keen terms because it has a secure and high credit-rating. The EIB is a very important source of long-term loans and has occasionally provided a guarantee for raising loans. Its loan terms depend upon the conditions prevailing on international capital markets and also on the projects themselves. Loans to industry are normally for a period of seven to 12 years and up to 20 years for infrastructure projects. Borrowing is at a fixed rate of interest and is a very useful source of funds for risky projects (Vanhove and Klassen 1980, p. 413). Repayment of the loan may also include a period of grace before any repayment of the principal needs to be made.

The Bank has been of greater significance in terms of total lending than some of the other much-heralded and better-known funds. Table 6.2 shows the extent of EIB lending, of which about 90 per cent has occurred within the EC rather than in conjunction with the EC's European Development Fund.

An appraisal of the EIB's activities, especially from the viewpoint of a regional dimension, would point to some of the following deficiencies. The Bank is not concerned solely with regional imbalance but with other functions (as laid down at the beginning of this section). It has financed common projects of joint interest to Community countries, such as the Airbus project. Much of this expenditure on new industrial investment often occurs outside weaker regions. Although the EIB is concerned with financing improvements to the infrastructure, again much of this occurs in developed regions; for example, the EIB has agreed to lend ECU 1.4 billion for building the Channel Tunnel, resulting in more investment in the south-east of England. If one wished to focus financial assistance purely on the problem regions then the multi-purpose role of the Bank would have to be diminished. For those who favour a more interventionist and subsidized approach to regional development, the EIB would appear to be too much of a commercial institution, providing repayable loans and not grants (except when supplemented by a small subsidy from the ERDF).

The EIB is never a source of the whole finance for a project, but provides up to half of the cost, with the borrower having to obtain the remainder from other financial institutions. The Bank's lending, now approaching World Bank levels, was focused initially upon large projects. Some of these have been extremely capital-intensive with the consequence that, apart from workers employed in the initial building work, they have failed to mop up surplus labour. It

Table 6.2 EIB financing provided (contracts signed), 1959–89 (in million ECUs)

Years	Total	Within the Community			Outside the Community	
		Lending from EIB own resources	Loans under mandate and guarantees	Lending from NCI resources[1]	Lending from EIB own resources	Operations mounted from budgetary resources
1959–72	2,836.7	2,340.1	110.1	–	155.7	230.8
1973–80	14,340.6	11,739.1	132.4	474.7	1,381.5	613.0
1981	3,531.4	2,523.8	–	539.9	377.9	89.8
1982	4,683.5	3,446.0	–	791.1	405.2	41.2
1983	5,921.8	4,145.9	97.6	1,199.6	426.0	52.7
1984	6,885.9	5,007.0	–	1,181.8	610.7	86.4
1985	7,181.5	5,640.7	–	883.7	581.3	75.9
1986	7,516.9	6,677.3	–	393.0	356.5	90.1
1987	7,778.0	6,965.1	–	425.2	184.4	203.3
1988	10,085.6	8,843.9	185.0	356.5	520.1	180.1
1989	12,246.1	11,555.9	–	78.3	485.9	126.0
Total	83,008.0	68,884.8	525.1	6,323.8	5,485.2	1,789.3

[1]The New Community Instrument has operated since 1979, through which the Commission transfers money to the Bank for specific purposes.

Source: EIB Annual Report, 1989 (1990)

has also been argued that too much finance has been canalized into polluting industries, such as the motor, chemical and nuclear power industries (Lewenhak 1982). With the benefit of hindsight, society is now much more conscious of the environmental externalities associated with these industries. But in any energy investment a difficult choice has to be made between coal, oil, gas and nuclear power, with none of them being completely immune from some undesirable environmental impact.

The emphasis on financing large projects gradually diminished after the introduction in the late 1960s of a global loan system for allocating funds to financial intermediaries to on-lend to medium-sized firms. These intermediaries can be of many types but are mainly banking institutions. As such, they are concerned primarily with the application of normal banking principles, especially with the capacity to repay loans. In some respects, from the perspective of promoting regional employment or steering funds to key sectors, they may be the wrong people to act as intermediaries. However, at least global loans were a step forward and a recognition that financing big projects *per se* was a mistake.

Large projects in 'growth-pole' locations have not only provided few jobs but have often added to overcapacity, with the same vulnerability to decline as many traditional industries. Smaller and medium-sized firms in contrast have offered more potential for stable indigenous growth. By the mid-1980s over half of all the Bank's industrial investment was under the global loan system. However, this again has not been as effective as expected in creating jobs and it has been suggested that more of its loans should be switched from manufacturing to the growing service sector (Pinder 1986).

The EIB is undoubtedly attractive to borrowers in countries which would have to pay high domestic interest rates and pay off loans over a short time-period. But while EIB loans can make investments look more favourable, the Bank is a market-based institution and can only respond when there is a demand from borrowers. In a recession when investment intentions are gloomy and pessimistic, investment is low and yet it is precisely at this time that investment needs to be stimulated. Despite innovations by the EIB in its lending policy, investment is demand-determined and has tended to fall away during recession. Some borrowers faced repayment problems, exacerbated by exchange rate changes, and to alleviate the latter, governments have provided some element of protec-

Table 6.3   ERDF financing in the EC, 1975–85

Type of investment	Amount granted (in million ECUs)	%
Industry, services and craft	2,481.52	17.7
Infrastructure	11,347.78	81.0
Studies	43.63	0.3
National programmes of Community interest	133.98	1.0
Total	14,006.91	100.0

Source: Commission, *ERDF in Figures 1975–85* (1985), p. 4

tive compensation for borrowers. The British government felt that this had become too costly and though some compensation was retained for loans to the public sector, it announced in 1985 that it was no longer willing to cover exchange risks on small loans: this policy change is somewhat inconsistent with the overall strategy of helping small businesses.

The European Regional Development Fund (ERDF). There was no explicit call for a common regional policy in the Treaty of Rome and it was only after the decision was taken to enlarge the Community that the ERDF was finally established in 1975. Its allocations have grown since then in terms of budgetary expenditure to over ECU 6 billion (or more than 10 per cent of the Budget) in 1991 (see Table 8.4). The ERDF (or FEDER – Fonds Européen de Développement Régional) has been assisted in its operation by two Committees comprising national officials: the Regional Policy Committee and the Fund Committee.

The ERDF covered some 60 per cent of the EC's land area and some 40 per cent of its population. It has provided grants for industry, services and crafts, and much of its investment has focused on infrastructure, such as transport, energy and water engineering projects. This is shown in Table 6.3.

ERDF grants are normally for half the investment costs, and up to 55 per cent for projects of exceptional regional significance. For projects with a large investment cost, the rate of grant available falls and generally lies between 30 and 50 per cent. The regions eligible for assistance are those designated by national governments, and ERDF funding is concentrated very heavily on a small number of regions, such as Italy and the UK; for example, from 1975–86 the three Italian regions – Campania, Sicilia and Calabria – received some 20 per cent of the ERDF expenditure quota. After the accession of Spain and Portugal in 1986 five of the ten most assisted regions were located in the Iberian peninsula (Commission 1987c, p. 43).

The system of fixed national quotas for ERDF expenditure was considered to be advantageous to Italy and the other new members of the Community which experienced severe regional problems. However, these quotas meant that the ERDF lacked sufficient discretion in allocating its finance and some critics have emphasised its disadvantages; for example, '*FEDER possédant une caractéristique unique parmi les instruments de la Communauté qui handicapant son actions: l'attribution aux États membres de certains quotas'* (Moussis 1982, p. 221). In 1979 some amendments were made which allowed the Community to introduce specific regional development policies, one of the most significant of which was the concept of a small non-quota section of 5 per cent of ERDF finance which could apply outside the nationally designated areas. This provided a very limited degree of additional flexibility, but was a significant step by the EC in trying to wrest regional policy away from tight national control (Keating and Jones 1985, p. 37). This led the Commission to propose an enlargement of the non-quota section to 20 per cent of the ERDF and it also sought to concentrate the quota expenditure on a smaller number of regions defined according to Community criteria; but these proposals were very controversial.

Eventually agreement was reached on a system of flexible quota guidelines. Instead of each country being given a fixed percentage quota, this is now based on minimum and maximum limits. The lower limit constituted the minimum which a country was entitled to receive and the upper limit was the maximum it could attain. The total minimum expenditure was set at 88.63 per cent so that the Commission had discretion over the small remaining marginal expenditure up to 100 per cent of the ERDF's funds. Countries submit many applications so that they can attract some of the 12 per cent marginal expenditure. Obviously the theoretical maximum set

Table 6.4   ERDF national shares: 1986 percentages

Country	Lower limit	Upper limit
Italy	21.62	28.79
Spain	17.97	23.93
United Kingdom	14.50	19.31
Portugal	10.66	14.20
Greece	8.36	10.64
France	7.48	9.96
Ireland	3.82	4.61
Germany	2.55	3.40
Netherlands	0.68	0.91
Belgium	0.61	0.82
Denmark	0.34	0.46
Luxembourg	0.04	0.06
Total	88.63	117.09

Source: ERDF *Twelfth Annual Report for 1986*, p. 5

at 117.09 per cent of the fund in 1986 was unattainable. Table 6.4 shows the range of national shares in ERDF in the enlarged Community.

Spain is now close to Italy in its ERDF entitlement, with nearly 75 per cent of its national territory and almost half of its population in assisted areas. From 1986 to 1989 Italy received ECU 2660 million from the ERDF, the UK ECU 2223 million, and Spain ECU 2183 million. Portugal has grown significantly in its entitlement and has shown an ability to put together viable projects for all its regions eligible for assistance (with the exception of Lisbon). This yielded ECU 1139 million from the ERDF 1986–9. Furthermore, if the amount of aid received was expressed per head, then countries like Portugal, Greece and Ireland would move up the league table of national shares, and others, like Italy and the UK, would move down.

ERDF expenditure has grown and between 1975 and 1986 it created or maintained nearly 764,000 jobs and most of these were newly created jobs (Commission 1987c, p. 75). The ERDF has moved to a preference for financing programmes rather than individual projects and it expects at least 20 per cent of a nation's share of Fund expenditure to be spent on programmes. It was hoped that this would improve co-ordination and coherence, reducing the time and effort spent in assessing each individual project. The programme approach increases the role of the Community in regional policy. Programmes are either Community programmes or national programmes of Community interest. There are also Integrated Development Operations bringing all loans and grants together to concentrate on particular areas; finally, there are Integrated Mediterranean Programmes.

While the ERDF has moved in the right direction, its financial resources are still far too small and only a fraction of those spent by member states (Armstrong 1983). The magnitude of agricultural expenditure has curtailed the finance available for the ERDF. In addition, it was easiest initially to reach a political compromise which gave all countries some share in the Fund's allocation – however small – diluting the limited finance available. EC regional expenditure should also add to regional expenditure by national governments, but unfortunately, instead of it being additional, it has often been substituted for some national regional spending. Nevertheless, governments like to claim that in considering their spending plans they make allowance for the inflow of EC funds and suggest that without them their regional spending would be even lower. Meanwhile, in the new Structural Funding for 1992 the additionality principle is to be applied more fully. Member states are to show a real additional regional impact, and by comparing the previous level of expenditure their funds should result in an equivalent increase in the total volume of structural expenditure. Enhancement of regional expenditure is to be welcomed, though without automatic carry-over of funds, expenditure may occur quickly, but not necessarily effectively.

E   Tackling social inequalities

The range of social policy. Social and regional inequalities sometimes overlap, but there are also separate and persistent social differentials. Social policy encompasses a wide range of issues, and at national level it includes social security expenditure which subsidizes income, such as pensions, sickness and unemployment benefits. In addition, there is provision of commodity subsidies for major selected social services, such as health, education, housing and so on.

The rationale is to alleviate poverty and to lessen inequalities by redistributing income. However, it is recognized that there is some trade-off in which greater equality may impede economic growth through a loss of incentives to enterprise. Furthermore, given the need to contain an excessive growth of public expenditure, this has led to greater consideration of the role of the private sector in providing merit goods.

In the EC, social policy is much more narrowly defined in scope and concentrates primarily on labour market issues. Although the Community has impinged upon educational and health matters, this has been marginal and often the by-product of other activities; for example, in promoting labour mobility, the EC has needed to involve itself educationally with the recognition of qualifications; or in industrial employment, there is the need to move on from specific health and safety requirements to a more general concern for citizens' health. From occasional meetings of ministers of education and health, other EC issues have been taken on board. Yet essentially the conception of EC social policy is still far more limited than that normally understood by social policy at a national level.

The development of social policy. The foundations of EC social policy can be found in the various Treaties which contain a general commitment to improving living and working conditions. The ECSC covered such matters as unemployment compensation, retraining, health and safety, and housing. But overall, like the subsequent Spaak Committee, it felt no need for a common social policy. Thus in the Treaty of Rome there were few precise commitments and no definite timetable drawn up for action. However, France was worried about the high level of social charges borne by its employers. They fretted that these would erode French industrial competitiveness unless some harmonization occurred. Though generally unsuccessful in its demands, France did manage to engage other member states to introduce equal pay for men and women– via Article 119 of the Treaty of Rome. Other Treaty clauses on holidays and overtime pay were gradually overtaken by events.

Gender inequalities in the labour market manifest themselves for women in terms of lower pay and horizontal employment concentration into a limited range of occupations, with a vertical clustering into lower grades. Proneness to unemployment arises from insufficient training, leaving the labour market to have children, and locational movements brought about by husbands' job changes. Women, like migrants, have been used as the most flexible marginal element in the labour market. Women have been attracted increasingly into employment by higher pay, smaller family size and new labour-saving technology in the home. Negative influences have been higher earnings for husbands and higher unemployment. While part of the gender inequalities can be attributed to supply-side differences, such as education and training, even after standardizing for these a significant level of discrimination still remains.

The many EC directives to tackle inequality have included the following: equal pay, 1975; equal opportunities in employment, recruitment, promotion and training, 1976; equal treatment for men and women in social security, 1977. Its various action programmes have increasingly recognized the links between employment and child care and in 1982 a directive was presented on parental leave which the Council was unable to approve. The EC has also sought to protect women's maternity leave so that they can return to their jobs and have the incentive to train. Its latest directive in 1990 concerned 14 weeks' paid maternity leave, though with a recognition that intervention is primarily that of national governments.

Another significant policy achievement in the context of making the market operate more efficiently was in promoting intra-EC labour migration. From the 1960s this was to a large extent from Italy, and the latter was concerned with social security provision and protection of working rights for migrants. However, especially since the 1970s, there has been a desire to go further in social policy, with some favouring a more redistributive system. In the early 1970s social policy was enhanced and the Paris Summit Conference of 1972 called for a Social Action Programme to be formulated. Its priorities were to create full and better employment; improvement of living and working conditions; and participation by employees in the process of decision-making. There was in addition a statement of many other proposals producing a worthy list of desirable social developments (Shanks 1977).

Implementing new developments was constrained by the background of a worsening economic climate. For example, the Draft European Company Statute, which was first presented to the Council of Ministers in 1975, failed to get approval; this would have set out a framework for industrial relations in European companies based on the German supervisory board model, including direct worker-participation. Likewise the Vredeling Directive on rights of workers to information and consultation in large companies was blocked, partly as a result of opposition from multinational companies. However, new developments did include the Council decision to establish a European Centre for the Development of Vocational Training (CEDEFOP), which began in 1977 in Berlin. In 1975 a Foundation for the Improvement of Living and Working Conditions was established in Dublin, and the Council has also supported a project of the European Trades Union Confederation to establish a European Trades Union Institute. Initiatives by the Commission in the 1980s were linked to other developments such as that of a People's Europe and the internal market programme.

The Social Charter. The Community has sought to consolidate basic social rights whose pillars are already enshrined in standards laid down by the UN, the ILO and the Council of Europe. In February 1989 the Economic and Social Committee (ESC) adopted a favourable position on this, followed in November 1989 by Commission proposals for the implementation of a Community Charter of Basic Social Rights for workers. These are grouped under various headings and in some matters, such as freedom of association and collective bargaining, the Commission did not propose any initiatives since it regarded these as matters for employers and unions in member states. In other areas the Commission has limited its 50 proposals which comprise the Social Charter mainly to directives or regulations, which will be introduced by 1992.

The EC monitors labour market trends in both employment and unemployment. For example, its Local Employment Development Action (LEDA) programme has identified and publicized successful local responses to employment problems. Other research has identified successful programmes or projects for long-term unemployed adults and for young people. Meanwhile, a long-established European system for the international clearance of vacancies and applications for employment (SEDOC) is to be improved.

The Commission has sought to establish basic levels of employment and remuneration. For example, there were two directives (unadopted) on voluntary part-time working and on temporary work/fixed-term contracts. The Commission has renewed its activities to introduce a standard contract on employment and to improve terms and conditions of workers employed on foreign contracts by sub-contractors. It also wishes to establish a minimum level of pay to avoid problems such as social dumping.

Improvement of living and working conditions has been tackled by directives to safeguard workers' rights in the event of transfer of firms or establishments, redundancies and insolvency of employers. Gaps are being filled, such as redundancies declared by employers restructuring their operations, but located in another member state. There was a Council recommendation in 1975 on the introduction of four weeks paid holidays. The Commission recommendations in the early 1980s to introduce and reorganize working time made little progress. The Commission's Social Charter would impose minimum rules on the maximum duration of work, rest periods, holidays, amount of overtime by night-work, weekend work, and so on. Also, to protect children and adolescents in particular, its latest initiative has been to set a minimum age of work, limits on working hours of juveniles (under 18) and prohibition of maximum night-work jobs. A policy of trying to provide equal treatment for all workers, whether full-time, part-time or temporary, would be costly in bringing nearly all employees into the national insurance system and pension schemes.

The EC Social Charter has proposed additional infilling of the few remaining minor gaps in relation to freedom of labour movement to level up conditions. There is a keen awareness of the need to protect workers and in September 1988 the EP requested the Commission to promote the introduction of a minimum income level. Many directives have also been encouraged to improve health and safety at work. Collective bargaining is encouraged, along with greater information and consultation by employers. Advantages have been identified from the development of employee participation via both financial schemes and workers' representation in decision-making.

The interests of disadvantaged groups, such as the elderly and the disabled, have also been considered, so that they can lead as independent a life as possible. For example, proposals have been made for an over-60s card; for the exchange of information on technical aids for the disabled; and for the continuation of the Helios Action Programme for the disabled.

Constraints in implementing some aspects of the Social Charter in the form of an action programme will arise from different practices between the member states. In addition, a key concern is to what extent setting some minimum standards, which are an improvement on equity grounds, are offset by higher unemployment if companies relocate outside the EC. For example, besides the NICs, there is now the attraction of location in low-cost countries in Eastern Europe. It is important for the Community to explore fully whether more extensive social policies are a natural complement to the internal market, or significantly detract from it by confronting businesses with higher labour costs. In small businesses which tend to be labour-intensive, the consequence in competitive markets will be greater unemployment. This partially offsets further benefits from the internal market in reducing other costs, such as capital through lower and convergent interest rates, and lower costs through economies of scale. In a Community where macroeconomic policies are being increasingly integrated, it may be preferable economically to leave the labour market relatively free to perform the main mechanism of economic adjustment.

Educational and training programmes.   Most significant in terms of social and economic benefits have been the continued commitments to raise skill levels via educational training schemes. For example, 1976 saw the first EC Action Programme in education establishing EURYDICE on educational information and exchange. It was also agreed to organize study visits for educational specialists under the ARION programme. Meanwhile, COMETT I 1987–9 and COMETT II 1990–4 provide support for transnational training, partnership and mobility between universities and industry in technology; EUROTECHNET deals with vocational training for technological change for workers in industry. The PETRA programme backs the training of young people to follow a course of vocational training for at least a year. The Commission intends to follow this up with supplementary vocational training for young people during working time. The EC over the years has sought the creation of comparability for vocational training in many sectors. Exchanges of young workers are encouraged (even with those in Eastern Europe), while student mobility and inter-university co-operation in higher education has been fostered by ERASMUS. The LINGUA scheme is also improving foreign language teaching. Another acronym in this area of education and training includes IRIS, to develop equal opportunities and vocational training for women. Meanwhile the European Centre for the Development of Vocational Training

(CEDEFOP) promotes the development of vocational training through information, research and co-operation.

The European Social Fund (ESF). The ESF has been in operation since 1958 and a full coverage of all its activities will not be given here, but merely signposts indicating the Fund's changing direction and emphasis. Originally it was not a proper instrument of positive regional policy, being concerned mainly with fostering labour mobility and in particular spending most of its expenditure on vocational training and retraining workers. In the early years West Germany, which was actively carrying out training and resettlement, was a major beneficiary.

A major turning point in ESF activities occurred after 1972 when the Fund was reformed with increased finance. This focused to a high degree on less-developed regions. The incidence of unemployment has risen, in particular affecting young people seeking to join the labour market for the first time, but also the duration of unemployment is even greater among older workers as long-term unemployment has become well entrenched. Hence the ESF now targets its expenditure increasingly on these two groups. For example, in 1987 about half of those unemployed in the EC had been unemployed for over a year and the Commission has aimed to reduce this downwards towards 30 per cent of the total unemployed. However, ESF financial assistance has reached only a small percentage of the long-term unemployed, and ESF help for vocational training for the unemployed was less than 10 per cent of national expenditure, though vocational training for the long-term unemployed has finally been recognized by member states. In addition, the Fund provides assistance to other disadvantaged groups: migrant workers, the disabled, women returning to employment and often requiring retraining, and workers adversely affected by new technology. The latter is a major preoccupation of the Community, and to improve technological performance and to mitigate any adverse labour market consequences the ESF now insists that all its training projects are not only to have a vocational orientation but must include a minimum amount of time devoted to new technology.

The ESF has recognized the regional dimension of its activities by allocating 44.5 per cent of its funds in the EC(12) to super-priority regions, while remaining expenditure also focuses mainly on areas of high unemployment and areas facing problems of readaptation. The depressed areas most adversely affected are those in Italy (1986–9 receiving ECU 1788 million) and Spain (receiving ECU 1354 million over the same period); also whole countries such as Greece, Portugal, the Republic of Ireland and Northern Ireland have benefited.

Thus it can be seen that the ESF is concerned with a very narrow interpretation of social policy. It focuses mainly on employment/unemployment and training rather than displaying the usual extensive concern of social policy with health and social welfare. Since the early 1970s resources have been channelled increasingly towards the poorer countries, such as Italy. For example, the distribution of ESF financing in 1986 continued to favour Italy, with a share of 21.72 per cent. The shares of other countries were: UK 16.23 per cent, France 14.82 per cent, Spain 13.93 per cent, Ireland 9.40 per cent, Portugal 8.76 per cent, and Greece 5.60 per cent.

The share of EC expenditure devoted to the ESF is still far too small and has faced demands far in excess of its resources. Iberia has begun to take a large slice of the Social Fund, putting together acceptable proposals far more quickly than had been anticipated by officials in Brussels. The funding to both the ESF and ERDF could be expanded significantly – if only agricultural expenditure could be reduced. Indeed, there may be a case for merging the two Funds and co-ordinating their operations more closely. This is because the Social Fund's pursuit of supply-side labour market measures can only be really effective if the ERDF succeeds in raising the level of regional investment demand; then the highly trained and retrained workers can be reabsorbed into the labour market. The ESF currently finances the running costs of schemes and not the capital costs, whereas the ERDF finances subsidies to capital costs of investment.

The main problem in the EC is the high level of aggregate unemployment and its uneven distribution which adversely affects the welfare of its citizens. Measures such as Community-wide finance and payment of unemployment benefits would be a significant step forward. Certainly Community problems have deepened and extended beyond some concerns in the ESF about whether workers are deriving sufficient job satisfaction, or are participating enough in their firms – too many workers are without any jobs and the Social Fund is overwhelmed by applications, often delaying the payments paid to applicants.

Those who regard the EC as a Community rather than as a

market, and seek an upward equalization of social standards, must be rather disappointed by the limited progress which is being made. At a time of high unemployment, when the need for social policy has grown, the meagre resources provided have failed to match these needs. Furthermore, many draft directives on social policy have been blocked in the Council by member governments opposed to active social intervention at Community level.

Part III   Inequalities in the UK
The UK has suffered from three particular problems. As the first European country to industrialize it has also become the first to deindustrialize. Its overcommitment to staple industries and their subsequent decline has resulted in deindustrialization with very severe effects on traditional regions. The second problem is that the rate of economic growth in the UK has been considerably lower than in other EC countries in the postwar years. Although during the 1980s the UK's relative rate of economic growth *vis-à-vis* its continental neighbours has greatly improved, much of the growth has been in the tertiary sector. Thirdly, the UK economy lies on the periphery of the Community's core area. Whereas the UK's location was central for trade with the Americas, the reorientation of trade towards the central areas of the Community has inevitably intensified the problem of regional imbalance.

The North–South divide has become very pronounced in the UK. The south-east and East Anglia were the only regions in the UK with GDP over £5000 per head in 1985 and an unemployment rate of under 10 per cent of the working population. If the depressed inner-city London boroughs were excluded, then the two-nations division would be accentuated further. Most of the traditional manufacturing jobs have been lost in the north, while most of the service jobs have been created in the south. For example, the sun-belt area stretching down the M4 corridor from Cambridge to Bristol reflects a growing concentration of high-technology sectors such as electronics. Some infrastructure demands in the south are high and the government needs to monitor the regional implications of its own expenditure.

A dilemma is that if the government does not maintain the attractiveness of the south-east by improving communications such as the Channel Tunnel then even that region may decline below the European average. The likely effect of the Channel Tunnel is to strengthen south-east England *vis-à-vis* the more depressed northern regions, handicapped by insufficient new rail infrastructure. The greatest beneficiary of all may well turn out to be French regions, such as Nord Pas de Calais, which has had one of the highest unemployment rates in France; at nearly 15 per cent in April 1989, its unemployment was exceeded only by Languedoc-Rouissillon (Eurostat 1990). The unemployment rate in Nord Pas de Calais was just over 10 per cent above that in south-east England; also, the former is less peripheral and with its lower costs will prove attractive for new business locations, leading to convergence downwards towards the rate of unemployment in south-east England. In any proposed transfrontier regional development programme between Kent and Nord Pas de Calais, the latter would still receive the bulk of ERDF expenditure.

A synthetic index based on GDP and unemployment for the EC(9) indicated that most UK regions had fallen below the EC average of 100. Between 1977 and 1981 the UK's most prosperous area, Greater London, reached a level of 72 per cent of Hamburg, whilst its poorest region, Northern Ireland, was only 23 per cent of Hamburg. New rank positions of regions for the EC(12) based on comparative GDP per capita (purchasing power parity) had Greater London as the UK's best-placed region, standing at 155.1, in relation to the best-placed regions of Hamburg (195.5) and Groningen (237.4) (Padoa-Schioppa *et al.* 1987, pp. 172–7). Regional performance is closely related to national performance, with the more prosperous regions tending to lie very much in West Germany and the poorer regions in the UK, Ireland and Southern Europe. For example, the poorest region on GDP per head in 1985 was Thrakis in Greece at 43.2. EC regional funding is at best a palliative, though in Ireland it is more significant when calculated per head of population. For the UK both the limited total regional funds available and their insufficient concentration on its problems have reduced the effectiveness of EC policy. UK regions now receive even less as a consequence of southern enlargement, and its rural areas, which are above the EC's new GDP per head level (for example, the Scottish Highlands and Islands) seem likely to suffer. The UK's depressed industrial areas will also be squeezed eventually. The UK even has problems in its capital city where depressed conditions have led to riots in Brixton and Tottenham, yet under EC regional policy capital cities have been exempt from aid (except Dublin).

Given the magnitude of regional problems in the UK it seems paradoxical that instead of the government increasing the level of regional expenditure it actually reduced it by about half in the 1980s. It was critical of the high costs of job creation, largely because of the heavy take-up of capital-intensive sectors. Regional policy was mainly redistributing employment rather than creating many new jobs. The assisted areas have been reduced to cover a smaller percentage of the working population and there was a move away from automatic investment grants to selective grants in 1984, linking assistance more directly to job creation. It was announced finally in 1988 under the Enterprise Initiative that automatic grants under the revised Regional Development Scheme were to be scrapped and Regional Selective Assistance was to be tightened further for large firms. The distinction between developed and intermediate areas has been greatly reduced, though new schemes are available to help small companies in development areas. It has been argued that the direction of governmental policy in the UK could be further improved by better co-ordination and by giving depressed English regions their own regional development agencies with wide powers (Armstrong and Taylor 1987).

Given the inadequate level of UK regional funding, depressed regions have had to tap EC regional funds. However, a full comparison of EC regional transfers shows a predominantly agricultural imprint, so that between 1973 and the end of 1986 the UK received £8632 million from the EAGGF, compared with only £1600 million from the ESF and £1519 million from the ERDF. A regional breakdown of ERDF commitments 1975–86 shows that Scotland received nearly a quarter of these, with 15 per cent each going to Wales and to the north of England, nearly 14 per cent to north-west England, and 10 per cent to Northern Ireland (Commission 1987c; for UK receipts from 1986–9, see Table 6.1).

To maximize the return from Community funds it is necessary to submit as many sound and well conceived projects as possible. Applications have been rejected where they have not been fully documented or failed to meet the formal conditions on assisted areas, costs, number of jobs created and so on. Awareness of the ERDF is high and in the UK applications for infrastructure projects are made via the Department of the Environment, and private sector applications are made via the Department of Trade and Industry. However, the House of Lords has concluded gloomily that 'the

Regional Fund caused very little to happen that would not have happened anyway, and that the principle of additionality was largely disregarded in practice' (House of Lords Select Committee 1984).

The European Social Fund was at first a less well known source of regional support – applications are made via the Department of Employment. In some ways the ESF offers fertile ground for applications since there are no national quotas – unlike the ERDF. Since the Fund is heavily oversubscribed, applicants may be safer to ask for only 25 per cent of their expenditure to be covered to be sure of receiving this, rather than asking for over 50 per cent.

Commission proposals in its Social Charter have had a mixed reaction in the UK, largely because the latter does not subscribe to the principle of a social market economy so typical, for example, in Germany. Although broader social rights are favoured by the Labour Party and the TUC, the Conservatives and business interests oppose excessive intervention and corporatism in the labour market. This is because it contradicts the deregulation of the British labour market in the 1980s which was successful in job creation, especially by small businesses – albeit many jobs were low paid. The government has also been concerned that some of the directives have been presented as health and safety measures which only require a majority vote, whereas as employment measures they would need unanimity and could therefore be blocked. Beneficial aspects of the Social Charter would be improved skill training and some elements of employee participation, such as equity participation and profit-sharing. Other elements such as industrial co-determination have never taken off in the UK since the Bullock Committee Report on Industrial Democracy in 1977.

The government squeeze on public expenditure has encouraged local authorities to establish direct links with the EC; more so than in France with its more centralized system (despite some steps to decentralize in the 1980s). Local authorities can use ERDF grants as a substitute for loans on which they would have to pay interest. While there are additional costs involved in seeking EC finance, those authorities which have appointed liaison officers, particularly in designated areas, have been most successful in tapping Community funds. This indicates that the employment of additional staff to put together viable programmes would be worthwhile as long as the inflow of EC funds exceeded the additional costs of employing them.

EC regional funding may at times appear something of a charade, with complaints about slow receipt of funds. Nevertheless, local authorities, especially those in areas unscheduled for national regional assistance, would probably prefer to have closer direct links with Brussels than with London. But there is no guarantee that their programmes would be approved by a larger bureaucracy dealing with regional affairs in Brussels because of limited funds and the excessive number of claimants. In conclusion, it is important that receipts from EC funds are fully maximized, and in order to improve the Community's image, areas need to be made aware of the specific contribution by the EC.

7 Monetary integration

Part I The characteristics of the international monetary system: fixed and floating exchange rates

The growth of trade between countries requires a system for currency exchange and essentially the choice is between some kind of fixed or floating mechanism. In the early postwar years the international economy opted for a system of fixed exchange rates, after the traumatic experience of the 1930s. This new international mechanism was very much an Anglo-American creation and led to the setting up of the International Monetary Fund (IMF). It was based upon a fixed exchange rate system in which the dollar was fixed in relation to gold, and the dollar as the pivot of the system was fixed in relation to other international currencies. Where countries experienced disequilibrium, financial assistance was forthcoming from the IMF, and when countries reached a position of fundamental disequilibrium they were expected to adjust their exchange rates.

The fixed exchange rate system served the international economy well in providing the certainty and stability which was needed by traders and investors. It provided a 'known element' in an uncertain world where there are too many variables. Nevertheless, it ran into specific difficulties since there was a misinterpretation of IMF rules, and countries in fundamental disequilibrium sought tenaciously to defend the parity of their currencies. The countries with balance-of-payments deficits were reluctant to accept the political consequences of devaluing their currencies. They had sizeable reserves trying to ward off speculation, but usually succumbed eventually. Problems were compounded by the lack of equivalent pressure on countries with balance-of-payments surpluses to revalue their currencies, and though one country's balance-of-payments deficit is matched by another country's balance-of-payments surplus, the countries in surplus did not rush to revalue for fear of making the task of their exporters too difficult.

The international monetary system was undermined by growing balance-of-payments deficits in the USA and a greater reluctance by other countries to hold dollars. This led ultimately to a crisis at the beginning of the 1970s with the break from gold and the devaluation of the dollar. Massive speculation and increasing divergence between national rates of inflation and economic performance brought the fixed exchange rate system to a state of collapse. Thus in the early 1970s the international economy moved over, with great euphoria, to a regime of floating exchange rates.

Floating the exchange rate seemed to offer an additional policy instrument, instead of being a policy target of economic management, enabling countries to pursue their own domestic economic policies. It was assumed that any balance-of-payments deficit/surplus would be adjusted automatically by appropriate exchange rate changes. It was assumed that markets were more likely to arrive at the 'right' exchange rate than were governments in administering a fixed rate – even if the latter were fixed at the correct level to begin with, the reluctance to alter it meant that it soon became the wrong rate of exchange. Countries would no longer need to hold massive reserves to defend their exchange rates, so floating exchange rates could help to alleviate the shortage of international liquidity. To the extent that there were uncertainties about exchange rates, for a small cost traders and investors could protect themselves in forward markets.

Like most fundamental changes, the claims made were far in excess of what could be delivered by a floating exchange rate. While firms can protect themselves against exchange rate fluctuations, the uncertainty and costs are a particular handicap to smaller firms in international trade. The system generally has been characterized by even more marked instability of currencies than of commodity prices, though less volatile than share prices. Exchange rates have fluctuated wildly in the short term and in the long term have still failed to settle at the correct levels, exemplified by the misalignment of sterling, particularly from 1979–81 and the dollar 1981–5. Countries have found it difficult to withstand the sheer volume of capital movements as speculative capital has flowed in and then out of their currencies. In countries with depreciating currencies, a nominal fall in exchange rate was not translated into the same effective exchange rate fall since it stoked up inflationary pressures. This resulted inevitably in the need for other policy instruments to be used, negating the very freedom which floating exchange rates were supposed to confer on domestic policy-makers. In countries with appreciating currencies, such as West Germany, this has not markedly affected its trade performance, partly because its specialization has been in exporting goods such as capital equipment where price is less important than the technical capacity of machines which are well designed, reliable and delivered on time.

Floating exchange rates have failed to live up to expectations and have imposed significant costs. These include: adjustment costs of temporary misalignments; greater uncertainty in trading products, which has contributed to a slowdown in capital formation; a rise in protectionism by countries whose exchange rates have been pushed up too far; and an additional increase in world inflation. Furthermore, any substantial degree of national monetary autonomy has been something of a 'myth' (Tsoukalis ed. 1986). Yet the great overhang of mobile capital has precluded a full return to international fixed exchange rates, though it has led to suggestions for a tax to dampen excessive capital mobility. What has occurred is an attempt to create some exchange rate stability between the major blocs, and in particular within the EC via the European Monetary System (EMS): in other words, to try to obtain internationally the best of both worlds from a blend of flexible and fixed rates and ultimately complete fixity.

Part II Economic and Monetary Union (EMU) and the European Monetary System (EMS)

A The characteristics of optimum currency areas

An optimum currency area (OCA) is a group of countries linked together through fixed exchange rates. Major academic contributions were made in this field during the 1960s and 1970s. They provided a useful background to consideration of the viability of EMU, even though this goes further than OCAs in seeking common economic policies and ultimately a common currency (Coffey 1977, p. 4).

The ability to create and maintain an OCA is based essentially upon the extent to which there are forces leading to convergence within the area, without necessitating an adjustment of the exchange rate. A key criterion used to justify an OCA was that of factor mobility (Mundell 1961). His pioneering theory is open to criticism on the grounds that the direction of factor flows is ambiguous, since capital may flow more to the dynamic region while labour may be relatively immobile and reluctant to move from the depressed region. Impediments still remain to the free mobility of labour in terms of linguistic difficulties, lack of skills, shortage of finance and so on. Although the EC has free labour mobility, much of the immigration has arrived from non-EC countries. However, the amount of capital mobility has increased significantly since the 1960s, with a growing trend currently towards the integration of capital markets.

A subsequent contribution stressed the importance of 'openness' in the economy (McKinnon 1963). Highly open economies which are very dependent on trade will be able to rely on fiscal and monetary policies without needing to alter their exchange rates. Highly open economies have a high marginal propensity both to import and to export products. Where a balance-of-payments deficit exists then deflation can rectify this, with only a small amount of deflation being required to restore a balance-of-payments equilibrium since much of the cut-back in expenditure will be on reduced imports. Countries will also prefer fixed exchange rates and eschew floating exchange rates where currency depreciation is highly inflationary (and workers do not have money illusion which would spark off wage inflationary pressure again). However, note that for stronger countries fixed exchange rates are more inflationary than allowing the exchange rate to appreciate in value.

EC countries have become much more open with the removal of intra-Community trading barriers; intra-EC imports and exports as a percentage of GDP more than doubled between 1960 and 1985. Intra-trade is particularly high for the Benelux countries, though lower for the UK. From the latter one may infer that the UK was correct not to join the EMS exchange rate mechanism (ERM), though in fact its growing trade with the Community means that there is not now a large difference between UK intra-trade with the EC compared with that conducted by other countries, such as Italy and France, with the Community.

Another criterion for an OCA which has been enunciated has been that of diversification (Kenen 1969). Highly diversified economies will be able to manage without having to rely on exchange rate changes, since if demand in one export sector falls, the effect will be small – assuming again a high mobility of labour and capital into other sectors. Although in a depression most export industries might be affected seriously, the larger economies in the Community are sufficiently diversified to withstand this to a greater extent than the smaller economies. It can be seen in examining individual EC economies that some countries may be prime members of an OCA on particular criteria, but not on others (Presley and Dennis 1976). For example, the Benelux countries are highly open, but they are much less diversified than the economies of the larger member states of the Community.

A far more important problem which has beset economies has been that of inflation, and it has been argued that a similar national propensity to inflate should be used as the main criterion for an OCA (Magnifico 1973, part 2 pp. 43–81). Inflation rates diverge since countries have different preferences and a different trade-off between unemployment and inflation. In any kind of monetary union some of the countries have to sacrifice their preferences, either conforming to one preference – usually that of the dominant country – or agreeing between themselves on a common objective. Greater problems arise where countries have different trade-offs, since even if they were to agree on the same unemployment preference, countries with Phillips curves closer to the origin, such as West Germany, have lower inflation. Institutional labour market practices partly underlie its lower wage-pushfulness; for example, its industrial unions and system of co-determination (*Mitbestimmung*).

Since the Phillips curve trade-off has partly broken down it has been argued that any success in reducing unemployment can only be temporary; hence, governments have little choice except to aim for price stability. This led to more persuasive views on the prospects for EMU (Presley and Dennis 1976). However, the monetarist approach of controlling the rate of growth of the money supply to create lower and convergent inflation has run into problems in defining and controlling money supply satisfactorily.

Where the four criteria for an OCA exist, then the case for EMU is strong. The USA provides a shining example to which the EC aspires, in which the dollar totally fulfils the true functions of money across a large geographical group of states. Furthermore, it has been argued that any misgivings one might harbour about abandoning the independent use of one's own exchange rate is misplaced where a complete union exists; that is, with economic policy co-ordination, a pool of foreign exchange reserves and a common Central Bank (El-Agraa ed. 1985). However, where workers do suffer from money illusion, where only a pseudo-union exists (that is, incomplete EMU) and where different trade elasticities exist, then it may still be argued that a multiplicity of currencies provides the most flexible adjustment to tackle regional disparities.

B   The case for monetary union

Monetary union comprises the essential ingredients of fixed exchange rates and the integration of capital markets. The case for monetary union is closely tied up with the CAP since changing exchange rates result in changing prices and incomes for farmers (see Chapter 4 on agriculture, and in particular the section on MCAs which were introduced to try to insulate agriculture from the consequences of these exchange rate alterations). Just as agriculture and monetary integration are closely linked, likewise other chapters show how monetary union needs integration in other spheres, such as regional and budgetary policies.

Although MCAs helped to hold the CAP together, they resulted in various complications, misallocating resources by encouraging further high-cost production in countries such as West Germany. France was particularly upset to see West Germany adding further agricultural gains to its existing large industrial benefits. The issue of MCAs was a source of disruption in the general cosy relationship between Schmidt and Giscard d'Estaing in March 1979.

By 1979 the EC had become increasingly disenchanted with the volatile system of floating exchange rates. It was also very concerned about the need to offer some alternative to the increasing problems afflicting the dollar. Apart from the traditional concern about the dominance of the dollar and dollar 'imperialism', which has often been expressed by countries such as France, there was growing recognition over time that the USA's economic situation was deteriorating. The USA shared the problem of many other countries in terms of rising costs of imported energy, and a high propensity to import goods from countries such as Japan. But what constitutes a special and continuous long-term burden to the USA is its very high defence expenditure. The likelihood of a continuing balance-of-payments deficit in the USA makes holders of dollars keen to switch into other reserve currencies. Other national currencies have been reluctant or unable to fulfil this role; hence countries such as West Germany, fearful of a rush of dollars driving up the mark in an excessive and unstable way, have sought to develop a common EC monetary position.

There are positive financial benefits which accrue from having

Table 7.1   Cost savings on intra-EC settlements by a single currency

	Billion ECU 1990 Estimated range	
1. *Financial transaction costs*		
Bank transfers	6.4	10.6
Banknotes, eurocheques, travellers' cheques, credit cards	1.8	2.5
Total	8.2	13.1
2. *In-house costs*	3.6	4.8
3. *Reduction of cross-border payment costs*	1.3	1.3
Total	13.1	19.2

Note:
Exchange transaction costs associated with several sources of in-house costs are not included in this table.

Source: 'One Market, One Money', *European Economy*, no. 49, Oct. 1990

fixity of exchange rates and eventually a single currency. The flow of goods and capital is facilitated and there are economies in the amount of reserve holdings since these are pooled. When one moves on from fixed exchange rates to the eventual outcome of a single EC currency, then money can fully perform its function as a medium of exchange by eliminating the costs of money conversion. Markets will operate far more efficiently. In addition, if the currency becomes a key currency, which is highly likely, then, like the dollar, benefits arise from seigniorage. Thus holders are prepared to hold that currency without pressing to exchange it, enabling the union, if it wishes, to run a balance-of-payments deficit.

Some of the advantages to the EC from having a single currency have been estimated, though not as comprehensively as those accruing from the single market. Transaction-cost savings range from ECU 13.1 billion to ECU 19.2 billion (see Table 7.1). They amount to around 0.5 per cent of EC GDP and are in excess of the gains from removing border controls of around 0.25 per cent of EC GDP. However, like border controls, their removal will be of greatest benefit to SMEs and small open economies. The single market needs to go hand in hand with EMU, and when all goods are priced in the same currency – so that consumers can easily compare prices – that will further reinforce the trend towards price convergence. Meanwhile, dynamic benefits will be reaped as the credibility and visibility of a single currency lead agents to modify their wage- and price-setting in a more disciplined way. This will increase business confidence, investment and the rate of economic growth in the Community.

C   The winding road to EMU

EMU was not mentioned explicitly in the Treaty of Rome and it did not provide for fixed and immutable exchange rates, though Articles 103–109 did set down the principles of unrestricted currency convertibility, abolition of restrictions on capital movements, and the co-ordination of economic policy. To facilitate the latter a Monetary Committee was established in 1958 and a Short-Term Economic Policy Committee in 1960. In 1964 there was formed a Committee of Governors of Central Banks, a Budgetary Policy Committee and a Medium-Term Policy Committee – these Committees were later merged into a new Economic Policy Committee.

While exchange rates remained fixed there was little point in initiating EMU and it was only when pressures built up in the late 1960s for exchange rate adjustments that the issue assumed some urgency. The devaluation of sterling in 1967 was followed in 1969 by the devaluation of the French franc and the revaluation of the D-mark. There was concern to prevent countries from resorting once again to protectionist measures, since France, for example, had introduced import controls in the immediate aftermath of the 1968 crisis.

In 1965 and 1969 both P. Werner and R. Barre came up with proposals for monetary reform, with the latter proposing, amongst other things, a system of monetary support and financial assistance to help economies experiencing balance-of-payments deficits. Both these personalities were to be influential over the next few years in shaping EMU, after the decision to introduce it which was made at the European Summit in late 1969, under the leadership of Brandt and Pompidou.

While member states were persuaded of the benefits of EMU there were significant differences in perspective, and to reconcile these a working party was established under P. Werner. The differences were largely between France and Germany, but alongside the French were Belgium and Luxembourg, while the German view was shared by the Dutch and sometimes by the Italians. These different perspectives have been given the label 'Monetarist versus Economist'. The monetarist position was to favour a commitment to fixed exchange rates and pooling reserves along the lines of the second Barre Plan, published in March 1970. The competing economist strategy was not to rush ahead with monetary union since this was 'putting the cart before the horse' before economic co-ordination had been achieved. The West German approach was enshrined in the Schiller Plan in March 1970. This detailed Plan divided the progress towards EMU into clear stages and it was only in the final stage that a common currency was to be introduced. West Germany has been concerned to persuade other countries to reduce their excessive rates of inflation, since under a fixed exchange rate system it felt that it was importing inflation from others. A greater co-ordination of macroeconomic policies, in particular to reduce wide national disparities in rates of inflation, has been an on-going concern of West Germany.

The Werner Committee had to resolve these different perspectives, coming up with a compromise described as one of 'parallelism' (Kruse 1980, pp. 70–5); that is, parallel advance on both fronts in co-ordinating economic policy and moving forward by narrowing exchange rate margins, integrating capital markets and finally establishing a common currency and a single Central Bank. In March 1971 EMU was born and a stage-by-stage timetable was over-optimistically drawn up for its full achievement by 1980.

The main outcome was the creation of the 'snake' in 1972. The international monetary order had already been shaken by the devaluation of the dollar and the Smithsonian Agreement in December 1971, after which there was a widening of the margins of currency fluctuations which had existed during the postwar period. The original ± 1 per cent margin (a band of 2 per cent) was now widened internationally to ± 2.25 per cent (a band of 4.5 per cent). EC countries themselves decided to limit the range of their own member currencies to a band of 2.25 per cent, hence the band for the snake was half the width of the 4.5 per cent 'tunnel'.

In preparation for the first enlargement of the Community, the UK, Denmark and Ireland were to be included. However, in June

1972 speculation drove both sterling and the Irish pound from the snake and the tunnel, followed a few days later by the Danish krone – though Denmark was able to rejoin the scheme later that year. Italy withdrew from it at the beginning of 1973 and in spring 1973 the international fixed exchange rate mechanism collapsed and was replaced by one of floating exchange rates. Although the snake continued between those EC countries which were able to participate, the system floated in relation to other currencies, and thus the snake ceased to be 'in the tunnel'. Between 1973 and 1978 there were widespread currency realignments and further departures from the snake: for example, by France on two occasions, 1974 and 1976; and Sweden, which had participated, withdrew in 1977. These have been described quite aptly as *'les vicissitudes du serpent monétaire'* (Moussis 1982, pp. 60–4).

The official target to achieve EMU by 1980 was dropped, but that did not prevent a plethora of new reports making further suggestions and recommendations. In 1974 Fourcade made a French proposal for a larger snake – a boa – which would have wider margins and allow countries to withdraw and re-enter the system. In 1975 a study group chaired by Marjolin reached the pessimistic conclusion that the prospects for EMU had been destroyed by discordant economic and monetary policies. Yet reports continued to circulate, with a group of prominent economists in 1975 suggesting the issue of a parallel currency – the Europa – for private use. A Belgian proposal by Tindemans in 1976 sought to strengthen the snake and suggested that a parallel currency might help. It also recommended greater co-ordination of economic policies, though it fell short of any target or deadlines for EMU. This was followed in the same year by a Dutch proposal (Duisenberg chairing the Council of Ministers) that European currencies ought to come closer together and that economic co-ordination might be improved by the creation of 'target zones'.

Despite adverse economic circumstances a series of reports and favourable public opinion provided continued momentum; for example, Eurobarometer surveys recorded public opinion in favour of a European currency. There was higher support for a European currency to replace weaker national currencies in countries such as Italy than in those with stronger currencies, such as West Germany. Although the ambitious goal for EMU was postponed, the Community made a renewed and modest start again via the EMS.

D   *Political initiatives to launch EMS membership*

The political initiative for the EMS was taken by Roy Jenkins in his capacity as President of the EC Commission. He argued in a speech in Florence in October 1977 that in the new situation of high inflation and high unemployment, the EMS could help to alleviate both macroeconomic problems. This reflected the new economic analysis starting from lower inflation and from which would come lower unemployment. This approach differed from and contradicted the original Phillips curve analysis in which inflation was inversely related to the level of unemployment.

The Community was in much need of redirection and the choice of the EMS was timely and appealed to West Germany, which Jenkins courted in his speech in Bonn in December 1977. His ideas were well received since it was clear that the dollar faced major problems and there was an international currency vacuum which could only be filled by a West German monetary initiative. In the past West Germany had accepted American monetary initiatives and American hegemony, showing a marked absence of responsibility for the international monetary system. The EMS provided it with a historic opportunity to take the leading role (Strange 1980), since it would gain very much both at an international level and also domestically from greater currency stability. West Germany was concerned about the damaging effects of overvaluation of the D-mark which were eroding its export competitiveness, and hoped that in the EMS it would be able to depress the value of the mark. Chancellor Schmidt became a major instigator of the EMS, but he had to contend with some internal scepticism; for example, there was concern about West Germany becoming more prone to inflation in the EMS, whereas with the floating D-mark, currency appreciation dampened inflation. There was also worry about the degree to which West Germany would have to support weaker currencies and weaker economies. Nevertheless, on balance the EMS seemed favourable and by co-operating with other EC countries West Germany hoped to reduce the pressure on key currencies such as the mark and the dollar.

The next crucial step was to engage the support of Giscard d'Estaing in France, since Franco-German co-operation has formed the heart of Community developments. Politically France wished to remain shoulder-to-shoulder with West Germany in the first division of world powers, rather than head the second division. It offered

France an opportunity to avoid a continual slide in the value of the franc, while a stronger franc would help the French to pursue an effective anti-inflationary strategy. It was naturally important to enlist other countries into membership of the EMS, though if that proved impossible then at least the range of credit facilities to support weaker members would not be dispersed so widely. It would be those weaker members which would enter the lower division of a two-tier Community.

Weaker countries, such as Italy, responded positively to avoid confirming its position in the second tier. Since Italy had taken the decision to become a founder member of earlier bodies such as the ECSC at a time when its steel industry could have been swamped by more competitive imports, it recognized the benefits of being in at the beginning of any new developments – in particular if special arrangements could be made. Italy also hoped that strict monetary obligations inherent in the system would be more effective than internal exhortations for restraint in dampening inflationary pressure. While Italy would have welcomed a really fundamental re-structuring of the Budget and the CAP to provide a greater transfer of resources, after a pause for reflection it joined the EMS. It did so on the basis of guiding the lira downwards to an undervalued level and operating with wide margins of ± 6 per cent (but now conforms to the standard ± 2.25 per cent, having gained sufficient anti-inflationary credibility to dismantle its wage-indexation system – the Scala Mobile – in the 1980s).

The entry of the three major EC countries into the EMS was accompanied by the smaller countries which joined fully into the system. They were enthusiastic, since small countries often manifest an even greater dependence upon trade as a percentage of GNP, and with high imports currency depreciation created inflationary instability. The Dutch have shared a close identity of interest with West Germany. Belgian influence was reflected by personalities such as Tindemans and van Ypersele who sought to reconcile the perspectives of different countries in a search for compromise and agreement. Denmark was also concerned with monetary discipline, though often less successful in actually achieving low inflation and currency stability.

The Irish decision to join the EMS manifested a resurgence of political confidence in seizing the opportunity to break free from its historic satellite currency link with sterling. In the past the Irish punt has been dragged down by successive devaluations of sterling, but there was now concern that the punt might appreciate in relation to sterling, adversely affecting Irish trade. In practice the opposite has occurred and since 1979 the punt has depreciated against sterling. Whilst this has favoured Irish trade, the pattern of its trade has diversified towards other EC countries. Ireland has welcomed this and felt that in the traditional currency arrangements of the British Isles, its economic fortunes were tied too closely to the slow-growing and inflation-prone UK economy. The balance between the two economies was maintained very much by the drain of free factor movements and by high interest rates in Ireland. In joining the EMS Ireland gained financial assistance, confident that if or when the UK decided to join, it would have illustrated its political and monetary independence from the UK. Having benefited so much from the CAP, it saw little to be gained by acceding to British requests for the EMS to be linked with agricultural and budgetary reform.

E   EMS: the mechanics of operation and the ECU

The design and mechanics of the EMS differ from those of its predecessor, the snake, in various ways. A most important and central new creation is the European Currency Unit (ECU) which has now replaced the earlier units of account which were used by the Community. Apart from its book-keeping function, the ECU acts as the denominator for the ERM; it provides the basis of the divergence indicator; it is the denominator for operations in both the intervention and credit mechanism; it is also accepted as a means of settlement between monetary authorities in the Community.

The ECU is composed of a fixed amount of each Community currency in its 'basket', whose individual percentage share is based on the country's respective GDP, trade and short-term credit quotas. While the weight of ECU currencies in the basket is fixed, changes in market exchange rates have resulted in an increasing weight of appreciating currencies, and the falling weight of depreciating currencies such as sterling. To avoid the risk that the ECU might become over-dominated by the strongest currency in the basket, arrangements were made for the shares of the ECU basket to be re-examined if the weight of one currency changed by 25 per cent

Table 7.2   Composition of the ECU

Currencies	Amounts of national currencies in the original ECU basket	Amounts of national currencies in the revised ECU basket, October 1990	% share of currencies in the basket 13 March 1979	% share of currencies in the basket October 1990
German mark	0.828	0.6242	32.98	30.4
Pound sterling	0.0885	0.08784	13.34	12.6
French franc	1.15	1.332	19.83	19.3
Italian lira	109.0	151.8	9.50	9.9
Dutch guilder	0.286	0.2198	10.51	9.5
Belgian franc	3.66 }	3.431	9.63	8.5
Luxembourg franc	0.14 }			
Danish krone	0.217	0.1976	3.06	2.5
Irish punt	0.00759	0.008552	1.15	1.1
Greek drachma	–	1.44	–	0.7
Spanish peseta	–	6.885	–	5.2
Portuguese escudo	–	1.393	–	0.8
			100.0	100.0

Sources: European Documentation, *The ECU*, Luxembourg; *Lloyds Bank Economic Bulletin*, no. 143, Nov. 1990

or more; it was also agreed that the composition of the basket would normally be re-examined every five years. The composition of the ECU is shown in Table 7.2.

The drachma has now been incorporated, with a very low share of the ECU, but a high rate of inflation in Greece has been an obstacle to its participation in the exchange rate mechanism. In contrast, the Spanish Prime Minister, Felipe Gonzalez, drove down the rate of inflation so that Spain could participate in the ERM. At first the peseta shadowed the D-mark and then in June 1989 Spain joined the ERM on a wide band of ±6 per cent. The peseta accounts for just over 5 per cent of the ECU, and it performed strongly in 1990, supported by high interest rates.

The ECU, the Exchange Rate Mechanism and the divergence indicator. Each currency participating in the EMS has a central rate expressed in ECUs; this was derived from the rates ruling in the snake, while for others it was based on those existing on 12 March 1979. From these central rates a grid of cross-parities is derived for each pair of currencies in the system. Around these parities margins of ±2.25 per cent are allowed, and for weaker currencies, such as Italy, a wider margin of ±6.0 per cent was agreed. Intervention occurs to enable currencies to operate within these parities. There was much discussion about whether the intervention should be based on the bilateral grid or on the deviation of a currency in relation to the ECU. There were various technical objections to the use of the latter (Ypersele and Koeune 1985, pp. 48–9). Some concern, for example, was expressed that the divergence of one currency against the ECU would not necessarily be accompanied by the divergence of another currency in the opposite direction and this would make it difficult to decide which currency to use for intervention purposes. It was decided, therefore, after the 'Belgian compromise', to use partially an ECU-based divergence indicator from which there would be a presumption to act, but that the bilateral grid would provide the automatic intervention. Thus the Central Bank of the country whose currency had appreciated to its full margin would buy the currency of the weak country which had depreciated, and the latter's Central Bank would sell the strong currency.

Both the ECU and the innovation of the divergence indicator constitute major differences from the earlier snake system, with the ECU having proved more important than the divergence indicator (Zis 1984). The maximum divergence spread of a given currency against the ECU is ±2.25 per cent and the divergence is set at 75 per cent of this spread. Some observers may be puzzled as to why the variations are not precisely three-quarters of this; this can be explained by each country's currency being a fixed part of the ECU basket. The formula to calculate the divergence limit is ±2.25 per cent multiplied by $(1 - w)$ where w is the weight of the currency for which the divergence spread is being calculated. The greater the weight of the currency, the smaller is its maximum spread. Thus, West Germany has the lowest percentage divergence limit. When the D-mark was 37.38 per cent of the ECU then the market ECU rate of the mark rose by 2.25 per cent × (1.00 − 0.3738) of this; that is, by

1.40895 per cent. The divergence indicator is three-quarters of this; that is, 1.0567. Italy had the widest divergence limit because of the ± 6 per cent applied to the lira.

In general, a currency will reach its divergence threshold before reaching its bilateral limit against another currency; but it is possible for it to reach its bilateral limit first when two currencies are at opposite poles, and all the other currencies are fairly stable. When a currency crosses its divergence threshold the authorities are expected to correct the situation by various policies: these include diversified intervention in different currencies to provide a better spread in the burden of intervention between EMS currencies; also, domestic policies, in particular interest rate changes, plus other measures such as incomes policy. Finally, changes in central rates may be made, but to ensure that these do not occur too frequently and are not carried out unilaterally, extensive financial assistance is provided so that countries can fulfil their EMS obligations. This financial assistance was more extensive than that available under the snake, in spite of Germany's attempts to limit the amount. Short-term finance was made available for 45 days, compared with 30 days under the snake. In the EMS, short-term financial support was offered for nine months and medium-term financial assistance for a period of between two and five years. Measures were also introduced to strengthen the economies of weaker member states. While the full demands of Italy and Ireland, in particular for large grants, could not be met, it was agreed that loans would be made available which could receive interest-rate subsidies from bodies like the EIB.

Various recommendations have been made on ways to strengthen the EMS: these could include some indicator of convergence measures, rather like the divergence indicator, with an expectation that the Commission would be obliged to issue warnings to members to take appropriate action. More concrete developments have actually included a restatement of the objective of EMU in Article 20 of the Single European Act. In addition, in September 1987 European finance ministers agreed on new measures to defend currencies in the EMS, before the weaker ones reached their floor. They also agreed on an increase in the short-term credits available to defend currencies, to extend the repayment period and to allow greater repayments in ECUs rather than West German marks.

The financial support available is derived from countries depositing part of their gold and dollar holdings with the European Monetary Co-operation Fund (EMCF) and the countries concerned are credited with ECUs. It was intended that the EMCF would be turned within two years into the European Monetary Fund (EMF) and that there would be full use of the ECU as a reserve asset and means of settlement. However, the transition to this second phase had to be delayed and the Community has faced real problems throughout in adhering to its timetable for EMU.

The ECU's attractiveness to users. The ECU carries out some of the functions of money, even though there are no ECU notes or coins circulating in member states. Belgium made a start in 1987 by minting commemorative ECU coins. Other progressive steps have been suggested, such as the issue of a limited amount of ECUs to be used by tourists and migrant frontier workers to save them the costs of currency conversion; also, that ECU postage stamps could be introduced.

The ECU offers many benefits in its usage, not merely as a standard measure for the operation of the Community, but also for private sector activities. Since the ECU is a weighted average of EC currencies, each member currency deviates less against the ECU than against each other; hence reducing exchange rate risks. Indeed, the private sector has made wide use of the ECU, with some multinational companies, such as the French company Saint-Gobain, drawing up their financial accounts in ECUs, and others such as Alcatel settling all intra-company transactions in ECUs The ECU is also used increasingly in addition to dollars by airlines for settling their accounts. Recently, more European joint ventures in the east have been denominated in ECUs. Even some bodies in distant countries have started to use ECUs and the Wheat Board in Australia denominates contracts in ECUs. Some European countries have also opted to invoice customers in ECUs since it reduces exposure to adverse exchange rate movements. In Italy nearly a third of companies sampled claimed to have done this; for example, in 1986 about $1 billion worth of Italy's exports were invoiced in ECUs.

Both savers and borrowers have recognized the advantages of operating through ECUs instead of national currencies. They receive a more stable return, avoiding the unforeseen effects of volatile changes in national exchange rates. Money placed in ECUs earns a weighted average of member countries' interest rates. Savers can open ECU accounts for fairly small amounts in Belgium and

Luxembourg, though West Germany initially restricted the opening of such accounts; it was opposed to any kind of index-linked savings, classing the ECU in that category. By 1987 West Germany showed some inclination to relax its opposition to ECU accounts, provided other countries in return would ease their controls on the movement of capital. Savers living in strong-currency countries will receive a higher interest rate in ECUs (though they may have to accept some depreciation against their own currency). Savers living in weak-currency countries and investing in ECUs will be better protected against losses by depreciation. Some savers in Belgium, Italy and France have become enthusiastic about ECUs.

The ECU offers advantages to borrowers and it has grown to become one of the major bond-issuing currencies, along with the dollar, D-mark, sterling and special drawing right (SDR). The composition of the SDR basket has been simplified but is so dominated by the dollar that the ECU has been favoured by investors looking for a dollar alternative. By using ECUs borrowers in weak currency countries are able to raise capital abroad more easily and at a lower interest rate than at home.

F   Evaluating the performance of the EMS
Any evaluation is limited by the difficulty of determining what the situation would have been like without the EMS; also, there are many facets of the EMS. In addition, much depends upon which end of the exchange rate spectrum one prefers, since if the aim is exchange rate fixity, then some would argue that the system has been too flexible, with overuse of adjustment in central rates (Padoa-Schioppa 1984). Nevertheless, the general experience of currencies operating outside the EMS has been one of far greater volatility in exchange rates.

Overall, the EMS is recognized as being fairly successful, despite early misgivings by those who preferred monetary union to take place through the introduction of a European parallel currency (Zis 1984, pp. 59–60). After the two devaluations of the Danish krone late in 1979, along with a small revaluation of the West German mark, no currency realignments were necessary in 1980. Circumstances were favourable, partly because weaker currencies, such as the lira, had entered the EMS at low central exchange rate levels, and with a wider margin for the lira. Italy survived without having to devalue until October 1981. West Germany continued to control its inflation with greater success than other countries, though the rise in oil prices severely affected its balance of payments, creating a massive external deficit in 1980. Apart from the D-mark weakening in 1980 against the EMS currencies, it also weakened against the dollar; this helped to take some of the speculative pressure off the mark as buyers purchased dollars. Indeed, the longer-term problems have arisen when the dollar has weakened, and investors have switched into the mark, driving up its value. In the medium and long term, the lower rate of inflation in West Germany has caused pressure for further revaluation *vis-à-vis* other EMS currencies.

Table 7.3 shows the changes in EMS central rates. Between 1981 and 1983 five currency realignments occurred; these mainly affected the franc and lira in devaluations and to a lesser extent the Danish krone and the Irish punt. These currency realignments resulted in agreed changes which were conducted quite swiftly and without major panic of the kind which had existed under the fixed exchange rate system of Bretton Woods. The alignments also resulted in more symmetry, with the stronger currencies also experiencing revaluation at the same time. The main revaluations have been to the West German mark and to a lesser extent to the Dutch guilder. The exchange rate adjustments have usually been accompanied by internal domestic policies to make the currency changes more effective and conducive to the maintenance of durable equilibrium.

There were no EMS currency alignments in 1984 and only one in 1985 – a significant depreciation of the Italian lira. April 1986 marked the ninth alignment in EMS, triggered mainly by weaknesses of the French franc, since French inflation had reduced the competitiveness of its manufactured goods. France had sought a larger devaluation than that eventually agreed upon; a collective package emerged in which there were accompanying currency readjustments, with the usual revaluations of the D-mark and the Dutch guilder. Italy's decision not to devalue the lira in 1986 aroused some misgivings by Italian businessmen fearing loss of competitiveness, which left the Italian lira vulnerable to a later devaluation.

The French franc and the German mark came under strong speculative pressure in January 1987, resulting in another realignment of the EMS. This became necessary because a weakening of the US dollar led to a flow of money towards the D-mark. The French government suggested that it was mainly a German problem and this was reflected by the revaluation of the D-mark by 3 per cent

Table 7.3 Changes in EMS central rates: dates of realignments (%)

	24/9 1979	31/11 1979	2/3 1981	5/10 1981	22/2 1982	14/6 1982	21/3 1983	21/7 1985	7/4 1986	4/8 1986	12/1 1987	1/1 1990
Belg/Lux franc	0.0	0.0	0.0	0.0	−8.5	0.0	+1.5	+2.0	+1.0	0.0	+2.0	0.0
Danish krone	−2.9	−4.8	0.0	0.0	−3.0	0.0	+2.5	+2.0	+1.0	0.0	0.0	0.0
German mark	+2.0	0.0	0.0	+5.5	0.0	+4.25	+5.5	+2.0	+3.0	0.0	+3.0	0.0
French franc	0.0	0.0	0.0	−3.0	0.0	−5.75	−2.5	+2.0	−3.0	0.0	0.0	0.0
Irish punt	0.0	0.0	0.0	0.0	0.0	0.0	−3.5	+2.0	0.0	−8.0	0.0	0.0
Italian lira	0.0	0.0	−6.0	−3.0	0.0	−2.75	−2.5	−6.0	0.0	0.0	0.0	−3.7
Dutch guilder	0.0	0.0	0.0	+5.5	0.0	+4.25	+3.5	+2.0	+3.0	0.0	+3.0	0.0

Source: Financial Times, 29 May 1986, updated

(along with the Dutch guilder), whilst leaving the French franc unchanged. West Germany bowed to speculative pressure, preferring the anti-inflationary effects of revaluation to reducing interest rates or increasing domestic expenditure. To limit the full manifestation of French weaknesses, other countries which preferred to revalue in January 1987 had their requests refused. A growing balance-of-payments deficit by some countries with West Germany, which could have turned the system further towards a crawling-peg mechanism, has been alleviated partly by the reduction in the united Germany's external balance.

There was some loosening of exchange controls under the EMS during the 1980s. These were the first significant movements since 1962 when the EC removed foreign exchange restrictions linked to trade and individual change in residence, but not those dealing with share placements, short-term investment and individual investment across borders. In November 1986 EC finance ministers agreed on a package obliging members to remove exchange controls on long-term credit and on buying and selling unlisted securities, unit trusts and other mutual funds. A full removal of control on capital movements is now the target for 1992. However, there is a danger that fully mobile capital flows – given continuing divergencies in economic performance – could destabilize the exchange rate mechanism.

Resorts to currency realignments in the EMS have been less frequent than critics predicted and they have been agreed collectively, so the onus has not fallen solely on the weaker countries facing devaluation. There has been more stability in the exchange rates between EMS countries than of other currencies such as sterling and the dollar. There has also been greater similarity in the level of interest rates and some consensus on the need to bring down the rate of inflation. Whilst the EMS may still not have created a sufficiently low and converging level of money supply and inflation rates, policy is moving in the right direction. The average growth rates of monetary aggregates have fallen since 1979 and inflation differentials have narrowed (Healey 1988).

During the period 1983–9, the average rate of inflation for the EC (12) was 4.1 per cent per annum, but 3.2 per cent per annum for members of the ERM. Table 7.4 shows inflation ranging from an average of 1.0 per cent per annum for The Netherlands to 5.9 per cent per annum in Italy. Spain became a potential member with an inflation rate of 6.5 per cent, but the double-digit inflation of Greece

Table 7.4 EC macroeconomic performance, 1983–9

% Annual average	Belg	Den	Ger	Gre	Spa	Fra	Ire	Ita	Lux	Neth	Port	UK	EC(12)
Total economic growth[1]	2.2	2.1	2.5	2.1	3.6	2.1	3.0	3.0	4.1	2.3	2.8	3.6	2.8
Inflation	4.1	4.0	1.2	16.3	6.5	3.3	3.8	5.9	2.1	1.0	12.3	4.6	5.4
Unemployment[2]	11.3	7.0	6.7	8.5	20.1	10.1	17.6	10.2	2.6	10.4	7.2	10.0	10.3

Notes:
[1]GDP market prices (at constant prices)
[2]Unemployment average, 1984–9

Source: Calculated from Eurostat (1990)

and Portugal precluded entry to the ERM – though their unemployment was below the EC average. The average rate of unemployment in the Community remained stubbornly high (averaging just over 10 per cent per annum). Unless lower inflation really does succeed in securing a faster rate of economic growth and lower unemployment, some countries will be unable to resist pressures to reflate their economies. For example, the tolerable trade-off between unemployment and inflation in Luxembourg, Germany and The Netherlands contrasts with an unfavourable trade-off in countries such as Ireland and Spain, with about one in five out of work.

Ultimately some countries' preferences and priorities are likely to turn towards the reduction of unemployment instead of the relentless pursuit of anti-inflationary policies. But their freedom to pursue independent economic objectives by national policies is constrained increasingly by the EMS and German Economic and Monetary Union, with the latter having dragged up interest rates to dampen inflationary pressure. There is recognition that it is only a much greater degree of economic convergence which can create the desirable conditions for EMU. Unless this can be achieved, the D-mark would remain the preferred currency to hold, whereas if other countries could achieve a similarly low rate of inflation, then the pressures for the D-mark to appreciate would be alleviated.

G   *Further stages of development*
According to the Delors Report there are three phases to EMU, and the first phase, from the beginning of July 1990, was to achieve closer co-operation within the existing EMS and greater macroeconomic convergence. However, after the Rome Summit the aim of getting all twelve EC currencies into stage I before proceeding has been diluted in favour of a vaguer objective of securing the greatest possible number of currencies in the ERM. Whilst this may involve Portugal's entry into the ERM, it provides exceptions which may continue to apply to Greece.

The first stage of monetary integration also entails making full progress to free capital mobility by removing exchange controls. When the EMS was established in 1979 all countries, except West Germany, The Netherlands and the UK, used tight controls on capital movements. Other countries, such as France, Italy and Belgium, have gradually liberalized their capital flows, with Spain and Ireland moving into line by 1992 and Portugal and Greece by 1994.

It has been recognized that capital controls tend to postpone eventual and more desirable long-run structural changes, and as economies converge there will be less need to resort to such controls. They also fit uneasily into the greater deregulation of financial markets.

The policy of setting target dates for various stages of EMU has continued in order to maintain momentum. The second stage should begin conditionally on 1 January 1994; it would involve the creation of new institutions, in particular a new European Central Bank (ECB). This ECB or Eurofed would ensure a common monetary policy, and governments would have to follow precise targets on public debt and the way in which public deficits are financed. Ceding financial power to a new central financial body is likely to be more effective and efficient than continuing weakly co-ordinated policies by existing national central banks. The constitution of a new ECB is much contested, especially in relation to whether it is to be independent or politically accountable. Germany naturally favours an independent central bank, modelled on the Bundesbank. The latter, like the Swiss Central Bank, has been very successful in delivering monetary stability and low inflation. While Germany has argued that an ECB agreed by the governments of the EC would provide a sufficient democratic base, others, such as France and the UK, have stressed the need for political accountability by any new ECB. Yet despite UK delaying tactics on EMU and political union, benefits from having a more independent central bank, even in the case of the Bank of England, were recognized by the then Chancellor of the Exchequer, Nigel Lawson. Any new ECB may be a close replica of the Dutch Central Bank. In the latter the Dutch government can ultimately override the Bank, and if it objects, the government has to publish the Bank's argument along with its own reasons for ignoring it. A new ECB would seek to ensure the maintenance of price stability which would be enshrined in its statutes, and it would have a high degree of independence from finance ministers. The latter would be allowed to overrule the ECB only in the most exceptional circumstances, supported by a majority in the Council and the EP.

The third stage of EMU, some time after 1997, is likely to involve the replacement of locked currencies (rather than the British preference for a common currency) by a single currency and a single monetary policy. The single currency is likely to be the ECU and various suggestions have been made for extending its usage steadily during the 1990s. A strategy for developing the ECU has been drawn up, commissioned by the Association for the Monetary Union of Europe; this was established under the auspices originally of Helmut Schmidt and Giscard D'Estaing. There is strong business support which is keen on a single currency – though banks will be affected in losing their profitable foreign exchange activities. To accelerate use of the ECU a clear timetable of developments is necessary for both public and private sector institutions during the 1990s. These would include initially enhanced information about the ECU; removing administrative barriers to its usage; and banks offering the full range of ECU services. That could be followed in 1992 by additional measures, such as insurance companies marketing ECU policies, and companies recording their Stock Exchange accounts in ECUs. In 1993 companies might be allowed to issue share capital in ECUs. Some businesses, such as the travel trade, are naturally likely to move towards ECU pricing. By 1994 commodity trade may be denominated in ECUs, and in 1995 companies should be encouraged to pay taxes in ECUs, invoice in ECUs and record their accounts in ECUs. 1996 would see the ECU as legal tender, with a new EC currency designed, machines converted and prices quoted in ECUs so that by 1997 the EC would attain a single currency.

Part III   UK ambivalence towards the EMS
There are some similarities between the UK's attitude to the formation of the EMS and the formation of the EC in the 1950s. The UK thought that there was a distinct possibility of both ventures foundering, and therefore it avoided the risks inherent in being a positive founder member. Thus sterling, though part of the ECU, did not participate in the ERM for a period of eleven years (March 1979 to October 1990). Evidence suggests that the UK's policy approach was short-sighted since both the EC and then the EMS 'took off' successfully. The UK belatedly joined the EC and always tends to be one step behind, participating eventually in the evolving stages of EC integration. To join later always implies reluctance, a lack of real commitment and a loss of political goodwill. Furthermore, it appeared an anomaly to belong to the EC and not to belong fully to the EMS exchange rate mechanism. The UK has preferred to see EMU as part of a looser form of *à la carte* integration. But on balance the EMS does not seem to manifest such adverse features as those associated with other aspects of sectoral integration which the UK has entered into, such as the CAP.

The UK attitude to the EMS was to lay down such stringent bargaining conditions for its membership that there was little likelihood of them being accepted. For example, the list of conditions in the Green Paper on the European Monetary System in 1978 may have been desirable, but there was no prospect of satisfying them all. The UK had doubts whether the weaker countries which had dropped out of the snake would be able to stay in. With the UK's tendency for wage inflation to outstrip productivity, it felt there was a need for exchange rate depreciation as a crucial policy instrument. There was a desire not to operate under an overvalued exchange rate, necessitating the imposition of deflationary domestic policies. In practice, however, non-participation in the ERM actually resulted in an overvalued exchange rate during the early 1980s!

The Labour government, already split in the past on the issue of the EC, simply lacked the confidence, support and vision to move forward in the process of European integration. It tried to link the introduction of the EMS to budgetary reform, though any progress on both fronts simultaneously was difficult. The UK also expressed concern about adverse effects of the EMS on the dollar, seeming to show even more concern about this than the Americans themselves. Nevertheless, there was general hostility to the EMS from other quarters in the UK; for example, the National Institute of Economic and Social Research agreed with most economists who had submitted evidence against the EMS to the House of Commons Committee which examined this in November 1978. Of even more emphatic influence was the opposition of the Treasury, though it had participated through Mr Cousins in the detailed discussions with Dr Schulmann and M. Clappier, the German and French representatives, about the precise construction of the EMS (Ludlow 1982).

The Labour government underestimated the unstoppable political momentum by the West German and French leaders towards the establishment of the EMS. They had become increasingly disillusioned with the UK's attitude and it was really only a desire of France to reduce the excessive weight of the D-mark in the ECU which helped to prevent the UK's total exclusion from the EMS. The UK settled for an intermediate position opting out of the ERM. Yet by joining this the UK could have prevented the currency split with Ireland; it could have pressed to join with wider margins, like the lira; and also have benefited from the financial aid available.

Mrs Thatcher and the EMS. While the reluctance of the Labour party to embrace the EMS was understandable, the lack of enthusiasm of the Thatcher governments required a somewhat different explanation. The predilection of the Conservative government for market forces was applied to the foreign exchange market, taking the view that the market was more likely than intervention to create the right exchange rate for sterling. The government removed exchange controls, resulting in an outflow of capital, and this appeared judicious in an attempt to restrain the rising value of sterling (as a petro-currency); even though the combination of both effects was to have a devastating impact on UK unemployment in the early 1980s. The Thatcher government also decided initially to introduce a Medium-Term Financial Strategy in which it sought to achieve its anti-inflationary strategy by using monetary targets instead of by using an exchange rate target. However, by 1986 the UK had started to move away from its main reliance upon money supply targets; this was because of the problems in attaining them successfully. Their defects are that more deposits are now held outside the banking system; also, the development of sophisticated corporate financial transactions means that a single act of borrowing may often be counted several times. Hence there was some recognition that instead of a money supply target there could be gains from pursuing an exchange rate target, yet the UK still did not join the ERM.

A major obstacle to UK participation is the distinctive nature of the economy as a significant oil producer – though The Netherlands has not found near self-sufficiency in energy any barrier to membership of the EMS. But the UK's dependence upon world oil prices has made sterling a volatile petro-currency which fluctuates widely, making it difficult to contain within the EMS. A continuous fall in world oil prices – brought about by the failure of OPEC to maintain a cohesive cartel – would lead to a long-run decline in the value of sterling. There is concern about the opposite effect of a change in oil prices on sterling and the D-mark, with a fall in oil prices leading to a rise in the D-mark. Both sterling and the D-mark have been used as reserve currencies, with the D-mark tending to eclipse sterling nowadays.

Any durable participation of the UK in the EMS is dependent on the UK reducing its rate of inflation towards the lower West German level on a permanent basis. Much depends, therefore, upon the willingness of the UK to pursue the same preference of low inflation, and also its ability to achieve this successfully. Under Conservative governments economic policy brought down the rate of inflation to a level compatible with its membership of the EMS by the mid-1980s. Given this, it was surprising that the UK postponed entry into the ERM for another five years. In addition, sterling began to shadow the D-mark and it was understood that a secret target zone for the movement of sterling against the D-mark had been agreed between the two countries around the time of the Group of Five meeting in Paris in February 1987. The central target rate for sterling was believed to be about 2.90 D-marks, but the successful managed float of sterling against the D-mark was finally breached in March 1988 when sterling was uncapped, amidst disagreement between Mrs Thatcher and the Chancellor of the Exchequer over interest rate policy.

Belated entry into the Exchange Rate Mechanism (ERM). Pressure on the UK to join the ERM increased with the inclusion of monetary articles in the SEA and the proposals for full capital mobility. Jacques Delors threatened that progress on this front could not occur if some countries would not conform to the monetary discipline of the EMS. The UK confirmed at the Madrid Summit in June 1989 that if certain conditions were met it would join the ERM. These comprised: a sharp fall in the UK's rate of inflation; completion of the single European market; the full implementation of a free market in financial services; the abolition of all exchange controls; and the strengthening of the Community's competition policy. Many of these conditions were aimed at the rest of the Community, but the one key condition applicable to the UK was to achieve a sharp fall in its rate of inflation.

The ERM continued to be a divisive issue in 1989 and Sir Alan Walters judged the EMS to be a 'half-baked scheme'. His controversial role as Mrs Thatcher's economic advisor and difference in view from the Chancellor of the Exchequer, Nigel Lawson, finally led to the resignation of both men in October 1989. On economic grounds, Walters's criticism of the EMS was that it would force interest rates down too much in high-inflation countries, such as the UK. Nigel Lawson, despite his innovative fiscal policy, failed to achieve entry into the ERM when it would have been most desirable, such as in 1985 when UK inflation was running at the low EC average of just over 5 per cent.

A groundswell of pro-ERM views helped to reinforce the more positive position of John Major in his short period as Chancellor of the Exchequer. For example, the National Institute of Economic and Social Research came round to the view that if the UK had joined the ERM, then inflation would have been much lower from the mid-1980s onwards, and membership would enable the achievement of price stability by 1992 (NIESR 1989). British business also advocated membership of the ERM to stimulate exports, arguing that it would reduce the costs of hedging against exchange rate movements. It was also necessary to consolidate London's role as Europe's leading financial centre, to keep it well ahead of places such as Paris and Frankfurt.

The economic arguments for ERM membership, of lower inflation and greater nominal exchange rate stability, were strengthened by the constellation of political changes in 1989–90. John Major was in a strong position since the government did not wish to lose another Chancellor, and he continued Nigel Lawson's path towards membership of the ERM. In November 1989 the government published its *Evolutionary Approach to Economic and Monetary Union*. It approved of stage 1 of the Delors Report, but disagreed with stages 2 and 3, proposing instead to build upon Lawson's earlier ideas of competing currencies. To have any influence on these later stages, some concession had to be made by joining the ERM. Since the timing of entry was less ripe economically than at certain points in the past, it meant engineering an appropriate dilution of the Madrid conditions regarding the UK's rate of inflation. The criterion was modified by notionally lowering the underlying rate of inflation by excluding mortgage rates and the community charge, and focusing on the future downward trend in inflation towards the EC level. Furthermore, since there were wide disparities in rates of inflation when countries first joined the ERM, the argument changed to one of the ERM itself leading to convergence. In other words, the causal link shifted to one of membership of the ERM not being conditional on a preceding low and immediately converging rate of inflation, but rather that the ERM would by itself subsequently drive down UK inflation, converging to the level in the EC.

The concern of Walters about the danger of lower interest rates overheating the British economy gave way to an opposite need to limit recession in 1990–1. But the latter is aggravated by a higher exchange rate and deflationary convergence towards the lower West German rate of inflation since these tend to outweigh any expansionist effect of lower interest rates – especially if the latter were partly offset by a tighter fiscal policy. The government in late 1990 found itself increasingly 'boxed in', seeking to achieve its prime economic target of lower inflation, and constrained by the electoral cycle of needing to manifest success by the beginning of 1992. In some respects the government had allowed the economy to become overheated in 1988, following its re-election in 1987 and the lowering of interest rates to avoid an economic decline after the Stock Market collapse in autumn 1987. From February 1987 to March 1988 the informal fixing of the pound against the D-mark and the strengthening of the pound had led to a sharp reduction in interest rates. Dampening this overexpansion had resulted by the end of 1990 in stagflation, but with membership of the ERM being seen as economically and politically expedient. Some financial commentators, such as Samuel Brittan of *The Financial Times*, have long awaited the discipline which membership of the ERM would impose on the UK to dampen its rate of inflation.

The Chancellor of the Exchequer was ready to exploit the first window of opportunity to join the ERM in order to influence the subsequent stages of evolution to EMU. For example, in June 1990 John Major, addressing an Anglo-German audience, seized the initiative in proposing a hard ECU, operating alongside national currencies. His pragmatic proposal was derived from Sir Michael Butler's plan based upon the hard ECU circulating in parallel alongside national currencies. The hard ECU would be guaranteed never to be devalued and it was proposed that it should be managed by a new European Monetary Fund. Whether a single currency then evolved would depend in the British view upon market choice.

On 5 October 1990 the government set a positive mood for the start of the Conservative Party conference by announcing that sterling would finally enter the ERM on 8 October. This stripped the Opposition parties of their own economic platforms on this issue. The government opted for a high exchange rate level; that is, D-mark 2.95, with bilateral central rates against other ERM currencies being shown in Table 7.5.

British business, while desiring exchange rate stability, is ham-

Table 7.5   Bilateral central rates of £ against other ERM currencies

Belgian franc	60.8451
Danish krone	11.2526
D-Mark	2.9500
Spanish peseta	191.750
French franc	9.89389
Italian lira	2207.25
Luxembourg franc	60.8451
Dutch guilder	3.32389

Source: Financial Times, 8 October 1990

pered by a high exchange rate, unless it pressurizes companies into resisting excessive wage awards on the basis of the very visible adverse effects that these would have in raising domestic unemployment. But business welcomed the accompanying initial 1 per cent reduction in interest rates. For the government the ERM appeared to offer a way out of their political dilemma of how to reduce excessively high mortgage interest rates, as a Party committed to raising private home ownership.

Some degree of flexibility has been provided by opting for a wide band of ± 6 per cent, previously enjoyed by Italy and subsequently by Spain. The choice was sensible given the difficulty in setting the right central rate, compounded by exogenous shocks, such as oil price effects; for example, following the invasion of Kuwait by Iraq. Theoretically the pound would trade against the D-mark between DM2.78 and DM3.13, but during 1990 the Spanish peseta was very strong, being some 3.5 per cent above its central rate against the D-mark, whilst the pound was about 1.25 per cent below its central parity against the peseta. Hence the pound cannot drop by more than 4.75 per cent before hitting its limit against the peseta. The pound is also limited in its movement against the ECU and if sterling were to rise 6 per cent against all other EMS currencies, its rise against the ECU would be only 5.25 per cent; this is because the pound constitutes one-eighth of the ECU basket.

If the pound cannot stay high enough, then devaluation may be necessary; for example, the pound fell during the 1980s on average by just over 5 per cent a year against the D-mark, and the new range of downward adjustment for the pound in the ERM would accommodate a similar initial depreciation. In the early weeks of sterling's trading in the EMS it soon dropped below its central rate. It will be difficult for the UK to maintain its central rate and especially to go further towards the narrower general band of fluctuation of ±2.25 per cent, unless the latter is done in the lower half of the existing 6 per cent-wide band (as Italy has done). By then the 'Schengen Five' of Germany, France, The Netherlands, Belgium and Luxembourg may have moved on to even narrower 1 per cent limits themselves.

The UK's inflationary problems, *vis-à-vis* countries such as Germany, arise from several sources. For example, strongly decentralized pay-bargaining in the UK was encouraged by the government during the 1980s. In most European countries industry-level bargaining usually occurs based upon national economic productivity. UK annual bargaining creates leap-frogging and would be better if it were synchronized in the first quarter of the year, with longer-term agreements. British unions are linking pay claims to past annual inflation, instead of accepting the lower projected governmental inflation rate within the ERM. Pay awards in the UK remain persistently inflationary because of a shortage of skilled labour in key sectors, and there is still a large public sector not subject to the visible exchange rate constraint of companies exposed to international competition. Meanwhile, financial profligacy after the abandonment of monetarism and financial deregulation in the late 1980s led to a massive growth in credit, over four times as large as in West Germany by 1990, despite higher UK interest rates.

In entering the ERM at a high rate of exchange everything hinges on dampening inflationary pressures, otherwise the British economy will experience mounting unemployment; for example, its chronic balance-of-payments deficit is exacerbated by price uncompetitiveness. Whilst inflationary pressures in the united Germany have increased slightly, because of the expenditure required to sustain the eastern part of Germany, the Bundesbank is committed to a restrictive monetary policy. The UK will find itself bereft of an independent monetary policy, particularly if it succumbs to pressure to accept stage 2: an independent central bank. The government's range of economic policy instruments has been severely constrained. In future it will have to be readier to use fiscal policy. Pressures to accelerate progress towards EMU have come from the rest of the Community, with the Rome Summit in November 1990 setting a precise date for the start of stage 2. This exposed the UK's isolation yet again, claiming that the UK was not set on a road leading inexorably towards a single currency. The consequence of the Rome Summit was the resignation of Sir Geoffrey Howe which was to undermine Mrs Thatcher's own position as Prime Minister. Her replacement, John Major, appears more pragmatic, but in pushing for the hard ECU he may have to recognize, after the inter-governmental conference in Rome, that if this is accepted it will be as a transitional step towards a single currency with a firm timetable for this. In other words, concessions will have to be made, perhaps surrendering the people's popular choice between competing currencies.

An alternative scenario might be one in which the UK not only fails to go beyond stage 1, but even within that stage is forced to devalue the pound. This could arise because of the very severe economic costs imposed upon the real economy in terms of depressed output and high unemployment. Entry to the ERM, instead of bringing down interest rates rapidly as some economists forecast, compounded the initial recession because of underlying economic weakness. Whilst devaluation is not the solution to fundamental economic problems, it can be beneficial; for example, UK economic growth improved markedly after the 30 per cent fall in the pound against the D-mark between July 1985 and February 1987. British unemployment started to fall in 1986, whereas unemployment in France and Italy rose eventually above the UK level. With a massive UK trade deficit of £19 billion in 1989 and a high pound (not only against European currencies but also against the dollar early in 1991), British companies are likely to become even less competitive, eroding their market share and leading to further job losses.

Even if some depreciation of the pound occurred, there is still likely to be some asymmetric imbalance if collectively other economies are reluctant to revalue sufficiently themselves – necessitating additional deflationary measures in the UK. Meanwhile it should be remembered that half of UK trade is conducted with the rest of the world with which exchange rates would still fluctuate freely. However, to deal with the problems of international exchange rate management since the mid-1970s the Group of Five, subsequently expanded to the Group of Seven (G7), has tried, among other things, to create greater exchange rate stability. For example, significant summit meetings were held at Versailles in 1982 which strength-ened multinational surveillance of exchange rates, followed in 1985 by the Plaza Agreement to reduce the overvaluation of the dollar, while the Louvre Accord in 1987 tried to stabilize the value of the dollar.

It would appear that, both at a European and wider international level, business requires greater stability of exchange rates. The key question is whether the exchange rate set for the pound is at the right level and, even with wide margins, whether it can remain at this level. If it cannot, then the prospects seem poor for permanently locking all exchange rates and achieving a single currency.

8 Fiscal policy: taxation and the Community Budget

Part I Fiscal policy issues

The term fiscal policy covers a wide range of public finance issues relating to both taxation and government expenditure. One of its main concerns has been with the allocation of resources since public goods have to be provided collectively. However, in recent years most EC countries have become concerned about the excessive size of the public sector, cutting the public sector borrowing requirement and trying to make room for the growth of the private sector. Even those countries which could indulge in high public expenditure in the past from energy revenue, such as The Netherlands and the UK, have had to moderate the level of public expenditure.

The concern of fiscal policy with macroeconomic stabilization has been the outcome of Keynesian economics. However, over recent years a scepticism has emerged about the effectiveness of Keynesian demand management policies when the outcome was invariably large budget deficits – such policies proved highly inflationary. Fine-tuning of the economy has been partly displaced in recent years by greater emphasis on budgetary balance and by using tax cuts as more a supply-side than a demand-side policy. Successful economies, as in West Germany, have been run along more orthodox lines, being less preoccupied with Keynesian macroeconomic stabilization policies, giving greater priority to monetary policy, within which at a microeconomic level freely competitive market forces could operate. West Germany is the dominant economy in the Community and the pivotal force, so that economic policy in the EC is influenced very much by the German example.

National governments have traditionally used fiscal policy to create a more equitable distribution of income by designing progressive taxation in terms of ability to pay, whilst trying to ensure that on the expenditure side benefits go mainly to the poor. Such policies have not always been successful, with often high marginal tax rates existing not only for the higher-paid groups but also for some of the low-income groups because of the poverty trap. Mean-

while, expenditure policies have often included indiscriminate subsidies going to all groups, not only to the poor.

This chapter will focus on tax harmonization and in particular on
the role of the Community Budget. Given the functions of national
budgets, is the role of the Community Budget to carry out these
same functions? What kind of activities does it carry out? Has it a
macroeconomic stabilization role? How has it affected the distribution of income? The Budget is still very much concerned with
financing the allocation of resources, rather than playing a major
role in economic stabilization and the redistribution of income.
Deciding on the appropriate level of budgetary powers and activities
is difficult and in the USA and Germany, for example, is highly
decentralized. In the latter, the balance between national and
regional provision tends towards the sub-national level represented
by the Länder. It is an even more difficult problem for the EC since
its federal nature could be enhanced with a larger budget, but those
countries contributing disproportionately to its finance remain luk-
ewarm. Nevertheless, there is scope for transferring to the Community level some activities currently financed at a national level.

Since national budgets are far bigger than the Community Budget,
to what extent is some co-ordination of the former necessary, or can
these be left as the independent element for national macroeconomic adjustment? Some co-ordination of budgetary policy has
occurred, especially since the Convergence Decision of the Council
in 1974 to establish target guidelines for budgetary policies. The
interdependence of Community economies has continued to grow
and therefore macroeconomic policies have large spillover effects on
other member states. For example, those economists whose prime
concern is with unemployment are worried about the dangers of
countries (already committed to restrictive German monetary policy
within the EMS) adopting over-tight fiscal policies than would be
desirable for the EC as a whole. This is because national expansion
would significantly worsen their balance of payments deficits; therefore the EC is driven to go beyond consultation towards some co-
ordination of fiscal policy.

Part II   Tax harmonization and the Community Budget
A   The rationale of fiscal harmonization
Fiscal harmonization is bound up with the achievement of the
customs union, the Common Market and the Economic and Politi-

cal Union. The first phase of removing customs frontiers remains incomplete, despite the elimination of intra-tariffs, since different rates of indirect taxation resulted in a continuing fiscal frontier. The creation of a single market has had to take this difficult problem on board.

The different excise duties levied on products such as wine and tobacco (plus tobacco monopolies in France and Italy) have distorted competition. Despite proposals to harmonize these, substantial differences have existed, since each country has been reluctant to relinquish its choice on the appropriate level of national taxation for these products on health grounds. Even assuming the same tax levels could be agreed, there would still be different tax yields according to the different patterns of consumption. Furthermore, countries' revenue requirements vary and are higher where these have to satisfy high public expenditure.

The creation of a free flow of factors of production within the Common Market led the EC to address particularly the issue of capital mobility, steering clear of any harmonization of direct taxation on labour. Finally, as more positive integration has occurred in different sectors, further tax harmonization has become necessary. For example, in agriculture, differences in value added tax (VAT) in the early 1980s meant that farmers in the UK and Denmark, unlike those in other member states, could not claim back a percentage of VAT which had been paid on factors of production.

The aim of the Community is not to standardize everything but to harmonize taxation as a means of achieving other objectives. But countries, having relinquished many important national economic policy instruments already as a consequence of integration, are naturally wary of any erosion of an independent fiscal policy to manage their economies. For example, EC members have surrendered their own national trade policies and most countries have largely given up their independent exchange rate policies within the EMS. Furthermore, continued integration within EMU will diminish the use of national monetary policy. Therefore it is important for economies to possess some key independent policy instruments, such as that of direct taxation. Nevertheless, tax harmonization has assumed added urgency since it is part and parcel of financing the revenue of the Community Budget. Meanwhile, progress towards integration in other areas such as EMU and the single internal market is facilitated by a large redistributive budgetary expenditure to help poorer countries.

B   Types of taxes

The EC has sought to promote the harmonization of three taxes: value added tax, excise duties and corporation tax. It has not proposed to harmonize income tax, since labour is less mobile than capital; hence, direct taxation provides the major independent policy instrument for national governments to use in managing their economies. However, it is intended that the overall fiscal stance between countries will be co-ordinated.

Value Added Tax (VAT). Value added tax or *taxe sur la valeur ajoutée* has been applied in France since 1954. The Neumark Report in 1963 recommended VAT and it was decided to introduce this as the sales tax for the Community by a Council Directive in April 1967. It was proposed that other member states which were operating different systems would change over to VAT by 1 January 1971; but extensions were necessary for Belgium and Italy and the latter did not introduce VAT until early 1973. It became tied up inextricably with Italy's other tax reforms and both the Mezzogiorno and export industries opposed VAT since under the existing turnover tax large rebates were possible. Other countries were much keener to introduce VAT, for example West Germany, even though their cumulative multi-cascade tax benefited exporters by generous rebates.

The disadvantages of cascade taxes (that is, taxes on total value), compared with VAT, were that they encouraged vertical integration of production by firms purely to minimize their tax payments. For example, assume three stages in production with the value of the product (excluding tax) at the end of the stages being £1000 (stage 1), £2000 (stage 2) and £3000 (stage 3). Assume a 10 per cent cascade tax was applied at each stage; hence tax payments would be £100 (stage 1), £200 (stage 2) and £300 (stage 3), making the total tax payable £600. To reduce the tax bill businesses engaged in vertical integration in order to pay only £300 tax on the total value of £3000. VAT is neutral with regard to the structure of economic activity. The tax is paid not on the total value at each stage but on the added value; hence, a 10 per cent VAT would yield £100 (stage 1), £100 (stage 2) and £100 (stage 3); that is, £300 VAT payable. Only in the case of the business being integrated is the cascade tax and the VAT bill the same. Without such integration a cumulative cascade tax yields more than VAT; in the example used, a 5 per cent cascade tax would have yielded the same as a 10 per cent VAT.

The replacement of cascade taxes by VAT has removed the incentive for the kind of integration which offered no economic gains apart from saving tax. Cascade taxes in encouraging integration increased monopoly structure (even though the latter is more likely to occur with horizontal than with vertical integration). '*Le remplacement des taxes cumulatives à cascade par la taxe à la valeur ajoutée a eliminé la source principale des discriminations au sens des articles 95 et 96 du traité CEE*' (Moussis 1982, p. 319).

A distinct advantage of VAT for the tax authorities is that it is difficult to evade since businesses have to make sure on invoices that tax has been paid at the previous stage of production so that their own tax payment is correct. VAT is also more favourable to fair trade than cascade taxes since the latter were often generously rebated for export, providing exporters with a hidden subsidy because of uncertainty about the exact amounts of tax which had been paid at each stage. With VAT the taxes rebated are clear and VAT is applied at the destination by the importing country. Unfortunately this means that a fiscal frontier still exists. If VAT were harmonized, then exports could take place smoothly from the country of origin.

The use of jurisdictional terms such as 'destination' and 'origin' is worth clarifying, though fuller details can be found elsewhere (Robson 1980, pp. 90–6). Where the destination principle is applied on all products in the country where they are consumed, both domestic and imported products face the same tax, while domestically produced goods for export are exempt from the tax. Under the origin principle, the taxes are imposed on the domestic production of all goods whether exported or not, and are not imposed on imports. Apart from the existence of a fiscal frontier with the destination principle, this is preferable where VAT rates have not been harmonized.

VAT is a general tax levied at all stages of production and distribution covering services (when the services affect the final price of goods) and consumer goods. Several directives have been introduced, such as the Sixth Directive in 1977 which was important in introducing a uniform basis for VAT. This sought to establish a

*Table 8.1   Rates of VAT in member states as applicable in
March 1991[1] (%)*

Member states	Reduced	Standard	Luxury/higher
Belgium	1 and 6	19	25[2]
Denmark	–	22	–
France	2.1, 5.5 and 13	18.6	22
Germany	7	14	–
Greece	3 and 6	18	36
Ireland	0 and 10	23	–
Italy	4 and 9	19	38
Luxembourg	3 and 6	12	–
Netherlands	6	18.5	–
Portugal	0 and 8	17	30
Spain	6	12	33
United Kingdom	0	17.5	–

Notes:
[1] Reduced rates are March 1990.
[2] Excludes 8% luxury tax on restricted selection of goods.

Sources: European Documentation, *Taxation in the Single Market*, June 1990.
The Economist, 8–14 June 1991, p.12

common list of taxable activities and a common list of exemptions.
This was necessary since the collection of the EC's own resources
from VAT receipts to finance the Community Budget can only be
equitable if all countries have the same basis of assessment. Hence
the VAT payable to the EC Budget is based on a common notional
structure, but has allowed countries to continue with their own
existing VAT rates and their existing derogations.

The differences in the rates of VAT charged and also in the
number of rates used in particular countries are shown in Table 8.1.

Denmark has had a very high rate of both direct and indirect
taxation, and the latter is also high in Ireland and especially in
Southern European countries such as Spain, Portugal and Greece.
Italy has been one of several countries which has had a luxury rate of
taxation, setting this at 38 per cent. Greece has chosen several rates
of VAT, though it delayed their introduction initially because of its
primitive book-keeping methods and worries that it would raise

Greek payments to the Community Budget. However, VAT replaces nearly half of the 500 indirect taxes existing in Greece.

Progress in harmonizing both the number and level of VAT rates has been constrained by two particular problems. First, member states using VAT as part of their economic policy are sometimes concerned about any inflationary effects from raising the rate – France has in the past suspended VAT on the retail sale of beef to keep down the rate of inflation. Secondly, countries differ in the extent to which they wish to define and tax products as luxuries or essentials. The latter may carry only low rates of VAT, be zero-rated or exempt from VAT. Those that are zero-rated are generally treated better than those which are exempt, since the latter are only exempt at their particular stage of production and they will have been charged VAT on the goods which have been bought in for processing or for resale.

Steps to equalize rates of VAT would have major budgetary implications for those countries heavily dependent upon VAT receipts, resulting in a budgetary shortfall. The Rogalla Report by the European Parliament in 1983 called for a standstill on any further widening of tax rates and a dual rate of VAT. However, to remove tax frontiers as part of the internal market programme Lord Cockfield's proposals in 1987 were to approximate VAT in two bands; a standard band between 14 and 20 per cent and a lower band from 4 to 9 per cent. The latter will apply to foodstuffs; energy products for heating and lighting; water supplies; pharmaceutical products; books, newspapers and periodicals; and passenger transport. These ranges are flexible since wide disparities are workable in local taxes in the USA, whilst taxes account for only a small part of the widely differing level of consumer prices that exist. The ultimate goal is the removal of fiscal frontiers by 1992 and the Commission has proposed a standard minimum rate of 15% VAT. However, an origin system would mean major exporting countries such as Germany benefiting tax-wise, unless some system of inter-country tax redistribution were provided. Hence the destination system is to remain, but instead of collecting the tax at the frontier the authorities will collect it later internally when tax declarations are made.

Excise duties. The five main excise duties are on beer, wine, spirits, tobacco and mineral oils. These account for most of the excise receipts, though there are variations between member countries; for example, Denmark has a high and important excise duty on cars, whilst Italy has numerous minor excise duties on products such as sugar, coffee, salt and matches. The imposition of excise duties can be based on the value, weight, quality or strength of a product. Excise duties are levied on products with a low price elasticity of demand, and the excise duty is usually shifted forward to the consumer. They represent a significant revenue-raising element for governments since the five main excise duties account for up to 25 per cent of consumer spending.

Excise duties both reflect and influence patterns of production and consumption; for example, wine producing countries tend to have no or only very low excise duties. Members of the EC(6) have tended to have lower excise duties, not only on wine but also on other alcohol and cigarettes, than those of the Northern European entrants to the EC (the UK, Ireland and Denmark). There have been very wide differences in excise duties, in particular between highly rated Denmark and the much lower rate in France. They reflect different governmental approaches to matters such as health, and in addition can be sources of tacit protectionism. Excise duties levied on mineral oils, though narrower between EC countries than other excise duties, have widespread effects since they are important inputs for many industries.

Tobacco taxation has constituted a high percentage of the final product price, but the basis of the taxation has differed; for example, some countries, such as the UK, Ireland and Denmark used specific duties based on tobacco content, whereas others relied more upon *ad valorem* taxes. The latter, favoured by countries such as Italy and France, tended to discriminate against more expensive and higher quality imported tobacco. From the early 1970s the EC agreed to limit the range of tobacco taxation. In 1978 the EC changed the system for tobacco, abolishing duties on raw tobacco leaf, and a new sales tax was introduced at the manufacturing level, combined with a specific tax per cigarette as well as VAT.

In general, rates of excise duties have varied more widely than VAT rates and, unlike the latter, excise duties are normally imposed in one operation at an early stage in the production process. It was suggested that some consideration might be given to replacing excise duties by special VAT rates (Prest in Coffey ed. 1983). However, this has not occurred and the EC has opted, unlike its original VAT proposals, to retain the destination principle for excise duties. To abolish tax frontiers, therefore, it is to adopt a Community system of interconnected warehouses. Proposals by Lord Cockfield were to

Table 8.2   Retail price changes from proposed excise duty harmonization (%)

	Petrol (super)	Popular cigarettes	Spirits	Wine	Beer
Belgium	17	25	1	−9	5
Denmark	−19	−44	−50	−45	−37
France	−9	70	6	11	18
West Germany	19	2	5	13	12
Greece	−5	170	145	13	8
Ireland	−4	−10	−41	−64	−51
Italy	−29	36	118	13	0
Luxembourg	32	51	26	3	14
Netherlands	0	18	−1	−10	−6
Portugal	−3	90	107	13	10
Spain	19	120	90	13	18
UK	15	−6	−37	−47	−37

Source: European Commission, from *The Financial Times*, 16 July 1987

harmonize excise duties at common rates and these would have major repercussions; for example, Danish prices would fall across the board, hitting government revenue heavily. Greece, on the other hand, would experience massive price rises for some products, such as cigarettes and spirits. The retail price changes which would occur in the EC(12) are shown in Table 8.2.

These price changes would be so disruptive for some countries' products that the Commission has recognized subsequently that some flexibility will have to be retained. However, it cannot allow such wide differences to continue in rates of excise duties on mineral oils because of its adverse effects on competition, and it will need greater uniformity in this area. However, in the case of products such as alcohol and tobacco there is scope for more flexibility, laying down some minimum rates, leading towards greater target convergence over time.

Corporation tax. One missing element of the internal market as we progress in the 1990s is that relating to a common taxation policy for companies. This absence has distorted the location of business investment, with some countries such as Ireland treating inward investment more favourably than others. Despite a draft directive in 1975 which was to create a range for corporation tax of 45–55 per cent, this was not adopted. In 1988 another draft directive addressed the different asset bases on which taxes are charged. The rationale for harmonizing corporation tax is that capital is highly mobile and countries with lower rates of corporation tax will attract capital; also, if the lower corporation tax were reflected in lower prices, then it would affect not only the capital market but the goods market as well. While corporate tax rates have fallen, they ranged from 35 per cent in the UK to 50 per cent in Germany (January 1990). Likewise, depreciation allowances differ, with some countries using accelerated depreciation allowances to subsidize capital investment.

Three different tax systems have been used in EC countries. First, there is the Classical system used in countries such as the Netherlands and Luxembourg, under which dividends paid to shareholders are subject to tax without any credit against corporate tax; that is, they are taxed twice. The Van den Tempel Report in 1970 favoured this system. Secondly, an imputation system: in the UK corporate tax is charged at one rate, and if profits are distributed, shareholders are given a tax credit which reduces their personal tax liability; in other words, part of personal tax has been included in the corporation tax payment. Thirdly, there is the split-rate or two-rate system in which distributed profits are charged a lower rate of corporation tax than undistributed ones. The Neumark Committee in 1963 favoured the split-rate system used in Germany.

Withholding taxes imposed by countries on the payment of dividends from a subsidiary to its parent company in another country have also differed; for example, French subsidiaries operating in Italy have had to face higher withholding taxes than Dutch subsidiaries operating in Italy when seeking to return money to their own countries. The EC has made little progress in implementing company tax harmonization, and as with other forms of taxation, governments are reluctant to harmonize when it involves sacrificing their own system and the flexibility which they believe it provides.

C   The Community Budget

Relationship to national budgets. The Community Budget differs from national budgets in two respects. The first is that the Community Budget is relatively small in size and Community expenditure is around 1 per cent of the EC's GDP – 1.15 per cent of the GDP of the EC(12) in 1988. EC budgetary expenditure has been little more than the budget of the largest Land in West Germany. This underdevelopment of the Community Budget is in marked contrast to the high and much increased levels of national expenditure as a percentage of GDP – up to some 45 per cent of their GDP. The key functions which one normally expects to be conducted in a federation, such as defence, are excluded from the Community. Defence lies in the province of national governments and organizations such as NATO.

The second important difference is that national budgets are functional budgets whereas that of the EC is an accounting type of budget which is expected to balance – despite difficulties in achieving this aim. Some borrowing facilities exist and these are extensive for the ECSC and Euratom, and for the EC they include the EIB, the Community loan instrument since 1975 and the new Community instrument since 1978. The Budget itself is concerned mainly to raise revenue to balance its financial expenditure and it is not engaged in macroeconomic Keynesian stabilization policies of running budgetary deficits to stimulate demand in order to reduce persistently high levels of unemployment. While a case could be made out for the EC to run deliberate budgetary deficits, some governments consider this to be undesirable because of its inflationary consequences. The Community Budget finances specific sectoral activities and exogenously determined factors have influenced the large agricultural expenditure. Indeed, it will be shown that the EC's major preoccupation in recent years has been to contain pressures towards budgetary imbalance.

Budgetary receipts. The separate budgetary arrangements for the ECSC, Euratom and the EEC were brought together into a General Budget after their merger in 1968. Both Euratom and the EEC were initially dependent for their receipts on national contributions and a key was constructed to determine these, based on national income and the degree of involvement in different activities. This was a reasonably fair system, but the Community decided in the mid-1960s to introduce its own direct sources of revenue. It started to use both customs duties and agricultural levies on imports from outside the Community. Customs duties and agricultural levies for the EC are collected at important entry points: ports such as Antwerp and Rotterdam. Since the goods' final destination is often elsewhere, such as Germany, it was decided that logically the revenue raised should accrue not to national governments but to the Community. The most open economies with high imports from extra-EC sources therefore contribute disproportionately to these revenue sources.

The EEC was influenced in its desire to have its own direct source of revenue by the ECSC which has imposed levies on coal and steel production, and these are now incorporated in the full EC budgetary receipts. It was decided to introduce the crucial new element of a percentage of VAT to raise the Community's revenue receipts and provide sufficient own resources. These have developed at an earlier stage in the evolution of the EC than in other unions, such as the USA or the German Zollverein. Own resources provide the EC with some independence, although it still depends on member states to collect the revenue for which they have received 10 per cent of the revenue collected – the Commission in 1987 proposed the elimination of this refund.

VAT tends to be a regressive tax, certainly when compared with the progressive nature of income tax. Although with VAT, higher-income countries which consume more tend to pay more than others, one has to bear in mind that VAT is excluded on investment and exports, both of which are usually higher in more successful economies. This has led to some criticism about the wisdom of relying so much upon VAT as the EC's main source of revenue (Brown in El-Agraa ed. 1985, pp. 312–13). Furthermore, reliance on VAT has grown and it became necessary to raise the VAT ceiling from 1 per cent to a maximum of 1.4 per cent from 1 January 1986; there was some pressure to have this raised again to 1.6 per cent in 1988 to finance the EC's growing commitments.

VAT is the major revenue source, outpacing customs duties and levies on agricultural imports which are insufficiently dynamic sources of revenue, because the EC has concluded a wide range of agreements with outside countries and negotiated tariff reductions in GATT. Furthermore, in agriculture levies are being more than spent up by export subsidies. The sources of budgetary receipts are shown in Table 8.3.

A search has been under way for additional revenue sources for the EC, such as those from excise duties. But progress in the field of taxation has been slow in an area where unanimous voting is required. The most significant proposal by the Commission is to introduce a fourth revenue source linked to GNP. This would be

Table 8.3 **Budgetary receipts of the European Communities (millions UA/EUA/ECU) (a)**

	ECSC levies and other	European Dev. Fund contributions	Euratom contributions (research only)	Miscellaneous and contributions under special keys	EC budget					Total
					Miscellaneous	Own resources			Total EC	
						Agricultural levies	Import duties	GNP contributions or VAT (b)(c)		
1958	44.0	116.0	7.9	0.02	—	—	—	5.9	5.9	173.8
1959	49.6	116.0	39.1	0.1	—	—	—	25.1	25.2	229.9
1960	53.3	116.0	20.0	0.2	—	—	—	28.1	28.3	217.6
1961	53.1	116.0	72.5	2.8	—	—	—	31.2	34.0	275.6
1962	45.3	116.0	88.6	2.1	—	—	—	90.2	92.3	342.2
1963	47.1	—	106.4	6.7	—	—	—	77.4	84.1	237.5
1964	61.3	—	124.4	2.9	—	—	—	90.1	93.1	278.7
1965	66.1	—	98.8	3.5	—	—	—	197.6	201.1	366.0
1966	71.2	—	116.5	3.9	—	—	—	398.3	402.2	590.0
1967	40.3	40.0	158.5	4.2	—	—	—	670.9	675.1	913.9
1968	85.4	90.0	82.0	—	—	—	—	2 408.6	2 408.6	2 666.0
1969	106.8	90.0	62.7	78.6	—	—	—	3 972.6	4 051.2	4 330.7
1970	100.0	130.0	67.7	121.1	—	—	—	5 327.3	5 448.4	5 746.1
1971	57.9	170.0	—	—	69.5	713.8	582.2	923.8	2 289.3	2 517.2
1972	61.1	170.0	—	—	80.9	799.6	957.4	1 236.6	3 074.5	3 305.6
1973	120.3	150.0	—	—	511.0	478.0	1 564.7	2 087.3	4 641.0	4 911.3
1974	124.6	150.0	—	—	65.3	323.6	2 684.4	1 964.8	5 038.2	5 312.8
1975	189.5	220.1	—	—	320.5	590.0	3 151.0	2 152.0	6 213.6	6 623.1
1976	129.6	311.0	—	—	282.8	1 163.7	4 064.6	2 482.1	7 993.1(d)	8 433.7
1977	123.0	410.0	—	—	504.7	1 778.5	3 927.2	2 494.5	8 704.9	9 237.9
1978	164.9	147.5	—	—	344.4	2 283.3	4 390.9	5 329.7	12 348.2	12 660.6
1979	168.4	480.0	—	—	230.3	2 143.4	5 189.1	7 039.8	14 602.5	15 251.0
1980	226.2	555.0	—	—	1 055.9(e)	2 002.3	5 905.8	7 093.1	16 057.5(f)	16 838.7
1981	264.0	658.0	—	—	1 219.0	1 747.0	6 392.0	9 188.0	18 546.0(g)	19 468.0
1982	243.0	750.0	—	—	187.0	2 228.0	6 815.0	12 197.0	21 427.0	22 420.0
1983	300.0	700.0	—	—	1 565.0	2 295.0	6 988.7	13 916.8	24 765.5(h)	25 765.5
1984	408.0	810.0	—	—	1 060.7(i)	2 436.3	7 960.8	14 594.6	26 052.4(j)	27 270.4
1985	453.0	710.0	—	—	2 491.0(k)	2 179.0	8 310.0	15 218.0	28 198.0	29 361.0
1986	439.0	897.0	—	—	396.5	2 287.0	8 172.9	22 810.8	33 667.2	35 003.2
1987	399.3	837.9	—	—	74.8	3 097.9	8 936.5	23 674.1	35 783.3	37 020.5
1988	567.0	1 000.0	—	—	1 377.0	2 606.0	9 310.0	28 968.0	42 261.0	43 828.0
1989	404.0	—	—	—	2 298.8	2 462.5	9 954.0	30 122.7	44 838.0	:
1990	391.0	—	—	—	1 080.4	2 283.3	11 329.9	32 115.0	46 808.7(l)	:
1991	495.0	1 467.0	—	—	561.0	2 187.6	11 872.8	37 802.5	52 423.9(m)	54 385.9

Notes: 1958–89. (a) UA until 1977, EUA/ECU 1978 onwards. (b) GNP until 1978, VAT from 1979 until 1987. GNP from 1988 onwards. (c) This column includes for the years to 1970 surplus revenue from previous years carried forward to following years. (d) As a result of the calculations to establish the relative shares of the member states in the 1976 budget, an excess of revenue over-expenditure occurred amounting to 40.5 million UA. This was carried forward to 1977. (e) Including surplus brought forward from 1979 and balance of 1979 VAT and financial contributions. (f) Including surplus of ECU 82.4 million carried forward to 1981. (g) Including surplus of ECU 661 million. (h) Includes surplus of ECU 307 million. (i) Includes ECU 593 million of repayable advances by member states. (j) See note (j) to Table 57 in *European Economy*, December 1990. (k) Includes non-repayable advances by member states. (l) Supplementary and amending budget No. 2 of 1990. (m) Draft general budget for 1991 (Council first reading).

From 1988 onwards agricultural levies, sugar levies and customs duties are net of 10 per cent collection costs previously included as an expenditure item.

Source: D. G. for Economic and Financial Affairs, *European Economy*, no. 46, December 1990.

provided from the difference between each country's GNP and its actual VAT base. The proposed ceiling would be set at 1.4 per cent of GNP (Commission August 1987(i)). It represents a significant increase in EC resources, and in 1988 comprised 16.5 per cent of budgetary resources, but is clearly less of an own resource than the other sources. GNP-related income is more equitable since GNP tends to possess greater progressiveness than VAT; also, it was intended to include Italy's 'black' economy. Since the EC will continue with VAT, the compromise of using both this and a return to GNP represents the usual Community fudge. Own resources for the period to 1992 were agreed at the Brussels Summit in 1988, and were not to exceed 1.15 per cent of EC GNP in 1989, 1.17 per cent for 1990, 1.18 per cent for 1991 and 1.20 per cent for 1992.

Budgetary expenditure. A small amount of expenditure goes on financing staff and administration, but the bulk of it finances common sectoral policies. The most significant area of expenditure has been on agriculture, as shown in Table 8.4. Its share of the Budget, for example, was about three-quarters in 1973 and around three-fifths in 1988. Claims on the Budget have become even larger when the dollar has fallen in value since the latter has increased the cost to the Community of disposing of its agricultural surpluses on the world market. The search for agricultural solutions has continued somewhat elusively, although some ingenious proposals have been made: a fighting fund to get rid of stocks; a proposal to substitute EAGGF payment in arrears for payment in advance which was implemented temporarily, with the *status quo ante* restored in the Brussels Agreement in 1988 with a longer time-lag (two-and-a-half months instead of two months) for the Community to pay over the money to the member states; automatic stabilizers to trigger action, such as price cuts whenever spending passes a given limit. Other Commission proposals to tax oils and fats were condemned because of their effects on both consumers and outside suppliers, such as the USA. The Brussels Council Agreement in 1988 laid down that the annual growth of EAGGF Guarantee expenditure should not exceed 74 per cent of the annual growth of Community GNP. EAGGF Guarantee commitments were set to rise from ECU 27,500 million in 1988 at current prices to ECU 32,000 million in 1992 (at constant prices).

Despite encroaching bankruptcy, there were pressures to increase

Table 8.4 *Budgetary expenditure of the European Communities (millions UA/EUA/ECU) (a)*

	ECSC operational budget	European Development Fund	Euratom (b)	EAGGF (c)	EC general budget Social Fund	EC general budget Regional Fund	EC general budget Industry, Energy, Research	EC general budget Administration (d)	Other	Total EC	Total
1958	21.7	—	7.9	—	—	—	—	8.6	0.0	8.6	35.5
1959	30.7	51.2	39.1	—	—	—	—	20.3	4.9	25.2	146.2
1960	23.5	63.2	20.0	—	—	—	—	23.4	4.9	28.3	135.0
1961	26.5	172.0	72.5	—	8.6	—	—	27.9	2.9	39.4	305.0
1962	13.6	162.3	88.6	—	11.3	—	—	34.2	46.8	92.3	356.8
1963	21.9	55.5	106.4	—	4.6	—	—	37.2	42.3	84.1	267.9
1964	18.7	35.0	124.4	—	7.2	—	—	43.0	42.9	93.1	271.1
1965	37.3	248.8	120.0	102.7	42.9	—	—	48.1	7.4	201.1	607.2
1966	28.1	157.8	129.2	310.3	26.2	—	—	55.4	10.4	402.3	717.3
1967	10.4	105.8	158.5	562.0	35.6	—	—	60.4	17.1	675.1	949.8
1968	21.2	121.0	73.4	2 250.4	43.0	—	—	91.8	23.5	2 408.7	2 624.2
1969	40.7	104.8	59.2	3 818.0	50.5	—	—	105.6	77.1	4 051.2	4 255.9
1970	56.2	10.5	63.4	5 228.3	64.0	—	—	114.7	41.4	5 448.4	5 578.5
1971	37.4	236.1	—	1 883.6	56.5	—	65.0	132.1	152.2	2 289.3	2 562.8
1972	43.7	212.7	—	2 477.6	97.5	—	75.1	177.2	247.1	3 074.5	3 330.9
1973	86.9	210.0	—	3 768.8	269.2	—	69.1	239.4	294.4	4 641.0	4 937.9
1974	92.0	157.0	—	3 651.3	292.1	—	82.8	336.7	675.2	5 038.2	5 287.2
1975	127.4	71.0	—	4 586.6	360.2	150.0	99.0	375.0	642.8	6 213.6	6 412.0
1976	94.0	320.0	—	6 033.3	176.7	300.0	113.3	419.7	909.5	7 952.6	8 366.6
1977	93.0	244.7	—	6 463.5	325.2	372.5	163.3	497.0	883.4	8 704.9	9 042.6
1978	159.1	394.5	—	9 602.2	284.8	254.9	227.2	676.7	1 302.4	12 348.2	12 901.8
1979	173.9	480.0	—	10 735.5	595.7	671.5	288.0	863.9	1 447.9	14 602.5	15 256.4
1980	175.7	508.5	—	11 596.1	502.0	751.8	212.8	938.8	2 056.1	16 057.5(e)	16 741.7
1981	261.0	658.0	—	11 446.0	547.0	2 264.0	217.6	1 035.4	3 024.6	18 546.0(f)	19 465.0
1982	243.0	750.0	—	12 792.0	910.0	2 766.0(g)	346.0	103.3	3 509.7	21 427.0(h)	22 420.0
1983	300.0	752.0	—	16 331.3	801.0	2 265.5	1 216.2	161.6	2 989.9	24 765.5(i)	25 817.5
1984	408.0	810.0	—	18 985.8	1 116.4	1 283.3	1 346.4	1 236.6	2 150.8	26 119.3(j)	27 337.3
1985	453.0	710.0	—	20 546.4	1 413.0	1 624.3	706.9	1 332.6	2 599.8	28 223.0(k)	29 386.0
1986	439.0	897.0	—	23 067.7	2 533.0	2 373.0	760.1	603.2	4 526.2	34 863.2	36 199.2
1987	399.3	837.9	—	23 939.4	2 542.2	2 562.3	964.8	740.0	3 720.5	35 469.2	36 706.4
1988	567.0	1 000.0	—	27 531.9	2 298.8	3 092.8	1 203.7	947.0	6 186.8	42 261.0	43 828.0
1989	404.0	:	—	29 682.5	2 950.0	3 920.0	1 363.0	2 150.0	4 772.5	44 838.0(l)	:
1990	391.0	:	—	30 204.9	3 321.9	4 704.5	1 787.5	2 400.6	4 389.3	46 808.7(m)	:
1991	495.0	1 467.0	—	34 236.0	4 069.0	6 309.0	2 018.9	2 560.3	3230.7	52 423.9(n)	54 385.9

Notes: 1958–89 Management accounts. (a) UA until 1977. EUA ECU 1978 onwards. (b) Incorporated in the EC budget from 1971. (c) This column includes for the years to 1970 substantial amounts carried forward to following years. (d) Commission, Council, Parliament, Court of Justice and Court of Auditors. (e) Including surplus of ECU 82.4 million carried forward to 1981. (f) Including ECU 1·173 million carried forward to 1982. (g) Including ECU 1·819 million UK special measures. (h) Including ECU 2·211 million carried forward to 1983. (i) Including ECU 1·707 million carried forward to 1984. (j) There was a small deficit in 1984 in respect of the EC budget due largely to late payment of advances by some member states. (k) There was a cash deficit in 1985 of ECU 1·25 million due to late payment of advances by some member states. (l) Includes a surplus of ECU 5,080 million carried forward to 1990. (m) Supplementary and amending budget No. 2 of 1990. (n) Draft general budget (or 1991 Council first reading).
Source: D. G. for Economic and Financial Affairs, *European Economy*, no. 46, December 1990.

221

spending in desirable areas, to raise the profile of the Community and to offset uneven distributional effects of the Budget. Although expenditure on the Social Fund predated agricultural spending, the introduction of agricultural spending by the EC in 1965 swamped that of the Social Fund (which constituted a higher proportion of the Budget in 1965 than in subsequent years). Non-agricultural expenditure can only be expanded either by taking steps to cut agricultural spending, or by increasing the overall level of Community expenditure. Then the Social Fund could be increased – perhaps even to finance unemployment benefits – and the Regional Fund could make a real impact, rather than a cosmetic one, on the magnitude of EC regional problems.

There are particular obstacles impeding the redirection of budgetary expenditure. Those countries, especially agricultural ones, benefiting from the existing pattern of expenditure, are reluctant to see these eroded. Agricultural countries benefit substantially in terms of total receipts, and the smaller countries, such as Ireland and Denmark, have fared particularly well in terms of per capita receipts. Such a redistribution of income on welfare grounds may be justified for Ireland but not for Denmark. Other small countries, such as Belgium and Luxembourg, have also gained significantly from being the host to Community institutions, though part of their income does not accrue to their own citizens but is repatriated by EC employees. Precise distributional effects of the Budget were initially uncertain and the President of the Commission, Jacques Delors, refused to publish net budgetary transfers for fear of encouraging '*juste retour*'. However, estimates were subsequently made and published elsewhere; for example, in the *Economist* (20 June 1987) and by the Court of Auditors, as shown in Table 8.5.

The Community is divided in its approach between the Commission, Parliament and the Southern European members which generally favour more – especially non-agricultural – expenditure. On the other hand, the UK, West Germany and more recently France, which pay most towards financing the Community, want to limit their excessive expenditure. Increasing the level of expenditure would enhance the Community's role, making agreement easier, though there are strong constraints on expansion. Governments are concerned about a rising proportion of budgetary expenditure as a percentage of Community GDP, even though this is far below the minimum proposed by the MacDougall Report. National govern-

Table 8.5   **Payments to member states and own resources from member states (1989)**

	Payments ECU million	%	Own resources ECU million	%
Belgium	683.3	2.0	1,807.2	4.1
Denmark	1,045.3	3.1	871.1	2.0
France	5,676.5	16.7	8,622.8	19.5
Greece	2,564.5	7.5	566.3	1.3
Ireland	1,711.7	5.0	370.9	0.8
Italy	6,177.1	18.1	7,605.9	17.2
Luxembourg	8.2	0.0	72.8	0.2
Netherlands	3,829.9	11.2	2,700.5	6.1
Portugal	945.5	2.8	458.3	1.0
Spain	3,544.4	10.4	3,575.1	8.1
United Kingdom	3,214.3	9.4	6,568.1	14.8
West Germany	4,579.8	13.4	11,110.4	25.1
Allocation not available	72.4	0.2		
Total	34,052.9	100.0	44,329.3	100.0

Source: Court of Auditors, Annual Report 1989, *Official Journal of the European Communities,* C313, 12 December 1990, pp. 76–7

ments involved in making cutbacks in domestic expenditure to make room for the private sector – which they perceive to be the basis of success of their major competitors in the USA and Japan – find it hard to acquiesce to more expenditure at Community level. Furthermore, such expenditure, even when initiated to remedy the adverse distributional effects of the Budget, is sometimes wasteful and on inappropriate objectives.

The EC wishes to plan its future development on the basis of adequate, stable and guaranteed resources. In February 1987 Jacques Delors unveiled to the European Parliament proposals for a new source of revenue linked to GNP, permitting a significant increase in the Community Budget up to 1992. While the rate of increase in spending would be no greater than from 1980–6, there would be more spending on structural funds to create greater cohesion, as a *quid pro quo* for progress in the internal market. But expenditure on agriculture will still remain too high, even though it is intended that its share of the Budget will fall to a half, while regional and social spending will double to reach about a quarter of the Budget. Agricultural spending guidelines took a generous base of 1988, and by concealing a few items this has also helped to ensure that agriculture fits into the budgetary constraints laid down up to 1992.

The role of the institutions in the budgetary process. The Commission has continued in its role of providing new initiatives for further integration, with an accompanying need to finance such developments. The Commission prepares preliminary draft budgets which are examined by the Council of Ministers. There is a special Budget Council which is composed of ministers from national finance ministries and it reaches its decisions by qualified majority voting. The Council of Ministers usually trims back budgetary expenditure and then passes on the draft Budget to the EP.

The EP has tried to increase its powers, particularly in the budgetary field. It has been given the last word on so-called 'non-compulsory expenditure' (NCE) – this differs from the 'compulsory expenditure' that is necessary to carry out the provisions of the Treaty. Thus, non-compulsory expenditure relates largely to EC spending on regions, social policy, energy, industry, transport and so on. The Brussels Agreement in 1988 has raised spending on structural funds into privileged NCE, or what has been called 'compulsory non-compulsory expenditure' (Shackleton 1990, p. 20). Compulsory expenditure is mainly on agriculture, especially on Guarantee spending and some Guidance spending. The Council therefore still controls the bulk of expenditure, and even on the NCE there is a limit to which this may be raised by the Parliament. The three objective criteria used to determine the maximum NCE are: the trend in GNP (in volume terms); the average variations in the budgets of member states; and the trend in the cost of living during the preceding financial year. The maximum rates fixed annually for NCE varied from 14.6 per cent for 1975 to 8 per cent for 1985.

Since 1979 the elected EP and the Council have been locked in a struggle almost every year over the size and shape of the Budget and their respective powers. Parliament has succeeded in raising annual expenditure marginally, even though its room for manoeuvre is mainly confined to NCE. For example, after Parliament's first reading of the Budget, the Council's second draft was some 10 per cent higher both in 1985 and in 1986.

Parliament and Council soon clashed in 1979 when the latter failed to obtain the qualified majority necessary to reject the EP's increase in the Regional Fund. The conflict between the two institutions became even more intense in 1980 when the EP rejected the Budget for the first time, by 288 votes to 64. Clashes continued in the early 1980s over contentious issues such as the CAP and the British budgetary rebate. The Fontainebleau Summit in 1984 in tackling the latter appeared to have settled the budgetary problem, paving the way to greater progress. In practice it failed to do this completely and there has been continuing turbulence over the Budget.

Expenditure claims have tended to overstretch resources and at the end of some years after 1984 it was not possible to agree satisfactorily on a Budget for the forthcoming year. For example, at the end of 1984 the proposed Budget for 1985 was rejected by the EP on the grounds that it contained sufficient funding for agriculture for a period of only ten months' and not twelve months' expenditure. Another dispute emerged between Council and Parliament in 1986; that time the EP denounced the Budget on the basis that it contained only enough money for ten members and not for an enlarged Community of twelve members. This dispute was referred to the Court of Justice and its judgment in March 1986 came down in favour of the Council having the final say in fixing the maximum rate. This disappointed the EP by nullifying its powers other than at the margin. However, the Council was not wholly satisfied, since in June 1986 the Advocate General condemned the Council's dictatorial behaviour. The Advocate General, Mancini, recommended that if agreement could not be reached between the Council and Parliament, the matter should be referred to the President of the Court of Justice for a decision. The Court's judgment in July 1986 prohibited both Council and Parliament from establishing a *de facto* situation unilaterally. The consequence of its judgment is that the Council and the EP must negotiate and achieve a result. They have to agree on a maximum rate of increase of resources, otherwise the Community is forced to survive under a system of provisional twelfths (the previous monthly funds).

Disagreements have been resolved by the use of creative accounting, with terms such as 'negative reserves' (to which appropriations not used by the end of the year would be transferred). Early in 1987 yet another subtle proposal was made by the Budget Commissioner, Henning Christopherson, to stick to the 8.1 per cent agreed maximum growth in non-farm spending, but to find some extra cash by pushing this to 8.149 per cent by ignoring small changes which did not alter the first figure after the decimal point!

Conflicting interpretations have arisen since the Council adopted accounting policies based on a stricter application than the EP, which has reflected the spirit of an evolving and expanding Community. Budgetary discipline provides a constraint on such developments and Euro-conflict has arisen over finance and the exercise of power. The EP has tried to exercise its budgetary influence on the Council in different ways: it has played on the divisions between the Council of Ministers dealing with budgetary and agricultural affairs; it has sought to exploit national divisions in the Council so as to muster a blocking minority, but has found it harder to get the qualified majority to increase the non-compulsory spending which Parliament favours. The EP has also continued to challenge the interpretation of what is compulsory and what is non-compulsory expenditure, trying to switch more elements into non-compulsory spending – even though a classification of these elements was agreed in 1982.

A clearer financial perspective was drawn in 1988 which should lessen the conflict between the Council and the EP. In that year there was an agreement signed between the institutions – that is, the Council of Ministers, the Commission and the EP – on budgetary discipline and improvement of the budgetary procedure. This set out not only the revised pattern of financial expenditure, with a ceiling reducing the share of compulsory expenditure on agriculture, but also accepted the maximum rates of increase set for other non-compulsory expenditure.

To monitor budgetary procedures, the Court of Auditors operates along with the Parliament's Committee of Budgetary Control. They are concerned to ensure that money is spent effectively to avoid waste, and certainly greater attention needs to be given to getting value for money from EC expenditure.

Part III   Taxation in the UK and the problem of the Community Budget

A   Taxation

Before the UK joined the EC its tax system was distinctive in showing a greater reliance on direct taxation than in other countries (particularly France and Italy), whilst its indirect taxation was based mainly on purchase tax across a wide range of consumer goods. This was levied at the wholesale stage and charged as a percentage of the wholesale price, originally at two rates, though both the rates and their number increased. Purchase tax came under criticism for its adverse effects on the performance of particular sectors, such as the motor industry. The problems of manufacturing industry and its excessive taxation in relation to services led to the introduction of the Selective Employment Tax (SET) in 1966 – this was a tax on the employment of workers in the service sector.

VAT offered the advantage of replacing these taxes by a single sales tax levied at the retail stage. But a disadvantage was that it proved more costly to collect since purchase tax had been collected from fewer than 100,000 taxpayers: a seven-fold increase in tax officers was needed to collect VAT from more taxpayers. When the Richardson Committee first examined the replacement of purchase tax by VAT in 1964 they actually concluded that purchase tax was preferable to VAT. In 1973 the UK altered its system (as it did in other areas, such as its agricultural deficiency payments), not so much because of major defects but as measures to harmonize within the EC. After 1979 the Thatcher government increased the rate of VAT from 8 per cent to 15 per cent (and to 17.5 per cent in 1991), with offsetting reductions in direct taxation as part of its new supply-side policy. Nevertheless, the government has shown some sensitivity to Community proposals to have two rates of VAT as part of the creation of a full internal market, since this would affect British zero-rating on a wide range of goods and services such as food, housing and so on. It has been estimated that phasing out zero-rating would raise VAT revenue by £4 billion a year and raise the retail price index by 2 per cent. But this will be largely offset by reduced excise duties resulting in a fall of government revenue of £2.3 billion a year and producing a net increase in the retail price index of about 0.75 per cent. For example, exact harmonization of excises would cut prices of alcohol and tobacco significantly, although mineral oils would rise in price, apart from diesel.

B   *Budgetary problems for the UK*

Budgetary problems have been a source of continual friction and strain in the UK's membership of the Community. Although in other EC countries few citizens consider that their own country benefits most from the EC, in the UK a large majority perceive not only that the UK benefits least but also contributes most (Hewstone 1986). Problems have arisen with regard to both revenue and expenditure.

On the revenue side, the UK has a highly open economy (especially in its trade with the rest of the world); it has contributed disproportionately to the EC's revenue in the form of customs duties and levies on agricultural imports. For example, during 1984–9 the UK was the second-largest source of customs duties (behind Germany) and was the second-largest source of agricultural levies (behind Italy). While the pattern of UK trade has changed, with greater imports from the Community, this has not really solved the problem. If the UK imports more foodstuffs from the EC, obviously no import levies are payable but the UK simply substitutes higher trade costs for higher budgetary costs. In other words, instead of importing low-cost foodstuffs from the rest of the world and paying an import levy to raise the price to the level prevailing in the Community, the UK pays the high price directly to import from a Community supplier.

The choice of VAT as the major source of Community revenue is also unfavourable to countries with high consumption and low investment and which have imports in excess of exports. From a UK perspective, some additional source of revenue may have been preferable, such as a tax on imports of oil. But this would have resulted in the Community having an energy policy similar to its agricultural policy and, given the criticisms of the latter, it would not be desirable to advocate yet another high-price policy. Furthermore, if the tax were imposed not on oil imports but on oil production, then the UK would actually suffer disproportionately. If a tax on oil (and other energy sources) were introduced, then from the viewpoint of conserving energy it would be better to tax consumption. While the latter would be a useful Community tax measure, unfortunately it would still not solve the UK's budgetary problems. In practice it is difficult to find additional revenue sources which are good taxes and which also result in a lower budgetary contribution by the UK (Denton in Cohen ed. 1983).

As a small agricultural producer, the UK has not been able to secure a net budgetary inflow from the overdeveloped level of CAP expenditure; for example, in 1989 EAGGF Guarantee payments to The Netherlands were almost twice those to the UK. Although a system of *'juste retour'*, in which every country receives exactly the same as it contributes, cannot be recommended, a system in which low-income countries are net contributors to the Budget is a very perverse outcome. It has proved extremely difficult to develop other common policies which are as favourable to the UK as the CAP is to the more agricultural countries. Although new areas of expenditure could be opened up, it is necessary to ensure that the Community level is appropriate to conduct these policies instead of the national level. Expenditure by the EC on defence, social expenditure and so on would particularly suit the UK. Changes like this would be fundamental and to date have been mainly piecemeal, since politically the EC has found it necessary to retain the expensive CAP, which has constituted an unfortunate restraint on expanding expenditure in other areas. But the UK has consistently been the largest beneficiary of ESF payments, with its payments from the ERDF being behind those of Italy (and now of Spain).

C Budgetary dialogue with the UK

When it joined the EC, the UK accepted that it would contribute to the Budget in accordance with a fixed percentage key, beginning at 8.78 per cent in 1973 and increasing to 19.24 per cent in 1977. The Labour government became concerned that this would represent an undue burden on the UK, since its relatively slow rate of economic growth meant that its share of Community GNP was likely to decline. This happened, particularly when measured using current exchange rates rather than rates designed to reflect the purchasing power parity of currencies. The government focused upon reducing UK contributions, because it was dubious about being able to change Community expenditure in a way more favourable to the UK. It pressed forward with renegotiation, and agreement was reached at the Dublin Summit in 1975 for a payback system for countries which oversubscribe to the Budget. It applied to gross contributions and a complex formula was established for a sliding scale reimbursement. Despite a favourable referendum vote in 1975, the UK's budgetary terms worked out badly.

Budgetary problems soon resurfaced and were brought to a head in 1979 by the new Conservative government, again at a Summit in Dublin. The UK pressed for a cut of £1 billion in its contribution, but the maximum reduction offered was £350 million. The government tried, relatively unsuccessfully, to increase Community expenditure in the UK by, for example, proposals for greater Community aid for investment in the coal industry. Budgetary confrontation resulted in stresses and acrimony, deflecting the Community's attention from much needed developments in other areas. Although the UK appeared to have a strong case in pointing to the inequities in the Budget, its pleas were frustrated; France constantly argued that the only concessions could be lump-sum, degressive and temporary (Butler 1986).

Early in 1980 the UK was offered a better deal after linking the Budget discussion to the setting of agricultural prices. On average, between 1980 and 1982 the UK received a refund of about 70 per cent of its net budgetary contribution. The British government agreed at the Brussels Summit in March 1984 that its contributions would be redefined to exclude the counting of levies and customs duties in its search for some permanent solution. It appeared that this had been achieved at the Fontainebleau Summit in 1984, and in return for agreement to raise the EC VAT contribution the UK obtained a guaranteed percentage rebate every year – whereas the earlier rebates received under the 1980 agreements had been for absolute financial amounts (Denton 1984). At Fontainebleau the UK accepted a budget rebate of ECU 1 billion for 1984; it agreed a compensation mechanism for 66 per cent of the difference between its share of VAT payments and its receipts from the Budget. The Fontainebleau agreement in its technically complex calculation of rebates to the UK created a special position which was resented by other countries. While German contributions to the British rebate have been reduced, Germany is still concerned about this, plus the fact that rich countries such as Denmark continue to be net beneficiaries from the Budget.

Some improved settlement had to be reached eventually to avoid an impasse which would distract the Community from new progress towards southern enlargement. It was recognized that the UK had a genuine grievance, but member states were upset by its tactics in demanding the return of its own money and threatening established pillars of the Community, such as the CAP. British policy continues to be based on keeping tight budgetary finance to encourage agricultural reform; it has been adamant about better husbandry before sanctioning further expansion in expenditure.

The resolution of the basic budgetary problem still falls short of UK aspirations, being inequitable to the extent that a country with a relatively low income per head remains a net contributor. Between 1973 and 1986 the UK's total budgetary imbalance with the EC was −£7,785 million. The UK's percentage share of annual contributions to the Budget compared with payments from it show the UK has had the largest net gap, apart from Germany. For example, the net gap in 1987 was 6.1 per cent, in 1988 4.0 per cent and in 1989 5.4 per cent (see Table 8.5 for 1989). Its attitude resulted in deadlock at the European Summit in Copenhagen in December 1987, since the UK's compensatory offer was less than that reached at Fontainebleau, though the use of the additional GDP base was welcomed. Fortunately, greater progress was possible, with a new agreement at the emergency European Summit in Brussels in February 1988. This has resolved budgetary disagreements up to 1992, after which a new agreement will be necessary. Subsequently it may prove difficult to continue the British abatement mechanism, perhaps necessitating a move away from the existing revenue-side system (through which all countries contribute to alleviating the British problem) towards expenditure-side policies.

9 World-wide trading links

Part I External background

Although the EC has been very much concerned with the process of internal integration and with fostering intra-trade, it has had to institute a common external policy towards the rest of the world. The EC is a giant in world trade and has created a distinctive preferential system in its extra-trade arrangements. It has focused its closest links with key areas with which the major ex-colonial powers, such as France and the UK, have had historic links. It was natural that the EC should seek to consolidate these links in using trade and aid to exercise its political influence in strategic areas such as the Mediterranean and Africa. They are important sources of supplies of energy and raw materials which need assistance, such as foreign investment from the Community, to develop more rapidly.

The Community's external policy has become intertwined with its policies in other sectors. For example, the consequences of the CAP have resulted in outside countries seeking to preserve their exports to some extent by reaching special trade arrangements with the EC. Outsiders have also sought to reduce the diversion of their manufactured exports caused by the Common External Tariff (CET). Modifications to the latter represent the Community's most potent weapon in dealing with outsiders. EC preferential agreements have multiplied to such an extent that very few countries are subjected to the full CET. However, an open trading policy has accelerated the decline of the Community's traditional industries, with related regional problems in those areas affected by imports. The EC has recognized the need to expand the new high-tech industries, but some countries such as France have made progress towards this conditional upon using the EC's Common Commercial Policy in a more protectionist way to outsiders (Pearce and Sutton 1986). There is concern by outside countries that the EC internal market programme may strengthen Community industry at external expense. Although outsiders will still possess some advantages in being able to subsidize their industries and not applying the same social measures as the EC, outside countries definitely need to review their trade strategies.

This chapter examines some of the EC's world-wide trading connections. How beneficial are these special trading arrangements to the Community, and what have been some of their effects on other countries? It pinpoints those areas which have special arrangements with the Community: for example, EFTA lies just outside the inner circle of the EC(12) but free trade exists and more members are likely to defect from EFTA. EFTA countries are most favoured, followed by the Mediterranean, with countries such as Cyprus and Malta also likely to join the Community fully. The Mediterranean agreements have been condemned for being against both the letter and the spirit of GATT (Pomfret 1986). A hierarchical ranking of links with outside countries has resulted in a clear 'pecking order' and in this chapter considerable emphasis is given to the links which the EC has established with those countries in Africa, the Caribbean and the Pacific (ACP). This is partly since EFTA has been referred to in Chapter 1 and Mediterranean enlargement of the EC is developed more fully in Chapter 10.

The geographical distribution of EC trade is shown in Table 9.1. More than half was intra-trade by 1973, and its major external trading partners are the USA, EFTA and the developing countries.

Part II   The EC's preferential and non-preferential links
A   The EC's non-preferential links with developed countries
The United States. The EC and the USA have enjoyed very close links because the USA has generally supported EC integration, but their harmonious relationship has deteriorated in recent years. Friction has arisen in specific economic sectors such as agriculture, and the USA announced in 1987 that it wanted an end to all farm subsidies by the end of the century. The EC's obstinate approach to agricultural protection manifested itself in the latest GATT tariff-cutting round of negotiations which were suspended in December 1990 in Brussels. In other industries, such as steel, the Americans have opted for import controls, arguing that European imports have been highly subsidized (Hine 1985, p. 234; Tsoukalis ed. 1986, p. 23).

In relation to Eastern Europe, the EC has adopted a less hostile view than the more distant Americans. The USA has been prepared to use trade sanctions as a way of putting pressure on the Soviet

Table 9.1 *EC(12): exports and imports by main country groups (in per cent[1])*

	Exports				Imports			
	1963	1973	1980	1985	1963	1973	1980	1985
EC(12)	48.4	56.1	55.8	54.7	43.1	53.2	49.4	52.9
EFTA(6)	13.4	11.3	11.0	10.0	9.0	8.3	8.6	9.3
Eastern Europe	3.0	3.8	3.5	2.8	3.4	3.1	3.7	3.9
United States	7.3	7.6	5.6	10.1	11.8	8.7	8.6	8.0
Japan	1.0	1.4	1.0	1.2	0.9	2.1	2.6	3.4
Developing countries	22.3	17.0	21.3	18.4	25.8	21.3	25.1	20.4
of which: OPEC	4.1	3.9	8.1	6.0	8.6	8.9	13.8	8.4
NICs	5.6	5.1	4.5	3.9	5.4	4.9	4.4	4.8
Rest of world	4.6	2.8	1.9	2.8	5.9	3.2	2.0	2.1

Note:
[1]Because of different data sources, some figures may deviate slightly from some of those in other tables.

Source: UN COMTRADE Data Base in A. Utne, *Efta Bulletin*, no. 4, vol. XXVII, Oct.–Dec. 1986

Union. Security-related exports are controlled through the Co-ordinating Committee on Multilateral Export Controls (COCOM). The attempt by the USA to control exports of high-technology products to Eastern Europe by its many business subsidiaries and by European companies operating under licence in the EC has resulted in disagreements between the EC and the USA. The USA likewise objected to Community countries subsidizing export credits and loans to Eastern Europe, though such opposition has lessened, with better relations since 1990.

Political/military differences between the USA and the EC became more apparent, in particular under President Reagan, and whilst the EC has supported UN action in the Gulf under President Bush there has been concern about the limited German commitment. While the two blocs remain allies with common interests, the traditional close-coupling between them is now questioned much more widely than in the past. Economically, the US faces massive budgetary and trade deficits, and the latter is likely to be cut only by reduced expenditure abroad, continued depreciation of the dollar and by further protectionist sentiments; these are likely to work against EC interests.

Japan. Japan began its trade dialogue with the Community in the early 1960s, although only bilateral deals were reached. The imbalance in trade has arisen since imports from Japan rose from under 1 per cent of EC imports in 1963 to 3.4 per cent in 1985, whereas EC exports to Japan showed only a minor increase from 1 per cent in 1963 to 1.2 per cent in 1985. While the virtue of a multilateral trading system is that it is unnecessary to achieve bilateral balance with each country, the EC and Japan agreed in 1983 to a voluntary export restraint (VER) on various sensitive products. By the mid-1980s VERs were applied to just over a third of Japanese exports to the Community. Despite these, Japan's trade surplus with the EC has continued to widen.

The trading problems can be attributed not only to Japanese non-tariff barriers (NTBs), but to the Community's own deficiencies. These include low capital investment in high-tech sectors and weaker marketing: for example, in the mid-1980s there were only some 2000 European businessmen in Japan, whereas Japan had some 33,000 businessmen in Europe.

Comecon. Comecon is the acronym which is usually used to describe the Council for Mutual Economic Assistance (CMEA) which was founded in 1949. It was a means of ensuring Soviet hegemony in Eastern Europe and its main membership has consisted of the USSR, Bulgaria, Czechoslovakia, Hungary, Poland, Romania and the German Democratic Republic (until reunification in 1990). The aim of Comecon, like that of the EC, was to promote integration of trade in order to prevent wasteful duplication in production. Thus the Soviet Union supplies much of the energy, raw materials and aircraft, and Hungary supplies buses. Disagreements have arisen over specialization, and Romania has pressed ahead, despite objections by the Soviet Union, with industries such as petrochemicals.

Compared with the EC, Comecon was a more intergovernmental and less supranational organization. The satellite states have preferred this, given the weight of the USSR. Factor mobility has also been less in Comecon, and although capital has flowed from the USSR to countries like the GDR and labour has moved from Poland to the GDR, these movements have been less easy than in the

EC. In 1986 53 per cent of Comecon trade was intra-trade and most of its members conducted more than half of their trade within the bloc. One exception to this has been Romania, which has significantly reorientated its trading pattern with the West.

Comecon's original autarkic view of trade eventually gave way to the realization that trade was a means of economizing on resources and of obtaining sophisticated products from the West. The EC offered trade agreements to individual states in 1974, though only Romania responded, in 1980. By 1986 12 per cent of Comecon trade was with the EC, but only 3 per cent of EC trade was with Comecon. The dominant trading country on the EC side is Germany and in Comecon it is the USSR. Trade has been stimulated since the Community granted most favoured nation treatment to Eastern European countries, enabling them to benefit from tariff reductions (Yannopoulos 1985, p. 30). However, the links between the EC and Comecon were bedevilled by a variety of limiting factors. Both systems are based on competing philosophies and they were loathe to recognize each other legally, since Comecon was dominated by the USSR. The links were mainly on a bilateral level between individual countries, or between the EC and Eastern European countries, in areas such as fisheries, in which countries like the USSR have entered into negotiations with the Community (Lodge 1983). The EC did not wish to legitimize Soviet hegemony in Eastern Europe by its actions, but under Gorbachev agreement was reached to give belated formal mutual recognition to the two organizations, with a mutual recognition agreement signed in Luxembourg in June 1988.

The trade of Comecon with the Community peaked in 1984 and has been inhibited by various elements such as Iberian enlargement of the EC, and the new protectionism affecting products such as textiles, clothing and so on. However, East European exports have suffered less from discriminatory trade agreements than from their own internal and fundamental deficiencies. For example, Comecon countries have lacked a proper pricing policy for their products, often under-pricing them to obtain Western currency, and partly to undermine Western markets – this has resulted in numerous anti-dumping cases against Eastern Europe. They have also faced problems in exporting agricultural products because of the CAP, though in some respects agricultural exporters fared better than those selling industrial products because of the generally poor quality of the latter and severe competition from the NICs. The import needs of Comecon for industrialization have generally exceeded their export capabilities. Currency inconvertibility led to bilateral deals involving different forms of countertrade; the latter involved complex and rather inefficient forms of trading.

The desire of Eastern Europe to catch up with the West led to massive borrowings to finance their industrialization. This resulted in major indebtedness because of rising interest rates and economic recession which reduced the propensity of Community countries to import from Comecon. Poland was the first country to experience problems in servicing its massive external debt. According to the Economic Commission for Europe, Poland's gross debt in 1988 was $38.9 billion, which was more than half Poland's GNP. The root cause of the Polish crisis was lack of incentive and poor morale (Drewnowski ed. 1982). Gross debts elsewhere in Eastern Europe in 1988 in US$ billion were: the GDR (19.9); Hungary (17.3); Bulgaria (7.6); Czechoslovakia (5.1); with Romania (2.7) being relatively underborrowed.

Since the disintegration in Eastern Europe and Comecon which began in 1989, the EC has become the forum for channelling aid there, including that from the USA. The PHARE programme was set up by the Group of Seven (G-7) Summit in July 1989 on behalf of 24 donor countries. The EC has invited the other G-24 members to participate in the TEMPUS programme of academic exchanges. Eastern Europe has also received financial support from the European Bank for Reconstruction and Development which was created in 1990 with a share capital of ECU 10 billion, based in London. It involves 40 countries plus the EC and the EIB; it has strong British support because of its lending commitment to stimulate development of the private sector.

The massive needs in Eastern Europe for aid and trade have major implications for LDCs in the rest of the world. For example, new trade agreements have been proposed for eastern Europe, along with the removal of import quotas (probably by 1994–5) and tariff reductions, to give imports from Eastern Europe the same entry conditions as those for developing countries – Romania enjoyed this privilege under Ceauşescu, and Poland and Hungary had to be treated similarly. By 1990 the EC replaced Comecon as Hungary's principal trading partner. These new trade agreements will lead on to association agreements (though excluding the USSR) creating free trade; economic and technical co-operation; financial assistance; and a political dialogue. It is important not to rush their full integration into the EC but to provide a sufficient breathing space for their adaptation, especially in the light of East Germany's difficult adjustment in even more favourable circumstances. Successful economic development will depend partly upon attracting sufficient new Western investment to benefit from low wage rates (for example, just over $2 an hour in Czechoslovakia). The latter has announced that it will manufacture to Western European norms and standards by the end of 1992. Meanwhile, the EC must brace itself for some structural readaptation in particular industries because of increased imports from Eastern Europe, such as glass from Czechoslovakia, cement from Poland and so on.

For the USSR itself a Trade and Economic Co-operation Agreement came into effect in 1990 with both sides granting the other MFN status, with the EC removing quotas and giving financial aid. This will be much needed because economic reform (*perestroika*), introduced after Gorbachev came to power in 1985, faces immense problems. His alluring offer of a 'common European home' needs cautious examination by the EC. An enlarged EC to include eventually the former East European satellite states would consolidate the Community as a major world power. However, to go further than this by incorporating the USSR, or even just the European part of the USSR, could create Soviet dominance, particularly if the American presence in Europe were to be displaced. Progress towards a 'common European home' will depend very much upon the German reaction, since it is no longer a prerequisite for German reunification, and it is the latter itself which is now the determinant of how rapidly closer East–West European links occur.

B   The EC's preferential trade relations
EFTA. The EC has accorded primacy to its trading links with EFTA, which lies at the apex of its trading hierarchy. Special arrangements had to be made for EFTA countries after the departure of the UK and Denmark into the EC in 1973. Free trade exists in industrial goods, with a single trade document being used. The Community has tended to run a balance-of-payments surplus in its trade with EFTA. In 1985 EFTA accounted for about 10 per cent of the EC's trade, whereas for EFTA the Community is far more important (in 1985 56 per cent of its trade was conducted with the EC). Nearly three-quarters of this EC–EFTA trade consists of

manufactured goods. While EFTA is more important as a group than in terms of individual countries, some of the latter are still significant since the Community sells more goods and services to Switzerland and to Sweden than to Japan, more to Norway than to Canada, and more to Finland than to China (*Economist* 21-7 Nov. 1987).

The Mediterranean. The importance of the Mediterranean to the Community has grown from the initial preferential trade links which France conducted with its former North African colonies in Morocco, Tunisia and Algeria. Algeria has the largest population and income per head of the three countries, drawing much of its revenue from oil exports. The agreement with these three Maghreb countries is separate from the Community's agreements with other countries in Africa under the ACP. Economically, countries like Tunisia have responded more positively to Community preferences than others such as Morocco. Morocco has also shown concern at Iberian enlargement of the Community, with estimates that this may cost Morocco some 2 per cent of its GDP (*Financial Times* 13 July 1987). In July 1987 Morocco surprised the Community by applying for membership, though this is impossible since membership is only open to European countries. Unfortunately the Community appears to have got itself into a zero-sum game in which trade concessions to certain countries are at the expense of others.

The signing of an Association agreement with Greece in 1961 established a precedent which has carried its association to full membership (this is discussed in Chapter 10). It became difficult to reject other preferential applications and one was reached with Turkey when it became an Associate Member of the EC by the Treaty of Ankara 1964. Its location is important strategically as a member of NATO, as is its population size of some 50 million people. Despite criticisms of its human rights record it was cleared by the Council of Europe in 1985. However, its economic weaknesses as the 'sick man of Europe' would create indigestible problems by full membership of the EC. Turkey's GDP per head is only slightly more than half that of Portugal (the poorest member of the EC). Much of Turkey's labour force has been employed in agriculture – more than the total in the whole EC(10) (Rustow and Penrose 1981). Industrially it has been unable to maintain the agreed reduction in its tariffs, and Turkish industries, apart from textiles, would suffer badly from stronger EC competition. Despite political advantages to the EC and Turkey, the Community rejected its application in 1989, ensuring by this delay that Turkish membership does not take place before the next century.

At first the Community was much preoccupied with internal integration, but its preferential agreements with African countries (under Yaoundé and later Lomé conventions) and the Maghreb (Morocco, Algeria and Tunisia), and with Greece and Turkey, led to other preferential agreements in 1970 with Spain and Israel. The Community has a free-trade agreement with Israel and the latter has gained significantly from this. To maintain a balance with Arab countries, co-operation agreements have been signed with the important Mashreq (Egypt, Lebanon, Syria and Jordan).

The proliferation of Mediterranean agreements in the early 1970s also included an association with Malta after 1970 and with Cyprus after 1972, and customs unions exist for free industrial trade with these two islands. Both have recorded good rates of industrial growth, though Malta· has been in a better position to raise its exports to the EC and has attracted inward investment, especially in industries such as clothing (Pomfret 1986, pp. 68–75).

Yugoslavia also signed a non-preferential agreement so that by the 1970s the only Mediterranean countries lacking special relations with the Community were Albania and Libya. The complicated pattern of individual agreements required some rationalization, and after Commission proposals in 1972 the Community sought to replace individual agreements by a more global approach to the Mediterranean. The Community has identified this area as one of strategic importance and has used its commercial policy to exercise political influence – whereas the USA has used its naval presence. The EC draws its oil and other raw materials from the area. The Mediterranean countries themselves have perceived economic advantages in securing access to the EC market to stimulate their own industrial development and agriculturally to offset some of the protectionist nature of the CAP. The EC has brought the Mediterranean into its orbit, though the extension of its influence in the area infringes GATT. It provides a poor example to other countries such as the USA which could also start to make greater use of preferential agreements as part of its own foreign policy (Pomfret 1986).

The general view was that the effects of preferential agreements would only be marginal, since tariffs have been lowered by GATT.

However, preferences have had a substantial impact on particular products where EC protection has been high, such as agriculture and textiles. The more outward-looking Mediterranean countries have been the ones to benefit most and they have provided an attractive source for multinational inward investment. Hence, it was a logical development for countries like Spain to move to full membership of the Community.

The southern enlargement of the Community aggravated its relations with outsiders such as the USA and other Mediterranean countries. The countries with products similar to those of the new entrants are the ones most vulnerable to displacement. New entrants to the Community not only add to its immediate problems, but dynamically the effects of higher Community agricultural prices are likely to increase supply, further threatening outside Mediterranean countries. The EC since enlargement has increased its self-sufficiency in many products, and imports from 'foreigners' seem likely to bear the brunt of future protectionism.

ACP countries: problems of trade and aid. ACP countries, as LDCs, are characterized by low income per head and over-dependence on agriculture. Most endure a precarious agricultural existence and some have suffered badly from drought in recent years. Many of the younger skilled and more mobile people have often been forced to emigrate from arid African countries to take advantage of opportunities elsewhere in countries like Senegal or the Ivory Coast.

The oil exporting countries have naturally benefited from the rise in oil prices (including ACP countries such as Nigeria, Congo, Gabon, Trinidad and Tobago). Other ACP countries which are oil importers have suffered and also their exports to OPEC have not consisted of sufficient industrial products to increase sales there significantly.

Apart from exogenous shocks, many LDCs have been moulded by their colonial inheritance. For example, high wages in the public sector, plus a legacy of minimum-wage legislation, have distorted resource allocation. Overseas multinationals have further reinforced the bias against investment in the indigenous private industrial sector. High wages militate against labour-intensive employment (yet labour is the abundant factor), and also generate inflationary pressure. ACP countries have tended to experience higher wage costs and inflation than many of the NICs in Asia.

LDCs require financial aid to fill both their savings–investment gap and their gap in foreign exchange. They can see the benefits from aid, even though they prefer to earn their living in the world to a greater extent by engaging in trade. Indeed, the latter is of far greater significance, since aid under Lomé has been equivalent to only about 3 per cent of ACP exports to the EC (Stevens ed. 1984).

Aid has created some problems with regard to debt servicing and over-dependence on donor countries. The EC Pisani Memorandum in 1982 noted that 'below a certain effectiveness and relevance, aid becomes an evil for it nourishes illusions and encourages passivity'. This is a very controversial issue: many development economists still maintain that the benefits exceed the costs and that the quality and quantity of aid should be improved. About 15 per cent of EC(10) aid was channelled through the Community. EC aid has been criticized on the grounds of its small size – in relation to keeping up with inflation and the growing membership of the ACP – and bureaucratic documentation which has resulted in slow disbursement. For example, in Lomé III by October 1988 only about 10 per cent of aid had been disbursed. Although in principle the ACP is responsible for selecting aid projects, the EC has used its financial powers to influence the choice and implementation of projects (Stevens ed. 1984, p. 16). Furthermore, some Lomé aid is being used to repay growing debts to the IMF and the World Bank.

EC association with the ACP. Links with LDCs were not provided for in the Spaak Report in 1956 but were proposed subsequently by France and included in the EC, since France regarded its colonial territories as a natural extension of France itself. It was also a means of ensuring that some of the financial costs of aiding overseas territories would be shared between EC countries. A European Development Fund (EDF) was established to channel aid to the associates, and over the first five years it was agreed that France and Germany should subscribe the lion's share equally.

France has been very successful in charging high prices for its exports to the associated countries. Where French production costs have been above the world price this has had the adverse effect of diverting trade towards less-efficient French producers. Close francophone co-operation has been maintained in Africa, helped by monetary union between France and the West African and Central African states. The large-scale presence of French advisors and a tendency to tie aid to French exports enabled France to supply on average 40 per cent of francophone imports between 1975 and 1982 and to enjoy a massive trade surplus with francophone Africa. Trade with associates has tended to provide a significant balance-of-trade surplus for the EC which has helped it to offset trade deficits with countries at a higher level of economic development, such as the USA and Japan.

From Yaoundé to Lomé. By the early 1960s many of the overseas territories had been given independence, and a new basis of association signed at Yaoundé (Cameroon) in 1963 came into effect in 1964. It covered 18 associated African states and Malagasy (AASM), and was later joined by Mauritius in 1971. Under Yaoundé I expenditure was 730 million units of account and under Yaoundé II from 1969–75 918 million units of account were spent. The aid was generous since most of it was given in grants and much of it went to heavily populated countries such as Zaire (the ex-Belgian Congo). Some of the interior states like Chad are very backward and much in need of aid, whereas many of the coastal states in Africa enjoy greater scope for trade (Cosgrove 1969).

Yaoundé was essentially neo-colonial, with no pretence of economic equality between the EC and the African associates. Trade relations were based on the reciprocity of trade advantages. However, under Lomé countries succeeded in ending the process of having to grant reverse preferences (Coffey 1975). The first agreement at Lomé (the capital of Togo) in 1975 was between the EC and 46 ACP countries; it was considered an inspiring and exemplary step forward towards a more balanced relationship with LDCs. Yet this is something of a façade since the ACP countries are so much more dependent upon the EC for trade and aid, whereas the ACP constitutes a much less significant trading partner for the Community. Nevertheless, the fact that the Caribbean and Pacific could form a joint group with the Africans was remarkable and their co-operation has created a group with some bargaining power and an ability to speak with one voice.

Nigeria, the Ivory Coast and Zaire account for nearly half of total ACP exports to the Community. The EC is much less important for the Caribbean countries for whom the USA is a greater trading partner. Poverty is endemic: about 40 per cent of ACP countries recorded no growth in income per head during the 1970s and by 1984 only 16 Lomé countries had an income per head of over $1000. Their dilemma is which path to take in development, since the formation of horizontal regional trading blocs separate from vertical links with the Community is very appealing and there is some very modest funding for regional economic integration in Lomé IV. Unfortunately, intra-trade between LDCs is low and disagreements have arisen over the location of industries. This has not been an insuperable problem in all horizontal trading blocs, but continuing difficulties have forced LDCs into traditional trade links with the Community.

Second, third and fourth Conventions were signed at Lomé, based upon the same principles of legality as the first agreement, though the duration of Lomé IV is increased from five to ten years. Although these agreements manifested improvements in some areas, the Community in recession could never match the aspirations and needs of the ACP. In Lomé II, on which agreement was finally reached on 31 October 1979, the EC exploited the divisions and lack of leadership in the ACP (Long ed. 1980, ch. 2). Negotiations were further protracted during Lomé III since the ACP was tied up with negotiations relating to the reduced funding from other international agencies at that time. Negotiations for Lomé IV began in October 1988 with the EC again being better briefed and organized than the ACP.

The financial endowment of the various Lomé agreements increased from ECU 3.5 billion under Lomé I to ECU 5.5 billion under Lomé II, ECU 8.5 billion under Lomé III and ECU 12 billion under Lomé IV. However, this has had to cover a growing ACP membership from 46 states under Lomé I to 68 states under Lomé IV (with additional provision for Namibia to join automatically, if it wishes, after full independence). Furthermore, ACP aid has to be measured against growing difficulties: falling commodity prices; a rising ACP debt burden (estimated at about $130 billion); and stagnation in many sub-Saharan African countries (necessitating since 1988 a special EC programme to aid some very highly indebted, low-income countries there). Many countries have also had to adopt painful macroeconomic restructuring programmes at the behest of international aid agencies.

Most of the EC financial aid (around two-thirds) has been pro-grammed, consisting mainly of outright grants or loans on soft

Table 9.2   Volume of aid for the first five years of Lomé IV in comparison with Lomé III

	Lomé III Value (million ECU)	%	Lomé IV Value (million ECU)	%
Aid	4,790	64.54	6,845[1]	63.38
Risk capital	635	8.58	825	7.64
STABEX	925	12.50	1,500	13.89
SYSMIN	415	5.61	480	4.44
Structural adjustment support	–	–	1,150	10.65
Soft loans	635	8.58	–	–
Total EDF	7,400	100	10,800	100
EIB	1,100		1,200	
Total resources	8500		12,000	

Notes:
[1]Part of it can be used for Structural Adjustment Support.
ACP states: Angola, Antigua and Barbuda, Bahamas, Barbados, Belize, Benin, Botswana, Burkina Faso, Burundi, Cameroon, Cape Verde, Central African Republic, Chad, Comoros, Congo, Djibouti, Dominica, Equatorial Guinea, Ethiopia, Fiji, Gabon, The Gambia, Ghana, Grenada, Guinea, Guinea Bissau, Guyana, Ivory Coast, Jamaica, Kenya, Kiribati, Lesotho, Liberia, Madagascar, Malawi, Mali, Mauritania, Mauritius, People's Republic of Mozambique, Niger, Nigeria, Papua New Guinea, Rwanda, St Christopher and Nevis, St Lucia, St Vincent, São Tomé and Principe, Senegal, Seychelles, Sierra Leone, Solomon Islands, Somalia, Sudan, Suriname, Swaziland, Tanzania, Togo, Tonga, Trinidad and Tobago, Tuvalu, Uganda, Vanuatu, Western Samoa, Zaire, Zambia, Zimbabwe; plus Haiti, Dominican Republic in Lomé IV.

Source: Lomé Briefing, no. 14, Jan.–Feb. 1990

terms. The remaining aid has been non-programmed, with the various categories under Lomé III and Lomé IV shown in Table 9.2.

A new feature of Lomé IV is the provision of 10.65 per cent of lending via the seventh EDF for structural adjustment support, rather than long-term development. Both Lomé III and IV have recognized the potential of a wide range of developments, including tourism and fisheries, but have focused mainly upon agriculture. The priority of rural development is shown in over three-quarters of the National Indicative Programmes drawn up for each state. These mainly reflect a centralized approach despite efforts to encourage more local participation. There is also a new emphasis on environmental protection in Lomé IV, though it seems doubtful whether environmentally damaging developments will be cancelled. Whilst each new agreement has tried to be innovatory to break new ground, constraints are imposed by the different perspectives of member states. For example, some EC members such as France and Italy favour the donation of more aid, whilst others such as Germany and The Netherlands would prefer to focus on the provision of better trade access into the Community market. Further liberalization of agricultural imports tends to be marginal because of the CAP. However, under Lomé IV there has been a significant improvement in the rum protocol, increasing the quantities to be imported duty-free, with plans for the abolition of the tariff quota in 1995.

STABEX. While the Community's Export Revenue Stabilization Scheme (STABEX) was predated by the IMF's own compensatory finance scheme, the conditions of STABEX have been less strict and it has given preferential treatment to very disadvantaged countries. The numbers of primary products covered under the scheme have been increased in each Convention, and 48 products are listed in the appropriate article of the third ACP–EC Convention. In addition, the restrictive threshold qualifications have been reduced. To obtain assistance the commodity must exceed a dependence threshold of export earnings in the previous year, and export earnings have to fall by a minimum amount below a reference level in the four years preceding the claim. The dependence threshold and reference level have been cut from 7.5 per cent in Lomé I to 6.5 per cent in Lomé II and 6 per cent in Lomé III. For the least developed, island and landlocked states, the dependence and reference levels have been reduced from 2.5 per cent in Lomé 1 to 2 per cent in Lomé II and 1.5 per cent in Lomé III.

A defect of STABEX is its limited funding and, with some falling commodity prices for products such as groundnuts and coffee, transfers have had to be scaled down significantly. For example, total STABEX spending allocated by the end of 1988 was already ECU 919 million. The importance of particular products in total STABEX expenditure is shown in Table 9.3 for the period 1975–85. These primary products have influenced the distribution of STA-

Table 9.3   STABEX, 1975–85: aggregate balance-sheet by product

	Total (in ECU)
All groundnut products	333,780,778
Coffee	282,196,654
All cocoa products	161,299,447
All cotton products	81,330,854
Iron ore	61,789,536
All wood products	45,349,687
Oil cake	45,303,777
All copra and coconut products	42,962,224
Sisal	33,118,052
Bananas	20,034,026
All palm products	18,165,476
Beans	17,838,522
Tea	17,243,689
Cajou kernals	11,458,241
Raw hides and skins	10,006,845
Vanilla	8,173,099
Sesame seeds	5,783,823
Cloves	5,212,874
Kante kernals	1,937,603
Essential oil	1,510,469
Mohair	1,290,959
Gum arabic	848,489
Prawns	710,289
Nutmeg	637,851
Pyrethrum	608,802
Total	1,208,592,066

Source: Eurostat, *ACP Statistics 1987*

BEX expenditure between ACP states, with Senegal topping the list of beneficiaries. This is shown in Table 9.4.

In some respects, the distribution is arbitrary since some poor

Table 9.4   The top ten beneficiaries from STABEX, 1975–85

	Receipts (in ECU)
Senegal	183,257,156
Sudan	125,042,319
Ivory Coast	113,324,801
Ghana	90,647,339
Ethiopia	53,807,619
Papua New Guinea	50,690,742
Tanzania	50,473,947
Kenya	44,865,565
Togo	41,775,242
Mauritania	37,000,450

Source: Eurostat, *ACP Statistics 1987*

countries which fail to meet the qualifications have suffered, *vis-à-vis* a few relatively more prosperous countries which have had their export earnings included. Many other criticisms have been levelled at STABEX, such as its bias against countries that have efficient domestic commodity policies and balance-of-payments management (McQueen 1977; Hewitt 1984; Hine 1985). In Lomé IV STABEX transfers no longer have to be repaid; there is an increased allocation to ECU 1.5 billion; and a few new commodities have been added; but all this will hardly cushion countries from the collapse of international commodity agreements for products such as cocoa and coffee.

SYSMIN. The Système Minérais (SYSMIN) was an innovation in Lomé II and is a scheme for mineral products similar to that for primary products in STABEX. Minerals, with the exception of iron ore, had been excluded from STABEX. Iron ore has been switched into SYSMIN along with various other mineral products, though the cost of financing these is less than if they had been included within STABEX (Long ed. 1980, pp. 104–6). The rationale of SYSMIN is to tackle the depletion of mineral resources, although the high demand in the 1960s and the 1970s was in fact dampened by slower economic growth during the 1980s. Africa is very well-endowed with minerals and metals, far more than the Caribbean or the Pacific. The scheme helps mineral producers where earnings fall below production costs and where production is threatened. A trigger threshold was set at 10 per cent with a dependence threshold of 15 per cent (and 10 per cent in the case of the least developed, island and land-locked states). The range of products included iron ore, copper, phosphates, manganese, bauxite, alumina and tin.

Criticisms have been levelled at the restrictive coverage of products and countries covered by the scheme. One modification made under Lomé III was the opening of a second 'window' for ACP countries that derived 20 per cent of their export earnings (12 per cent for the least developed, island and land-locked countries) from a combination of mining products – other than precious minerals, oil and gas, but not necessarily those mentioned specifically in the Convention. This was expected to broaden the number of beneficiaries, since in the first four years of SYSMIN only four countries benefited: Zambia, Zaire, Guyana and Rwanda. The modified scheme was considered likely to benefit ACP states such as Botswana, Niger and Zimbabwe. It was also agreed that SYSMIN funds could be used to tackle problems emanating from adverse developments such as new technology. In addition, SYSMIN ceased to be concerned solely with maintaining productive capacity, and where it was in the interests of the ACP, orderly reductions in capacity could be financed.

The consequences of association with the ACP. ACP countries in association with the EC have naturally derived some economic benefits, although the trading benefits have been less than anticipated. Under both the Yaoundé and the Lomé agreements the associates' share of total EC imports has fallen, and surprisingly they have had a slower rate of export growth to the Community than those from some other developing countries. ACP performance has been disappointing in several respects. Its share in all extra-EC imports fell from 8.1 per cent in 1974 to 5.5 per cent in 1982 (Hewitt 1984; *The Courier* 1986). The ACP share of world trade also fell from 2.5 per cent in 1970 to 1.6 per cent in 1982, excluding Nigeria. Furthermore, the degree of intra-ACP trade has remained low – only about 4 per cent – with a high proportion of this being conducted in regionally integrated blocs such as the Economic Community of West African States (ECOWAS).

The apparent liberalism of the Lomé agreements, with their lack of formal quantitative restrictions, conceals certain weaknesses. For example, most ACP exports – tropical foodstuffs and raw materials – enter the EC duty free in any case. Exports of energy and mineral products come in zero-rated, meaning that many countries, such as Zambia, have benefited very little. For those products where the ACP does enjoy an advantageous margin of preference over other LDCs, this has been reduced by multilateral tariff reductions under GATT, plus other special arrangements such as the Generalized System of Preferences (GSP). The CAP has been mentioned as one obstacle to agricultural exports, while industrially many ACP countries have been unable to benefit significantly because of their low level of industrial development. Furthermore, restrictive rules of origin were imposed under Lomé I, whereby 50 per cent of value-added had to take place within ACP states. This was a high level of added value to set for countries with limited manufacturing industry and which needed to co-operate with other non-Lomé states. The EC has responded by making the rules more flexible where they were found to be inhibiting industrial development. Under Lomé IV, requests can be made for a derogation reducing the ACP value-added to 45 per cent and the EC must respond within 60 working days, otherwise the request will be deemed to have been accepted.

In industries favoured by LDCs, such as textiles, the ACP share of exports by LDCs to the Community has been very low. Furthermore, a few countries, such as Mauritius, have accounted for a high proportion of these exports, having attracted considerable inward investment into the textile industry. The benefits derived by Mauritius eventually led to national safeguards being imposed in the form of VERs by the UK and France. Another country which has been quite successful in developing and diversifying its trade has been the Ivory Coast. Hence the consequences of Lomé depend upon which countries are examined, and to focus on overall ACP performance, dominated by some countries with poor performance such as Ghana, Zaire and Zambia, may result in a misleading conclusion (Stevens ed. 1984, ch. 2).

While ACP trade gains may have been relatively limited, this has not placated other countries which have expressed continuing concern that in the long run their own exports will tend to be displaced from the Community market. Furthermore, some trade diversion has been observed in particular products (Balassa 1975).

However, in many products the ACP preference is ineffective either because the ACP is quite competitive without the preferences or, at the opposite extreme, because even with the benefit of the preferences it still remains insufficiently competitive. The ACP preference has been decisive for about a third of exports, especially products such as palm oil, coffee, cocoa and bananas, in which countries such as Senegal, the Ivory Coast, Kenya and Zimbabwe have raised their competitiveness.

The ACP importance as a supplier to the Community is particularly high for specific products. For example, in 1985 it supplied 83 per cent of EC sugar imports (though only to top up heavily protected EC beet output), but it has been of benefit to countries such as Mauritius, Swaziland, Belize and Fiji. The ACP also supplied 79 per cent of EC cocoa imports, 64 per cent of its aluminium imports, 41 per cent of its coffee imports and 24 per cent of its copper imports.

Outside (non-ACP) countries have considered it vital to try to reach some agreement with the Community to minimize perceived disadvantages and to safeguard their interests. To outsiders the attraction of the large Community market is very clear and there has been a scramble to reach some kind of trading agreement with it.

C   The Generalized System of Preferences (GSP)

Those LDCs not in association with the EC have been eligible under the GSP. Both the EC and the UK introduced a GSP scheme in 1971, though the former scheme was less extensive in coverage. The enlarged Community operates one GSP which gives tariff concessions on industrial and agricultural imports – though the agricultural imports are highly restricted by the CAP. The GSP has offered much less than either Yaoundé or Lomé: it is more restrictive and excludes many of the products which are important to the associates. It has quotas and covers fewer products, with restrictions on products such as textiles. The GSP lacks the binding and permanent nature of Lomé. Although the GSP covers a given time period, the Community can make withdrawals from it at any time without breaching its legal obligations. Where there has been a surge in imports from the successful NICs the Community has introduced safeguards. The EC also applies rules of origin which do not allow cumulation apart from the imports of regional groupings.

The effects of the GSP have generally been very limited (Balassa 1975; Hine 1985). Most LDCs naturally have only a limited base for the production of industrial exports and it is the NICs which have been most successful; the latter, whilst being relatively efficient, are often not the neediest countries. Seven countries – Yugoslavia, Malaysia, Hong Kong, India, South Korea, Brazil and Romania – have been responsible for over half the Community's GSP imports (Hine 1985, p. 210).

China is now covered by the GSP. It has been seeking closer links with the Community to offset the dominance of the superpowers. In 1978 a non-preferential trade agreement was signed with China, followed in 1985 by a trade and co-operation agreement (Redmond 1987).

Part III   The British Commonwealth
When the UK joined the EC in 1973 it was natural that some arrangements would be made to fit the British Commonwealth into a modified association with the Community. What was at issue was whether this was to embrace both the less-developed and the developed countries in the Commonwealth which had enjoyed Imperial Preference. Provisions had been made by the EC largely to suit French overseas interests and the overall outcome has tended to reflect a French view of the outside world; but also West Germany's special interests in trade with the GDR were catered for. The UK successfully negotiated agreements to replace its special links with most less-developed countries and in addition special treatment was provided for New Zealand, despite dissatisfaction of French farmers about imports of New Zealand dairy products. The old dominions, Canada and Australia, though important suppliers of products such as minerals to the EC, have refocused their links in their own region, establishing closer relationships with countries such as the USA and Japan.

Even before the UK entered the Community some less-developed Commonwealth countries had already reached their own agreements with the EC. They had been encouraged to do so in the expectation that the UK would enter the Community. It was paradoxical that in the 1960s some of these LDCs were successful in joining the EC and began to discriminate in favour of the EC and against the UK. Nigeria was the first Commonwealth country to appreciate the benefits of an agreement with the expanding Community market which was importing more than twice as much of its important cocoa exports than the UK. There was recognition of the need to become associated to prevent a displacement of sales by competitors already enjoying association under the Yaoundé Convention.

By 1969 the three East African countries – Tanzania, Uganda and Kenya – had reached agreement with the EC, but their terms were less favourable than those accorded to the Yaoundé associates. They were only able to reach an agreement on trade (not on aid), and in trade they not only had to accept quotas on some of their exports which were in strong competition with the Yaoundé producers but also had to grant even more beneficial reverse preferences to the EC.

The incorporation of 21 Commonwealth countries into the first Lomé Convention helped to bridge Anglo-French divisions which had resulted in a carving up of the African continent. The Commonwealth associates were in many cases more developed than their counterparts and less prepared to accept a subservient position. The UK has helped to turn the Community into a more outward-looking bloc. Prior to UK entry into the Community, imports from LDCs were about a quarter of the UK's total imports, whereas about a fifth of total EC imports came from LDCs. The liberal trading policy of the UK, and support from the USA, moved the Community towards the approach of those two countries of requiring no reverse preferences from associated countries. Although today the UK is still a major importer from LDCs, the growth of its imports from ACP countries has been relatively slow. France has overtaken the UK as the major market for the ACP, while West Germany imports more manufactured goods from the ACP than does the UK (*The Courier* 1986).

Whereas there was no sugar agreement in the Yaoundé Convention – the Congo being the only significant producer until Mauritius joined in 1972 – the Commonwealth sugar agreement with the UK was used as the basis of a new ACP agreement. The Community agreed to buy 1.2 million tonnes from the ACP; this was about 60 per cent of total exports. While the price had to be negotiated between ACP exporters and EC consuming countries, it could not be lower than the price agreed by the Community for its own producers. The guarantees have been helpful, though unfortunately offset by the EC's overproduction of beet sugar and its dumping on the world market which has tended to depress world prices.

One area of the Commonwealth that has suffered is the part in Asia which was deemed ineligible for inclusion in Lomé. It was argued that Bangladesh, India, Malaya, Pakistan, Sri Lanka, Singapore and Hong Kong differed in economic structure and their inclusion in Lomé would dilute the benefits enjoyed by other ACP associates. They are covered instead by the EC's GSP scheme, though this was tighter than the UK's own GSP. Over time, the UK has fallen in line with a less liberal policy towards those countries not covered by the EC's preferential arrangements. Those groups (ACP) for which the UK was able to negotiate special terms have been able to increase their share of trade with the Community; but other LDCs have been squeezed by such preferential agreements and by the primacy accorded to trade with other blocs such as EFTA and the Mediterranean.

10 Enlargement and integration: prospect and retrospect

Part I The new Community

The original Six (West Germany, France, Italy, Belgium, The Netherlands and Luxembourg) reflected many differences; for example, Italy with its particular problems in the Mezzogiorno for which special provisions were necessary. Nevertheless, the Six constituted a much more homogeneous and optimal grouping than the current twelve members of the Community. The first enlargement of the Community in 1973 enhanced its northern bias, bringing in the United Kingdom, Ireland and Denmark. Subsequent enlargement in the 1980s shifted the balance of influence towards Southern Europe after the entry of Greece in 1981 and the accession of Spain and Portugal in 1986. The reunification of Germany in 1990 focused attention eastward.

Why has the Community doubled its membership? It is open to any European country to apply for membership of the EC. Countries outside the Community regard it with awe, seeing it as a much stronger, united and more attractive organization than it often appears once they have gained membership. The EC has generally looked on applications favourably, since its image is strengthened by its new found popularity, and it has been flattered by applications to join. It has become a more powerful actor with an enhanced capacity to exercise its economic and political influence in international affairs. The EC has been greatly strengthened in size and potential power; for example, its population is 339 million and its share of world trade (excluding intra-EC trade) is 21 per cent of exports and 22 per cent of imports.

Unfortunately, enlargement of the EC has also multiplied its problems, making it a less optimal grouping. The addition of more members has aggravated procedural difficulties. A system of majority voting on particular issues will help, encouraged by the Single European Act, though there will be ill-will if countries are outvoted on issues which they perceive to be important. The incorporation of extra members has resulted in new official languages, with the multiplication of interpretation and translation services. The EC now has nine official languages: Danish, Dutch, English, French, German, Greek, Italian, Portuguese and Spanish. Economic disparities have similarly been increased with a lower income per head and wider national and regional variations within an even more agricultural Community.

The countries in Southern Europe have been highly dependent upon the EC, relying upon tourist receipts and migrant remittances to support their low income levels. As full members of an enlarged single market, there are likely to be significant readjustment costs with trade leading to the decline of less-efficient nascent technological sectors in Southern Europe. Whereas in Chapter 3 attention was drawn to the predominance of intra-industry trade, the more significant differences in factor endowments between Northern and Southern Europe are likely to see Southern Europe specializing in more labour-intensive industries. There are also dangers from this inter-industry specialization that the less-competitive countries that have joined the EC will push it towards more protectionism against non-members. To avoid the growth of such protectionism requires enhanced structural funding to cushion the costs of readjustment.

The focus on Southern Europe in the 1980s is likely to be diluted in the 1990s by a switch in emphasis towards Eastern Europe. A reunified Germany will be the hub of the Community, inevitably refocusing it eastwards as investment is redirected to areas with lower wage costs and skilled labour, which are centrally located for European sales. Despite the special trading relationship which has long existed between the two Germanies, a reunified country has major implications for EC policies because of wider regional disparities, adverse environmental problems, the need to cut industrial state subsidies, and the dangers of adding to agricultural overproduction.

Part II   Enlargement and integration

A   Enlargement

Greece. The entry of Greece as the tenth member of the EC in 1981 completed its links with the Community. These had been established twenty years earlier with the signing of the Athens Agreement in 1961 which commenced its association. Greece has encountered both political and economic problems. Politically it moved from a military coup in 1967 back to a democratic civil regime in 1974. Economically, Greece has a larger percentage of its labour force in agriculture than either Portugal or Spain; furthermore, the contribution of agriculture to Greek GNP is much lower than its contribution to total employment. Nevertheless, Greece enjoyed both a food surplus in its trade with the Community and also with the rest of the world (Tsoukalis ed. 1981). Greece submitted a memorandum to the EC in 1982 outlining the problems of the Greek economy and the inadequacy of Community policies; this included the CAP market organization which covered only 75 per cent of Greek agricultural production compared with 95 per cent of agricultural production in other member countries (Nicholson and East 1987, p. 198). Greece has an overdeveloped service sector, whilst its industry manifests serious deficiencies, with some economists referring to its deindustrialization before it has even reached the stage of industrial maturity.

The dissatisfaction of Greece with some aspects of the Community has been alleviated by a positive response to dealing with its problems. Currently there seems little likelihood of any withdrawal by Greece from the EC since its net impact on the Greek economy has generally been positive and it is a net beneficiary from the CAP (Yannopoulos ed. 1986). Greece used its bargaining position to obtain favourable treatment in the Integrated Mediterranean Programmes (IMPs) before agreeing to Iberian enlargement of the EC. Greece has also enjoyed leverage in the Community over its rival, Turkey, and it has taken a hard line because of the occupation by Turkish forces of the northern part of Cyprus.

The coming to power of the New Democracy Party in 1990 led to a switch towards more liberal economic measures, including privatization. Macroeconomic policies continue to strive for a reduction in government debt and inflation to single figures, with attempts to force greater austerity on Greece in return for EC financial help. The objective is to enable the drachma to enter the ERM, probably in 1993 on the wide ±6 per cent margins used by Spain and Britain.

Portugal. Unlike Greece, which enjoyed close links with the EC over many years, Portugal enjoyed a more outward-looking role towards its empire in Africa. Like Britain, it had its back to the continent, facing the open sea. Within Western Europe it retained its close links with the UK by joining EFTA. At that time Portugal lacked a democratic political system. It fared well in EFTA since it had a long timetable for cutting its tariffs on imports, whereas those tariffs against its exports were eliminated more quickly.

Portugal's decision to become a full member of the EC coincided with its more European outlook and the shedding of its colonial empire, even though immense trading opportunities still remain in mineral-rich Angola and Mozambique. The trade agreement between Portugal and the EC in 1973 offered less generous terms than those which had been granted to Greece. With the return to full democracy in Portugal after the departure of Caetano in 1974, public opinion gave wide support to pursuing full membership of the EC – even to a greater extent than in Greece.

Unlike Greece, Portugal is weaker in agriculture but stronger industrially. Portugal has by far the lowest income per head in the Community but has had a good rate of economic growth since joining the EC. It has benefited from its low labour costs, helping industries such as textiles and ship repair and proving attractive to foreign investment – though some of the latter may now be diverted towards Eastern Europe. In 1986 on its entry to the EC, Portugal lost its narrow trade surplus with the Community, and in key sectors such as textiles (which accounts for about a third of Portugal's export earnings) there is strong competition; for example, the granting of a large EC textile quota to Turkey has been unpopular.

Investment priority to industry led to low agricultural investment, and for many years Portugal has been a net importer of food. After 1974 its food imports rose again to help feed the people displaced from the colonies (*retornados*). Agricultural productivity is low and production of wheat per hectare, for example, is only about one-quarter of that in countries such as The Netherlands. The dairy industry is particularly inefficient, with on average only three or four cows per farm. Portugal has benefited significantly from EC Guidance expenditure and has been adapting over a ten-year transition period to lower EC prices such as for cereals, which are 50 per cent lower than in Portugal. To ease the burden the EC has agreed to extend the transition period to 2001 provided that the extra support is given through direct income aids and not through guaranteed prices. Portugal will need continuing massive structural assistance for both agriculture and industry (for example, when the PEDIP expires in the early 1990s). Without financial help Portugal will face continuing economic difficulties in placing the escudo in the ERM.

Portugal also seems likely to suffer in some respects from the opening-up of trade in Iberia with Spain. Historically, their joint trade has been low, and in 1984 only 4.4 per cent of Portugal's exports and 7.2 per cent of its imports were conducted with Spain. For Spain, 2.4 per cent of its exports and 0.7 per cent of its imports were with its Portuguese neighbour. Although Portugal has the advantage of lower wages, few of its companies do much marketing outside Spain or have set up abroad. Meanwhile, Spain benefits from its larger home market and stronger companies, reinforced by an influx of much multinational investment in recent years.

Spain. Spanish membership of the Community was a justified reward for its return to democracy, but Spain probably poses the greatest economic challenge for the EC – certainly since digesting the UK in 1973. Spain under Franco was very much a closed economy, and until 1970 it had not established trading links with either EFTA or the EC. In 1970 it began a trade agreement with the EC which reduced tariffs, but with some exceptions in sensitive products and with a slower pace for dismantling tariffs on the Spanish side.

Full membership of the Community provides new export opportunities for Spain, but also much stiffer import competition, previously contained by higher tariffs. This tariff protection was particularly high in sectors such as the car industry and in 1986 the tariff was cut from 36.5 per cent to 22.5 per cent as a first stage towards its eventual removal. The introduction of EC policies such as VAT and abolition of the former tax rebate, plus weak expertise in marketing, handicap Spain's export potential and is likely to result in a long-term trade deficit. Community exporters such as Germany have taken full advantage of the opening-up of the Spanish market, with Germany replacing the USA as its major supplier. In its first two years of Community membership the Spanish economy grew rapidly with high investment, though the surge of imports resulted in a huge trade deficit. Spain has about a 30 per cent gap in productivity compared with the Community average and also low quality standards. The issue of renegotiation with the EC has already been raised, since its budgetary gains are being outweighed by its massive trade imbalance.

The size of Spanish output in agriculture and fishing and in industry poses problems for the Community. Although agricultural production in Southern Europe is to some extent complementary to that in Northern Europe, there are likely to be some adverse effects, especially in southern France and Italy. An even greater problem is the prospect of generating additional farm surpluses; for example, Spanish olive oil production is almost as large as that in the rest of the Community. The dilemma for the Community has been the extent to which it should extend price support to Southern European products (Leigh and van Praag 1978). Spanish producers possess a worrying capacity to add to overproduction, and its fishing fleet tends to complicate agreements to control overfishing. Industrially, Spain is a major world producer in some staple industries such as steel and shipbuilding in which the EC has already had to introduce policies for restructuring because of overcapacity. Spain will also be a major competitor in other traditional industries such as footwear and textiles.

A united Germany. The German Democratic Republic (GDR) enjoyed a special trading relationship with West Germany, but these intra-German links have now taken on a new significance with reunification in 1990. They have accelerated pressures for faster EC integration to lock Germany rigidly into the Community. Reunification has elevated Germany to an even stronger position as the Community's dominant economic power. West Germany's total exports were already in excess of those of Britain and France combined, but now Germany will be by far the biggest in terms of population size (77.8 million) and labour force (36.5 million). Its total share of EC GDP is around 30 per cent – even though the East German GNP was only about 7 per cent of that in West Germany. Berlin, which was a pawn in the struggle between East and West, is now likely to become a central influence, moving power eastward from London, Paris and Brussels.

Reunification took place swiftly, because the exodus of people which began in August 1989 was weakening the GDR and aggravating problems in the receiving West Germany. Hence reunification after the Berlin Wall was breached in November 1989 occurred more quickly than was really justified by economic conditions. In March 1990 there were free elections in East Germany; monetary union in July; and in September a treaty was signed between the two Germanies and the four wartime allies. By the end of the year, in the first all-Germany postwar elections, Helmut Kohl was re-elected Chancellor.

EC integration is not unfamiliar with the problems which arise for a weaker economy when it is linked to a highly developed economy. However, in the case of German economic and monetary union (GEMU) from 1 July 1990, this has involved not only the joining together of a weak eastern economy to a strong western economy, but also a switch from a centrally planned system; that is, it is a capitalist takeover by the West. Furthermore, monetary union has preceded economic convergence, with a common monetary system based on the D-mark (which has replaced the Ost-mark) in the east of the country. The Bundesbank was overruled and accepted somewhat reluctantly a generous exchange rate conversion between Ost-marks and D-marks. For adults, this was a one-to-one conversion rate up to 4000 Ost-marks, with the rest at two-to-one. For children, the one-to-one limit was 2000 Ost-marks and for pensioners, 6000 Ost-marks. In terms of demand and supply analysis, immediate problems arose from excess monetary demand and inadequate supply of goods in the east because of the lack of competitiveness and the collapse of many firms. Other sources of inflation have arisen from the removal of subsidies on basic goods in the east and pressure for higher wages, partly to compensate for higher food prices, but also in comparability claims with workers in the west of Germany. Eastern Germany has found that having the D-mark is illusory wealth, since an already feeble economy has become even more uncompetitive through higher costs. By 1994 wages in the two Germanies are likely to be fully equalized, but productivity gaps will remain into the next century. Hence unemployment has soared and by 1991 nearly one-third of the workforce in the east was either unemployed or on short time.

There are some potential advantages for firms from locations in eastern Germany, such as relatively low labour costs. In the motor industry Volkswagen, Opel and Mercedes-Benz have all announced plans to produce cars in the east. However, unfortunately there is a lag between the opening of new plants, such as the Opel plant in Eisenach, and contraction of existing plants such as Wartburg, creating heavy unemployment. Furthermore, basic infrastructure deficiencies and legal problems over ownership of capital have led many businesses, especially the smaller ones in western Germany, to take the less risky option of supplying their highly demanded goods directly from the west. The outdated and polluting chemical and power-generating industries face decimation because of their conflict with environmental standards. GNP in eastern Germany fell into decline by about 10 per cent in 1990, with a further 5 per cent fall likely in 1991.

West Germany has taken over an economy with some useful assets, particularly in the longer term. However, hopes that a fifth of East German industry could be competitive were too optimistic and even some of the stronger sectors have had to be slimmed down radically. Also, East Germany has a similar type of industrial economy to West Germany, with the east being weaker technologically; for example, the machine tool industry is also strong in eastern Germany but has lacked the modern electronic controls on the machines incorporated by the more advanced western producers. The Treuhandanstalt is disposing of industry in eastern Germany, privatizing firms often at 'knock-down' prices, mainly to West German companies.

The immediate needs in the east are for both increased investment and social transfers to cushion the unemployment and social discontent. This expenditure will constitute a drain on the German budget deficit (likely to exceed D-mark 150 billion in 1991). Furthermore, if the Treuhandanstalt were to change its priority from closing inefficient companies to restructuring them, this would require some D-mark 400 billion during the 1990s decade. Increased expenditure is likely to raise the overall rate of German inflation slightly. Dampening inflationary tendencies will place pressure on interest rates to rise. Also, the huge West German capital surplus is likely to be reorientated towards eastern Germany, driving up interest rates world-wide.

B   Differentiated and flexible integration

Enlargement is likely to accelerate the more pragmatic and flexible approach to integration. However, a range of basic common policies have formed the building blocks of the Community. Countries have to conform to the Treaties and to the ongoing legislation from Community institutions. The basic foundations of the EC, such as the principle of non-discrimination against its members, have to be respected and countries cannot reimpose trading barriers against other members of the Community. Unless these principles are applied, the EC cannot operate effectively and will be undermined. Nevertheless, a pursuit of excessive common standardization and an attempt to impose uniformity for its own sake is undesirable and certainly less practicable for a Community of twelve different countries. The Community has acknowledged this, using various instruments such as gradual and phased directives, plus some derogations, and some national discretion in how measures are to be applied (Wallace 1985).

Some differentiation in approach has also existed in other organizations, such as French and Spanish arrangements in NATO. The crucial issue, however, is how much flexibility is possible and whether it can be provided without creating so many exceptions and special cases that ultimately it distorts and discredits the whole organization. In the new Community the less standard and more diverse pattern of integration which has had to emerge is likely to be reinforced in the future. The first enlargement of the EC in 1973 created a situation of differential treatment by the transition phases of adjustment. It is no coincidence that this first enlargement resulted in greater discussion about a two-speed Europe which was suggested by W. Brandt in West Germany in 1974; this was followed by the Tindemans Report in 1976 in which there were further proposals for differentiated development. In a two-speed Europe at least there is an obligation on those countries which are forging ahead faster to help the weaker countries, for example, by greater regional assistance.

There is little doubt that since enlargement the EC has shown a tendency to split into at least two tiers. There is not only a reluctance to support weaker countries sufficiently, but also doubts about whether such fiscal transfers would actually produce long-run convergence. The pattern that is inevitably emerging is one in which some countries, usually the original Six, are better able to push forward with policies in new areas. The two countries, France and Germany, which have taken most initiatives have provided the momentum in fields such as the EMS, though the Bundesbank since German reunification has become conscious of the costs imposed on the real economy for weaker areas. Countries not participating in new initiatives are free to join and encouraged to take up the option when conditions become more propitious for them. The Schengen Treaty which was signed in 1985 by France, West Germany and Benelux was another example of the more progressive countries pressing on ahead to abolish frontier controls from 1 January 1990. The two-tier approach may even prove to be the most practical way of progressing in other fields, such as that of removing tax barriers; otherwise the deadline of 1992 will be difficult to achieve. Tax rates and yields on VAT and excise duties have been much wider in the UK, Denmark and Ireland than in the original Six.

The Community is likely to be confined to core policies, though there is no consensus over what they should be; for example, R. Dahrendorf's list in a Europe *à la carte* included foreign policy, trade, monetary policy and overseas development. France approved a variable-geometry Community in the 1970s, particularly in industrial and technological policy. The *'acquis communautaire'* applies to core policies, but in other areas countries may choose whether to participate or not. Even some non-members of the EC have participated in the EUREKA project and projects of nuclear fusion, such as the Joint European Torus (JET).

The new Community of twelve cannot be optimal for all activities. It has striven hard to obtain basic agreement in key areas and indeed it is surprising in some respects that the Community has been able to make as much progress as it has, given the differences and at times the unco-operativeness of new members. A much looser pattern of integration seems inevitable in the future and the UK may look back wistfully on why it could not attain flexibility to a greater extent in the first place in sectors such as agriculture. A more variegated pattern of integration enables the more dynamic countries to press on ahead, acting as catalysts to new policy areas and providing a way of breaking the soul-destroying deadlock and paralysis of the EC (Langeheine and Weinstock 1985). Perhaps the SEA, with more use of majority voting, will help to overcome a damaging split of the Community into two groups.

C The EC: prospect and retrospect

Integration in the EC has been a major contributor in restoring postwar prosperity after two disastrous world wars. Nations were prepared to surrender some degree of power to supranational institutions, though hopes for a federal Europe have been dashed by the continued dominance of the Council of Ministers in the Community's decision-making process. Progress towards rendering the EC's decision-making more democratic has been painfully slow – 27 years elapsed before provisions for direct elections to the European Parliament finally materialized in 1979. Since then the EP has gradually sought an accretion of its powers, and these, such as the co-operation procedure, have been manifested in the Single European Act.

The economic benefits from the customs union and the growing intra-trade are likely to be enhanced further with the completion of the internal market by 1992. Unfortunately, the CAP, which is a cornerstone of the Community and its most fully developed policy, has faced continuing problems. Economic events have changed greatly since its inception as worries over food shortages have been replaced by massive surpluses. These have arisen as a result of inexorable technical progress and over-generous price-support policies. They have had increasingly adverse effects on the pattern of agricultural trade with the rest of the world. Agricultural reforms have tended to be piecemeal and belated, always falling short of really fundamental changes in policy. Prospects for successful reform are limited, with West Germany holding the Presidency of the Council in 1988 and being expected to solve some of the agricultural problems for which it was partly responsible. The CAP has swallowed up the finance which could have been used far more effectively in other ways, such as much-needed support to expand high-technology industry to keep pace with the USA and Japan. The Budget is dominated by agriculture, with spending tending to outgrow revenue, and even by 1992 agriculture is still expected to account for half of budgetary expenditure. Despite attempts to reorientate the Budget towards industrial and regional policies, spending on these is still small compared with national expenditure, and regional policy still bears a marked agricultural imprint.

Progress in the Community has been gradual and largely incremental, running into periodic crises. Proposals for a great leap forward towards a major transformation, such as that towards EMU in the 1970s, failed, partly as a result of the oil crisis and a move to floating exchange rates. But in 1979 a new initiative led to the EMS which operated more flexibly during the 1980s. The success of the ERM reactivated the elusive goal of full EMU. However, enlargement of the Community has held back progress as new members have become preoccupied with their own particular problems, and Greece and Portugal have lagged behind. Nevertheless, while any annual appraisal of progress might indicate that this has occurred at a snail's pace and at time the Community has had to back-pedal, when one cumulates the developments retrospectively over a period of 30 years it indicates a massive step forward. On its thirtieth anniversary on 25 March 1987, the EC could look back on the outcome of its complex bargaining. It is a Community enlarged from six to twelve members which has manifested not only its durability but also its attractiveness to other countries. In addition, countries outside have recognized the EC as the world's economic trading giant and have clamoured to reach some kind of trading arrangement with it.

Any temporary loss of momentum towards integration is inevitable at times, and especially after the early idealism and the dynamism of super-economic growth of the 1960s. The most recent attempt to restore a new sense of direction to the Community has been provided by the Single European Act which came into force in 1987. This is much less ambitious than many supporters of European union had hoped for, and in some respects is the lowest common denominator which could be agreed by the Twelve. Even so, it represents a recommitment to real completion of the internal market; to co-operation in economic and monetary policy; economic and social cohesion; research and technological development; the environment; and greater political co-operation, leading towards a common foreign policy. It became necessary to refocus the Community's activities, since some new policies had begun to operate outside the Community's framework, with also a trend towards inter-governmental integration. A greater use of majority voting became a prime requirement if the enlarged Community were to work more effectively and not become almost paralysed in its decision-making. Majority voting has been introduced in areas which are important in revitalizing the EC, such as the internal market. The fact that a vote can be taken is likely to encourage compromise, though there are still many areas where unanimity is necessary. While the co-operation procedure with Parliament injects greater democracy into the Community, this may tend to prolong decision-making.

There is little doubt that the internal market will become the prime focus of economic interest and activity over the next few years since it has given the EC a new lease of life. Glittering economic prospects for 1992 have been painted from the realization of a single domestic market in the European Community (Pelkmans and Winters 1988; Cecchini 1988). For example, potential microeconomic gains in welfare of some ECU 216 billion have been estimated for the EC(12) equal to some 5.3 per cent of GDP. A virtuous circle of benefits is expected, especially in the long term, from industrial reorganization, the reaping of economies of scale and through greater innovation. At a macroeconomic level the benefits accruing from the successful completion of a single market are likely to help the EC to attain a better trade-off between conflicting policy objectives. The rate of inflation can be lowered (an average of 6.1 per cent); economic growth can be raised (on average by 4.5 per cent), leading to the creation of new employment opportunities (some 1.8 million jobs). The constraints provided by both budgetary and balance-of-payments deficits will be loosened. Although in the short run some job change and displacement will occur, in the medium and long term the employment gain could be enormous (some 5 million new jobs, if accompanied by reflationary policies) (Cecchini 1988). However, it must be borne in mind that the realization of these optimistic gains is not automatic but depends upon the validity of the necessary underlying assumptions. Outside countries will also wish to share in these benefits, adopting new trading and investment strategies.

The EC is aware that it needs to confine itself to those areas where it can demonstrate clear superiority of competence and performance over nation states. The principle of subsidiarity needs to be enshrined to determine their different levels of activity. In moving forward into new areas the Community cannot assume or take for granted that all the problems have been solved in existing areas of integration. In addition, the enlarged Community is likely to experience greater internal problems since it now comprises a much less optimal grouping in its membership; for example, doubts remain about whether sufficient structural funding will be forthcoming for the weakest Southern European economies to enable them to participate fully in EMU. It would appear that only a looser pattern of integration is compatible and suitable for the new Community in the future, particularly if it is to see continuing enlargement, such as that incorporating additional membership by some countries in Eastern Europe.

Part III   Integration and the UK

Each chapter has tried to present the story of the unfolding links between the EC and the UK. The latter in joining the EC in 1973 had to adjust to an organization which it had not initiated itself and which was not the one most suited to displaying its strengths. Meanwhile, politically the UK has been reluctant to embrace further rapid progress towards a more supranational Community. The concern with agriculture in the EC seems singularly inappropriate for the UK with such a small agricultural sector, and the budgetary consequences largely accruing from this have resulted in the UK being a net contributor. By the time the UK joined, its industrial competitiveness had diminished and the pace of EC economic growth had started to slacken. Nevertheless, the UK has continued to seek industrial gains; it has become a favoured location for inward investment; and it is also trying to exploit its comparative advantage in the tertiary sector of the economy, such as financial services. This partly explains why the UK has become a major proponent of opening up the internal market.

If the UK is to take full advantage of the internal market, steps will have to be taken to improve its competitiveness further, after years of underinvestment in capital and the skills of employees. In terms of better communications, the Channel Tunnel may make a marginal improvement to the competitiveness of UK exports on the continent. It is yet another indication of how the UK is being brought ever closer to continental Europe. Economically, the EC has offered only potential opportunities for business from a larger market, with no guarantee of economic success. Without major efforts to keep up with the implications of the internal market, British business will continue to lag behind its major European competitors.

There has not been much evidence of major economic benefits to the UK and if it has become more '*communautaire*' this is partly relative to the situation of some other new members, for example, Greece and Denmark, which refused initially to sign the Single European Act, though later relented after the Danish referendum. Use of a referendum in Denmark, and also in the UK in 1975, has proved a significant supportive element in confirming membership of the Community. After the Fontainebleau Summit in 1984 the UK enjoyed a better phase in its relationship with the Community, taking advantage of its Presidency of the Council of Ministers in 1986 to provide a new direction. It is attuned to specific liberal developments such as the internal market. But essentially, apart from this, the UK has mainly been in the position of responding defensively and minimally to many new developments. In the early years especially it failed to recognize that progress could best be made through the traditional interlinking of issues, making it an 'awkward partner' (George 1990). However, in the mid-1980s the UK recognized that it had to take more initiatives and that unless it became more accommodating to the pace of integration there was the danger of others pressing on ahead, Britain thereby losing influence on events. A basic stumbling block between the EC and the Thatcher government arose over interventionist policies; for example, the CAP, the EMS and the Social Charter. Any future Labour government might encounter different problems, finding more difficulties with Community integration in areas such as the internal market but being more approving of interventionist policies in fields such as social policy.

The case of the EMS has been illuminating, with the UK initially missing the natural linkage between the EMS and enhanced regional funding, which it could have obtained when the EMS was first set up. The belated decision to enter the first stage of the ERM in 1990 partly represented a wish to avoid its isolation and inability to influence other stages of monetary development about which the UK still has major reservations. Hence it is still seen as dragging its feet over a common European currency and a single central bank.

Mrs Thatcher's vision of Europe as reflected by her speech at Bruges in 1988 was based upon the limited co-operation of independent states, being opposed to any federal and bureaucratic European superstate. The UK still prefers to see a widening of EC membership, including further EFTA countries and countries from Eastern Europe, perhaps favouring this in order to delay and dilute the deepening process of integration. However, in practice it could accelerate particular developments such as greater majority voting to ensure that a larger Community is workable. Certainly the division between majority voting on the internal market and the need for unanimity in other areas such as social policy appears arbitrary. Perhaps with the removal of Mrs Thatcher the conflictual British policy style will be modified on various issues, such as social policy, though Euro-pessimists doubt whether there will be a significant change in the substance of British policy overall.

The UK's relative GDP per head continued to deteriorate in the EC(9), though economically there was a relative improvement in the UK's performance during the 1980s in the EC(12). This is partly a reflection of a long-overdue improvement in UK economic performance, but is mainly a consequence of the lower GDP per head of the three new Mediterranean entrants: Greece, Spain and Portugal. Given that the UK in the past tended to consider itself a special case, meriting distinctive budgetary treatment, it has in retrospect provided an unfortunate precedent. The new Mediterranean entrants have even greater special needs, and meeting these is likely to result in further problems in constraining agricultural and budgetary expenditure, while redirecting regional finance from declining industrial areas to underdeveloped Mediterranean areas. For example, Spain is now the leading recipient from the ERDF.

Enlargement tipped the balance of Community influence towards the problems of Southern Europe in the 1980s and is likely to result in additional difficulties for the UK. Although UK farmers are not directly affected by Mediterranean-type agricultural competition as are farmers in the south of France and Italy, the financial implications of integrating Southern Europe are enormous. The undoubted gains lie in expanding UK industrial exports to Southern Europe, and the British Overseas Trade Board has pinpointed several areas of potential growth. Nevertheless, industrial competitors such as West Germany appear better placed to take advantage of these new export opportunities, if past UK performance is any guide. Much hinges on a positive business response and there is some evidence of considerable British investment in traditional markets, such as Portugal. Furthermore, existing companies have started to develop new strategies; for example, Unilever has decided to close its labour-intensive soap-making operations in Spain and to produce in Portugal where labour costs are lower, and to concentrate its more capital-intensive scouring-powder production in Spain. Some investment is also being displaced from Southern Europe towards Eastern Europe, and whilst the UK is not in the forefront of this, there have been examples of a British push into Eastern Europe; for instance, GKN has purchased the motor components-maker Gelenkwellenwerk Mosel (GWM) in eastern Germany to take advantage of the growing investment and projected growth in car output in Eastern Europe in the 1990s.

The British economy seems destined to continue with high unemployment and major regional imbalance, since any British attachment to the exchange rate mechanism of the EMS is likely to necessitate high unemployment to dampen the inflation-prone tendencies of the British economy towards the lower level of West Germany. The UK economy also faces stiff intra-EC competition which will grow more intense in the single internal market, and which is likely to exacerbate regional imbalance. There is strong extra-competitiveness in down-market products from the NICs and any incapacity to compete effectively by member states such as the UK could result in an even more protectionist policy by the

Community towards outside countries. So far the EC has not proved as inward-looking as many feared, and recently it has turned down some of the adverse reciprocity measures of the single market. However, it would be unfortunate if progress towards an internal market were maintained only at the expense of externalizing its problems, leading to some disintegration in the Community's trading relationship with the rest of the world.

Bibliography

Ackermann, C. and Harrop, J. (1985) 'The Management of Technological Innovation in the Machine Tool Industry: A Cross-National
Regional Survey of Britain and Switzerland', *R and D Management*, Vol. 15, No. 3, July.

Albert, M. and Ball, R. J. (1983) *Towards European Economic
Recovery in the 1980s*, Report for the European Parliament, Brussels.

Aldcroft, D. H. (1978) *The European Economy, 1914–1970*, London,
Croom Helm.

Allen, H. (1979) *Norway and Europe in the 1970s*, London, Global
Book Resources.

Arbuthnott, H. and Edwards, G. (1979) *A Common Man's Guide to
the Common Market*, London, Macmillan.

Ardagh, J. (1982) *France in the 1980s*, Harmondsworth, Penguin.

Armstrong, H. W. (1983) 'The Assignment of Regional Policy
Powers within the EC', in A.M. El-Agraa (ed.), *Britain within the
European Community: The Way Forward*, London, Macmillan.

Armstrong, H. and Taylor, J. (1986) 'An Evaluation of Current
Regional Policy', *Economic Review*, Vol. 4, No. 2, November.

Armstrong, H. and Taylor, J. (1987) *The Way Forward*, London,
Employment Institute.

Balassa, B. (1967) 'Trade Creation and Trade Diversion in the
European Common Market', *Economic Journal*, Vol. 77.

Balassa, B. (1975) *European Economic Integration*, Amsterdam,
North-Holland.

Barber, J. and Reed, B. (eds) (1973) *European Community: Vision
and,Reality*, London, Croom Helm.

Barclays Bank (1985) 'Comecon', *Barclays Bank Review*, August.

Bayliss, B. T. (1985) 'Competition and Industrial Policy', in A. M.
El-Agraa (ed.), *The Economics of the European Community*,
Oxford, Philip Allan.

Blackwell, M. (1985) 'Lomé III: The Search for Greater Effectiveness', *Finance and Development*, Vol. 22, No. 3, September.

Booz Allen and Hamilton Inc. (1986) *Europe's Fragmented Markets:*

A Survey of European Chief Executives, The Wall Street Journal/ Europe.

Bourguignon-Wittke, R., Grabitz, E., Schmuck, O., Steppat, S. and Wessels, W. (1985) 'Five Years of the Directly Elected European Parliament: Performance and Prospects', *Journal of Common Market Studies*, Vol. XXIV, No. 1, September.

Bracewell-Milnes, B. (1976) *Economic Integration in East and West*, London, Croom Helm.

Brewin, C. and McAllister, R. (1986) 'Annual Review of the Activities of the European Communities in 1986', *Journal of Common Market Studies*, Vol. XXV, No. 4, June.

Brown, A. J. (1985) 'The General Budget', in A. M. El-Agraa (ed.), *The Economics of the European Community*, Oxford, Philip Allan.

Buckwell, A., Harvey, D., Thomson, K. and Parton, K. (1982) *The Costs of the Common Agricultural Policy*, London, Croom Helm.

Budd, S. A. (1987) *The EEC: A Guide to the Maze*, London, Kogan Page.

Butler, M. (1986) *Europe: More than a Continent*, London, Heinemann.

Butt Philip, A. (1983) 'Industrial and Competition Policies: A New Look', in A. M. El-Agraa, *Britain within the European Community*, London, Macmillan.

Cairncross, A., *et al.* (eds) (1974) *Economic Policy for the European Community: The Way Forward*, London, Macmillan.

Capstick, M. (1970) *The Economics of Agriculture*, London, Allen & Unwin.

Castles, S. and Kosack, G. (1973) *Immigrant Workers and Class Structure in Western Europe*, London, Oxford University Press.

Cecchini, P. (1988) *The European Challenge, 1992*, Aldershot, Wildwood House, Gower.

Central Statistical Office (1987) *United Kingdom Balance of Payments*, (Pink Book), London, HMSO.

Chalkley, M. (1986) 'Selling Mountains and Lakes', *Economic Review*, Vol. 4, No. 2, November.

Coffey, P. (1975) 'The Lomé Agreement and the EEC: Implications and Problems', *Three Banks Review*, No. 108, December.

Coffey, P. (1976) *The External Relations of the EEC*, London, Macmillan.

Coffey, P. (1977) *Europe and Money*, London, Macmillan.

Coffey, P. (1979) *Economic Policies of the Common Market*, London, Macmillan.

Coffey, P. (ed.) (1983) *Main Economic Policy Areas of the EEC*, The Hague, Martinus Nijhoff.

Coffey, P. and Presley, J. (1971) *European Monetary Integration*, London, Macmillan.

Cohen, C. D. (ed.) (1983) *The Common Market – Ten Years After*, Oxford, Philip Allan.

Collins, C. D. E. (1985) 'Social Policy', in A. M. El-Agraa, *The Economics of the European Community*, Oxford, Philip Allan.

Commission of the European Communities (1984) *Working for Europe*, Luxembourg.

Commission of the European Communities (1986a) *The Agricultural Situation in the Community*, Brussels.

Commission of the European Communities (1986b) *Single European Act*, Brussels.

Commission of the European Communities (1987a) *Bulletin*, Vol. 20, Nos 1, 2 and 3, Brussels.

Commission of the European Communities (1987b) *Twentieth General Report on the Activities of the European Communities (1986)*, Brussels/Luxembourg.

Commission of the European Communities (1987c) *Twelfth Annual Report of the Regional Development Fund for 1986*; also earlier Reports.

Commission of the European Communities (1987d) *Report by the Commission to the Council and Parliament on the Financing of the Budget*, COM(87) 101 Final 1/2, Brussels.

Commission of the European Communities (1987e) *Commission Communication on Budgetary Discipline*, COM(87) 430 Final, Brussels.

Commission of the European Communities (1987f) *Reform of the Structural Funds*, COM(87) 376 Final, Brussels.

Commission of the European Communities (1987g) *Making a Success of the Single Act*, February, Brussels.

Commission of the European Communities (1987h) *A New Frontier for Europe*, COM(87) 100 Final, Brussels.

Commission of the European Communities (1987i) *Own Resources Decision*, COM(87) 420 Final, Brussels.

Commission of the European Communities (1987j) *Review of Action*

Taken to Control the Agricultural Markets and Outlook for the Agricultural Policy, COM(87) 410 Final, Brussels.

Commission of the European Communities (1987k) *Research and Technological Development in the Less Favoured Regions of the Community, (STRIDE)*, Final Report, Brussels.

Commission of the European Communities (1988) Research on the *Cost of Non-Europe*, Brussels, 16 volumes.

Commission of the European Communities (1990) *EC Research Funding*, 2nd edn, Brussels.

Coombes, D. (1970) *Politics and Bureaucracy in the European Community*, London, Allen & Unwin.

Cooper, C. A. and Massel, B. F. (1965) 'A New Look at Customs Union Theory', *Economic Journal*, Vol. 75.

Cosgrove, C. A. (1969) 'The EEC and Developing Countries', in G. R. Denton (ed.), *Economic Integration in Europe*, London, Weidenfeld & Nicolson.

Cosgrove-Twitchett, C. (1981) *A Framework for Development?: The EEC and the ACP*, London, Allen & Unwin.

The Courier (1986) No. 98, July–August.

Daltrop, A. (1982) *Politics and the European Community*, London, Longman.

Dearden, S. (1986) 'EEC Membership and the United Kingdom's Trade in Manufactured Goods', *National Westminster Bank Quarterly Review*, February.

Dennis, G. (1985) 'The European Monetary System', in A. M. El-Agraa (ed.), *The Economics of the European Community*, Oxford, Philip Allan.

Denton, G. (ed.) (1969) *Economic Integration in Europe*, London, Weidenfeld & Nicolson.

Denton, G. (ed.) (1974) *Economic and Monetary Union in Europe*, London, Croom Helm.

Denton, G. (1984) 'Restructuring the European Community Budget', *Journal of Common Market Studies*, Vol. XXIII, No. 2, December.

Denton, G., Forsyth, M. and Maclennan, M. (1968) *Economic Planning and Policies in Britain, France and Germany*, London, Allen & Unwin.

Department of Industry (1981) *An Investigation into the Woollen and Worsted Sector of the Textile and Garment Making Industries in the United Kingdom France, Germany and Italy*, London.

Dinkelspiel, U. (1987) 'Eureka: Co-operation in High Technology', *EFTA Bulletin*, Vol. XXVIII, No. 1, January–March.

Dosser, D., Gowland, D. and Hartley, K. (eds) (1982) *The Collaboration of Nations*, Oxford, Martin Robertson.

Drewnowski, J. (ed.) (1982) *Crisis in the Eastern European Economy*, London, Croom Helm.

Duchêne, F., Szczepanik, E. and Legg, W. (1985) *New Limits on Agriculture*, London, Croom Helm.

The *Economist*, various issues.

Einzig, P. (1971) *The Case against Joining the Common Market*, London, Macmillan.

El-Agraa, A. M. (ed.) (1983) *Britain within the European Community: The Way Forward*, London, Macmillan.

El-Agraa, A. M. (ed.) (1985) *The Economics of the European Community*, Oxford, Philip Allan.

The European (1987) Vol. 1, No. 3, May–June, and No. 5, September–October.

European Documentation, (1986) *The European Community's Budget*, Luxembourg.

European Economy (1988 and 1990) Nos 34, 35 and 49, Luxembourg.

European Investment Bank (1989 and 1990) *Annual Report*, Luxembourg.

European Parliament (1978) *Powers of the European Parliament*, London.

Eurostat (1986) *ACP, Basic Statistics*, Commission, Brussels.

Eurostat (1990) *Basic Statistics of the Community*, Commission, Brussels.

Evans, D. (ed.) (1973) *Britain in the EC*, London, Gollancz.

Fennell, R. (1979 and 1988) *The Common Agricultural Policy of the Community*, London, Granada.

Fennell, R. (1985) 'A Re-consideration of the Objectives of the Common Agricultural Policy', *Journal of Common Market Studies*, Vol. XXIII, No. 3, March.

Financial Times, various issues.

Foley, P. (1990) 'UK Open for Business', *Lloyds Bank Economic Bulletin*, No. 138, June.

George, K. D. and Joll, C. (1975) *Competition Policy in the United Kingdom and the European Economic Community*, Cambridge University Press.

George, K. D. and Joll, C. (1978) 'EEC Competition Policy', *Three Banks Review*, March.

George, K. D. and Ward, T. S. (1975) *The Structure of Industry in the EEC*, Cambridge Occasional Paper.

George, S. (1985) *Politics and Policy in the European Community*, Oxford, Clarendon Press.

George, S. (1987) *The British Government and the European Community since 1984*, University Association for Contemporary European Studies, No. 4.

George, S. (1990) *An Awkward Partner*, Oxford University Press.

Greenaway, D. (1987) 'Intra-Industry Trade, Intra-Firm Trade and European Integration', *Journal of Common Market Studies*, Vol. XXVI, No. 2, December.

Groeben, H. von der (1985) *The European Community: The Formative Years*, Commission, Brussels/Luxembourg.

Grubel, H. G. and Lloyd, P. J. (1975) *Intra-industry trade: the theory and measurement of international trade in differentiated products*, London, Macmillan.

Han, S. S. and Liesner, H. H. (1971) *Britain and the Common Market*, Cambridge Occasional Paper, No. 27.

Harrop, J. (1973) 'The Rise and Fall of EFTA', *Bankers' Magazine*, March.

Harrop, J. (1978a) 'Convergence in Europe', in R. D. Wilson (ed.), *Workbook on Testing Ten Economies*, Sutton, Economics Association.

Harrop, J. (1978b) 'The European Investment Bank', *National Westminster Bank Quarterly Review*, May.

Harrop, J. (1978c) 'An Evaluation of the European Investment Bank', *23A Société Universitaire Européenne de Recherches Financières*, Tilburg, Netherlands.

Harrop, J. (1985) 'Crisis in the Machine Tool Industry: A Policy Dilemma for the European Community', *Journal of Common Market Studies*, Vol. XXIV, No. 1, September.

Hartley, K. (1982) 'Defence and Advanced Technology', in D. Dosser, D. Gowland and K. Hartley (eds), *The Collaboration of Nations*, Oxford, Martin Robertson.

Hay, R. (1989) *The European Commission and the Administration of the Community*, Office for Official Publications of the European Communities, Luxembourg.

Healey, N. M. (1988) 'The Case for Britain Joining the EMS', *Economic Affairs*, February–March.

Heertje, A. (ed.) (1983) *Investing in Europe's Future*, Oxford, Basil Blackwell.

Heller, R. and Willat, N. (1975) *The European Revenge: How the American Challenge was Rebuffed*, London, Barrie & Jenkins.

Henderson, P. D. (1977) 'Two British Errors: Their Probable Size and Some Possible Lessons', *Oxford Economic Papers*, No. 2, July.

Henig, S. (1980) *Power and Decision in Europe*, London, Europotentials Press.

Heseltine, M. (1989) *The Challenge of Europe – Can Britain Win?*, Weidenfeld & Nicolson, London.

Hewitt, A. (1984) 'The Lomé Conventions: Entering a Second Decade', *Journal of Common Market Studies*, Vol. XXIII, No. 2, December.

Hewstone, M. (1986) *Understanding Attitudes to the European Community*, Cambridge University Press.

Hill, B. E. (1984) *The Common Agricultural Policy: Past, Present and Future*, London, Methuen.

Hine, R. C. (1985) *The Political Economy of European Trade*, Brighton, Wheatsheaf.

Hodges, M. (ed.) (1972) *European Integration*, Harmondsworth, Penguin.

Hoffman, G. (ed.) (1983) *A Geography of Europe*, 5th edn, New York, John Wiley.

Holland, S. (1976a) *Capital versus the Regions*, London, Macmillan.

Holland, S. (1976b) *The Regional Problem*, London, Macmillan.

Holland, S. (1980) *Uncommon Market: Capital, Class and Power in the European Community*, London, Macmillan.

Holland, S. (ed.) (1972) *The State as Entrepreneur*, London, Weidenfeld & Nicolson.

Holmes, P. (1983) 'The EEC and British Trade', in C. D. Cohen (ed.), *The Common Market: Ten Years After*, Oxford, Philip Allan.

Holt, S. (1967) *The Common Market*, London, Hamish Hamilton.

House of Commons (1971) White Paper: *The United Kingdom and the European Communities*, Cmnd 4715, London, HMSO.

House of Commons (1978) Green Paper: *The European Monetary System*, Cmnd 7405, November, London, HMSO.

House of Lords (1983) Select Committee on the European Communities, *European Monetary System*, Fifth Report.

House of Lords (1984) Select Committee on the European Communities, *The Common Fisheries Policy*, December.

House of Lords (1985) Select Committee on the European Communities, *The 1985 Farm Price Proposals: Agricultural Price Review*, 2 vols, March.

House of Lords (1986) Select Committee on the European Communities, *Socio-Structural Policy in Agriculture*, July.

Hu, Yao-Su (1981) *Europe Under Stress*, London, Butterworths.

Ionescu, G. (ed.) (1979) *The European Alternatives*, The Netherlands, Sijthoff and Noordhoff.

Jacquemin, A. P. (1974) 'Size, Structure and Performance of the Largest European Firms', *Three Banks Review*, June.

Jacquemin, A. P. and de Jong, H. W. (1977) *European Industrial Organisation*, London, Macmillan.

Jay, D. (1968) *After the Common Market*, Harmondsworth, Penguin.

Jenkins, R. (1978) 'European Monetary Union', *Lloyds Bank Review*, January.

Jenkins, R. (ed.) (1983) *Britain and the EEC*, London, Macmillan.

Johnson, C. (1982) 'The Fall in Farm Prices', *Lloyds Bank Economic Bulletin*, No. 41, May.

Johnson, C. (1987) 'How Well Are We Doing?', *Lloyds Bank Economic Bulletin*, No. 100, April.

Johnson, H. G. (1973) 'An Economic Theory of Protectionism, Tariff Bargaining and the Formation of Customs Unions', in M. B. Krauss (ed.), *The Economics of Integration*, London, Allen & Unwin.

Jones, A. J. (1979) 'The Theory of Economic Integration', in J. K. Bowers (ed.), *Inflation, Development and Integration: Essays in Honour of A. J. Brown*, Leeds University Press.

Jones, A. J. (1985) 'The Theory of Economic Integration', in A. M. El-Agraa (ed.), *The Economics of the European Community*, Oxford, Philip Allan.

Josling, T. (1984) 'US and EC Farm Policies: An Eclectic Comparison', in K. J. Thomson and R. M. Warren (eds), *Price and Market Policies in European Agriculture*, Dept. of Agricultural Economics, University of Newcastle-upon-Tyne.

Josling, T. (1986) 'Agricultural Policies and World Trade', in L.

Tsoukalis (ed.), *Europe, America and the World Economy*, Oxford, Basil Blackwell for the College of Europe.

Josling, T. and Harris, J. (1976) 'Europe's Green Money', *Three Banks Review*, March.

Kaldor, N. (1971) 'The Truth about the Dynamic Effects', *New Statesman*, 12 March.

Kangaroo News, various issues.

Keating, M. and Jones, B. (1985) *Regions in the Community*, Oxford, Clarendon Press.

Kenen, P. B. (1969) 'The Theory of Optimum Currency Areas: An Eclectic View', in R. A. Mundell and A. K. Swoboda (eds), *Monetary Problems of the International Economy*, Chicago University Press.

Klassen, L. H. and Molle, W. T. (1983) *Industrial Mobility and Migration in the European Community*, Aldershot, Gower.

Krauss, M. B. (ed.) (1972) *The Economics of Integration*, London, Allen & Unwin.

Kreinin, M. E. (1974) *Trade Relations of the EEC*, London, Praeger.

Kruse, D. C. (1980) *Monetary Integration in Western Europe: EMU, EMS and Beyond*, London, Butterworths.

Langeheine, B. and Weinstock, U. (1985) 'Graduated Integration: A Modest Path Towards Progress', *Journal of Common Market Studies*, Vol. XXIII, No. 3, March.

Layton, C. (1969) *European Advanced Technology*, London, Allen & Unwin.

Lee, R. and Ogden, P. E. (1976) *Economy and Society in the EEC*, Farnborough, Saxon House.

Leigh, M. and van Praag, N. (1978) *The Mediterranean Challenge: 1*, Sussex European Research Paper No. 2.

Lewenhak, S. (1982) *The Role of the European Investment Bank*, London, Croom Helm.

Lewis, D.E.S. (1978) *Britain and the European Community*, London, Heinemann.

Lodge, J. (1983) *Institutions and Policies of the European Community*, London, Frances Pinter.

Lodge, J. (ed.) (1986) *European Union: The European Community in Search of a Future*, London, Macmillan.

Lodge, J. (ed.) (1989) *The European Community and the Challenge of the Future*, London, Frances Pinter.

Lodge, J. and Herman, V. (1978) *The European Parliament and the European Community*, London, Macmillan.

Long, F. (ed.) (1980) *The Political Economy of EEC Relations with African, Caribbean and Pacific States*, Oxford, Pergamon Press.

Ludlow, P. (1982) *The Making of the European Monetary System*, London, Butterworths.

Lundgren, N. (1969) 'Customs Unions of Industrialised West European Countries', in G. R. Denton (ed.), *Economic Integration in Europe*, London, Weidenfeld & Nicolson.

Mackel, C. (1978) 'Green Money and the Common Agricultural Policy', *National Westminster Bank Quarterly Review*, February.

Maclennan, R. (1978) 'Food Prices and the Common Agricultural Policy', *Three Banks Review*, September.

Macsween, I. (1987) 'The Common Fisheries Policy', *Royal Bank of Scotland Review*, No. 154, June.

McKinnon, R. I. (1963) 'Optimum Currency Areas', *American Economic Review*, No. 53.

McQueen, M. (1977) *Britain, The EEC and the Developing World*, London, Heinemann.

Magnifico, G. (1973) *European Monetary Unification*, London, Macmillan.

Mahotière, S. de la (1970) *Towards One Europe*, Harmondsworth, Penguin.

Marques Mendes, A. J. (1987) *Economic Integration and Growth in Europe*, London, Croom Helm.

Marsh, J. S. and Swanney, P. J. (1980) *Agriculture and the European Community*, London, Allen & Unwin.

Mathijsen, P. S. R. F. (1985) *A Guide to European Community Law*, London, Sweet & Maxwell.

Mayne, R. (ed.) (1972) *Europe Tomorrow*, London, Fontana/Collins.

Midland Bank (1977) 'European Monetary Union', *Midland Bank Review*, Winter.

Midland Bank (1986) 'On Joining the EMS', *Midland Bank Review*, Winter.

Midland Bank (1987) 'Setting Priorities for Science and Technology', *Midland Bank Review*, Winter.

Millington, A. I. (1988) *The Penetration of EC Markets by UK Manufacturing Industry*, Aldershot, Gower.

Molle, W. (1990) *The Economics of European Integration*, Aldershot, Dartmouth.

Morgan, A. (1980) 'The Balance of Payments and British Membership of the EEC', in W. Wallace (ed.), *Britain in Europe*, London, Heinemann.

Morgan, A. (1984) 'Protectionism and European Trade in Manufactures', *National Institute Economic Review*, No. 109, August.

Moussis, N. (1982) *Les Politiques de la Communauté Economique Européenne*, Paris, Dalloz.

Mundell, R. A. (1961) 'A Theory of Optimum Currency Areas', *American Economic Review*, No. 51.

Myrdal, G. (1957) *Economic Theory and Underdeveloped Regions*, London, Duckworth.

National Institute of Economic and Social Research (NIESR) (1983 and 1989) 'The European Monetary System', *National Institute Economic Review*.

Nevin, E. (1990) *The Economics of Europe*, London, Macmillan.

Nicholson, F. and East, R. (1987) *From the Six to the Twelve: The Enlargement of the European Communities*, Harlow, Longman.

Nicoll, W. (1984) 'The Luxembourg Compromise', *Journal of Common Market Studies*, Vol. XXIII, No. 1, September.

Noel, E. (1985) *The Institutions of the European Community*, Luxembourg.

Noort, P. C. van den (1983) 'Agricultural Policy', in P. Coffey (ed.), *Main Economic Policy Areas of the EEC*, The Hague, Martinus Nijhoff.

Nugent, N. (1989) *The Government and Politics of the European Community*, London, Macmillan.

Open University (1973) *The European Economic Community: History and Institutions, National and International Impact*, Milton Keynes, Open University Press.

Owen, N. (1983) *Economies of Scale, Competitiveness and Trade Patterns within the European Community*, Oxford University Press.

Padoa-Schioppa, T. (1984) *Money, Economic Policy and Europe*, European Perspective Series, Commission, Brussels.

Padoa-Schioppa, T. *et al.* (1987) *Europe in the 1990s: Efficiency, Stability and Equity, a Strategy for the Evolution of the Economic System of the European Community*, Oxford University Press.

Palmer, M. and Lambert, J. (1968) *European Unity: A Survey of the European Organizations*, London, Allen & Unwin.

Parr, M. and Day, J. (1977) 'Value Added Tax in the United Kingdom', *National Westminster Bank Quarterly Review*, May.

Pearce, J. (1981) *The Common Agricultural Policy*, Chatham House Paper No. 13, London, Routledge & Kegan Paul.

Pearce, J. and Sutton, J. (1986) *Protection and Industrial Policy in Europe*, London, Routledge & Kegan Paul.

Pelkmans, J. and Winters, A. C. (1988) *Europe's Domestic Market*, Chatham House Paper No. 43, London, Routledge.

Petith, H. C. (1977) 'European Integration and the Terms of Trade', *Economic Journal*, Vol. 87.

Pinder, D. A. (1986) 'Small Firms, Regional Development and the European Investment Bank', *Journal of Common Market Studies*, Vol. XXIV, No. 3, March.

Pinder, J. (1987) 'Is the Single European Act a Step Towards a Federal Europe?', *Journal of Policy Studies*, Vol. 7, Part 4, April.

Pollard, S. (1974) *European Economic Integration, 1815–1970*, London, Thames & Hudson.

Pomfret, R. (1986) *Mediterranean Policy of the European Community*, London, Macmillan.

Postan, M. M. (1967) *An Economic History of Western Europe, 1945–1964*, London, Methuen.

Presley, J. R. and Coffey, P. (1974) *European Monetary Integration*, London, Macmillan.

Presley, J. R. and Dennis, C. E. J. (1976) *Currency Areas: Theory and Practice*, London, Macmillan.

Prest, A. R. (1983) 'Fiscal Policy', in P. Coffey (ed.), *Main Policy Areas of the EEC*, The Hague, Martinus Nijhoff.

Pridham, G. (1986) 'European Elections, Political Parties and Trends of Internalization in Community Affairs', *Journal of Common Market Studies*, Vol. XXIV, No. 4, June.

Priebe, H. (1980) 'German Agricultural Policy and the European Community', in W. L. Kohl and G. Basevi (eds), *West Germany: A European and Global Power*, Lexington, Mass., D.C. Heath.

Pryce, R. (ed.) (1987) *The Dynamics of European Union*, London, Croom Helm.

Ransom, C. (1973) *The European Community and Eastern Europe*, London, Butterworths.

Redmond, J. (1987) 'Trade Between China and the European

Community: A New Relationship?', *National Westminster Bank Quarterly Review*, May.

Ritson, C. (1977) *Agricultural Economics*, St Albans, Granada.

Roarty, M. J. (1987) 'The Impact of the Common Agricultural Policy on Agricultural Trade and Development', *National Westminster Bank Quarterly Review*, February.

Robson, P. (1980) *The Economics of International Integration*, London, Allen & Unwin.

Rustow, D. and Penrose, T. (1981) *Turkey and the Community, The Mediterranean Challenge: V*, Sussex European Research Centre, Paper No. 10, Brighton.

Science et vie économie (1987) No. 25.

Scott, A. (1986) 'Britain and the EMS: An Appraisal of the Report of the Treasury and Civil Service Committee', *Journal of Common Market Studies*, Vol. XXIV, No. 3, March.

Seers, D. and Vaitsos, S. (1980) *Integration and Unequal Development*, London, Macmillan.

Servan-Schreiber, J. J. (1968) *The American Challenge*, London, Hamish Hamilton.

Shackleton, M. (1990) *Financing the European Community*, London, Frances Pinter.

Shanks, M. (1977) *European Social Policy Today and Tomorrow*, Oxford, Pergamon Press.

Sharp, M. (ed.) (1985) *Europe and the New Technologies*, London, Frances Pinter.

Shonfield, A. (1972) *Europe: Journey to an Unknown Destination*, Harmondsworth, Penguin.

Stevens, C. (ed.) (1984) *EEC and the Third World: A Survey*, No. 4, ODI/IDS, London, Hodder & Stoughton.

Strange, S. (1980) 'Germany and the World Monetary System', in W. L. Kohl and G. Basevi (eds), *West Germany: A European and Global Power*, Massachussets, Heath Lexington.

Svennilson, I. (1954) *Growth and Stagnation in the European Economy*, Geneva, United Nations Economic Commission for Europe.

Swann, D. (1983) *Competition and Industrial Policy*, London, Methuen.

Swann, D. (1984) *The Economics of the Common Market*, 5th edn, Harmondsworth, Penguin.

Tarditi, S. (1984) 'Price Policies and European Economic Integration', in K. J. Thomson and R. M. Warren (eds), *Price and Market Policies in European Agriculture*, Dept. of Agricultural Economics, University of Newcastle-upon-Tyne.

Taylor, P. (1983) *The Limits of European Integration*, London, Croom Helm.

Treaties Establishing the European Communities (1987) abridged edition, Brussels/Luxembourg.

Tsoukalis, L. (1977) *The Politics and Economics of European Monetary Integration*, London, Allen & Unwin.

Tsoukalis, L. (ed.) (1981) *The European Community and its Mediterranean Enlargement*, London, Allen & Unwin.

Tsoukalis, L. (ed.) (1986) *Europe, America and the World Economy*, Oxford, Basil Blackwell for the College of Europe.

Tugendhat, C. (1986) *Making Sense of Europe*, Harmondsworth, Penguin.

Turner, G. (1986) 'Inside Europe's Giant Companies: Cultural Revolution at Philips', *Long Range Planning*, Vol. 19/4, No. 98, August.

Utne, A. (1986) 'EFTA's Importance as a Trading Partner for the EC', *EFTA Bulletin*, Vol. XXVII, October–December.

Vanhove, N. and Klassen, L. H. (1980) *Regional Policy: A European Approach*, Farnborough, Saxon House.

Wallace, H. (1985) *The Challenge of Diversity*, London, Routledge & Kegan Paul.

Wallace, H., Wallace, W. and Webb, C. (eds) (1977) *Policy-Making in the European Communities*, London, John Wiley.

Wallace, W. (ed.) (1980) *Britain in Europe*, London, Heinemann.

Whitby, M. (ed.) (1979) *The Net Cost and Benefit of EEC Membership*, London, Wye College.

Williams, M. (1977) *Teaching European Studies*, London, Heinemann.

Winters, A. (1987) 'Britain in Europe: A Survey of Quantitative Trade Studies', *Journal of Common Market Studies*, Vol. XXV, No. 4, June.

Yannopoulos, G. N. (1985) 'EC External Commercial Policies and East–West Trade in Europe', *Journal of Common Market Studies*, Vol. XXIV, No. 1, September.

Yannopoulos, G. N. (ed.) (1986) *Greece and the EEC*, London, Macmillan.

Ypersele, J. van and Koeune, J. C. (1985) *The European Monetary System*, Cambridge, Woodhead–Faulker.

Zis, G. (1984) 'The European Monetary System, 1979–1984: An Assessment', *Journal of Common Market Studies*, Vol. XXIII, No. 1, September.

Index

C000018612

Madrid

Spain

EVERYMAN
CITY GUIDES

EVERYMAN CITY GUIDES
Copyright © 1998 David
Campbell Publishers, London

ISBN 1-85715-828-8

*First published February 1998
Revised and updated Feb. 1999*

Originally published in
France by Nouveaux Loisirs,
a subsidiary of Gallimard,
Paris 1997, and in Italy by
Touring Editore, Srl.,
Milano 1997.
Copyright © 1997
Nouveaux Loisirs,
Touring Editore, Srl.

SERIES EDITORS
EDITORIAL MANAGER:
Seymourina Cruse
MADRID EDITION: Vincent de
Lapomarède, Caroline Cuny
and David Beytelmann
GRAPHICS
Élizabeth Cohat, Yann Le Duc
LAYOUT: Olivier Lauga, Yann
Le Duc
MINI-MAPS, AIRPORT MAPS:
Kristoff Chemineau
MADRID MAPS:
Édigraphie
STREET MAPS:
Touring Club Italiano
PRODUCTION
Catherine Bourrabier

Translated by Laura Ward
Edited and typeset by Book
Creation Services, London

English edition revised by
First Edition Translations Ltd,
Cambridge, UK

Printed in Italy by
Editoriale Lloyd

*All rights reserved. No part
of this publication may be
reproduced, stored in a retrieval
system or transmitted, in any forms
or by any means, electronic,
mechanical, photocopying, recording
or otherwise, without the prior
permission of the copyright owners.*

Authors
MADRID
Things you need to know:
Pilar Careaga (1)
Author of travel guides on CD-Rom, Pilar
Careaga spent her teenage years guiding
visitors around the Prado museum.

Where to stay and where to eat: Victor de la Serna (2)
Victor de la Serna has written about food
for the Spanish newspapers *El País*, *Diario 16*
and *El Mundo*. He was the Spanish
correspondent for the London magazine
Decanter and a columnist for the Spanish
Sibarita magazine. He is now joint editor of
the daily *El Mundo*.

After dark: Jaime Iglesias (3)
Jaime Iglesias trained as a lawyer and
journalist and is now a publicity director.
He has been among Madrid's night-owls for
many years.

What to see:
Mariano Navarro (4)
Consultant to the Spanish TV program
Trazos e Imágenes, exhibition curator, editor
of books for bibliophiles and writer of
supplements on Velázquez, Goya and
Gauguin for *El País Semanal*, Mariano
Navarro is currently arranging Madrid's
latest exhibitions of 20th-century art.

Further afield:
Consuelo Álvarez de Miranda (5)
Art historian and expert on Baroque
architecture, Consuelo Álvarez de Miranda
has taught in various schools, edited the six-
volume *Historia del arte hispánico* (1976–
1980) and was joint author of the guide
Madrid práctico – Todo Madrid (1995).

Where to shop:
Paloma Sarasúa (6)
Author, journalist and sociologist, Paloma
Sarasúa has just published *Trabaja, mujer,
trabaja* for Acento Editorial, an essay on
women's work in modern-day society. She
was also joint author of the guide *Madrid
práctico – Todo Madrid* (1993).

*Note from the publisher:
To keep the price of this guide as low as
possible we decided on a common edition for
the UK and US, which has meant
American spelling.*

Symbols

- ☎ telephone
- ➡ fax
- ● price or price range
- 🕐 opening hours
- ▣ credit cards accepted
- ▣ credit cards not accepted
- Ⓥ toll-free number
- @ e-mail/website address
- ★ tips and recommendations

Access

- **M** subway stations
- 🚍 bus (or tram)
- **P** private parking
- 🅿 parking attendant
- ♿ no facilities for the disabled
- ➘ train
- 🚗 car
- 🚤 boat

Hotels

- ☎ telephone in room
- 📠 fax in room on request
- 🍸 minibar
- 📺 television in room
- ❄ air-conditioned rooms
- 🕐 24-hour room service
- 🔑 caretaker
- 👶 babysitting
- 🛋 meeting room(s)
- 🐾 no pets
- 🍴 breakfast
- ☕ open for tea/coffee
- 🍽 restaurant
- 🎵 live music
- 💿 disco
- 🌳 garden, patio or terrace
- 🏋 gym, fitness club
- 🏊 swimming pool, sauna

Restaurants

- 🥗 vegetarian food
- 🏔 view
- 👔 formal dress required
- 🚬 smoking area
- 🍸 bar

Museums and galleries

- ⊞ on-site store(s)
- 🎫 guided tours
- ☕ café

Stores

- 🔀 branches, outlets

The Insider's Guide is made up of **8 sections** each indicated by a different color.

Things you need to know (mauve)
Where to stay (blue)
Where to eat (red)
After dark (pink)
What to see (green)
Further afield (orang)
Where to shop (yellov
Finding your way (purple)

M Goya **Modern Spanish** 9–11.30pm; closed Aug. 1 1

Practical information is given for each particular establishment: opening times, prices, ways of paying, different services available

How to use this guide

The section **"In the area"** refers you (➡ 00) to other establishments that are covered in a different section of the guide but found in the same area of the city.

In the area

Located north of Retiro Park, this developed into an upmarket shop
■ Where to stay ➡ 2
■ Where to shop ➡
➡ 138 ➡ 140 ➡ 144

Serrano/Velázquez   D DI - F AI

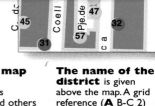

The small map shows all the establishments mentioned and others described elsewhere but found "in the area", by the color of the section.

The name of the district is given above the map. A grid reference (**A** B-C 2) enables you to find it in the section on Maps at the end of the book.

Not forgetting

■ **La Trainera (32)** Lagasca 60,
A rustic tasca serving up excellent se

The section "Not forgetting" lists other useful addresses in the same area.

"Bargain!"
This star marks good value hotels and restaurants.

The opening page to each section contains an index ordered alphabetically (Getting there), by subject or by district (After dark) as well as useful addresses and advice.

The section "Things you need to know" covers information on getting to

Madrid and day-to-day life in the city.

Theme pages introduce a selection of establishments on a given topic.

The "Maps" section of this guide contains 9 street plans of Madrid followed by a detailed index.

▶Getting there

Pets

To bring a dog or cat into Spain, you need a rabies vaccination certificate and certification, issued within the previous three months, to show that the animal is in good health.

Electric current

In line with the rest of Europe (except the United Kingdom) the voltage is 220, using two-pin plugs.

Average temperatures
Summer temperatures range from 12°C to 39°C (53°F to 102°F); winter temperatures are between -8°C and 17°C (18°F and 63°F).

Things
you need to Know

Passports
EU nationals can stay in Spain for up to six months if they have a national identity card, and for an indefinite period if they have a valid passport. US and Canadian tourists visiting Spain for up to three months do not currently require a visa. Others should enquire about visa requirements before departure.

Health
EU nationals are covered for urgent medical treatment and should take form E111 with them ➡ 15. Non-EU nationals are not covered and are therefore advised to take out adequate medical insurance before departure.

Driving
Motorists should carry a national or international driver's license and a green card issued by their insurers.

Madrid's only international airport, Madrid-Barajas, lies about 10 miles to the east of the city. Internal flights with Iberia (Spain's national airline) or Aviaco also operate from this airport, forming a network with Spain's major cities, other European capitals (such as London, Paris, Geneva and

Getting there

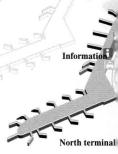

Information

Information
☎ 91 305 83 43
or 91 305 83 44
Left luggage
In the arrivals area of the international terminal.
Tourist office
☎ 91 305 86 56
🕒 Mon.–Fri. 8am–8pm; Sat. 9am–1pm
In the arrivals area of the international terminal.
Lost property
☎ 91 393 61 19
🕒 Mon.–Fri. 8am–3pm; Sat. 8am–2pm
Opposite the left luggage.
Police
The office is located near the Iberia desk in the departures area of the international terminal.

Telephones

Payphones take coins or cards. The cards are on sale in the kiosks or from dispensers in the international arrivals and domestic departures areas (taking 1000 peseta and 2000 peseta notes).

Currency exchange

Automatic cash dispensers are located in both domestic and international terminals.
Argentaria
☎ 91 305 55 51
Two offices are open from 6am to 11pm and two open 24 hours (inside the terminals). Exchange rates are slightly higher than in the city.

Airlines

American Airlines
☎ Madrid 91 597 20 68
☎ UK 0345 789789
☎ US 800-433-7300
Aviaco
Domestic flights
☎ 91 305 86 85
British Airways
☎ Madrid 91 431 75 75
☎ UK 0345 222111
☎ US 800-247-9297
Iberia
☎ Madrid 91 240 05 00
☎ UK 0345 222111
☎ US 212-644-8839

TWA
☎ Madrid 91 310 30 94
☎ UK 0171-439 0707
☎ US 800-892-4141

Getting into the city
Buses
☎ 91 431 61 92
Yellow buses run between the airport and Plaza de Colón (the terminus is under

the Jardines del Descubrimiento). The journey takes about 30 minutes when traffic flows freely. Buses also stop at Canillejas, Avenida de América, María de Molina and Velázquez.
🕒 First bus at 4.45am, second at 5.45am, then every 15 minutes from 5.45am to 7am,

North terminal

Brussels), and with major cities in
North America.

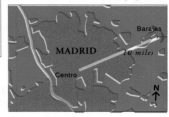

Airport hotels

Barajas
Avenida Logroño
305, 28042
☎ 91 747 77 00
➡ 91 747 87 17
24-hour transport.
Sofitel
Campo de las
Naciones, 28042
☎ 91 721 00 70
➡ 91 721 05 15
Courtesy bus.

Car rental

Hertz
☎ 91 393 72 86
Avis
☎ 91 393 72 22
Eurodollar Atesa
☎ 91 393 72 32
Europcar
☎ 91 393 72 89

then every 10
minutes from 7am
until 10pm, and
every 30 minutes
from 10pm until
1.30am. ● One-
way fare: 370 Ptas.

Taxis
Outside the
airport. Official
taxis are white

with a red stripe.
A supplement is
charged for picking
up at the airport
and for baggage.
All taxis must be
equipped with a
meter. Fares are

usually shown on
a list on one of
the rear windows.
The fare to Plaza
de Colón is about
2000 Ptas,
including baggage
supplement.

2nd level

1st level
Check-in

Information

Information

first floor
Arrivals

International terminal
P **1**

Domestic terminal
P **2**

P **6**

N1, M40, Pl. Castilla

P **5**

Madrid / Barajas
Airport **Madrid**

P Parking

🚌 Bus

🚕 Taxis

🚗 Car rental

RENFE, Spain's national rail company, runs standard and high-speed trains. There are two overnight services from Paris to Madrid. Arriving by car can be straightforward, but roads in the city are congested and parking can be difficult.

▶ Getting there

Trains

Information for all train services and all stations can be obtained from a centralized telephone bureau, open 24 hours:

RENFE
(*Red Nacional de Ferrocarriles Españolas*)
☎ 91 328 90 20
Ask about special deals on fares.

AVE
Alta Velocidad Española (Spain's own high-speed train).

Estación de Chamartín
Agustín de Foxá, 28036
Ⓜ *Chamartín*

Trains for Europe, Spain and Madrid suburbs
Situated in the north of the city, Chamartín links Madrid with most of Spain and with other countries throughout Europe. The *cercanías*, or local network, can be the quickest way to travel within the city, and links up with the subway system. An underground train connects Chamartín and Atocha Stations, with stops at Nuevos Ministerios and Recoletos-

Colón. To reach the rest of the city take the subway (the station for this is in the main-line station), taxi or bus (found outside the main-line station).

Estación de Atocha
Plaza Emperador Carlos V, 28012
Ⓜ *Atocha Trains for Portugal, southern Spain and Madrid suburbs*
Opened in 1851, Atocha is Madrid's oldest station but is also now its most modern. It consists of two stations: Atocha-

Mediodía (for regular trains) and Puerta de Atocha (for the high-speed AVE). Both connect with the subway. Atocha boasts one of the world's most beautiful waiting rooms ➡ 98 and a restaurant, Samarkand overlooking tropical greenhouses. Buses and taxis depart from Plaza Carlos V.

Principe Pío
(or Norte)
Paseo de la Florida, 28008
Ⓜ *Principe Pío*
Suburban services.

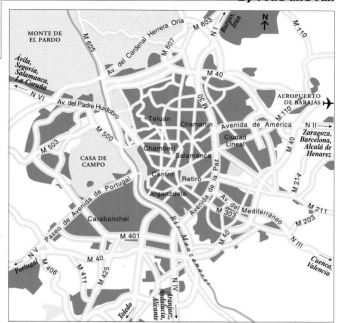

Cars

Madrid is located at the hub of six main roads radiating across Spain. Distances from the capital are measured from the center of Puerta del Sol. Two ring roads – the M-30 and M-40 – encircle the city and are less congested than the main thoroughfares of central Madrid. The N-1 (Hendaya) enters the city from the north via Plaza de Castilla. The N-11 (Figueras) comes from the northeast and joins the Barajas freeway and Avenida de América.

Traffic information

Ⓥ *900 123 505*
☎ *91 742 12 13*
🕐 *24-hour service*

Gasoline

A liter of premium costs around 120 Ptas. Most gas stations sell premium (*super*) unleaded (*sin plomo*) and diesel (*gasoleo*).

Safety

Deposit your luggage in the hotel at once on arrival; don't leave it in the car.

Long-distance buses

Cheap but not very fast.
Estacion Sur de Autobuses
Méndez Álvaro, corner of Calle Retamar, 28043
Ⓜ *Méndez Álvaro*
☎ *91 468 42 00*
This is the bus station for arrivals and departures of Euroline (international) company buses and Spanish domestic services. For detailed information, the monthly *Guia de Horarios*, which is available from most news-stands, lists all bus routes and times (it has information about train and airline times as well). Tickets for long journeys should be bought in advance from the bus station. Bus services are much reduced on Sundays. When planning a trip, watch out on timetables for the words *diario* (daily) and *domingos y festivos* (Sundays and holidays). The word *laborables* means "workdays and Saturday".

Bonometro and *bonobus* tickets (each allowing ten journeys) work out cheaper than buying one-way subway or bus tickets for each trip. Licensed taxis are white with a red stripe on the side.

Getting around

Subway

☎ 91 552 59 09
The Madrid subway is Europe's third-oldest subway system after London and Paris. *El Metropolitano* was opened in 1919 by King Alfonso XIII. It has 129 stations (now mostly air conditioned), carries over a million passengers every day and is the quickest way to get around town.

Tickets
One-way ticket 130 Ptas for any journey. The pink and white *Metrobus diez viajes* entitles you to ten trips for 670 Ptas. Subway tickets can be bought at subway stations, *estancos* (tobacconists), EMT (*Empresa Municipal de Transportes*) information offices, and newsstands. These tickets can also be used on the buses.

Timetables
The subway runs daily from 6am to 1.30am.
Rush hours: 7–9.30am; 1.30–2.30pm.

Taking the subway
There are ten subway lines, each with its own number and color code. The *circular* line (no. 6, gray) runs around the city, while the rest run from north to south, or from east to west. Pick up a free color map (*plano del metro*) of the subway system from any station. They are easy to read even if you have no Spanish.

Buses
The heavy city-center traffic is slow going, but the bus is still a practical way of getting along the main thorough-fares, such as the Paseo de la Castellana. Buses are air-conditioned in summer.

Tickets
Fares are the same as the subway. The ten-trip ticket (*Metrobus*) is a long cardboard strip which is punched every time you take the bus. These tickets cannot be bought on the bus. They are available from special sales points; *estancos* (tobacconists), EMT information offices and newsstands. One-way tickets can be bought on the bus.

Timetables
Buses run from 6am to midnight. Between midnight and 2am night buses run every 30 minutes from the Puerta del Sol. Between 2am and 5am they run hourly.

Waiting for the bus
Bus-stops can be recognized by a blue sign showing the number of the bus route, with the main stops listed underneath. Spaniards wait in line for the bus.

Biobus
A unique Madrid experience – some EMT buses run on vegetable-based fuel (a mixture of diesel and sunflower oil). There are plans to extend the same fuel to private cars.

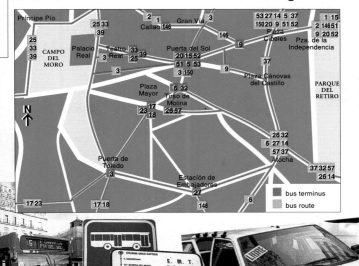

Taxis

Radioteléfono
☎ 91 547 82 00
Radio-taxi
☎ 91 447 51 80;
91 447 32 32
Tele-taxi
☎ 91 371 21 31

Taking a cab

Taxis are usually white, but some are black with a red or green diagonal stripe on the side. They can be found at stands near hotels or major tourist attractions, or can be hailed in the street. A green sign on the windshield shows that a cab is free. A red notice shows which way the driver is heading if they are about to go off duty. The driver will only accept passengers bound for the same destination. At night, when the subway is closed and there are only night buses, taxis become thin on the ground.

Fares

Supplements are charged at night, on Sundays and public holidays, and for picking up at stations, the airport, stadiums and bullrings. Tips (normally about ten per cent) are appreciated but they are not expected. All fees should be clearly posted in the taxi. If, when you reach your destination, you feel you have been overcharged, ask for an official receipt (a white form bearing the city coat-of-arms and perforated with a license number) and send to city hall: *Área de Circulacion y Transportes, Plaza de la Villa 4, 28005.*

Cars

Parking

Few hotels have private parking lots. Take advantage of those that do by leaving the car there except for excursions out of the city, and getting around by taxi or public transportation. The symbol **P** identifies Madrid's numerous municipal parking lots (Plaza de Colón, Plaza de España y Princesa, Plaza Mayor, Plaza de Santo Domingo, Plaza de las Cortes, Plaza de Santa Ana, Sevilla, Auditorio Nacional and Orense). Madrid is regulated by ORA (*Operación de Regulación del Aparcamiento*), which limits parking

Mon.–Fri. 9am–8pm; Sat. 9am–2pm. Parking permits can be obtained from *estancos.* To save parking fees when renting a car for a day trip or a longer tour, arrange for it delivered to the hotel on the day of departure.

Car rental

Atesa
☎ 91 559 78 26
Avis
☎ 91 348 03 48
Europcar
☎ 91 555 99 31
Hertz
☎ 91 101 001
Rentalauto
☎ 91 441 36 02

Breakdown services

Grúas ADA
☎ 91 519 33 00
Radio-Grúa
☎ 91 508 42 42
Real Automovil Club (RACE)
☎ 91 593 33 33

13

Madrid has plenty of automatic cash machines and places to change money, but many Madrid banks are not open in the afternoons. Stores are generally open until late, but many close for an hour or more at lunchtime. A 24-hour news-stand is located in the Puerta del Sol (2)

Getting by

Money
Currency exchange
232 Ptas = £1, 140 Ptas = $1 (October 1998) Most banks exchange cash, traveler's checks and Eurocheques. ⊙ Mon.–Fri. 8am–2pm; some banks are open until 4.45pm; some branches are open on Sat. 9am–noon. Currency can be exchanged in travel agencies, hotels, department stores and 24 hours a day at the airports ➡ 8.

Tipping
Tip at your discretion in bars and taxis. 50 Ptas to 100 Ptas in modest restaurants, and 5 to 10 % of the bill in upmarket ones. 25 Ptas for restroom attendants and cinema attendants. 100 Ptas per person for ushers in theaters and concert halls.

Media
Spanish press
Principal dailies: *El Mundo; ABC La Vanguardia; El País.* Weekly supplements: *Blanco y Negro; La Revista; El País Semanal.*

Radio
RNE (state radio, 5 stations) *SER* (commercial station, part of the *El País* and *Canal +* group) *COPE* (station operated by the Catholic Church) *Onda 0* (belongs to a group of charities)

Television
Public broadcasting channels: *TVE1* and *La 2.* Commercial channels: *Canal +* (subscription), *Antena 3 Televisión* and *TV 5.* Local channel: *TELE Madrid*

Telephone
Area codes
The former area code 91 must now be dialed for all numbers in Madrid, either from inside the city or outside. National inquiries ☎ 003 International inquiries ☎ 025

Public telephones
Payphones take coins or phonecards. Phonecards are available on sale at tobacconists (*estancos*), news-stands, post offices and *7 Eleven* stores.

Tariffs
In hotels charges are often higher. In public payphones a 50% reduction is given on calls made Mon.–Fri., 10pm–8am; Sat. from 3pm.
Telefónica (3)
Gran Vía 30, 28012
⊙ 9am–midnight

International phonecards
Calls from hotels are often higher than standard rates.
Worldtalk
☎ 900 97 44 08
● 2000 Ptas
In bureaux de change Chequepoint (Puerta del Sol). Mainly international calls.

Mail
Letters can be mailed from large hotels. Post offices are identified by the word *correos* above the door. Mail boxes have the same word and are yellow. Postage stamps (*sellos*) can also be bought at tobacco stores.

Main post office (4)
Palacio de Comunicaciones, Plaza de Cibeles, 28014
☎ 902 197 197
⊙ Mon.–Fri. 8am–10pm; Sat. 8.30am–2pm

(international newspapers are on sale in the city center).

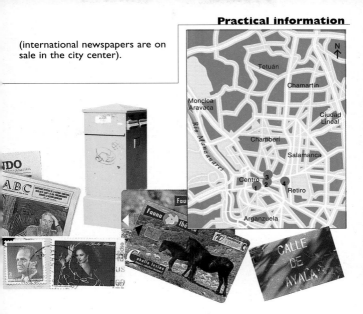

(some departments close earlier).

Neighborhood post offices

Mon.–Fri. 8.30am–8.30pm, some open 8.30am–2.30pm

Postal rates

To mail a letter weighing 20g: 35 Ptas (Spain); 70 Ptas (Europe); 114 Ptas (USA).

Getting around

Streets are numbered from the Puerta del Sol end. To ask the way, give the name of the neighborhood (Chamartín, Chamberí, Salamanca or Centro) or the name of the subway station.

Business hours

Stores

🕐 9.30am–2pm, 4.30–8pm

Opening times vary in summer.

Department stores

🕐 Mon.–Sat. 10am–9pm (1st Sunday in the month noon–8pm)

Tourist offices

Oficina Municipal de Turismo
Plaza Mayor 3, 28012
☎ 91 588 16 36
🕐 Mon.–Fri. 10am–8pm; Sat. 10am–2pm

Oficina de Información Turística de la Comunidad de Madrid
Duque de Medinaceli 2, 28014
☎ 91 429 49 51; or 91 429 31 77
🕐 Mon.–Fri. 9am–7pm; Sat.. 9am–1pm

Patronato Municipal de Turismo
Mayor 69, 28013
☎ 91 588 29 00
🕐 daily 9am–1pm

Información Turística

General de España

☎ 91 300 600
🕐 Mon.–Fri. 8.30am–5.30pm; Sat.–Sun. 9am–6pm

Gays and lesbians

Colectivo de Gais y Lesbianas de Madrid
Fuencarral 37 primera planta, 28004
☎ 91 522 45 17
🕐 Mon.–Sat. 6–10pm

GAI-INFORM
☎ 91 523 00 70
🕐 Mon.–Fri. 5–9pm

Medical care

Municipal ambulances
☎ 91 588 44 00

Red Cross Ambulances
☎ 91 479 93 61

Pharmacies

🕐 Mon.–Fri. 8am–1.45pm; Sat. 9am–1.45pm

For a list of pharmacies, see *Guía del Ocio* (the

weekly listings magazine), daily newspapers or pharmacy windows.

Useful phone numbers

Fire service (Cuerpo de bomberos)
☎ 080

Police (Policia)
☎ 091

Lost property
☎ 91 588 43 46

International codes
Calling Spain from abroad:
From the USA, dial 011 followed by 34 followed by the number.
From the UK, dial 00 followed by 34 then the number.
From Australia dial 0011 34, from New Zealand 0044 34.
To call abroad from Spain, dial the international prefix 001 for the USA, 0044 for the UK, 00353 for Ireland, 0061 for Australia, then the number.

Breakfast

Thick, hot chocolate or coffee and pastries filled with cream or jam is usually served. Some hotels also offer Spain's famous *churros*, long fritters made from doughnut batter ➡ 66. Order *café solo* for black coffee, *café cortado* for coffee with a dash of milk, and *café con leche* for a large cup of coffee with plenty of milk.

Reservations

Reserve rooms in advance. This is advised especially during the high season (*temporada alta*), from June to September and the week before Easter (*Semana Santa*).

Prices For all the hotels we list the number of rooms, the price range, the number of suites, the lowest price for a room, and the cost of the cheapest breakfast. Prices given are for a double room inclusive of taxes (VAT at 7%). Most of the large Spanish hotel chains (NH, Meliá or Tryp) and many independent hotels offer special low season and weekend rates.

Hotels

THE INSIDER'S FAVORITES

Hotel classification

Madrid offers a wide range of places to stay. *Hotels* listed here carry between one and five stars. *Hostales* are more modest hotels, also graded by a star system. *Pensiones* are family-run guest houses offering the cheapest accommodation.

Youth hostels

Madrid has two youth hostels. Information and reservations can be obtained from the REAJ (Spanish Youth Hostels Association):
Red Española de Albergues Juveniles
Alcalá 32, 28014
☎ 91 580 42 16
➡ 91 580 42 15

In the area

A number of Madrid's great classic hotels lie close to the city's three major museums – Museo del Prado ➤ 96, Museo Thyssen-Bornemisza ➤ 96, and Centro Cultural Reina Sofia ➤ 98. ■ Where to eat ➤ 40 ■ After dark ➤ 70 ➤ 74 ➤ 76 ➤ 78 ■ What to see ➤ 94 ➤ 96

▶ Where to stay

Ritz (1)
Plaza de la Lealtad 5, 28014 ☎ 91 521 28 57 ➧ 91 532 87 76

Ⓜ *Banco de España* Ⓟ *129 rooms* ●●●●● *29 suites 102,000 Ptas* 🔲
3300 Ptas ▤ ⊙ ▦ ☎ Ⅲ 🛄 Ⅲ 🍴 *Goya* ➤ 40 🌂 🔲 ✖ ✖ ✚ ✖ ✦

This spectacular white palace, built under the supervision of King Alfonso XIII and César Ritz and designed by Charles Mewes in 1910, created a revolution in the hotel business. Its elegance, grand public rooms and personal service make it Spain's most celebrated hotel. In summer, the terrace and garden are a popular meeting place for Madrid's smart set.

Palace (2)
Plaza de las Cortes 7, 28014 ☎ 91 360 80 00 ➧ 91 360 81 00

Ⓜ *Banco de España* 🈂 *396 rooms* ●●●●● *44 suites 128,400 Ptas*
🔲 *3200 Ptas* ▤ ▦ ☎ 🛄 Ⅲ 🍴 *La Cupola* 🌂 🔲 ✖ ▦

The Palace, built in 1912, has a much more modern ambience and attitude than its traditional rival, the Ritz. An ambitious renovation program is currently in progress, aimed at restoring the hotel to its former glory and equipping it with state-of-the-art facilities. It has a good Italian restaurant.

Villa Real (3)
Plaza de las Cortes 10, 28014 ☎ 91 420 37 67 ➧ 91 420 25 47

Ⓜ *Banco de España, Sevilla* 🈂 *115 rooms* ●●●● *12 suites 69,550 Ptas*
🔲 *2140 Ptas* ▤ ⊙ ▦ ☎ 🛄 Ⅲ 🍴 🌂 🔲 ✖ ✚ ▦

The Villa Real was only recently converted into a hotel. It blends well into this *belle-époque* corner of Madrid, harmonizing with its prestigious neighbors, the Spanish Parliament, the Palace Hotel and the Ritz. Fine antique furniture and marble bathrooms maintain its sense of period grandeur, but it also has the best facilities in terms of modern fixtures and fittings.

Tryp Reina Victoria (4)
Plaza de Santa Ana 14, 28014 ☎ 91 531 45 00 ➧ 91 522 03 07

Ⓜ *Sol* Ⓟ 🈂 *201 rooms* ●●●● *4 suites 53,500 Ptas* 🔲 *1650 Ptas* ▤ ▦ ☎
🛄 Ⅲ 🍴 🌂 🔲 ✖ ✖ ✖ ✍ ✚ ✖

The Reina Victoria's greatest claim to fame is that it is one of the favorite haunts of the bullfighting fraternity. Following recent renovations, this early 20th-century building can now boast elegant, modern facilities and interiors.

Not forgetting

■ **Regina (5)** Alcalá, 19, 28014 ☎ 91 521 47 25 ➧ 91 522 40 88 ●
■ **Suecia (6)** Marqués de Casa Riera 4, 28014 ☎ 91 531 69 00
➧ 91 521 71 41 ●●●

■ Where to
shop ➡ 126
➡ 128 ➡ 132

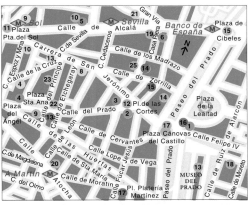

The beautiful cupola
of the Palace,
inaugurated in 1912
by Alfonso XIII,
crowns a belle-
époque rotunda.

19

This modern thoroughfare (built in 1910) cuts through the tangled streets of Old Madrid. ■ Where to eat ➡ 38 ■ After dark ➡ 72 ➡ 80 ■ What to see ➡ 90 ➡ 92 ➡ 94 ■ Where to shop ➡ 128 ➡ 132 ➡ 134 ➡ 136

▶ Where to stay

Arosa (7)
Salud 21, 28013 ☎ 91 532 16 00 ➡ 91 531 31 27

Ⓜ *Callao, Gran Vía* 🏠 *139 rooms* ●● 🎟 *1250 Ptas* 🔲 🔳 ☎ 📶 Ⅲ 🍴 ☒ 🔲 ✕ ✚

The Arosa is always undergoing an extensive program of modernization. The rooms are now very well sound-proofed and here it is essential. The hotel shares a building with the largest bookstore in Madrid, Casa del Libro ➡ 132, but the upstairs reception area and separate side entrance help to maintain discretion. There are two restaurants: one, inside the hotel, which is adequate; the other, La Joya de Jardines, a few yards away on Calle Jardines, is more adventurous.

Gaudí (8)
Gran Vía 9, 28013 ☎ 91 531 22 22 ➡ 91 531 54 69

Ⓜ *Gran Vía 88 rooms* ●●● *2 suites 37,450 Ptas* 🎟 *1500 Ptas* 🔲 ⓞ 🔳 ☎ 📶 Ⅲ 🍴 🔲 ✏ ✚ ✕

A small, modern hotel tucked away behind the financial district of Calle Alcalá, the Gaudí is well suited to the business traveler. Unusually for accommodation in this area, the hotel has both a gym and a sauna.

Style Santo Domingo (9)
**Plaza de Santo Domingo 13, 28013
☎ 91 547 98 00 ➡ 91 559 22 16**

Ⓜ *Santo Domingo* 🅿 *120 rooms* ●●● 🎟 *1500 Ptas* 🔲 🔳 ☎ 📶 Ⅲ 🍴 ☒ 🔲 ✕ ✖ ✏ ✚ @ *sdomingo@stnet.es*

In spite of its size, this brand new independent hotel can certainly be described as 'characterful'. Fine furniture, antiques and modern paintings blend well. The lounges retain the impressive granite walls of the apartment block that was once here.

Tryp Ambassador (10)
**Cuesta de Santo Domingo 5, 28013
☎ 91 541 67 00 ➡ 91 559 10 40**

Ⓜ *Ópera, Santo Domingo* 🅿 *180 rooms* ●●● *2 suites 68,500 Ptas* 🎟 *1800 Ptas* 🔲 🔳 ☎ 📶 Ⅲ 🍴 ☒ 🔲 ✕ ✏ ✚

A superb 19th-century mansion in which the Granada de Ega family once lived. It features an interior courtyard, covered by a glass roof, and a conservatory housing a charming restaurant. The Teatro Royal opera house ➡ 92 is located nearby.

Not forgetting
■ **El Coloso (11)** Leganitos 13, 28013 ☎ 91 559 76 00 ➡ 91 547 49 68 ●●
■ **Mayorazgo (12)** Flor Baja 3, 28013 ☎ 91 547 26 00 ➡ 91 541 24 85 ●

10

7

HOTEL AROSA

7

8

9

9

Where to stay

Santo Mauro (13)
Zurbano 36, 28010 ☎ 91 319 69 00 ➡ 91 308 54 77

Ⓜ *Alonso Martínez, Rubén Dario* 🉑 *26 rooms* ●●●●● *11 suites 49,220 Ptas* 🉑 *2500 Ptas* 🔲 ⓞ 🔲 ☎ 🔼 Ⅲ 🎴 *Belagua* ➡ *52* 🆈 ⓒ 🔣 🔏 ➕ ♒ ✦ ➡ *68*

Built as a palace for the dukes of Santo Mauro, this elegant and imposing building was then used by a sequence of foreign embassies before being transformed into a luxury hotel in 1991. The original formal architecture coexists extremely well with the newly designed and fashionably modern interiors. The vast bedrooms that retain their great marble fireplaces have been decorated in a rather unusual style, which is not always to everyone's taste. The glass pavilion serving as entrance to the inner courtyard creates a light and graceful ambience. What was once the library is now a good restaurant, and the gardens and terrace provide an ideal meeting place as well as a delightful setting to rest or relax on a fine day.

NH Embajada (14)
Santa Engracia 5, 28010 ☎ 91 594 02 13 ➡ 91 447 33 12

Ⓜ *Alonso Martínez 101 rooms* ●● 🉑 *1700 Ptas* 🔲 🔲 ☎ 🔼 Ⅲ 🎴 ⓒ ➕

The ideally-located Embajada has an interesting and attractive design, which dates from the Madrilenian Belle Epoque, when the Spanish regional style with its Castilian and Andalusian features was highly prized. The style achieves its most distinctive expression in the wrought-iron balconies that adorn rooms facing the street. The rooms themselves are modern and functional, in the style of the Spanish chain NH, of which Embajada is a part.

Tryp Fénix (15)
Hermosilla 2, 28001 ☎ 91 431 67 00 ➡ 91 314 31 56

Ⓜ *Serrano* 🉑 *214 rooms* ●●●● *14 suites 57,250 Ptas* 🉑 *1800 Ptas* 🔲 🔲 ☎ Ⅲ 🔼 🎴 🆈 🔣 ➕ ▦

The distinctive style of the Tryp Fénix's reception area and its marble-clad lounges evokes the 1950s, a time when the hotel bar was a favorite watering-hole and meeting place of journalists, writers and bankers. Its name derives from the huge bronze imperial phoenix that perches on its rooftop. A few years ago, this venerable if somewhat aging establishment announced a long-awaited relaunch under the wing of the Spanish Tryp chain. The vast bedrooms, which are quiet and well-equipped, have been completely redecorated, and the hotel once again counts itself among the liveliest and most interesting in the capital. Note that the local branch of the Hard Rock Café, which occupies part of the ground floor of the building, has no direct access to the reception area, thereby preserving peace in the hotel.

Not forgetting
■ **NH Sanvy (16)** Goya 3, 28001 ☎ 91 576 08 00 ➡ 91 575 24 43 ●●●

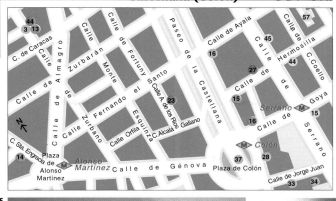

In the area

The streets of this eastern section of Madrid are laid out on a grid plan, designed by the Marqués de Salamanca. The area that takes his name is today Madrid's most upmarket residential and shopping area. ■ Where to eat ➡ 44 ➡ 46 ➡ 48 ➡ 50 ■ After dark ➡ 70 ➡ 74 ➡ 80 ■ What to see ➡ 98

Where to stay

Villa Magna (17)
Paseo de la Castellana 22, 28046☎ 91 576 75 00 ➡ 91 431 22 86

Ⓜ *Colón, Rubén Dario* 🄼 *182 rooms* ●●●●● *16 suites 96,300 Ptas* 🄼 *2950 Ptas* ◨ Ⓘ ▦ ☎ ▮ ▥ ▥ *Tse-Yang, Le Divellec* ➡ *50* Ⓨ ▣ ✖ ✳ ⊞ ★ @ *villamagna@compuserve.com*

The Villa Magna is a modern hotel set in a park of ancient cedars that once belonged to an old palace on the Castellana. The rooms are exceptionally comfortable, and the lounges have a classical English elegance, while the entrance and reception areas reflect a sense of calm opulence that relaxes the senses at the same time as it inspires confidence in the management. This is justified, and the Hyatt chain, which owns the Villa Magna, has excelled itself here in many respects, especially in the culinary field. It has placed Jacques Le Divellec in charge of the exceptional restaurant, and has also opened a branch of the Geneva-based Chinese restaurant, the Tse-Yang, in the hotel.

Wellington (18)
Velázquez 8, 28001 ☎ 91 575 44 00 ➡ 91 576 41 64

Ⓜ *Velázquez, Príncipe de Vergara, Retiro* Ⓟ *296 rooms* ●●●●● *7 suites 53,300 Ptas* 🄼 *2200 Ptas* ◨ Ⓘ ▦ ☎ ▮ ▥ ▥ *El Fogón* ➡ *46* Ⓨ ▣ ✖ ✂ ★ ✳ ⊞ ★

This traditional hotel, in the heart of the elegant Salamanca district, has recently been modernized while retaining many of the most-loved features of its former style. Located close to the Ventas bullring ➡ 100, it has long been popular with bullfighters and their followers, and is always full during the Feria de San Isidro in May and June. The service is impeccable, the bedrooms are spacious, and – unusually for Madrid – there is also a swimming pool.

Gran Hotel Velázquez (19)
Velázquez 62, 28001 ☎ 91 575 28 00 ➡ 91 575 28 09

Ⓜ *Velázquez* Ⓟ 🄼 *146 rooms* ●●● *75 suites 34,500 Ptas* 🄼 *1600 Ptas* ◨ ▦ ☎ ▮ ▥ Ⓨ ▣ ✖ ✂ ★ ⊞

The Gran Hotel Velázquez, situated in the heart of the Salamanca district, attracts large numbers of visitors during the major art exhibitions held at the nearby Juan March foundation ➡ 74. It also hosts numerous social activities for a predominantly Spanish clientele. The huge rooms are attractively old-fashioned (1940s in style); the restaurant is adequate if not exceptional. An additional attraction is that tea is served daily in the *salón*.

Not forgetting

■ **Pintor (20)** Goya 79, 28001 ☎ 91 435 75 45 ➡ 91 576 81 57 ●● *Recently renovated* ■ **Convención (21)** O'Donnell 53, 28009 ☎ (91) 574 84 00 ➡ 91 574 68 00 ●●

■ Where to
shop ➡ 130
➡ 138 ➡ 140
➡ 144

Where to stay

Emperatriz (22)
López de Hoyos 4, 28006 ☎ 91 563 80 88 ➡ 91 563 98 04

Ⓜ *Rubén Darío* 🅿 *153 rooms* ●●●● *5 suites from 75,000 Ptas* 💲 *1800 Ptas*
▣ ▣ ▣ ▣ ▥ ▦ ▸ ▣ ▨ ✚

Like its neighbor, the Inter-Continental ➡ 28, this comfortable, white-fronted hotel was built in the mid-1950s. It was refurbished in 1996, and the rooms today are bright and cheerful, with pale furniture, soft-colored drapes and three original vestibule panels by Eduardo Vicente, Madrid's chief style interpreter (also responsible for the frescos in the restaurant El Schotis ➡ 36).

Apartahotel Eraso (23)
Ardemáns 13, 28028 ☎ 91 355 32 00 ➡ 91 355 66 52

Ⓜ *Diego de Léon* 🅿 *31 studio appartments* ● 💲 *850 Ptas* ▣ ▣ ▥ ▨

The Eraso certainly lives up to the reputation of the Barcelona-based Husa hotel chain. Its affordable studio apartments, with lounge and kitchenette, are ideal for short visits or long stays in the Spanish capital. Although not ultra-luxurious, they are well maintained, modern and comfortable, with none of the impersonal atmosphere of so many *apartahotels*.

Rafael Ventas (24)
Alcalá 269, 28027 ☎ 91 326 16 20 ➡ 91 326 18 19

Ⓜ *El Carmen* 🍴 *110 rooms* ● *I suite 26,725 Ptas* 💲 *1300 Ptas* ▣ ▣ ▣
▸ ▥ ▦ ▣ ✚ ♒ ✴ ♿ ▨ @ *hotel@rafaelventas.com*

The *fin-de-siècle* version of the Wellington ➡ 24. The new Rafael is closer to the bullring ➡ 100, and numerous toreros and their impresarios have taken to staying in this steel-and-concrete establishment, as have their fans. The rooms are bright and pleasant.

NH Parque de las Avenidas (25)
Biarritz 2, 28028 ☎ 91 361 02 88 ➡ 91 361 21 62

Ⓜ *Ventas, Parque de Avenidas* 🅿 *198 rooms* ●●●● *I suite 32,100 Ptas*
💲 *2000 Ptas* ▣ ◍ ▣ ▣ ▸ ▥ ▦ ▣ ▣ ▨ ✚ ♒ ✴

This is one of the most recent of the 12 hotels owned by the NH chain in Madrid, and one of the most successful in terms of its ultra-functional style. The rooms are spacious and comfortable, the small bar is lively, and the modern restaurant serves modern Basque cuisine. Well positioned midway between the bullring ➡ 100 and the residential district of Parque de las Avenidas.

Not forgetting
■ **Meliá Confort Los Galgos (26)** Claudio Coello 139, 28006 ☎ 91 562 66 00 ➡ 91 561 76 62 ●●●●
■ **NH Príncipe de Vergara (27)** Príncipe de Vergara 92, 28006 ☎ 91 563 26 95 ➡ 91 563 72 53 ●●
■ **Abeba (28)** Alcántara 63, 28006 ☎ 91 401 16 50 ➡ 91 402 75 91 ●

C. de María de Molina — Av. de América
C. del Serrano · C. del General Oráa · 27 · Calle de Ardemáns · C. de Brescia
C. de Velázquez · 7 · C. de Azcona
C. Diego de León · Diego de León · C. Cartagena · Calle de Martínez Izquierdo · 25
C. de Maldonado · Calle de Azcona · AV. DE LA PAZ
1 · 41 · C. de · 14 · 33 · Silvela · Avenida de los Toreros · 27 · 24
38 16 17 · Bravo · 26 · AV. ALCALÁ
23 · 39 · 28 · C. de Londres · Ventas — M — Calle de Alcalá
18 · Calle de Padilla · El Carmen

Paseo de la Castellana

27

25

24

24

22

27

This residential district parallels Salamanca, though it has no shopping avenue to compare with that of Calle Serrano. The site of embassies and ministries, it is also home to the charming Museo Sorolla. ■ Where to eat ➡ 52 ➡ 56 ■ After dark ➡ 68 ■ What to see ➡ 106

Where to stay

Castellana Inter-Continental (29)
Paseo de la Castellana 49, 28046
☎ 91 310 02 00 ➡ 91 319 58 53

Ⓜ *Rubén Darío, Gregorio Marañón* 🅿 *285 rooms* ●●●●● *20 suites 90,000 Ptas* 🈂 *2800 Ptas* 🔲 🔘 🔳 🔲 🔲 🔲 🔲 🔲 🔲 🔲 🔲 🔲 @
albor@line/pro.es

The Castellana Inter-Continental has recently been modernized, but it still boasts some of the rarest examples of tasteful 1950s style to be found in Madrid: the red and black marble facings are unique, and the courtyard garden features sculptures by Angel Ferrant – a member of 1950s avant-garde. The garden offers excellent, shaded dining – try the famous club sandwiches. An establishment with a big personality, much loved in Spain.

Miguel Ángel (30)
Miguel Ángel 20, 28010 ☎ 91 442 00 22 ➡ 91 442 53 20

Ⓜ *Gregorio Marañón* 🅿 🈂 *232 rooms* ●●●●● *30 suites 45,368 Ptas* 🈂 *2500 Ptas* 🔲 🔘 🔳 🔲 🔲 🔲 🔲 🔲 🔲 🔲 🔲 🔲 🔲 🔲 🔲

The Miguel Ángel has a modern exterior combined with an elegant, classical interior that is impressively decorated with Baroque-style carpets and furniture. The well-proportioned bedrooms have recently been refurbished, the service is of a high standard and the management is professional – making this palace on the Castellana one of the most reliable addresses in Madrid. It also boasts a superb indoor swimming pool and gymnasium.

NH Zurbano (31)
Zurbano 79-81, 28003 ☎ 91 441 55 00 ➡ 91 442 91 48

Ⓜ *Gregorio Marañón* 🈂 *264 rooms* ● *10 suites 24,610 Ptas* 🈂 *1700 Ptas* 🔲 🔳 🔲 🔲 🔲 🔲 🔲 🔲 🔲

Vuelta de España drivers and other professional sporting teams often stay in this comfortable, NH-style hotel close to the Castellana. Its sporting reputation means that it is livelier and more colorful than many of the other hotels in the chain.

Style Esculptor (32)
Miguel Ángel 3, 28010 ☎ 91 310 42 03 ➡ 91 319 25 84

Ⓜ *Rubén Darío 59 rooms* ●●● *2 suites 37,450 Ptas* 🈂 *1450 Ptas* 🔲 🔳 🔲 🔲 🔲 🔲 🔲 🔲 🔲 🔲

A small, basic but comfortable hotel, the Style Esculptor looks out over the Glorieta Rubén Darío, now the most expensive residential square in town.

Not forgetting

■ **NH Prisma (33)** Santa Engracia 120, 28003 ☎ 91 441 93 77 ➡ 91 442 58 51 ●●

Statue of Gregorio Marañón, endocrinologist and Madrid historian.

In the area

The wide thoroughfare of the Paseo de la Castellana is lined with government ministries and hotels geared toward the business traveler. Two skyscrapers – the 43-story Torre Picasso and the twin-towered Puerta de Europa – stand as symbols of Madrid's modernity.

Where to stay

Meliá Castilla (34)
Capitán Haya 43, 28020 ☎ 91 567 50 00 ➠ 91 567 52 51

🅼 *Plaza de Castilla* 🏨 *899 rooms* ●●●● *14 suites 60,445 Ptas* 🅿 *1600 Ptas*
▢ ◉ ▣ ☎ ⬆ Ⅲ 🍴 Ⅎ ▣ 🎌 ✚ ♨ ⊞ ◉ ➠ *82*

An uninspiring skyscraper from the outside, the Meliá Castilla rewards closer inspection. It offers attentive service, comfortable, tastefully decorated rooms, two reputable restaurants and a famous cabaret venue and nightclub.

Hotel Cuzco (35)
**Paseo de la Castellana 133, 28046
☎ 91 556 06 00 ➠ 91 556 03 72**

🅼 *Cuzco* 🏨 *30 rooms* ●●● *8 suites 32,100 Ptas* 🅿 *1350 Ptas* ▢ ▣ ☎ Ⅲ
🍴 Ⅎ ▣ 🎌 ▨ ✚

The names of the lounges (Tolteca, Maya, Azteca, Inca) are in keeping with that of the hotel which, unsurprisingly, refers to the Spanish Conquest of South America. Guests will love the richly decorated entrance hall with its allegorical 17th- and 18th-century tapestries, the comfortably modern bedrooms and the restaurant with its weekend 'family menu' offering special reductions for the under-11s.

Holiday Inn (36)
**Plaza de Carlos Trías Beltrán 4, 28020
☎ 91 456 80 00 ➠ 91 456 80 01**

🅼 *Nuevos Ministerios 282 rooms* ●●●● *31 suites 37,611 Ptas* 🅿 *2400 Ptas*
▢ ▣ ☎ ⬆ Ⅲ 🍴 Ⅎ 🎌 ✚ ♨ ▨ ⊞

A modern building, ideally located close to the Torre Picasso, Spain's highest skyscraper, opposite the Real Madrid stadium and the Palacio de Congresos, and right in the heart of Azca, Madrid's largest business complex ➠ 108. American-style comfort: large beds, a swimming pool, rooftop solarium and a gym.

Castilla Plaza (37)
**Paseo de la Castellana 220, 28046
☎ 91 323 11 86 ➠ 91 315 54 06**

🅼 *Plaza de Castilla* 🏨 *234 rooms* ●●●● *7 suites 31,000 Ptas* 🅿 *1900 Ptas*
▢ ▣ ☎ Ⅲ ⬆ 🍴 Ⅎ ✚

This recently opened hotel (1994) lies at the foot of the two leaning towers of the Puerta de Europa ➠ 108, modern Madrid's most talked-about landmark. It is well equipped, and the ultra-modern rooms are softened by wooden fittings and plants. A tapas bar with a surprisingly good menu adds an unexpected, but welcome, Madrilenian touch.

Not forgetting

■ **Orense (38)** Orense 38, 28020 ☎ 91 597 15 68 ➠ 91 597 12 95 ●●●
■ **Aitana (39)** Paseo de la Castellana 152, 28046 ☎ 91 344 00 68
●● *Recently renovated.*

■ Where to eat ➡ 60 ➡ 64 ■ After dark ➡ 68 ➡ 80 ➡ 82 ■ What to see ➡ 108 ■ Where to shop ➡ 142

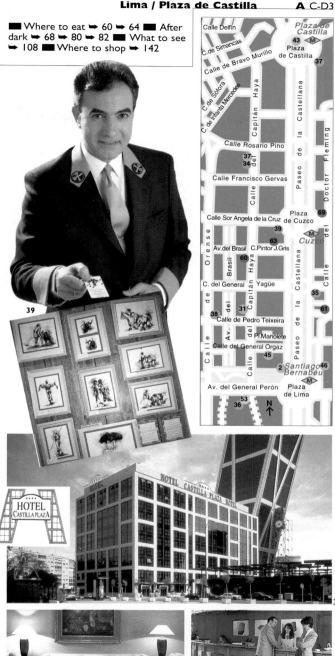

In the area

The Real Madrid district is a prime example of the Madrilenian 'boom' of the 1960s, when anarchic urban planning schemes were implemented. Both a shopping district and a residential area, its real treasures, tucked away at its center, are the *colonias*, with their villas and secluded gardens.

▶ Where to stay

NH Eurobuilding (40)
Padre Damián 23, 28023 ☎ 91 345 45 00 ➡ 91 345 45 76

Ⓜ *Cuzco* 🅿 🖅 *428 rooms* ●●● *52 suites 33,000 Ptas* 🅿 *2000 Ptas* ▢ ⓪
▢ ▢ ▢ ▥ ▥ ▯ ▢ ▨ ▢ ▨ ▦ ▢

Occupying an entire block of houses just off the Castellana, this is more of a city than a hotel. If this may seem a disadvantage to those looking for a more intimate environment, this can be countered by the advantages of the impressive raised terrace-garden, with a beautiful outdoor pool – a rarity in Madrid – which combine to give Eurobuilding the edge over its competitors. In addition, the hotel has numerous conference rooms, restaurants, shops, the most famous bridge club in Madrid, and a renowned debating society. Many business travelers return here again and again for the hotel's impressive facilities.

La Residencia de El Viso (41)
Nervión 8, 28002 ☎ 91 564 03 70 ➡ 91 564 19 65

Ⓜ *República de Argentina* 🅿 *12 rooms* ● 🅿 *800 Ptas* ▢ ▢ ▢ ▥ ▥ ▯
▢ ▢ @ *elviso@estancias.es*

La Residencia de El Viso is a remarkable cubist-style, salmon-pink villa that typifies the rationalist architecture of the 1930s. In addition to this architectural distinction, the hotel provides a green and quiet refuge from the noisy, bustling capital, even though it is situated right in the city center. Its small bedrooms are functional and modern. A garden-view restaurant serves fresh market produce.

Aristos (42)
Avenida Pío XII 34, 28016 ☎ 91 345 04 50 ➡ 91 345 10 23

Ⓜ *Pío XII* 🅿 *24 rooms* ●● *1 suite 24,000 Ptas* 🅿 *1000 Ptas* ▢ ⓪ ▢ ▢
▢ ▥ ▥ *El Chaflán* ▯ *El Chaflán* ▢ ▨ ▨ ▨ ▢

Situated at the end of an avenue that once marked the northern limits of the city, the Aristos has a deserved reputation as a charming place to stay for a romantic visit to Madrid. The rooms are impeccable, the garden delightful, and the restaurant excellent. Since the early 1990s, a burgeoning business district on the nearby M30 bypass has attracted a lively new clientele to this small hotel.

NH Habana (43)
Paseo de La Habana 73, 28036 ☎ 91 345 82 84 ➡ 91 457 75 79

Ⓜ *Colombia* 🅿 *156 rooms* ●● 🅿 *1700 Ptas* ▢ ▢ ▢ ▥ ▥ ▯ ▢ ▨ ▢

Frequented especially by sportsmen and by Basque and Catalan business travelers, the Habana is the Charmartín representative of the ubiquitous NH hotel group. This establishment is modern and is also more luxurious than others in the chain. One attraction for sports enthusiasts is that the concierge has an amazing ability to procure tickets for even the most oversubscribed Real Madrid football matches ➡ 108.

■ Where to eat ➥ 36 ➥ 60 ➥ 64
■ After dark ➥ 70 ➥ 72 ■ What to
see ➥ 108 ■ Where to shop ➥ 142

41

42

41

41

41

The Bauhaus and art deco
movements have left their
imprint on the El Viso area.

41

Tipping

Although service (12% of the total) is always included in the bill, it is usual to leave at least 5% more.

 # Where to eat

IVA

Some restaurants give prices inclusive of IVA (VAT at 7%); others add it to the total. The menu should state whether or not IVA is included.

Parking

It is not unusual for restaurants, especially the upmarket kind, to have doormen to park diners' cars for them. Otherwise parking is difficult in the narrow, winding streets of old Madrid.

Busy times

It is worth reserving a table, especially at lunchtime. The locals take a very late lunch (often not until around 2.30pm), but they no longer dine around midnight like they used to, preferring to eat around 9.30pm. Nevertheless, restaurants are quite accustomed to taking earlier reservations from foreign visitors.

73

Restaurants
THE INSIDER'S FAVORITES

Basic facts

In the 19th century, tascas were the wine leftovers used to concoct such basic dishes as the *cocido*, a stew made from cabbage, *chorizo* (spicy sausage) and chickpeas. The word 'tasca' is now applied to small restaurants, called *tascas ilustradas*. There is still a large number of these in Madrid, often

Where to eat

Casa Lucio (1)
Cava Baja 35, 28005 ☎ 91 365 32 52 ➡ 91 366 48 66

La Latina **Tasca** ●●●● 🔲 🕓 *Mon.–Fri., Sun. 1.15–3.45pm, 9pm–midnight; Sat. 9–11.30pm; closed in Aug*

This historic inn was renovated in the 1970s by the great Lucio Blázquez, who has transformed it into one of the best-known and most fashionable Madrilenian restaurants. The owner is a colorful character of such renown that he has been made the subject of a book, a copy of which he is proud to produce. The established ritual for most regulars begins with a plate of *patatas revolconas* (sautéed potatoes with scrambled eggs), followed by red meat, milk-fed roast lamb or fried hake, washed down by a carafe of Valdepeñas. To soak up the atmosphere, ask for a table in the main brick-vaulted dining room.

El Schotis (2)
Cava Baja 11, 28005 ☎ 91 365 32 30 ➡ 91 365 72 44

Tirso de Molina, La Latina **Tasca** ●● 🔲 🕓 *Mon.–Sat. 1–4.30pm, 8.30pm–12.30am; Sun. 1–4.30pm*

The splendid frescos depicting scenes from old Madrid (painted by Eduardo Vicente in the 1940s) add a lively touch to this *tasca*, a local-style restaurant which has influenced numerous other similar eating houses in the area. The waiters are 'old-timers' who have become co-owners and are most attentive. Try the stuffed sweet peppers and excellent red meats.

La Fuencisla (3)
San Mateo 4, 28004 ☎ 91 521 61 86

Tribunal **Tasca** ●●● 🔲 🕓 *Mon.–Sat. 1.30–4pm, 9pm–1am; closed in Aug.*

Modern paintings of questionable artistic merit and bullfighting mementoes adorn the walls of this tiny dining room. Señor and Señora De Frutos serve up excellent home cooking, which reflects the traditions of Segovia ➡ 120, their native town. While the proprietor presides over the front-of-house, as he has for the last 40 years or so, his wife creates meals in the kitchen. Try the grilled chops of milk-fed lamb or oven-baked *ventresca* (fillet) of tuna. The Rioja wines are exceptional.

De la Riva (4)
Cochabamba 13, 28016 ☎ 91 458 89 54

Colombia **Tasca** ●● 🔲 🕓 *Mon.–Fri. 1.30–6pm; closed in Aug.*

De la Riva has moved to the north of the city where, in a nondescript building in the modern district of Chamartín, its eponymous owner has re-created the atmosphere of a traditional *tasca*. When ordering, trust his advice as he recites the dishes of the day, among them *chipirones* (squid) in their ink, roasted fillet of veal, and the famous Castilian conger eel. This *tasca* is closed in the evenings.

plainly decorated with colored *azulejos*, (ceramic tiles), offering an atmospheric place to meet but little in the way of comfort.

4

Lucio Blázquez makes a point of offering his customers those tables at which famous guests have sat.

Where to eat

Botín (5)
Cuchilleros 17, 28005 ☎ 91 366 42 17 ➡ 91 366 84 94

Ⓜ *Sol, Tirso de Molina* **Castilian cuisine** ●●● ▭ ◐ *daily 1—4pm, 8pm—midnight*

This traditional establishment, founded in 1725, was entered in the *Guiness Book of Records* as 'the oldest restaurant in the world'. Happily, though, its four floors, exposed beams, wood oven and Castilian decoration in no way resemble a dusty museum. Delicious milk-fed lamb and roasted suckling pig are served to a mixed clientele of tourists and Madrileños.

Caripén (6)
Plaza de la Marina Española 4, 28013 ☎ 91 541 11 77

Ⓜ *Santo Domingo* 🔌 **French bistro cuisine** ●● ▭ ◐ *Mon.–Sat. 9pm–3am*

In a genuine art deco dining room Daniel Boute serves up the best French-style bistro cooking in Madrid. The Caripén is also one of the Madrid's most appealing restaurants in another sense, because you can eat here well after midnight when most other restaurants have closed. Sample specialties such as mussels in a cream sauce, excellent and copious fresh pasta, deliciously fresh steak tartare, mouthwatering skate in black butter and, to round out the meal, a very good apple tart... The cellar has some good French wines including a wonderful, reasonably priced vintage Médoc.

La Esquina del Real (7)
Amnistía 2, 28013 ☎ 91 559 43 09

Ⓜ *Ópera* **French cuisine** ●●● ▭ ◐ *Mon.–Fri. 2–4pm, 9–11.30pm; Sat. 8pm–midnight; closed Aug. 15–31*

Located a few yards from the Teatro Real ➡ 92, the Esquina del Real is one of Madrid's well-kept culinary secrets. The 17th-century building is one of the oldest in Madrid, with impressive granite walls that are nearly six feet thick. Marcel Margossian serves classic and resolutely French dishes, including Dublin Bay prawns with raspberry vinegar, delicious home-made foie gras, fricassée of veal sweetbreads, and as a specialty, flambéd Tarte Tatin.

Not forgetting

■ **Bajamar (8)** Gran Vía 78, 28013 ☎ 91 548 48 18 ●●●●● *Sublime fish and shellfish, simply cooked. Expensive.*
■ **Entre Suspiro y Suspiro (9)** Plaza de la Marina Española 4, 28013 ☎ 91 542 06 44 ●●● *Genuine Mexican home cooking – a far cry from the local 'Tex Mex'.*
■ **La Bola (10)** Bola 5, 28013 ☎ 91 547 69 30 ● *A* Taberna *(inn) with an old-style tasca atmosphere* ➡ *36. Serves up an excellent cocido madrileño (Madrilenian stew).*
■ **Cornucopia (11)** Flora 1, 28013 ☎ 91 547 64 65 ●● *Although Debora Hansen has left this Edwardian setting, there is still a distinctly New England flavor to this restaurant which is in fact more like a tearoom. European and American cuisine.*

11

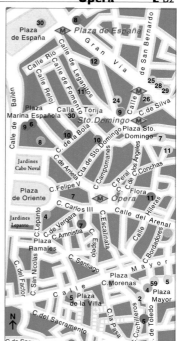

10

LA BOLA TABERNA

10

11

11

5

9

In the area

This is the artistic hub of Madrid, and the political heart of the capital, home to the Palacio de Congresos, scene of the attempted coup of February 23, 1981. ■ Where to stay ➡ 18 ➡ 20 ■ After dark ➡ 70 ➡ 72 ➡ 74 ➡ 76 ➡ 78 ■ What to see ➡ 94 ➡ 96 ➡ 98

Where to eat

Viridiana (12)
Juan de Mena 14, 28014 Madrid ☎ 91 523 44 78 ➡ 91 532 42 74

Ⓜ *Retiro, Banco de España* **Modern Castilian cuisine** ●●●●● ▢
Ⓢ *Mon.–Sat. 1.30–4pm, 9pm–midnight; closed Easter week, Aug., Christmas*

Everything here is dedicated to the memory of Luis Buñuel. The movie-mad proprietor Abraham García is a colorful character, always on the look out for new and exotic ingredients and techniques (the menu changes fortnightly), while remaining rooted in his native Castile. The result is the most inventive cuisine in Madrid. The cellar is exceptional, stocked with wines from around the world.

El Cenador del Prado (13)
Prado 4, 28014 ☎ 91 429 15 61 ➡ 91 369 04 55

Ⓜ *Sevilla* **Mediterranean cuisine** ●●●● ▢ Ⓢ *Mon.–Fri. 1.45–4pm, 9pm–midnight; Sat. 9pm–midnight; closed one week in Aug.*

Abandoning their haute cuisine, the Herranz brothers have opted for a cheaper, neo-Madrilenian version. Yet their clam and potato ragout, venison medallions with quince jelly, and chocolate stuffed with pear ice-cream never disappoint, and the three dining rooms are sumptuous.

Errota-Zar (14)
Jovellanos 3 (1st floor), 28014 ☎ / ➡ 91 531 25 64

Ⓜ *Banco de España, Sevilla* **Basque cuisine** ●● ▢ Ⓢ *Mon.–Sat. 1–4pm, 9pm–midnight; closed Easter week*

Errota-Zar belongs to Euskal Etxea, the home of Basque cuisine in Madrid. In this plush, traditional setting, the Olano family serves up excellent meats and popular Basque dishes, such as Tolosa kidney beans, almond cardoons, and Bay of Biscay cod.

Paradis Madrid (15)
Marqués de Cubas 14, 28014 ☎ 91 429 73 03 ➡ 91 429 32 95

Ⓜ *Banco de España* **Catalan cuisine** ●●● ▢ Ⓢ *Mon.–Fri. 1.30–4pm, 9pm–midnight; Sat. 9pm–midnight; closed Easter week, Aug., public holidays*

With its Catalan-style décor and old mosaic-tiled floor, this Madrid branch of the Barcelona-based restaurant chain is a worthy ambassador of the cuisine and wines of the principality: broad beans sautéd with squid, sea bream cooked on a hot slate, Catalan cream, Penedés and Priorato wines.

Not forgetting

■ **Goya (16)** Hotel Ritz, Plaza de la Lealtad 5, 28014 ☎ 91 521 28 57 ●●●●● *A splendid wood-paneled dining room overlooking Madrid's most beautiful summer garden.* Cocido, callos *(tripe)* a la madrileña…*the menu changes daily.*
■ **La Vaca Verónica (17)** Moratín 38, 28014 ☎ 91 429 78 27 ● *Decorated in the style of a Madrid mansion of the early 1900s. Featured on the lunchtime menu are salads, bourgeois dishes and excellent Argentinian meats.*

■ Where to shop ➡ 128 ➡ 132

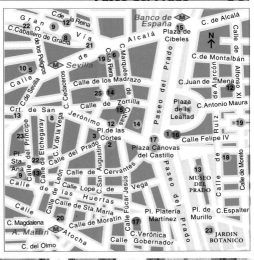

16

17

17

14

12

41

In the area

Cibeles is dominated by two symbols of Madrid – the fountain of Cybele, showing the goddess in a chariot, and the granite Puerta de Alcalá. ■ Where to stay ➡ 18 ➡ 20 ■ After dark ➡ 72 ➡ 74 ➡ 76 ■ What to see ➡ 94 ➡ 96 ➡ 98 ■ Where to shop ➡ 132 ➡ 138

➡ **Where to eat**

San Carlo (18)
Barquillo 10, 28004 ☎ 91 522 79 88 ➡ 91 522 73 01

Ⓜ *Banco de España* **Modern Italian cuisine** ●●● ☐ Ⓒ *daily 1–4.30pm, 9–11.30pm* Ⓨ

A newcomer in a category that is well represented but often disappointing in Madrid, the San Carlo offers authentic trans-alpine cooking. The impressive interior calls to mind the Teatro San Carlo in Naples, a city that was for a long time ruled by Spain. Light pizzas are served up in the first room; in the second, a modestly updated Italian cuisine, with fresh tomato sauce and beef *tagliata* with rocket. Musical evenings at weekends.

Nicolás (19)
Villalar 4, 28001 ☎ ➡ 91 431 77 37

Ⓜ *Banco de España, Retiro* **Creative Spanish cuisine** ●● ☐ Ⓒ *Tue.–Sat. 1.30–4pm, 9pm–midnight; closed Easter week, Aug.*

Formerly a bistro in a working-class neighborhood, Nicolás has now become a comfortable restaurant with minimalist decor and Guinovart prints on the walls. The cuisine served up by Juan Antonio Méndez is as simple and elegant as ever: lamb sweetbreads in breadcrumbs, cassoulet of squid and chickpeas, duck's liver with pears, and perfect cod *ajoarriero* (in garlic).

La Gamella (20)
Alfonso XII 4, 28014 ☎ 91 532 45 09 ➡ 91 523 34 90

Ⓜ *Retiro* **Spanish and American cuisine** ●●● ☐ Ⓒ *Mon.–Fri. 1.30–4pm, 9pm–midnight; Sat. 9pm–midnight; closed Easter week*

A truly postmodern eating house with scarlet walls. The restaurant, run by Richard Stephens, combines the best of Spanish and American cuisine. The latter is fairly predictable (steak tartare with bourbon, excellent cheesecake), while the former is more inventive (eggplant with Manchego cheese and Xérès brandy and a tomato coulis).

Horcher (21)
Alfonso XII 6, 28014 ☎ 91 522 07 31 ➡ 91 523 34 90

Ⓜ *Retiro* **Traditional German cuisine** ●●●●● ☐ Ⓒ *Mon.–Fri. 1.30–4pm, 8.30pm–midnight; Sat. 8.30pm–midnight; closed in August*

The Horchers arrived in Madrid in 1943, when allied bombs were falling on the family restaurant in Berlin. A cozy conservative Saxon atmosphere in which to sample traditional German cuisine served up by Carlos Horcher: herrings with *kartoffelpuffer*, game, Viennese strudels.

Not forgetting

■ **Club 31 (22)** Alcalá 58, 28014 ☎ 91 531 00 92 ●●●●●
International cuisine with a classic finish served in a luxury-style canteen to a well-heeled clientele.

18

18   18

20   NICOLAS   19

Villalar, 4
Teléfono 431 77 37
28001 Madrid

➡ Where to eat

Jockey (23)
Amador de los Ríos 6, 28010 ☎ ➡ 91 319 24 35

🅼 *Colón* **Classic Spanish and French cuisine** ●●●●● ▣ 🕒 *Mon.–Fri. 1–4pm, 9pm–midnight; Sat. 9pm–midnight; closed public holidays, Aug.*

The green, velvet benches and equestrian prints have been here since the restaurant opened in 1945. For over half a century, it has maintained its position at the top of Madrid's restaurant league under the direction of the Cortés family. The cuisine is ultra-conservative, but the well-roasted fatted chicken served up by chef Jesús Barbolla has definite appeal. Private dining rooms, and a clientele of bankers and politicians.

Ciao Madrid (24)
Argensola 7, 28004 Madrid ☎ 91 308 25 19

🅼 *Alonso Martínez* **Italian trattoria** ● ▣ 🕒 *Mon.–Fri. 1.30–3.45pm, 9.30pm–midnight; Sat. 9.30pm–12.30am; closed Easter week, Aug.* 🔼 *Apodaca 20, 28004* ☎ *(91) 447 00 36*

When it comes to authentic, family-run Italian *trattorias*, Ciao Madrid wins hands down. The decor is unremarkable and the service brisk, but the cooking is good and ranges from pasta (*gnocchi al pesto* and ravioli with zucchini) to meat dishes (carpaccio and a robust *cotechino* with lentils). The cellar stocks a good Rosso di Montalcino. The related establishment on Calle Apocada serves excellent pizzas.

El Mentidero de la Villa (25)
Santo Tomé 6, 28004 ☎ 91 308 12 85 ➡ 91 319 87 92

🅼 *Alonso Martínez* **Modern Franco-Spanish cooking** ●● ▣ 🕒 *Mon.–Fri. 1.30–4pm, 9pm–midnight; Sat. 9pm–midnight; closed Aug. 15–31*

The charming proprietor Mario Martínez has created a fairy-tale interior with the aid of *trompe l'oeil* murals and carousel horses. The culinary style is modern Franco-Spanish, featuring unusual but simple fish dishes and perfect cuts of lamb. An excellent cellar stocked with Spanish wines.

Al Mounia (26)
Recoletos 5, 28001 ☎ 91 435 08 28

🅼 *Colón, Banco de España* **Moroccan cuisine** ●●● ▣ 🕒 *Tue.–Sat. 1.30–4pm, 9–11.30pm*

The ornate decorative motifs conceived by Moroccan craftsmen are alone worth a visit, but the best North African restaurant in Madrid has other delights to offer: the *b'stella etheree* (Castilian lamb prepared Moroccan-style) is excellent and the couscous is light and flavorsome. The wines are expensive but not of the standard of the food.

Not forgetting
■ **La Alpargatería (27)** Hermosilla 7, 28001 ☎ 91 577 43 45 ● *Italian-style pasta, Argentinian beef and a no-fuss atmosphere. Modest prices.* ■ **Pelotari (28)** Recoletos 3, 28001 ☎ 91 578 24 97 ●●●●● *Classic Basque cuisine with excellent beef grills.*

■ Where to shop
➡ 136

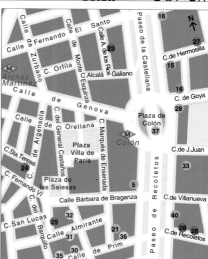

26

At Al Mounia the interior, atmosphere and food will transport you to the Maghreb. An essential 'detour' for those wanting to learn more about Spanish history while in Madrid.

26

24

26

PELOTARI

28

Located north of Retiro Park, this part of the Salamanca district has developed into an upmarket shopping area specializing in designer items and luxury goods. It is here that the most prestigious commercial art galleries are located.

Where to eat

El Amparo (29)
Puigcerdá 8, 28001 ☎ 91 431 64 56 ➡ 91 575 54 91

Ⓜ *Goya* **Modern Spanish cuisine** ●●●●● ▢ ◐ *Mon.–Sat. 1.30–3.30pm, 9–11.30pm; closed Aug. 11–17*

One of the finest and most innovative restaurants in Madrid, El Amparo was relaunched following the arrival as culinary adviser of Martín Berasategui, one of the most outstanding young chefs to emerge from the Basque Country in recent years. Several intimate dining areas are laid out on different levels around a covered interior courtyard. Choose from the prawn and wild mushroom salad, the white tuna and lobster mousse or the grilled turbot with spinach and a shellfish-and-saffron coulis. The menu also includes a selection of choice cuts of meat. Luis Miguel Martín, one of the best sommeliers in Madrid, runs a well-stocked wine cellar that includes bottles of *prioratos* and *riberas*, some of the latest labels to cause a stir.

La Paloma (30)
Jorge Juan 39, 28001 ☎ 91 576 86 92

Ⓜ *Goya, Principe de Vergara* **Creative gourmet cuisine** ●●● ▢ ◐ *Mon.–Sat. 1.30–4pm, 9–11.45pm; closed Easter week, Aug., public holidays*

Segundo Alonso was head chef at El Amparo, but has now opened his own restaurant nearby. La Paloma is less luxurious, and not as beautifully decorated, but the menu is less expensive, while the service is impeccable, and Alonso's cooking is as robust and appealing as ever. This undisputed master of variety meats – notably pigs' trotters – excels equally at wood pigeon stuffed with foie gras, lasagna with spider crab and spinach and watercress coulis. He also creates some mouthwatering desserts.

Teatriz (31)
Hermosilla 15, 28001 ☎ 91 577 53 79

Ⓜ *Serrano* **Italian cuisine** ●●● ▢ ◐ *daily 1.30–4pm, 9pm–1am; closed in Aug.* ▯

A fashionable restaurant where many of the regulars are being squeezed out by crowds of newcomers visiting this old theater – often less for its superb cuisine than for its extraordinary modern decor, designed by Philippe Starck in the early 1990s. Not least among its wonders must be a visit to the *servicios* (W.C.s), in the center of which stands a throne-like fountain of gold, marble and silver, all bathed in a bluish light – you could be forgiven for thinking this was a nightclub.

Not forgetting

■ **La Trainera (32)** Lagasca 60, 28001 ☎ 91 576 05 75 ●●●●
A rustic tasca *serving up excellent seafood. A good* Jabugo *(cured ham) for meat-lovers, plus langoustines, sole and turbot, all delicately prepared.*
■ **El Fogón (33)** Hôtel Wellington, Villanueva 34, 28001 ☎ 91 575 44 00
●● *A good hotel restaurant serving up classic Spanish dishes. Service is smooth.*

29

29

33

32

31

The Teatriz (above) was designed by Philippe Starck, the French architect and interior designer, who attaches great symbolic importance to shapes and spaces.

In the area

Goya is a large upmarket residential district, much of it built in the early 1900s. Its northern perimeter is marked by a splendid plaza dedicated to Salamanca – the man behind this urban grid-plan. The district stretches south to Retiro Park, and is also the most direct route to the bullring.

➡ **Where to eat**

El Buey I (34)
General Pardiñas 10, 28001 ☎ 91 431 44 92

Ⓜ *Príncipe de Vergara* **Grills** ● ▤ 🕓 *daily 1–4pm, 9pm–midnight*

Despite its origin as a 'formula' restaurant, El Buey I has managed to rise above the negative connotations of such a label, as the clientele attests. The long, narrow dining room, resembling a railroad dining-car, is always packed. Diners flock here for the tender slabs of beef roasted over a wood fire, served up in unusually generous portions. A good *estofado de ternera* (beef stew) helps vary the meat theme, but beef is not the only ingredient on the menu. There is onion soup as a starter, a choice of specials (the game and mushroom lasagna is excellent), and lemon sorbet to finish off with, all washed down with a good Duero *ribera* house wine.

Combarro (35)
José Ortega y Gasset 40, 28001 ☎ 91 577 82 72 ➡ 91 435 95 12

Ⓜ *Nuñez de Balboa* **Fish and shellfish** ●●●●● ▤ 🕓 *Mon.–Sat. 1–4.30pm, 8pm–midnight; Sun. 7pm–2am* 🚗 *Reina Mercedes 12, 28020 Tel. 91 554 77 84 Fax. 91 534 25 01*

Did the stone for the façade really come from Galicia? It did according to Manuel Domínguez Limeres who, after almost twenty years in the north of the city where he has won the acclaim of the profession, has opened a second restaurant under the same name. The new Combarro merely enhances his reputation. The very freshest seasonal produce is meticulously prepared to create traditional Galician dishes – from baked bass to *coquilles Saint-Jacques* – while the vast wine cellar is well stocked with excellent French and Spanish wines.

Castelló 9 (36)
Castelló 9, 28001 ☎ / ➡ 91 435 91 34

Ⓜ *Príncipe de Vergara* **Modern Spanish cuisine** ●●● ▤ 🕓 *Mon.–Sat. 1.30–4pm, 9pm–midnight; closed Easter week, public holidays*

Castelló 9 provides a smart setting in which to sample Franco-Spanish food in the style of the Jockey genre ➡ 44. For particular specialties, try the wild-mushroom omelette with lobster or the hake tartare with caviar; neither will disappoint.

El Pescador (37)
José Ortega y Gasset 75, 28006 ☎ 91 402 12 90 ➡ 91 401 30 26

Ⓜ *Lista* **Fish and shellfish** ●●●● ▤ 🕓 *Mon.–Sat. 1–4pm, 8.30pm–midnight; closed Easter week, Aug.*

The rustic setting of El Pescador, with fishing nets hanging from the ceiling, conjures up the dockside taverns of Spain's northern ports. Here, you can sample the same seafood cooking as at O'Pazo ➡ 56, but at slightly lower prices. Enormous fresh sole served up *lenguado Evaristo*-style is unbeatable.

■ Where to stay ➟ 24
■ After dark ➟ 70 ➟ 74
➟ 82 ■ What to see ➟ 98

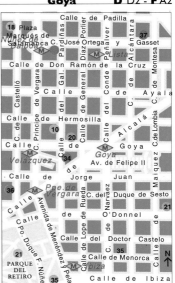

36

37

37

In the area

An extension of the shopping district of Serrano, this is the most attractive section of the Castellana. ■ Where to stay ➡ 24 ➡ 26 ➡ 28
■ After dark ➡ 68 ➡ 70 ➡ 72 ➡ 74 ➡ 80 ■ What to see ➡ 106
■ Where to shop ➡ 130 ➡ 140

Where to eat

Suntory (38)
Paseo de la Castellana 36-38, 28046 ☎ 91 577 37 34 ➡ 91 577 44 55

Ⓜ *Rubén Darío* **Japanese cuisine** ●●●● 🔲 🕓 *Mon.–Sat. 1.30–3.30pm, 8.30–11.30pm; closed public holidays*

With its minimalist décor and maximally attentive service, this exceptional restaurant is a worthy ambassador of the famous Japanese chain which now has branches worldwide. Talented chef Ken Sato presides over three different dining areas (sushi bar, Teppan Yaki, Shabu-Shabu). The superlative quality of the fish and shellfish in the local markets is a source of delight to Japanese chefs in Madrid, and allows them to create exquisite sushi, red tuna sashimi and Mediterranean-prawn tempura. An unforgettable experience, even though it is an expensive one.

Pedro Larumbe (39)
Serrano 61, 28001 ☎ 91 575 11 12 ➡ 91 576 60 19

Ⓜ *Rubén Darío, Núñez de Balboa* **Creative cuisine** ●●●● 🔲 🕓 *Mon.–Fri. 1.30–4pm, 9pm–midnight; Sat. 9pm–midnight; closed public holidays*

Pedro Larumbe, the Navarrese chef who used to preside over the kitchen at the Cabo Mayor ➡ 64, now has his own restaurant, with his own name. The three dining rooms (the stunning Patio Andaluz, the Salón Pompeyano and the Salón Fundador) have retained the *belle époque* interior of the former headquarters of the *ABC* newspaper ➡ 130. The cuisine is appropriately *fin de siècle* too: warm lobster salad with almond mayonnaise or casserole of *kokotxas* (hake cheeks). The wine list is good, if still on the young side.

Le Divellec (40)
Hotel Villa Magna, Paseo de la Castellana 22, 28046
☎ 91 576 75 00 ➡ 91 431 22 86

Ⓜ *Rubén Darío, Serrano* **French cooking, fish and shellfish** ●●●●● 🔲
🕓 *daily 1–4pm, 8.30–11.30pm* ➕ 🔛

The Hyatt chain chose Jacques le Divellec to relaunch the Berceo, at the Hotel Villa Magna, making it one of the most attractive dining venues in Madrid. Decked out in wood, deep-blue fabrics and beautiful Chinese lamps, its magnificent banquet rooms have breathtaking views of the city. After Thierry Buffeteau, it is now Frédéric Fétiveau who has embraced the challenge of creating a seafood-based, French-style cuisine in a city renowned for its fish and shellfish. Since his arrival in 1996 the restaurant has developed innovative dishes such as oven-baked mullet with eggplant and pine-nut ravioli and a julienne of crisp chives.

Not forgetting

■ **La Giralda III (41)** Maldonado 4, 28006 ☎ 91 577 77 62 ●●●●
Fried fish and Andalusian dishes served up in a relaxed décor. Cuisine similar to that of nearby Giralda I (Claudio Coello 24): fluffy rice with clams or hake in sherry.

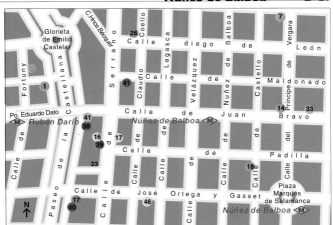

39

The Pedro Larumbe with its stately entrance hall, sophisticated Salón Fundador and banqueting area, La Redacción.

39

39

40

40

In the area

The three most desirable neighborhoods – Salamanca, Chamberí and Chamartín – converge on the verdant Plaza del Doctor Marañón. The area combines noisy thoroughfares and peaceful oases, such as the area around the Museo Nacional de Ciencias Naturales, or the tiny garden of

Where to eat

Zalacaín (42)
Álvarez de Baena 4, 28006 ☎ 91 561 48 40 ➡ 91 561 47 32

Ⓜ *Rubén Darío, Gregorio Marañón* **Haute cuisine** ●●●●● ☐ Ⓢ *Mon.–Fri. 1.30–3.45pm, 9–11.45pm; Sat. 9–11.45pm; closed Easter week, Aug., public holidays*

Since the Zalacaín opened in 1974 it has been the undisputed leader among the top restaurants in Madrid. Although in its early days it cut a radical figure in what was then a traditional field, chef Benjamín Urdiaín's cuisine is today regarded as classic. The interior is reminiscent of a rich 19th-century bourgeois residence, the service is impeccable, and the intelligent wine advice of Custodio Zamarra is a bonus. Memorable culinary encounters include hake sprinkled with thyme, warm salad of young pigeon and foie gras, turbot on a soubise of wild mushrooms and herb butter, crunchy chocolate and warm pineapple desert – each dish is presented with care. The prospect of dining on the new veranda is a pleasant additional attraction.

El Bodegón (43)
Pinar 15, 28006 ☎ 91 562 88 44 / 91 562 31 37 ➡ 91 562 97 25

Ⓜ *Rubén Darío, Gregorio Marañón* **Modern Basque cuisine** ●●●●● ☐ Ⓢ *Mon.–Fri. 1.30–4pm, 9pm–midnight; Sat. 9pm–midnight; closed public holidays, Aug.* 🅨

The elegant yet simple cuisine of Hilario Arbelaitz, who advises El Bodegón from his peaceful retreat in the Basque province of Guipúzcoa (in Oyarzun, Zuberoa), is interpreted admirably in Madrid by chef José Machado. The modern paintings of proprietor Plácido Arango, one of Spain's great collectors, are a treat, while the menu offers a mouthwatering feast for the palate. Snout of Zuberoa veal, soft-boiled eggs on pickled vegetables, oven-baked hake with red pepper coulis or mille feuille with creamed rice and cinnamon ice-cream are on a par with the masterpieces of the Centro Nacional de Arte Reina Sofia ➡ 98.

Belagua (44)
Hotel Santo Mauro, Zurbano 36, 28010
☎ 91 319 69 00 ➡ 91 308 54 77

Ⓜ *Alonso Martínez* **Modern Basque-Navarran cuisine** ●●●●● ☐ Ⓢ *Mon.–Sat. 1.30–3.30pm, 8.30–11pm; closed Easter week, public holidays* 🎫 ➡ 68

A magnificent town-house interior ➡ 22 with postmodern touches. The cuisine varies with chefs. Several special dishes are worth a mention: foie gras sautéd with celery and redcurrants, partridge *en escabeche* (marinated in vinegar with bay leaves) and veal snout with fried chickpeas. In summer the restaurant opens its pleasant terrace. A word of caution: prices are steep.

Not forgetting

■ **Doña (45)** Zurbano 59, 28010 ☎ 91 319 25 51 ● *A delightfully roguish cuisine reminiscent of the Casa Benigno ➡ 58. In 1996, the Doña changed its decor and its menu which became resolutely Mediterranean. The lobsters, prawns and sardines prepared by chef Emilio Serrano are complemented by one of the 89 Spanish wines from the well-stocked cellar.*

the Museo Sorolla. ■ Where to stay ➡ 22 ➡ 26 ➡ 28 ■ After dark ➡ 68 ➡ 70 ■ What to see ➡ 106

43

43

44

The gardens of the Santo Mauro (above) provide the Belagua with a superb summer setting. At tables under the white pergola you can have a full meal, while on the terrace you can sample items from the *pica pica* menu (tapas ➡ 70).

In the area
To the east, Glorieta Cuatro Caminos, once a working-class neighborhood, is now home to the middle classes. To the west, the university district is now surrounded by a new business zone.
■ Where to stay ➡ 28 ■ After dark ➡ 82 ■ What to see ➡ 102

Where to eat

Las Cuatro Estaciones (46)
Paseo San Francisco de Sales 41, 28003
☎ 91 553 63 05 ➡ 91 553 32 98

Ⓜ *Guzmán el Bueno* **Creative gourmet cuisine** ●●●● ▱ Ⓘ *June–Sep: Mon.–Fri. 1.30–4pm, 9pm–midnight / Oct.–May: Mon.–Fri. 1.30–4pm, 9pm–midnight, Sat. 9pm–midnight / closed Jan. 1, Easter week, Aug.*

Francisco Arias reigns over this modern, flower-decked dining space. Although it opened in 1981, the somber colors give it the air of a 1970s disco, but dancing is far from the thoughts of the diners as they tuck into some of the best food in Madrid, served up by young Francisco Vicente. From ravioli with asparagus to bull's tail with breadcrumbs and sautéed potatoes, or cod cased in pastry, the choice is wide-ranging and imaginative. Impeccable service at all times.

Las Batuecas (47)
Avenida Reina Victoria 17, 28003 ☎ 91 554 04 52

Ⓜ *Guzmán el Bueno, Cuatro Caminos* **Spanish cuisine** ● ▱ Ⓘ *Mon.–Fri. 1–4pm, 9–11pm; Sat. 1–4pm*

The building and its interior are unremarkable, but the wholesome and unpretentious cuisine are certainly noteworthy. This *casa de comidas* (literally, 'meal house') has proved itself time and again. Las Batuecas opened its doors in 1954 and has survived by virtue of its above-average *comidas* – a culinary genre that, sadly, is becoming increasingly rare. The clientele remains faithful from one generation to the next, dining out here on home cooking at low prices: traditional specialties include fried whiting, squid in its own ink, omelette with potatoes (*tortilla española*) and asparagus accompanied by *callos* (tripe) *a la madrileña*. A first-class eatery.

San Mamés (48)
Bravo Murillo 88, 28003 ☎ 91 534 50 65

Ⓜ *Cuatro Caminos* **Spanish cuisine** ●●● ▱ Ⓘ *Mon.–Fri. 1.30–4pm, 8.30–11pm; Sat. 2.30–4pm; closed public holidays, Aug.*

Nine tables are crammed into two small rooms decorated with multi-colored *azulejos* (ceramic tiles): signs that this is a good, honest *tasca* ➡ 36. Santiago García, however, is not content with serving up basic *tasca* cuisine. Occasionally too grand (take the fillet with duck liver, for example), the cooking is perfect when it relies on regional recipes: hotpot of haricot beans, black pudding and chorizo from Ávila, or sautéed meadow mushrooms and tripe *a la madrileña*.

Not forgetting

■ **Sal Gorda (49)** Beatríz de Bobadilla 9, 28040 ☎ 91 553 95 06 ●
The dining area resembles a bourgeois dining room and the cuisine is suitably in keeping: superb menestra of fresh vegetables, excellent roast beef, bacalao ajoarriero (salt cod with garlic) and apple tart. Service is attentive, and the prices reasonable.

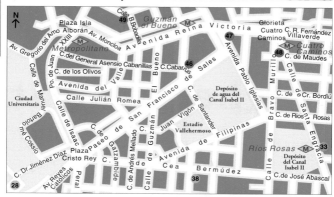

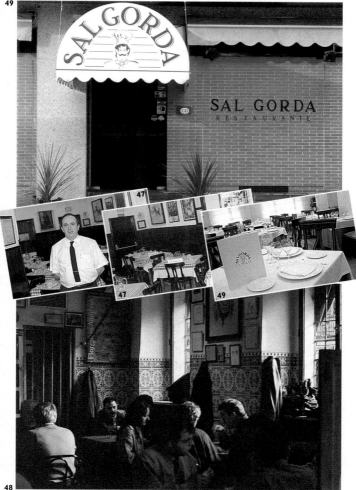

In the area

This immense ministerial complex, begun in the 1930s and completed under General Franco, together with the Azca commercial complex, its contemporary equivalent, form the hub of the modern city's expansion. The 'Manhattan of Madrid', this second city center is where the

Where to eat

O'Pazo (50)
Reina Mercedes 20, 28020 ☎ 91 553 23 33 ➡ 91 554 90 72

Ⓜ *Nuevos Ministerios, Alvarado* **Fish and seafood** ●●●● ▭ Ⓒ *Mon.–Sat. 1–4pm, 8.30pm–midnight; closed in Aug.*

Evaristo García – a fishmonger in his youth and now a big name in Spain's upmarket fish trade – supplies the best restaurants in the land. In this English-style dining room, one corner of which is a library, he is in his element. His chef Francisco Monje prepares simple, perfectly cooked fish and shellfish. The oven-baked turbot with olive oil and vinegar is exquisite.

Goizeko Kabi (51)
Comandante Zorita 37, 28020 ☎ 91 533 01 85 ➡ 91 533 02 14

Ⓜ *Alvarado* **Basque cuisine** ●●●●● ▭ Ⓒ *June 16–Sep. 15: Mon.–Fri. 1.30–4pm, 8.30pm–midnight, Sat. 8.30pm–midnight / Sep.16–June 15: Mon.–Sat. 1.30–4pm, 8.30pm–midnight*

The Madrid branch of the famous Bilbao restaurant. The squid with onions, red meat, fried hake or woodcock roasted in Jesús Santos' old brandy are in the best Biscay tradition. English-style décor, but a small room. Book in advance.

Gaztelupe (52)
Comandante Zorita 32, 28020 ☎ 91 534 90 28 ➡ 91 554 65 66

Ⓜ *Nuevos Ministerios, Estrechos* **Rotisserie, Basque specialties** ●●● ▭ Ⓒ *June 16–Sep. 15: Mon.–Sat. 1.30–4pm, 8.30pm–midnight, Sun. 1.30–4pm / Sep.16–June 15: Mon.–Sat. 1.30–4pm, 8.30pm–midnight*

The emphasis here is on the spectacular – or, if you like, 'Hollywood' – version of the popular Biscay inns, with all the expected classics of the genre: tender kidney beans from Tolosa, *zancarrón* (ragout) of veal, *marmitako* (a soup of tuna, potatoes and green peppers), and rice pudding. Very good wines.

Babel (53)
Alonso Cano 60, 28003 ☎ 91 553 08 27

Ⓜ *Ríos Rosas* **Armenian specialties, grilled meats** ●● ▭ Ⓒ *Mon.–Fri. 1.30–4pm, 8.30pm–midnight; Sat. 8.30pm–midnight; closed Aug.*

The regulars know what to expect with Armik Hamparzoumian: perfect roasts of Galician beef, which have made this one of Madrid's best meat-eating establishments, and exotic hors d'oeuvres, such as the tender Armenian-style eggplants. Good red wines.

Not forgetting

■ **Da Nicola (54)** Orense 4, 28020 ☎ 91 555 76 37 ● *Huge underground premises offering good, authentic Italian cuisine at low prices.*
■ **Alborán (55)** Ponzano 39, 28003 ☎ 91 399 21 50 ●● *A tiny dining room in which to enjoy good Andalusian seafood.*

multinational corporations are located. ■ After dark ➡ 86 ■ What to see ➡ 108

O'Pazo (above) is among the fish and seafood restaurants that have earned Madrid its gastronomic reputation. Though situated at the center of the Iberian peninsula, nearly 200 miles from the nearest sea, Madrid is considered by seafood aficionados to be the best 'port' in the country.

Where to eat

Príncipe y Serrano (56)
Serrano 240, 28016 ☎ 91 458 62 31 ➡ 91 458 86 76

Ⓜ *Concha Espina, Colombia* **Modern Castilian cuisine** ●●●● ▭ 🕙 ⭐
Mon.–Fri. 2–4pm, 8.30pm–midnight; Sat. 8.30pm–midnight; closed in Aug.

The view of lawns and flower beds, seen through the restaurant's bay window, make it difficult to believe that you are dining in central Madrid. Service is attentive, the setting classic and luxurious, and yet Príncipe y Serrano is still affordable, thanks to intelligent management by Salvador Gallego's two daughters. Gallego, the 'guru' of haute cuisine in the Sierra of Madrid, keeps a discreet eye on this, the second of his family establishments. The cuisine is simple yet sophisticated, in the very best Spanish tradition – try the *txangurro* (spider crab cocktail), or boned oxtail in flaky pastry. The cellar is interesting, with some very good and unusual Iberian wines, such as Veigadares, a vat-fermented white wine from Galicia.

Casa Benigna (57)
Benigno Soto 9, 28002 ☎ 91 413 33 56 ➡ 91 416 93 57

Ⓜ *Concha Espina* **Mediterranean cuisine and Scandinavian specialties**
●●●● ▭ 🕙 *daily 1.30–4pm, 9.30–11.45pm*

The bright colors of this simple bistro and the landscape paintings on the wall divert attention from the low ceiling, which might otherwise seem oppressive. By the side of his mother, ever present beside the stoves, Norberto Jorge (who comes from Alicante but has lived for 20 years in Norway and still commutes between Madrid and Oslo) offers some of the most exquisitely prepared dishes in town. The dual influence – resulting in dishes that could be termed Hispano-Scandinavian – produces a unique menu. For instance, the marinated herring with horseradish contrasts with sumptuous vegetarian paellas, prawns *en papillote* and scampi *al ajillo* (in garlic mayonnaise). There is always an excellent fish of the day and the international wine list includes some interesting finds at a democratic range of prices.

La Atalaya (58)
Joaquín Costa 31, 28002 ☎ 91 562 87 45

Ⓜ *República Argentina* **Cantabrian cuisine** ●● ▭ 🕙 *Tue.–Sat. 1–4.30pm, 9pm–midnight; Mon. 1–4pm; closed public holidays and one week in Aug.*

The walls of La Atalaya are covered with modern paintings – the owners come from Santander, a city where virtually every restaurant and bar resembles an art gallery. The atmosphere is restrained but hospitable and the cuisine comes straight from Spain's verdant north, with specialties such as *maganos* (minuscule squid) prepared with onions, and fried anchovies stuffed with *piquillos*. At lunchtime, La Atalaya offers a cheap but interestingly authentic menu, based on the rustic dishes of Cantabria (the region south of the Bay of Biscay in the province of Santander). Choose a Thursday or a Saturday for your visit in order to savor *cocido montañés*, a hearty cabbage soup with haricot beans, sausage and black pudding.

■ What to
see ➡ 108
■ Where to
shop ➡ 142

Norberto Jorge
runs the Casa
Benigna ('gentle
house') like the
Sancho, his other
Oslo restaurant,
with a master's
hand. Here he is
the chef as well
as the owner,
and sometimes
even provides
the evening's
entertainment by
playing the guitar.

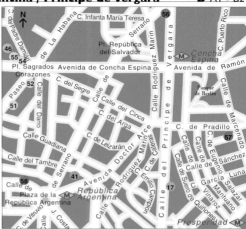

The Palacio de Congresos and the immense Bernabéu football stadium, home of Real Madrid, extend the city northward. The shops of the Castellana and of the streets running parallel rival those of the Serrano district. ■ Where to stay ➡ 30 ■ After dark ➡ 80

➡ Where to eat

El Comité (59)
Plaza de San Amaro 8, 28020 ☎ 91 571 87 11 ➡ 91 435 43 27

Ⓜ Santiago Bernabéu **Creative gourmet cuisine** ●●● ▣ Ⓞ *Mon.–Fri. 1.30–4pm, 9pm–midnight; Sat. 9pm–12.30am; closed in Aug.*

Old photos of revolutionary parties and women's charitable committees adorn the walls of this bistro, where Agnès Masso and her French chef Claude Maison d'Arblay offer elegant dishes to a devoted clientele. These include monkfish with mascarpone and a red wine sauce and julienne of fried pears, followed by hazelnut Charlotte with a coffee-flavored coulis.

La Tahona (60)
Capitán Haya 21, 28020 ☎ 91 555 04 41 ➡ 91 556 62 02

Ⓜ Cuzco **Castilian cuisine** ●● ▣ Ⓞ *Mon. –Sat. 1–4pm, 9pm–midnight; Sun. 1–4pm; closed in Aug.*

Madrid has several Hollywood-style restaurants, but La Tahona, designed to resemble a basilica, is inimitable. A branch of the restaurant chain created in Aranda de Duero, and home to tender, Castilian milk-fed lamb, the place is itself a temple dedicated to the glory of this traditional Spanish roast.

Príncipe de Viana (61)
Manuel de Falla 5, 28036 ☎ 91 457 15 49 ➡ 91 457 52 83

Ⓜ Santiago Bernabéu **Basque and Navarin cuisine** ●●●●● ▣ Ⓞ *Mon.–Fri. 1–4pm, 9–11.45pm; Sat. 9–11.45pm; closed Easter week, Aug., public holidays*

Ramón Quintanilla, the chef who trained here before launching another successful restaurant, has returned to the fold in order to maintain the highest quality of popular cuisine in the city. In this distinctive and cheerful setting, the *menestra* of fresh spring vegetables and oven-baked fish merit the highest culinary accolades. Attentive service.

El Cenachero (62)
Manuel de Falla 8, 28036 ☎ 91 457 59 04

Ⓜ Santiago Bernabéu **Mediterranean cuisine** ●● ▣ Ⓞ *Mon.–Fri. 1.30–4pm, 9.30pm–midnight; Sat. 9.30pm–midnight; closed in Aug.*

This kind of small, unpretentious restaurant, perfect for an intimate dinner, is rare in Madrid. El Cenachero offers the flavors of maritime Andalusia (in Malaga a *cenachero* is a port peddler), interpreted delicately by chef Alberto Chicote: broad beans and snow peas with smoked duck breast, tomatoes stuffed with crab, tuna with a compote of tomato and basil, and sea bream with oven-roasted vegetables. Exceptional quality at reasonable prices.

Not forgetting

■ **Asador de Roa (63)** Pintor Juan Gris 5, 28039 ☎ 91 555 39 28 ●● *Castilian cuisine. Specialties: milk-fed oven-roasted lamb and roast piglet.*

■ What to
see ➡ 108
■ Where to
shop ➡ 142

RESTAURANTE EL C...

Calle Sor

Angela de la Cruz

Plaza de Cuzco

Av. de A. Alcocer

Jiménez

39

Ⓜ Cuzco

Calle de Huesca

Orense

Varela

Brasil

Haya

C. Pintor Juan Gris

63

60

Doctor Fleming

Calle de Juan Ramón

Calle Panamá

Calle del General Yagüe

C. de Prof. Waksman

35

Plaza San Amaro

C. General Cabrera

General del Capitán

Pedro Teixeira

Paseo de la Castellana

Calle

61

62

C. del Padre Damián

59

38

31

Calle del General

Orgaz

Avenida

de

Pl. Manolete

Calle

C. Rafael Salgado

Calle

Calle

45

Palacio de Congresos y Exposiciones

2

Estadio Santiago Bernabéu

46

Ⓜ Santiago Bernabéu

N ↑

Avenida del General Perón

Plaza de Lima

Av. de Concha Espina

36

53

59

59

59

La Tahona

60

62

60

'...in true Spanish inns,
naturally you can eat and
drink, but you also enjoy what
others bring to the place.'
Abraham Bengio

In the area

The Ciudad Lineal – a model district of villas and broad, pine-shaded avenues dating from the early 1900s – has been dramatically altered by sprawling urban developments. Mayor Arturio Soria would no longer recognize his own town. Despite this, the district is still very pleasant.

Where to eat

Casa d'a Troya (64)
Emiliano Barral 14, 28043 ☎ 91 416 44 55

Ⓜ *Avenida de La Paz* **Galician cuisine** ●● ▨ Ⓧ *Mon.–Sat. 1.30–3.30pm, 8.30–11pm; closed July 15–Aug. 31, Christmas, public holidays*

With the exception of a fine rustic-style slate façade, the setting is unremarkable and resembles that of an ordinary restaurant in a new suburb. However, appearances are deceptive because this is a high temple of Galician tradition. Pilar Vila serves octopus, *camarones* (small shrimps), hake, pork knuckle with turnip tops, and almond tart of the highest quality, yet at reasonable prices, using produce sent daily from northwestern Spain. Understandably the regular clientele is devoted so be sure to book well in advance.

La Misión (65)
José Silva 22, 28043 ☎ 91 519 24 63 ➡ 91 416 26 93

Ⓜ *Arturo Soria* 🔲 **Classic Basque cuisine** ●●●● ▨ Ⓧ *Mon.–Fri. 1.30–4pm, 9pm–midnight; Sat. 9pm–midnight; closed Easter week, Aug.* ✖

The charming décor, complete with pink stucco and exposed beams, conjures up the image of a Spanish 17th-century mission in California. Yet the cuisine at La Misión makes no allusions to new-wave Californian cuisine. Indeed it is firmly rooted in Hispanic tradition, with a heavy Basque accent. Our gastronomic recommendation is the excellent oven-baked turbot, one of the star dishes on the menu.

Nicomedes (66)
Moscatelar 18, 28043 ☎ 91 388 78 28 ➡ 91 388 78 28

Ⓜ *Arturo Soria* **Estremaduran specialties, creative cuisine** ●●● ▨ Ⓧ *Sun.–Mon. 1.30–4pm; Tue.–Sat. 1–4pm, 9–11pm* ✖

A modern villa with huge bay windows opening onto a flower-filled garden, the restaurant of Elena and Concha Suárez has a strong New World flavor, with 1940s jazz playing gently in the background. The cuisine is thoroughly modern, and incorporates imaginative touches from the region of Extremadura. Especially memorable dishes include Iberian pork and the exquisitely soft farm cheese, *Torta del Casar*, made from ewe's milk. The service, presided over by the two sisters, is charming and friendly, and the cellar boasts a fine selection of many of the best 'new' Spanish wines.

Don Víctor (67)
Emilio Vargas 18, 2843 ☎ 91 415 47 47 ➡ 91 320 93 10

Ⓜ *Arturo Soria* 🔲 **Fish, Galician cuisine** ●●●●● ▨ Ⓧ *Mon.–Fri. 1–4.30pm, 9–11pm; Sat. 9–11pm; closed in Aug.*

Don Víctor's modern bistro is one of the few culinary options available in a new business district still badly served by restaurants. The Galician owners offer superb fish and excellent red meats roasted in a crust of coarse salt. The high quality is reflected in the check.

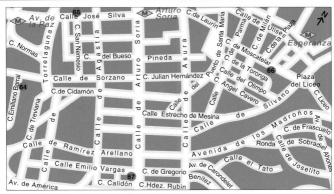

Av. de la Paz · Calle José Silva **65** · M · Arturo Soria · C.de Laurín · Calle de Milán · Calle de Ulises Plaza
C. Normas · Torrelaguna · C. San Nemesio · C. de Agastia · del Bueso · Calle de Arturo Soria · Pineda · C. de Asura · C. de Moscatelar · C. de Parma · C. de la Plata · Esperanza
64 · C.Emiliano Barral · C.de Treviana · Calle de Sorzano · C. de Cidamón · C. Julián Hernández · Calle del Puerto de Santa María · Calle de la Toronga · Calle del Olimpo · **66** · Plaza del Liceo · C. Liceo
Calle de Ramírez · Arellano · Calle Estrecho de Mesina · C. Angel Cavero · Calle · de · Silvano · Calle de los Madroños · C. de Frascuelo
Calle Emilio Vargas · Calle · Avenida de los Madroños · Ronda · Calle de Sobradiel · Añorbes · Calle de Joselito
Av. de América · **67** · C. Calidón · C. de Gregorio · C.Hdez. Rubín · Benítez · Av. de Carondelet · Calle el Tato

65

65

66

64

66

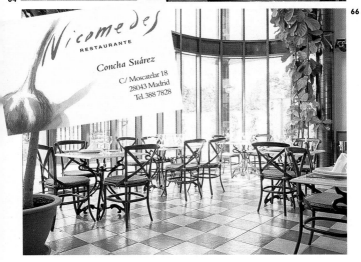

Nicomedes
RESTAURANTE

Concha Suárez

C/ Moscatelar 18
28043 Madrid
Tel. 388 7828

In the area
The shaded streets of this quiet district are frequented mainly by office workers who, at various times of day, leave their work to chat or relax at the tables of the local terrace bars. ■ Where to stay ➡ 30 ➡ 32
■ After dark ➡ 70 ➡ 80

Where to eat

El Olivo (68)
General Gallegos 1, 28036 ☎ 91 359 15 35 ➡ 91 345 91 83

🅼 *Cuzco, Plaza de Castilla* **Mediterranean cuisine** ●●●● ▢ 🛇 *Tue.–Sat. 1–4pm, 9pm–midnight; closed Aug. 15–30* 🆈

The vocation of this olive-green restaurant is clear: virgin olive oils and Xérèz wines constitute its main culinary theme. Born in Bordeaux and raised in Andalusia, Jean-Pierre Vandelle's Franco-Spanish background produces some superb results. Don't miss the springtime specialty, lamprey in Ribera del Duero wine, or the monkfish *a la plancha* (grilled on a hot plate) with a black olive coulis.

Aldaba (69)
Avenida Alberto Alcocer 5, 28036 ☎ 91 345 21 93 ➡ 91 350 83 03

🅼 *Cuzco* **Basque and Navarin cuisine** ●●●● ▢ 🛇 *Mon.–Fri. 1–4pm, 9pm–midnight; Sat. 9pm–midnight; closed in Aug.*

This intimate little restaurant was renovated by the team from Zalacaín ➡ 52, headed by José Luis Pereira. It lays on some of the best cuisine in Madrid, with an emphasis on regional and market produce: cod salad with a compote of tomatoes and spiced oil, and lasagna of monkfish and king prawns with sage.

Cabo Mayor (70)
Juan Ramón Jiménez 37, 28036 ☎ 91 350 87 76 ➡ 91 359 16 21

🅼 *Cuzco* **Creative cuisine** ●●●● ▢ 🛇 *Mon.–Sat. 1–4pm, 9pm–midnight; closed Easter week, Aug. 15–31, public holidays*

The cavernous, nautical-themed interior of this restaurant is decorated in the style of a Santander farmhouse. The son and daughter of founder Victor Merino maintain the tradition of modern regional cuisine, aided by chef Carlos Barasoain's passion for spices: try the turbot with asparagus and squid or supreme of young pigeon.

Asador Frontón (71)
Pedro Muguruza 8, 28036 ☎ 91 345 36 96

🅼 *Cuzco* 🉐 **Basque grilled meats and fish** ●●● ▢ 🛇 *Mon.–Sat. 1–4pm, 9pm–midnight; Sun. 1–4pm* 🆑 *Jesús y María 1, 28012* ☎ *(91) 369 23 25*

Madrid is a meat-eater's paradise. With its superb Basque-style grilled meats and slabs of beef, the Frontón is the front runner in this field. The fish is equally good. A busy and noisy atmosphere. Book ahead.

Not forgetting
■ **Sacha (72)** Hurtado de Mendoza 11, 28036 ☎ 91 345 59 52 ●● *Galician cuisine served up by Pitila Hormaechea and son Sacha: clams with creamed turnips, partridge with mushrooms and rice.*
■ **Alborada (73)** Henri Dunant 23, 28036 ☎ 91 359 18 42 ●● *From Tuesday to Saturday, simple, fresh ingredients and Mediterranean flavors prepared by the former chef of El Olivo.*

69

69

As you go down into the Cabo Mayor (below), look up at the bronze sculptures (left) of children preparing to leap into the water to fish out the coins thrown there by passers-by – a once-familiar scene in Santander.

70

70

72

71

La Filmoteca Española
International movies in the original language.
Cine Dore *Santa Isabel 3, 28012* ☎ *(91) 369 11 25*

➤ After dark

Listings magazines
To check out day-to-day
cultural events:
La Guía del Ocio,
weekly from news-stands.
¿ Que Hacer en Madrid ?,
*free monthly from the tourist
office in Plaza Mayor (bilingual
Spanish-English).*

Open to all
There are no private clubs in Madrid.
Some places try to discourage
customers by putting up *aforo completa*
(full) notices, but no door can resist
the determined night owl.

'Vamos de juerga' say
Madrileños as they prepare for a night
on the town. Not too fond of private
parties, they cram the countless bars.
They say there are more bars in one
Madrid neighborhood than in the
whole of Switzerland.

Chocolate con churros

Follow an old city tradition and indulge in this late-night treat: long, crunchy fritters dunked in a steaming cup of thick hot chocolate.

Chocolatería San Ginés *Pasaje de San Ginés 5, 28013* ☎ *91 365 65 46*
🔲 *Oct.–May: Tue.–Thur. 7pm–10pm; Fri.–Sun. 7pm–7am; July-Aug: Tue.–Sun. 10pm–7am; June, Sep, Tue.–Thur. Midnight–7am, Fri.–Sun. 7pm–7am.*

Nights out

THE INSIDER'S FAVORITES

Cultural events calendar

May–June Madrid City Rock Festival *Mastertrax* ☎ *91 304 95 17* Madrid Dance Festival *Información del Ayuntamiento* ☎ *010*
Summer (Sunday Concerts by the Banda Municipal in the Parque del Retiro) *Información del Ayuntamiento* ☎ *010*
July Johnny Walker Music Festival *Caja de Cataluña* ☎ *902 38 33 33*

July–Sep. Summer in the City *Información del Ayuntamiento* ☎ *010*
Sep.–Oct. Autumn Festival *Información del Ayuntamiento* ☎ *010*
Oct.–April Chamber and polyphonic music concerts *Auditorio Nacional de Música* ☎ *91 337 01 00*
Nov. Jazz festival *Caja de Cataluña* ☎ *902 38 33 33*

Basic facts

With the arrival of the first fine days of summer, which is always early in Madrid, the capital's inhabitants take to the streets, and re-acquaint themselves with their summer haunts. Chairs and parasols spill out onto the sidewalk as the *terrazas* re-open between April and June. This is

After dark

Terraza Bulevar (1)
Paseo de la Castellana 37, 28046 ☎ 91 308 51 45 / 91 308 52 58

Ⓜ *Rubén Darío* Ⓢ *May 15–Sep. 30: daily noon–5am* ▱ Ⓜ *Serrano 41–45, 28001 ☎ (91) 578 18 65 ; Paseo de la Castellana 12, 28046*

Summer visitors to Madrid are drawn inexorably to the colorful crowds filling the *terrazas* of the Castellana, the city's vital artery. Lately El Bulevar has become *the* spot to visit on a summer's night, frequented by stars and personalities such as Richard Gere, Michael Jackson and Samantha Fox. Any day of the week, however, the movers and shakers from the world of business, bullfighting, sports or showbiz come to drink here. After celebrity spotting at the Bulevar, wander down the Castellana for a drink at the terrace bars of the Bolero, Embassy or Castellana 8 ➡ 72. Here you can sample the beach-style holiday atmosphere of Madrid, complete with blaring music.

Fortuny (2)
Fortuny 34, 28010 ☎ 91 310 18 49

Ⓜ *Rubén Dario* Ⓢ *daily 1.30pm–6am* �𝍄 *Mon.–Thur. 1.30–4pm, 9pm–12.30am; Fri.–Sun. 1.30–4pm, 9pm–1.30am ☎ 91 319 05 88* ▱

The Fortuny occupies a 19th-century mansion (1896) that offers a unique setting less than 100 yards from the Castellana. The three-story building, whose vast terrace holds up to 1,000 people, stands in a district of former private mansions that now house foreign embassies. Guests can simply enjoy a drink, dine in the lively restaurant or hold a private function. Since it opened in May 1997, Fortuny has been one of Madrid's most popular venues. From the vaguely to the seriously glamorous, as well as the simply curious, all come to enjoy the cool freshness of the magnificent garden.

Hotel Santo Mauro (3)
Zurbano 36, 28010 ☎ 91 319 69 00

Ⓜ *Alonso Martínez* Ⓢ *May–Sep.: daily 10–3am* ▱ �𝍄 *Belagua* ➡ 52

In summer the delightful garden of the hotel Santo Mauro ➡ 22 is transformed into a *terraza*. One part is reserved for restaurant diners, while the other contains a bar. Shaded by magnificent chestnut trees, this is one of the most elegant and intimate places for a romantic rendezvous in the city, or simply for an opportunity to enjoy a relaxed drink with friends.

Not forgetting

■ **Cafe de Oriente (4)** Plaza de Oriente 2, 28013 ☎ 91 541 39 74
In May this is one of the best terrazas in the city. Service is impeccable. A classic Madrileño café in a newly pedestrianized area.
■ **El Espejo (5)** Paseo de Recoletos 31, 28004 ☎ 91 308 23 47
Like the famous Café Gijon further down the Paseo, El Espejo terraza recreates the ambience of a belle-époque literary café. The splendid glass pavilion is worthy of admiration in its own right.

where the *Madrileño* puts the world to rights over a coffee or cool drink, and where the visitor can taste an authentic slice of Madrid life.

Below the elegant glass roof of the famous *belle-époque* pavilion of El Espejo, it is sometimes difficult to find a seat.

3

5

5

4

Basic facts

Various anecdotes are used to explain the origin of tapas. One theory is that *tapear* – getting a bite to eat – became popular in the reign of Charles III, when in the army it became obligatory to have something to eat with a drink in order to 'moderate' the effect of the alcohol.

After dark

José Luis (6)
Serrano 89-91, 28006 ☎ 91 563 09 58

Ⓜ *Rubén Darío* 🈁 Ⓢ *daily 9–1am* ▬ Ⓨ ⟨▸⟩ *Paseo de la Habana 4, 28036 ☎ 91 562 75 96; Paseo San Francisco de Sales 14-16, 28003 ☎ 91 442 67 90; Rafael Salgado 11, 28036 ☎ 91 458 80 28; Teatro Real ➡ 78*

For years now, the tapas served up at José Luis have been an unmissable treat come snack-time. When you don't feel up to a full-blown meal and are looking for a relaxed atmosphere, there is always a José Luis nearby. The four branches in Madrid tend to be permanently packed, proof of the quality of the *pinchos* (literally, 'little pieces of something'), which are both varied and copious. Sirloin, hake, crab salad, fritters, salmon or potato *tortillas* are all popular, but the list is endless.

Handicap (7)
General Oráa 56, 28006 ☎ 91 562 21 59

Ⓜ *Diego de León* Ⓢ *Mon.–Sat. 1–4pm, 8pm–1am; closed public holidays, Aug.* ▤

The owner was a dancer at the Paris Lido in the 1950s, has performed for the Queen of England and was a triumph at Las Vegas. A fan of French refinement, his restaurant resembles a tiny Parisian bistro. Yet this is not to say that Juan Contreras has turned his back on Spain when it comes to culinary matters, for it was he who introduced to Madrid those tiny baguettes, called *bocadillos* (then later *pulgas*), which serve as a base for smoked meats, pâtés, black pudding or sirloin steak with Dijon mustard. His 'astronaut potatoes' (fried potatoes with scrambled eggs)

11

Another, more simple, explanation is that to *tapear* is a natural urge for the Spanish.

and *Kung-fu* (marinaded tuna with mayonnaise and vinaigrette) have been a resounding success. The cramped premises can be a problem at busy times, but this is no reason to miss out on the experience.

Punto Cero (8)
Serrano 93, 28006
☎ 91 561 27 89

Ⓜ *Rubén Darío, Avenida América*
🕒 *daily 7–2am* ⬛ ✴

A shopping street, a nearby business school, a pleasant owner and a wide range of *pinchos*, both hot and cold: all this explains why the Punto Cerro is full at 9pm every evening. Here, a glass of wine becomes a reason to *tapear*, which later on becomes an excuse for a full-blown meal. Outdoor seating between April and September – sometimes later – when the crowded *terraza* is noisy, but convivial.

Not forgetting

■ **Cervecería Alemana (9)** Plaza Santa Ana ☎ 91 429 70 33
To tapear in this bar, or in the next-door Cerveceria Santa Ana or Naturbier, is one of the delights of Madrid.
■ **La Daniela (10)** General Pardiñas 21, 28028 ☎ 91 575 23 29
An authentic Spanish taberna serving excellent tapas: stuffed olives, bread rubbed with garlic or topped with fresh tomato.
■ **Las Cumbres (11)** Avenida Alberto Alcocer 32, 28036
☎ 91 458 76 92 *To be sampled seated or at the bar: Jabugo (cured ham), oxtail, cheese, home-made fritters, squid, lettuce hearts with anchovies. A little corner of Andalucía.*

Basic facts

Every day of the week from about 8pm in the evening, when the tapas hour is over, hundreds of places open their doors to those wanting to *ir copas* (have a drink) and listen to some music. This is the time of the night when the *Madrileños* meet up with friends and launch into

After dark

Cock (12)
Reina 16, 28004 ☎ 91 532 28 26

🅜 *Gran Via, Banco de España* 🕑 *Mon.–Thur. 7pm–3am, Fri.–Sat. 7pm–4am*
● *950 Ptas* 🔲

This cocktail bar never disappoints. This is partly due to its charming surroundings – the high ceiling and old oak furniture that are the dominant features of its elegant 1920s interior. The key to its success is also the *mojitos* and other delicious cocktails that can be sampled here. It attracts a mixed clientele from a spectrum that can range from politicians to actors of stage or screen.

Honky-Tonk (13)
Covarrubias 24, 28010 ☎ 91 445 68 86 ➡ 91 445 68 86

🅜 *Bilbao, Alonso Martínez* 🕑 *daily 9pm–5am* ● *800 Ptas–900 Ptas* 🔲 🎵
Sun.–Fri. after midnight, rock, blues, fusion 🍴 *Honky-Tonk Café*

After nine years as one of the city's top venues, the Honky Tonk is still one of the best disco-bars in Madrid. Its formula: good cocktails and other drinks, live bands and exhibitions of photos and paintings. Its program satisfies lovers of country music, swing, jazz, rock or blues; as if this is not enough, it also features magicians and one-person shows. It attracts a regular crowd of sports personalities, actors and night owls, between the ages of 18 and 45.

El Viso Madrid (14)
Juan Bravo 31, 28006 ☎ 91 562 23 79 ➡ 91 562 23 79

🅜 *Diego de Léon* 🕑 *daily 9pm–5am* ● *900 Ptas* 🔲 🎵 *Wed. 10.30pm* 🔲 ✪

One of the latest bars to hit the scene. It was bought recently by the owners of the El Viso terrace bar, and the regular clientele followed. It is known less for its hi-tech décor than for the animated crowds jamming its entrance. Upstairs, there is a quiet area for chatting. The ground level is the place to parade or people-watch, and you can let your hair down on the downstairs dance floor.

Gayarre (15)
Paseo de la Castellana 118, 28046 ☎ 91 564 25 15

🅜 *Nuevos Ministerios* 🕑 *Mon.–Thur. 6pm–3am; Fri., Sat. 6pm–4am*
● *1000 Ptas* 🔲

This former cinema opened as a bar in 1992. The spacious premises are decorated with bowls of fruit and rustic kitchen utensils and the candlelight and gentle background music combine to create an atmosphere that is popular with the over-35s. ★ Twice a week, but never the same day, a surprise buffet is served up free of charge.

Not forgetting

■ **Castellana 8 (16)** Paseo de la Castellana 8, 28046 ☎ 91 431 30 54 *A warm welcome and intimate ambience in this bar.*

animated conversations,
setting the world to rights.

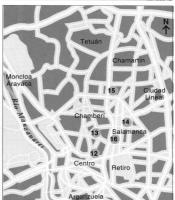

73

Basic facts

When it comes to classical music, Spain is known more for its opera than for its symphonic orchestras. Nowadays, however, the choice during the season (October to June) is seemingly limitless. Concerts are held almost daily, either in the capital's main concert halls or in more unusual

After dark

Auditorio Nacional de Música (17)
Príncipe de Vergara 146, 28002 ☎ 91 337 01 00

🅼 *Cruz del Rayo* 🕔 **Concerts** *7.30pm; 10.30pm* **Information** *daily 8am–10pm* **Box office** *Mon. 5–7pm, Tue.–Fri. 10am–5pm, Sat. 11am–1pm (for some concerts 100 tickets are on sale 1 hr before the show)* ● *4200–8100 Ptas* **Concerts Ibermusica** ☎ 91 359 09 64 ▣ ▣

Founded in 1988, the auditorium contains two halls, one for symphonic music and the other for chamber music, with 2200 and 700 seats respectively. In the former, which is almost rectangular in shape, the ceiling has been designed to achieve maximum acoustic effect, and to allow different sections of the orchestra to be heard more precisely. The semi-circular chamber hall is designed to maintain proximity between orchestra and audience. The National Auditorium is home to the Spanish National Orchestra (the *Orquestra Nacional de España,* or ONE) and its associated choir, who play here from October to June. In tandem, the group Ibermúsica organizes the *Orchestras del Mundo* between October and May, featuring major international orchestras. Though in theory reserved for season-ticket holders, some of the upmarket hotels should be able to procure tickets. Elsewhere in the capital, the *Pro-Música* cycle and programs at the Polytechnic, Complutense and Autónoma universities are usually of interest. Finally, the concerts organized by the *Orquestra Nacional de España* and the *Liceo de Cámara* between October and June offer music lovers of all types the opportunity to enjoy both chamber and polyphonic music.

Fundación Juan March (18)
Castelló 77, 28006 ☎ 91 435 42 40 ➡ 91 576 34 20

🅼 *Núñez de Balboa* 🕔 *Sep.–June : Mon.–Sat. 10am–2pm, 5.30–9pm; Sun., public holidays 10am–2pm* ● *free*

Renowned for its exhibitions of contemporary art, the Fundación Juan March, one of the leading cultural centers in the city, also hosts numerous chamber music concerts.

Círculo de Bellas Artes (19)
Marqués de Casa Riera 2, 28014 ☎ 91 360 54 00

🅼 *Banco de España* 🕔 **Exhibitions** *Tue.–Fri. 5–9pm; Sat. 11am–2pm, 5–9pm; Sun. 11am–2pm* ● *100 Ptas* **Movies, theater, concerts** *telephone or see the magazine* Minerva *for details* ● *prices vary*

This multifunctional cultural institution offers a literary café, exhibition spaces, an arts cinema, workshops and conferences, plays and top-notch concerts. Ask for a program.

Not forgetting

■ **Teatro Monumental (20)** Atocha 65, 28012 ☎ 91 429 81 19 *Home of the Orchestra and Choir for Spanish Radio and Television (OCTRVE). Also used by the Orchestra and Choir of the Comunidad de Madrid.*

venues. Check the programs
of the major museums, for
instance, as they occasionally
host classical concerts.

18

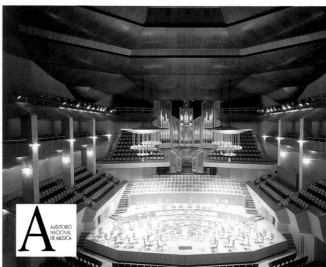

17

18

Basic facts

Taking into consideration all the national, municipal, private and public venues in the capital, Madrid is home to more than 30 different theaters. This means that it is possible to take in a first-rate production every evening. The repertoire is sufficiently wide-ranging to accommodate all

After dark

Teatro María Guerrero (21)
Tamayo y Baus 4, 28004 ☎ 91 310 29 49 ➡ 91 319 38 36

Ⓜ *Chueca, Colón* ◑ *Performances Sep.–July: Tue.–Sat. from 8pm, Sun. from 7pm* **Box office** *Tue.–Sat. 11.30am–1.30pm, 5–8pm* **Reservations by telephone** *902 488 488* ● *1650 Ptas–2600 Ptas* ▦

Inaugurated in 1885 as the Teatro de la Princesa, this building is one of the best examples in Madrid of a 19th-century wrought-iron structure. The classical façade conceals a neo-Mudéjar theater which can accommodate a large audience. When it was purchased by the Spanish State, the theater was renamed Teatro María Guerrero, after the great Spanish actress who performed here for many years in the early part of this century. It is now home to Spain's Centro Dramático Nacional. The program covers the different trends in international and contemporary Spanish drama. The theater basement has a café that is quiet and friendly, frequented by both actors and theatergoers.

Teatro Español (22)
Príncipe 25, 28012 ☎ 91 429 62 97 ➡ 91 429 62 50

Ⓜ *Sevilla* ◑ *Performances Tue.–Thur., Sun. 7pm; Fri.–Sat. 7pm, 10.30pm* **Box office** *daily 11.30am–1.30pm, 5–8pm* ● *up to 2200 Ptas* ▦ ▣

One of the oldest theaters in Europe, the Teatro Español is, with the María Guerrero, one of the most important theaters in the city. It was inaugurated as an open-air theater in 1583, and was known as the Corral de La Pacheca, or Corral del Príncipe. In 1745 it was given a roof, and was renamed Teatro del Príncipe. In 1849 it became the Teatro Español, and many of the new Romantic plays were premiered here. It became a municipal theater in 1975. In 1980 it was enlarged to accommodate 763 spectators. The program features contemporary Spanish works.

Teatro de la Comedia (23)
Príncipe 14, 28012 ☎ 91 521 49 31 ➡ 91 522 46 90

Ⓜ *Sol* ◑ *Performances Sep.–June: Mon.–Tue., Thur.–Sat. 8pm; Sun. 7pm* **Box office** *daily 11.30am–1.30pm, 5–6pm* ▦ ● *from 1300 Ptas; Thur. –50%* ▣

Housed in a 19th-century building, the Teatro de la Comedia is the home of Spain's Compañía Nacional de Teatro Clásico. This was created in order to fill a gap in the city's theater program – that of a sorely needed classical repertoire. As a result, since 1985 works by Spanish Golden Age authors such as Calderón de la Barca, Lope de Vega and Tirso de Molina have been resurrected in Madrid, and performed before the 619 spectators that the Teatro de la Comedia can accommodate.

Not forgetting

■ **Teatro de Bellas Artes (19)** Marqués de Casa Riera 2, 28014 ☎ 91 532 44 37 *A theater linked to the Círculo de Bellas Artes* ➡ *74. Run by director José Tamayo, it reflects both his personality and that of his troupe, the Campañía Lope de Vega, which performs also in major theaters around the country. A repertoire of Spanish authors.* ■ **Teatro Nuevo Apolo (24)** Plaza Tirso de Molina 1, 28012 ☎ 91 369 06 37 *Popular shows and musicals.*

tastes, from the traditional to the avant-garde.

23

21

22

Luces de Bohemia by Don Ramón del Valle Inclán, directed by José Tamayo at the Teatro de Bellas Artes.

19

23

Basic facts

The *zarzuela* is a form of light opera unique to Spain and not to be missed. Like other Mediterranean countries, Spain has a strong vocal tradition and some superb singers. It excels equally at dance with the world-class Ballet Nacional de España.

After dark

Teatro de la Zarzuela (25)
Jovellanos 4, 28014 ☎ 91 524 54 00 ➡ 91 429 71 57

Ⓜ *Banco de España, Sevilla* **◐** *Performances* Nov.–July: Tue.–Sun. 8pm ● *1200 Ptas–4500 Ptas* **Box office** *daily noon–6pm; performance days noon–8pm* **▱** **Ⓨ**

This beautiful theater stages an exclusive program of *zarzuela*, the light romantic operetta so popular in Madrid. Its annual repertoire consists of a dozen or so carefully selected works (often repeated by popular demand) and at least one little-known piece. The scenery is often spectacular and the productions extremely imaginative. The theater also presents individual singers and organises series of *lieder*.

Teatro Real (26)
Plaza de Oriente 1, 28013 ☎ 91 516 06 60 ➡ 91 516 06 51

Ⓜ *Opera* **◐** *Performances* Oct.–July **Box office** *daily 10am–2pm, 5–8pm* ● *Operas 2000 Ptas – 20000 Ptas; Recitals and concerts 500 Ptas – 5000 Ptas; Ballets 1000 Ptas – 16000 Ptas* **▱** **Ⅲ** *José Luis* ➡ *70* **▱** *every morning 300 Ptas* **✚**

Opened in 1850 by Queen Isabel II, the Teatro Real enjoyed its golden age during the second half of the 19th century. It was closed in 1925 and finally restored to its former glory in 1997 when it was entirely renovated. A multi-level scene mechanism enabling it to present three plays concurrently without having to change the sets has placed it at the cutting edge of technology and made it a world-class opera venue. It has a seating capacity of 1700 and excellent acoustics wherever you are sitting and whatever you are watching – opera, ballet or a concert. The Teatro Real also has a fashionable restaurant and tearoom, while its private rooms stage regular exhibitions of works of art loaned by the Museo del Prado ➡ 96, the Centro Nacional de Arte Reina Sofia ➡ 98 and the Patrimonio Nacional.

Teatro Calderón (27)
Atocha 18, 28012 ☎ 91 369 14 34

Ⓜ *Tirso de Molina* **◐** *Performances* Sep.–July: Tue.–Sat. 8pm; Sun. 7pm **Box office** *daily 11am–2pm, 4–9pm* ● *3000 Ptas–8000 Ptas* **▱** **▱**

Bought by the municipality in 1996, this theater hosts a program of events ranging from popular *zarzuelas* (in the summer) to well-known operas (during the rest of the year). Its repertoire features popular operas such as *Madama Butterfly* or *La Bohème*, Spanish operettas such as *Bohemios* or *La Alegría de la Huerta* and moving recitals by Isabel Pantoja.

Not forgetting

■ **Centro Cultural de la Villa (28)** Plaza de Colón, 28001 ☎ 91 575 60 80 *Hidden beneath the monument to Columbus and the fountains of this square* ➡ *104 is a remarkable purpose-built cultural center which, from time to time, hosts zarzuela and flamenco shows* ➡ *80. It is also the home of Banda Sinfonica Municipal of Madrid. See program for details.*

27

25

26

28

Basic facts

Nearly every performing company in Spain ends its tour by coming to Madrid, including the country's best flamenco and *sevillana* shows. Seize an opportunity to spend an evening in a *tablao* (literally, 'stage') or *sala rociera*. In a *tablao*, or Andaluz bar, you will be applauding the footwork of

After dark

Corral de la Morería (29)
Morería 17, 28005 ☎ 91 365 84 46

Ⓜ *Latina, Ópera* 🕐 *daily from 9pm* **Performance** *10.45pm–2am* ● **Dinner performance** *11,000 Ptas* **Bar performance** *4000 Ptas* 🔲

Hidden away at the Corral de la Morería in the Castilian district of Las Vistillas is one of the more surprising flamenco *tablaos*, both for its long tradition and for the purity of its performance. The ballet that founded the place in 1956 included famous dancers such as Pastora Imperio. Other great names, such as Antonio Gades, La Chunga and Lucero Tena, followed. The star of the moment is Blanca del Rey. The small room is ideally suited to the smouldering intimacy of a flamenco dance, while the Castilian-style décor is sober and elegant.

Café de Chinitas (30)
Torija 7, 28013 ☎ 91 559 51 35

Ⓜ *Santo Domingo* 🕐 *Mon.–Sat. dinner served from 9pm* **Performance** *10.30pm–2am* ● **Dinner performance** *9500 Ptas* **Bar performance** *from 4300 Ptas* 🔲

Art and history interweave to great effect in this 17th-century palace, now renovated and decorated with valuable paintings, sculptures in bronze and marble, bullfighting memorabilia and a superb collection of Manila shawls ➡ 128. The famous dancer La Chunga appeared at its opening in 1969. Since then, flamenco stars such as Manuela Vargas, Enrique Morente, José Mercé and Pastora Vega have performed here.

Al Andalus (31)
Capitán Haya 19, 28020 ☎ 91 556 14 39

Ⓜ *Cuzco* 🕐 *daily 10.30pm–6am; closed 15 days in July.–Aug.* ● *Sun.–Wed. 2000 Ptas; Thur.–Sat. 3000 Ptas (with one drink)* 🔲

Al Andalus is more of a *sala rociera* than a *tablao*, where you can dance passionate *sevillanas* or athletic rumbas with the *rocieros*. It is impossible to stay seated. Al Andalus transports you to the lively streets of Andalusia with the bar's southern *mosaicos* (Andalusian tiles), white-washed balconies, flowers, roasts and the fiesta flamenca.

Corral de la Pacheca (32)
Juan Ramón Jiménez 26, 28036 ☎ 91 359 26 60

Ⓜ *Plaza Castilla, Cuzco* 🕐 *daily 9pm–2.30am* ● **Dinner performance** *9500 Ptas–12,500 Ptas* **Bar performance** *4200 Ptas* 🔲

A famous *tablao* on two floors. The ballets performed here are of the highest standard. The *bailaoras* (female dancers) are splendidly costumed in spotted dresses and colored shawls.

Not forgetting

■ **Almonte (33)** Juan Bravo 35, 28006 ☎ 91 563 54 04 *Somewhere to practise the sevillana, rumba or salsa!*

the audience; in a *sala rociera* you may find yourself joining in with the dancers on the floor.

29

29

30

29

29

30

29

Basic facts

You will find fewer cabarets in Madrid than any other European capital. A reason for this could be that the Spanish, who are by nature fidgety and talkative, are restless spectators. Those that do exist, however, are worth seeing. The shows are invigorating and of a high quality. Madrid

After dark

Berlín Cabaret (34)
Costanilla de San Pedro 11, 28005 ☎ 91 366 20 34

Ⓜ *La Latina* 🅿 🕐 *Mon.–Thur. 11pm–5am; Fri.–Sat. 11pm–6am*
Performances *from 1.30am* ● *1200 Ptas* 🎵

An evocation of the Prohibition era, with exotic shows, near-naked women, drag-queens, dancing, magic tricks, plenty of humor and a dose of 1930s social satire. The Berlin Cabaret is the perfect place for a drink in a unusual setting. It is not a traditional cabaret, nor a café, but a bar, dance club and meeting-place all rolled into one. In short, somewhere to be thoroughly entertained.

Florida Park (35)
Paseo de coches del Retiro, 28009 ☎ 91 573 78 05

Ⓜ *Ibiza* 🕐 *Mon.–Sat. from 9pm* **Performance** *10.30pm–3am* ● **Dinner performance** *9500 Ptas* **Bar performance** *4500 Ptas* 🎵

Located right in the heart of the Parque del Retiro ➡ 98, Florida Park was for a long time the place to hear major Spanish and international artists such as Lola Flores, Chavela Vargas, Liza Minelli, Plácido Domingo and Diana Ross. Today, flamenco ➡ 80 and other types of Spanish dance music are on the program, and the orchestra is as happy to play old bolero and salsa classics as it is to play the latest tunes.

Clamores Jazz (36)
Albuquerque 14, 28010 ☎ 91 445 79 38

Ⓜ *Bilbao* 🕐 *Sun.–Thur. 5pm–3am, Fri.–Sat. 5pm–4am, Sun. dancing from 10pm,* ● *500 Ptas* 🎵 *Tue.–Sat.* ● *prices vary* 🎵

Jazz, country, salsa and blues are just some of the different types of live music on offer at the Clamores. Here, you can hear Ismaël Serrano, Jayme Marqués, Pedro Iturralde, Jorge Drexler, Lonnie Smith, Billy Brooks and many others. Should you wish to seize the microphone, a pianist will accompany you until the audience gives in and applauds.

Scala Meliá (37)
Rosario Pino 7, 28020 ☎ 91 571 44 11

Ⓜ *Plaza de Castilla* 🅿 🕐 *Tue.–Sat. from 8.30pm* **Performances** *Tue.–Fri. 10.45pm; Sat. 10.45pm–12.30am* ● **Dinner performance** *10200 Ptas* **Bar performance** *5300 Ptas* 🎵

A spectacular setting, with a skating rink, swimming pool, water cascades, bridges, floating staircases, hydraulic platforms, featuring exotic beauties, dancers, musicians and other artistes, always of a high standard. Excellent variety shows. An unusual venue that is a must for night owls.

Not forgetting

■ **Galileo Galilei (38)** Galileo 100, 28015 ☎ 91 534 75 57
Café concerts. An extensive program featuring a variety of shows. Salsa evenings.

has a selection of off-the-beaten-track venues offering everything from live concerts to exotic shows in good-humored spirit.

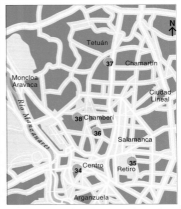

Basic facts

When people talk of Madrid as the 'party capital', they are usually referring to the huge number of clubs and their one great advantage over their European counterparts: their long hours. The clientele is varied, though there are some places where the 'urban tribe' look is *de rigueur*.

After dark

Joy Eslava (39)
Arenal 11, 28013 ☎ 91 366 54 39 ➡ 91 366 54 40

Ⓜ *Sol* ◕ *daily 11.30pm–6am* **Performances** *Thur.–Sun. around 2am*
● *Sun.–Wed. 1500 Ptas; Thur.–Sat. 2000 Ptas* ▣

The star of the Madrid scene, Joy Eslava is housed in a former variety theater. The interior has retained its tiered balconies, which overlook the dance floor, and its 19th-century Romantic décor, and serves as a backdrop for social gatherings, cultural events, fashion shows, movie premieres and concerts. The clientele is the most cosmopolitan of all Madrid night spots, comprising movie stars, theater actors, dancers, literary figures, politicians, TV personalities and members of Madrid's jet-set.

Empire (40)
Paseo de Recoletos 16, 28001 ☎ 91 435 84 50

Ⓜ *Colón* ◕ *daily 11pm–5am* ● *Fri.–Sat. 1500 Ptas, Sun.–Thur. 1000 Ptas* ▣

The Empire is a mix of traditional and modern, in both its clientele and its décor. It once played host to luminaries such as Gloria Estefan, Prince, Omar Shariff, Antonio Banderas, Pedro Almodóvar and Steven Seagal. It has preserved its theatrical charm, and still draws a mixed crowd. Plenty of *marcha* (ambience) and good music.

Pachá (41)
Barceló 11, 28004 ☎ 91 446 01 37

Ⓜ *Bilbao* ◕ *Wed.–Thur. 12.30pm–6am; Fri.–Sat. 11.30pm–6am* ● *Wed.–Thur., Sun. 1500 Ptas; Fri.–Sat. 2000 Ptas (with one drink)* ▣ ▤

'When you go by Pachá, don't forget to visit Madrid.' This famous saying tells you a lot about the reputation of this club with *Madrileños* and visitors alike. Attractive people, good music, and a packed dance floor – Pachá has become the late-night legend of Madrid.

Nells (42)
López de Hoyos 25, 28006 ☎ 91 562 49 54

Ⓜ *Avenida de América, Cruz del Rayo* ◕ *Tue.–Sat. midnight–6am* ● *5000 Ptas*
▣ ▼

This small, recently opened club, with its élite clientele, is to Madrid what private clubs are to other European capitals. This is where the beautiful people meet: mostly over-25s, jackets but no ties, glamorous, well-dressed women and good music. ★ At weekends, book a table in advance to avoid being suffocated at around 3am. On Tuesdays there is a flamenco *fiesta* ➡ 80, usually by invitation only.

Not forgetting

■ **Palacio de Gaviria (43)** Arenal 9, 28013 ☎ 91 526 60 69
A gorgeous 19th-century palace hosting tea dances, disco nights and salsa evenings.

Bono museo
You can buy a pass for the Centro Cultural Reina Sofía, the Prado and Museo Thyssen-Bornemisza at any of the three museums ● 1050 Ptas

 # What to see

Bus tours

Privately-operated buses run regularly between Palacio Real and Plaza de Colón. Take the whole tour, or get off at any stop and take the next bus.
Madrid Vision Avenida Manoteras 14, 28050 ☎ (91) 767 17 43
● 1600 Ptas for a panoramic tour, 2000 Ptas for one day, 2500 Ptas for two days.

46
Sights
THE INSIDER'S FAVORITES

Guided tours

Asociación de Guías de Madrid
Genova 3, 28004
☎ 91 308 17 66
🕐 Mon.–Fri. 8am–7pm; Sat. 9am–1pm
● Pick your own itinerary. From 12000 Ptas for a three-hour walking tour for up to 30 people.

Helicopter trips

You can hire a helicopter from
Empresa Hispanica de Aviación
Aeropuerto de 4 Vientos, Avenida del Valle 13, 28003 ☎ 91 553 85 01
● 162400 Ptas for a one-hour flight, maximum 5 people.

> "And finally, Madrid! That beloved city, welcoming you into its arms like a lover! A city that still offered the traveler a uniquely gentle way of life. A city of contrasts with its Plaza Mayor, its Género chico, its skyscrapers and its local bistros still haunted by the shadowy figure of Federico García Lorca!" *Alejo Carpentier*

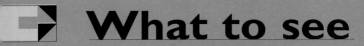

▶ What to see

Born from water

The fortress of Mayrit ('source of water') was built by the Moors in the rich, fertile valley of the Mazanares river facing the Sierra Guadarrama. The Muslim city stood on the present site of the Palacio Real. Today, all that remains of the Moorish occupation are a few remnants of the outer wall and the Mudéjar tower of the Iglesia San Pedro El Viejo. Recaptured by Alfonso VI in the 11th century, Mayrit was converted to Christianity and renamed Magerit. Gradually, the city developed around the original Moorish walls, forming a dozen or so parishes that functioned as separate districts.

A royal capital

There was nothing to suggest that Madrid was destined to become a capital. In the 16th century, it still resembled a medieval town with its cob buildings, its narrow, winding streets leading to small, enclosed market squares, and only 4,000 inhabitants. However, in 1561, Philip II, son of Charles V, chose it as his capital with the intention of making it a cosmopolitan city that would absorb all regional differences. But Madrid still lacked the buildings equal to its city status.

A monumental city

The Hapsburg dynasty (1516–1700) built the Plaza Mayor ➡ 92, constructed churches and laid out gardens. During the reign of the Bourbons (1701–1808), vast palaces (Palacio Real ➡ 90), promenades (Paseo del Prado ➡ 96) and gardens (Parque del Retiro ➡ 98) were built to celebrate the absolute power of the monarchy. In the 19th century, the face of Madrid was radically altered as the Castro plan rationalized urban development. Monumental squares were constructed and new districts based on a regular grid layout (e.g. Salamanca) were built alongside the old districts of the city center. The city's population had by now reached 250,000. The early 20th century saw the construction of the city's main thoroughfares – the Castellana and the Gran Vía – and such modern buildings as the impressive Palacio de Communicaciones ➡ 96 and the Compañía Telefónica ➡ 94.

Francoism

When the parties of the left came to power in 1936, they fought bitterly amongst themselves while the Carlists, Falangists and Monarchists formed an alliance. With the outbreak of civil war, Barcelona fell in early January 1939 but Madrid held out until March 28. General Franco seized power and ruled until his death in 1975. His severe centralist government drastically altered the face of Madrid. The carefully preserved city center was marred by towers (Torre de España) and an increasing number of business districts (Nuevos Ministerios ➡ 108), while the outskirts were overrun by dormitory towns. Madrid's population tripled in the space of forty years.

The districts of Madrid

The city of Madrid is in fact composed of a large number of 'villages'. In the narrow, winding streets of the old working-class districts of La Latina, Lavapiès, Malasaña and Chueca, isolated from the hustle and bustle of the grand boulevards, time seems to stand still. But not for long! After dark, the narrow streets become the preserve of the districts' night birds. To the north lies modern Madrid with the business centers of the Castellana and the elegant middle-class districts of Salamanca and Chamberí. The main thoroughfares of the Paseo del Prado, the Gran Vía and the Castellana bridge the gaps between these vastly different areas of the city.

The festival tradition

There are over 10,000 bars in Madrid, not counting nightclubs and *tascas*. Although the summer heat undoubtedly contributes to the city's frenetic lifestyle, the fall of Franco marked the end of dictatorship and moral harassment, and gave rise to a more liberal approach. This found its best form of expression in the festivals of the 1980s when the *movida* was born. However the festival tradition dates from much earlier. Since time immemorial the people of Madrid have always celebrated their popular saints: Isidro, the plowman, the city's patron saint since the 11th century, and the Virgen de la Almudena, who watches over the city. The countless public holidays associated with these festivals are an integral part of life in Madrid.

In the area

The history of *La Villa* (Madrid) begins here, for it was on this site in the 9th century that Muhammad I erected his *Kasbah*. Though the settlement expanded over the centuries, the rocky promontory overlooking the Manzanares river – now little more than a trickle – has remained the

What to see

Palacio Real (1)
Bailén, 28005 ☎ 91 542 00 59 ➡ 91 542 69 47

Ⓜ *Opera* 🕙 *Oct. 1–Mar 31: Mon.–Sat. 9.30am–5pm, Sun. 9am–2pm / Apr. 1–Sep 30: Mon.–Sat. 9am–4pm, Sun. 9am–3pm; closed on official ceremony days* ● *850 Ptas; over 65s, students, children 350 Ptas; Wed. free* 🚩 🔔 *950 Ptas* ♿ 🏛

The Palacio Real (Royal Palace) is one of the most majestic monuments in the city. It was built on the ruins of the Alcázar (fortress) of Madrid, destroyed by fire in 1734. Completed in 1764, in the reign of Charles III (1759–88), the palace was designed by Italian architect Gianbattista Sacchetti, and construction was supervised by architects Ventura Rodríguez and Francisco Sabatini. The neoclassical structure was modified to suit the difficult terrain – a hill sloping steeply to the Manzanares river. Away from the river, on the other side of the palace, is the Plaza de Oriente. An equestrian statue of Philip IV – a superb piece of 18th-century sculpture by Pietro Tacca – stands at its center.

Inside the palace, highlights include the Throne Room, which has a superb view of the Campo del Moro, the sumptuous Dining Room (Comedor), the Porcelain Room, the Sala Gasparini, the grand staircase (each step cut from a single block of marble), and the Chapel, which has a remarkable collection of stringed instruments. In the various rooms hang paintings by Velázquez, Goya, El Greco, Rubens and Tiepolo. The palace's collection of tapestries is the largest in Europe, and charts the development of this decorative art from its Gothic origins to the late-18th century. One of the most impressive exhibits in the palace is the Armería Real (Royal Armoury), which exhibits weaponry from the Middle Ages through to the modern day. If there is time, try to visit the Farmácia (Royal Pharmacy), which has a display of Talavera ceramic jars, and the Museo de Carruajes (Carriage Museum), which houses a collection of 18th- and 19th-century vehicles (access is via the Sabatini gardens).

The Palace Gardens, or Campo del Moro, are attached to the west wing of the palace. Laid out under Isabel II (1833–68), they reflect the English landscape style that was popular in Madrid at the time. Note the splendid fountains, as well as the fantastic view of the palace's west face. Access to the gardens is via a grand flight of steps; another, toward the north side, leads down to the French-style Sabatini gardens, embellished with statues and fountains. These formal gardens were laid out in the reign of Alfonso XII (1874–85).

Not forgetting

■ **Catedral de la Almudena (2)** Mayor 90, 28005 🕙 daily 10am–2pm, 6–8pm *Work on the cathedral began in 1874. The plans were modified so many times during construction, however, that it was consecrated only in 1992.*
■ **El Viaducto (3)** Calle Bailén/Calle Segovia, 28071 *This viaduct is one of the city's marvels of civil engineering. Built in 1932 along 'rationalist' lines, it straddles the canyon-like Calle Segovia, and links the Royal Palace with the southern part of the city.*

main residence for all Spanish
monarchs, except the
present king, Juan Carlos.
■ After dark ➡ 68 ➡ 80

The State Dining
Room is one of the
palace's most
magnificent rooms.

In the area

This district in Old Madrid, a warren of streets and famous squares (once the setting for official ceremonies and public events) is one of the most beautiful and unspoiled areas of the city. ■ Where to stay ➡ 20 ■ Where to eat ➡ 38 ■ After dark ➡ 68 ➡ 80 ➡ 84

What to see

Plaza Mayor (4)

Ⓜ *Sol, La Latina*

The Plaza Mayor is the largest square in the historic center of Madrid. Its present appearance is the result of work by Juan de Villanueva (1789–1811), the architect of the Prado ➡ 96. It comprises a medieval marketplace (adjacent streets are named after confraternities and guilds), the *Casa de la Panadería* (headquarters of the bakers' guild) and the *Casa de la Carnicería* (headquarters of the butchers' guild). The square evolved into the social hub of the city, hosting public spectacles, jousts and even bullfights ➡ 100. Today its shops, restaurants and architecture draw many visitors. The front of the Casa de la Panadería is decorated with frescoes by Carlos Franco depicting the classic symbols of Madrid: allegories of water and the countryside, *majos* and *majas* (elegant 17th-century men and women), *toreros* and 'cats' (the nickname given to the *madrileños*).

Plaza de la Villa (5)
☎ 91 588 10 00

Ⓜ *Ópera, La Latina* 🕐 *Casa de la Villa / Casa de Cisneros Mon. 5–7pm* ● *free* 🛈 *Patronato municipal de turismo ☎ 91 588 29 00*

The buildings around Plaza de la Villa (Town Square) include several examples of the architectural style favored by the Hapsburgs. The *Ayuntamiento* (Town Hall) – also called the *Casa de la Villa* – is built on two levels around a patio, and flanked by pinnacle towers decorated with coats of arms. Inside, the grand staircase, the *Patio de Cristales*, the former chapel and the *Allegory of 2nd of May* (Francisco de Goya) merit close inspection. The *Casa de Cisneros*, built in 1537, is one of the finest examples of the Plateresque style (from *platero*, the Spanish word for silversmith), characterized by its intricate detail. Opposite the *Ayuntamiento* is the tower of Los Lujanes. It has two portals – one Gothic and the other, with an overreaching arch, that is typically Moorish. The statue in the center of the square represents Alvaro de Bazán, admiral of the 'invincible' Armada of Philip II (1556–98).

Not forgetting

■ **Monasterio de las Descalzas Reales (6)** Plaza de las Descalzas 3, 28013 ☎ 91 542 00 59 🕐 Tue.–Sat. 10.30am–12.30pm, 4–5.30pm *A convent housing a rich collection of paintings, sculptures, tapestries and reliquaries. One of the finest Baroque collections in Spain.*
■ **Iglesia San Ginés (7)** Arenal, 28013 ☎ 91 366 48 75 🕐 Sep.–June: daily 9am–1pm, 6–9pm / July.–Aug.: daily 9am–1pm, 7–9pm *The Iglesia San Ginés was rebuilt in the 17th century. Its Capilla del Cristo (Christ's chapel) houses paintings and sculptures reflecting 17th-century Spanish art, including El Greco's Christ Cleansing the Temple.*
■ **Monasterio de la Encarnación (8)** Plaza de la Encarnación 1, 28013 ☎ 91 542 00 59 🕐 Wed., Sat., Sun. 10.30am–12.45pm, 4–5.30pm *An Augustin convent. Parts of the cloisters are open to the public. A remarkable collection of 17th-century Madrid School paintings. An impressive and ornate reliquary.*

■ Where to shop ➡ 126 ➡ 128 ➡ 144

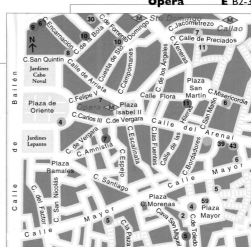

93

What to see

Gran Vía (9)

Ⓜ *Gran Vía, Callao, Plaza de España*

The Gran Vía is a broad, mile-long thoroughfare that links Plaza de Cibeles ➡ 96 with Plaza de España ➡ 102. Work was carried out in three phases, each corresponding to a different section. Along the first section, from the Plaza de Cibeles to Red de San Luis (at the intersection of Calle de Fuencarral and Calle de Hortaleza), the buildings resemble Parisian apartment blocks of the late-19th century. The Edificio Metrópolis (no. 39), located at the corner of Gran Vía and Calle de Alcalá, typifies this exuberant and theatrical style. On Calle de Alcalá (no. 42) to the left of it, is the Círculo de Bellas Artes ➡ 74, a striking building designed by architect Antonio Palacios. From the Red de San Luis the buildings resemble, on a reduced scale, the first skyscrapers of Chicago. The Compañía Telefónica building (no. 28), housing Spain's national telephone company, was the first skyscraper to be erected in Madrid, though its façade is more Madrid Baroque than avant-garde. Closing this second section of the Gran Vía are three unusual buildings: Palacio de la Prensa; Palacio de la Música; and the Callao Cinema. The brick Palacio de la Prensa (no. 46) was the fist Madrid apartment block to be given an art deco façade, revealing its debt to German Expressionism. Huge cinema posters conceal the curious façade of Palacio de la Música (no. 35), whose decorative details were inspired by the Madrid Baroque. The Art–Deco interior of the Callao Cinema is worth seeing. The third section of the Gran Vía begins at the curved corner of the Edificio Carrión (no. 78), which now houses the Capitol Cinema (no. 41). It ends at the pared-down Edificio Coliseum (no. 78), yet another cinema. This last section is the most colorful part of Madrid.

Real Academia de Bellas Artes de San Fernando (10)
Alcalá 13, 28014 ☎ 91 522 14 91

Ⓜ *Sevilla, Sol* 🕐 **Museum** *Mon., Sat.–Sun. 9am–2.30pm; Tue.–Fri. 9am–7pm* ● *Mon.–Fri. 400 Ptas; children 150 Ptas; over-65s, students, Sat.–Sun. free* **Exhibitions** *Mon., Sat.–Sun. 10am–2pm, Tue.–Fri. 10am–2pm, 5–8pm* ● *free*

The second most important museum in Madrid after the Prado ➡ 96. The collection includes thirteen canvases by Francisco de Goya, numerous 17th-century sculptures and paintings (Zurbarán, Murillo, Pedro de Mena, Rubens and Van Dyck), a series of Italian paintings from the 16th century (including the only Archimboldo in Spain) and a series of academic paintings from the 18th, 19th and 20th centuries.

Not forgetting

■ **Puerta del Sol (11)** *The geographical center of Madrid and, up until the 1950s, the scene of historic events. Statues of Mariblanca and the oso and madroño (bear and arbutus tree), which feature on the city's coat of arms. Monument dedicated to King Juan Carlos.*
■ **Plaza de las Cortes (12)** *The Chamber of Deputies (1850) is the most important building on this square. Designed by Pascual y Colomer, it has a colonnaded portico and a classical pediment.*

■ Where to shop ➡ 126 ➡ 128 ➡ 130 ➡ 132

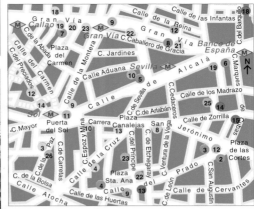

9

9

12

At the beginning of this century an entire district was demolished to make way for the Gran Vía. The Compañía Telefónica building was erected in 1929 by Ignacio Cárdenas. It rises to a height of 266 feet.

12

95

This shady avenue is often referred to as the Paseo del Arte (literally, the 'Art Walk'), and with good reason, for it is home to Madrid's great art museums. ■ Where to stay ➡ 18 ■ Where to eat ➡ 40 ➡ 42 ■ Where to shop ➡ 138

What to see

Museo del Prado & Casón del Buen Retiro (13)
Paseo del Prado, 28014 ☎ 91 330 28 00 ➡ 91 330 28 58

Ⓜ *Atocha, Banco de España* 🕒 *Tue.–Sat. 9am–7pm; Sun., public holidays 9am–2pm* ● *500 Ptas; students 250 Ptas; over-65s, children free* 🖼️ 🏛️ 🎫 🏢 🍽️ 🖼️

Designed in 1785 by Juan de Villanueva, the building houses one of the world's leading art museums. The collections (originally part of the Spanish royal art collection) cover three great schools of painting. The Spanish School numbers among its works many El Grecos, the world's largest Velázquez collection (over sixty canvases, including his most famous painting *Las Meninas*) and works by Goya (court portraits and 'dark paintings'). The glorious Italian collection includes works by Fra Angelico, Raphael and Titian. The Flemish School has some superb pieces by Bosch and Rubens. The Prado also contains around 500 sculptures of Graeco-Roman, Renaissance and Baroque origin. The nearby annexe was once the ballroom of the palace of El Casón del Buen Retiro. Now run by the National Museum of Modern Art, it contains Spanish sculptures and paintings from the 19th century.

Museo Thyssen-Bornemisza (14)
Paseo del Prado 8, 28014 ☎ 91 420 39 44 ➡ 91 420 27 80

Ⓜ *Banco de España* 🕒 *Tue.–Sun. 10am–7pm* ● *700 Ptas; over‑65s, students 400 Ptas; children free* 🖼️ 🏛️ 🎫 🖼️ 🖼️

Since 1992 the Palacio de Villahermosa has housed the superb private collection of baron von Thyssen-Bornemisza. Over 800 works of western art are on display in the museum. Among them are *Saint Catherine of Alexandria* by Caravaggio, Venetian views by Canaletto, *Venus and Cupid* by Rubens and *Easter Morning* by Caspar David Friedrich. There is a good collection of Impressionist and post-Impressionist art, an impressive canvas by Mark Rothko, a leading American Abstract Expressionist, and an eclectic display of Soviet avant-garde works.

Not forgetting
■ **Plaza de Cibeles (15)**
A Castilian square designed by Ventura Rodríguez in 1775. Fountain dedicated to the goddess of nature, Cibeles.
■ **Puerta de Alcalá (16)** Plaza de la Independencia, 28001
Symbol of Enlightenment Madrid. A neoclassical granite gate by Francisco Sabatini (1778).
■ **Plaza de Cánovas del Castillo (17)**
The twin sister of Cibeles, by Ventura Rodríguez (1780). Fountain dedicated to Neptune.
■ **San Jerónimo el Real (18)** Moreto 4, 28014 ☎ 91 420 35 78
🕒 *daily 9am–1pm, 5–8.30pm*
Built over the ruins of a monastery. The church was erected under the Catholic Monarchs and was modified in the 19th century. Juan Carlos I was crowned here.
■ **Museo del Ejército (19)** Méndez Núñez 1, 28014 ☎ 91 522 89 77
🕒 *Tue.–Sat. 10am–2pm An extensive military collection.*

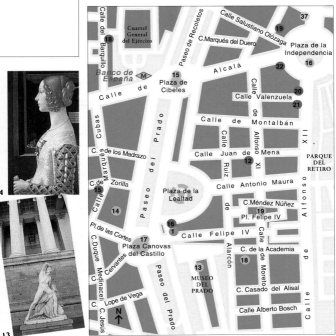

In the area

The Glorieta (roundabout) of Charles V, known simply as Atocha, marks the city's southern perimeter. The Centro Cultural Reina Sofía completes the so-called 'Golden Triangle' bordered on its other sides by the Prado and Thyssen-Bornemisza museums.

What to see

Museo Nacional Centro de Arte Reina Sofía (20)
Santa Isabel 52, 28012 ☎ 91 467 50 62 ➡ 91 467 84 31

🅼 *Atocha* 🕒 *Mon., Wed.–Sat. 10am–9pm; Sun. 10am–2.30pm ● 500 Ptas; students 250 Ptas; over-65s, children, Sat. after 2.30pm, Sun. free* 🔳 🔳
Reservations ☎ *91 527 72 05* 🔳 🔳 🔳 🔳

Designed by Francisco Sabatini in 1776, this former hospital today houses Madrid's National Museum of Contemporary Art. The 19th-century and 20th-century collections include the famous *Guernica* by Picasso, a number of important Spanish Surrealist and avant-garde works, including early works by Dalí, Miró paintings from the 1970s, and a fine collection of Cubist sculptures by Julio González. Major works by Antoni Tàpies and by Spain's two greatest living sculptors, Jorge de Oteiza and Eduardo Chillida are also on show. The museum hosts regular retrospectives of both major artists and up-and-coming talent.

Parque del Retiro (21)

🅼 *Retiro, Príncipe de Vergara, Atocha, Ibiza* 🕒 *24 hours* ***Palacio de Velázquez***
☎ *91 573 62 45 ● free* 🔳 🔳 🔳 🔳 🔳

The garden of the palace of the same name, built as a pleasure retreat for Philip IV (1621–55) ➡ 96. Retiro Park was opened to the public in 1869 by Isabel II, in exchange for a rent of 5 Ptas a year. In the center is a boating lake presided over by a monument to Alfonso XII which features an equestrian statue of the king by Mariano Benlliure and some magnificent examples of 19th-century Spanish sculpture. Exhibitions were held in the park buildings up until 1882. Today, the only two buildings still used for this purpose are Palacio de Velázquez and Palacio de Cristal. The latter is an iron-and-glass structure inspired by London's Crystal Palace and designed as a huge hothouse. Both palaces are decorated with *azulejos* (enamelled ceramic tiles) by Daniel Zuloaga.

Not forgetting

■ **Estación de Atocha (22)** Plaza del Emperador Carlos V, 28012 *19th-century railway architecture, transformed by Rafael Moneo in 1992. The old wrought-iron structure was designed by Alberto del Palacio with the aid of Gustave Eiffel, and housed a winter garden. Opposite is the Ministry of Agriculture, a 19th-century building decorated with azulejos (ceramic tiles) and a large sculptural group.*
■ **Jardín Botánico (23)** Plaza de Murillo 2, 28014 ☎ 91 420 30 17 🕒 *daily 10am–8pm A remnant of Charles III's grand scheme for a scientific complex. Buildings and gateways by Juan de Villanueva. A peaceful botanical garden in which to examine a huge variety of plant species.*
■ **Observatorio Astronómico (24)** Alfonso XII 3 et 5, 28014 ☎ 91 527 01 07 🕒 *Mon.–Fri. 9am–2pm Part of the Botanic Garden. Built in 1790, and reconstructed in 1978.*
■ **Museo de Etnología (25)** Alfonso XII 68, 28014 ☎ 91 530 64 18 🕒 *Tue.–Sat. 10am–7.30pm, Sun. 10am–2pm The building dates from 1875. Exhibits from Africa, Asia and the Americas, including an interesting collection from the Philippines.*

■ Where to eat ➡ 40
■ Where to shop ➡ 144

21

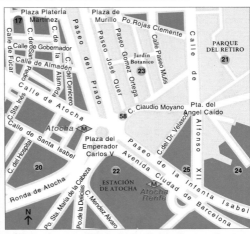

Plaza Platería Martínez
17
Calle de Gobernador
C. de San Pedro
Calle de Almadén
Calle de Fúcar
C. del Cencorro
Sta. Inés
Calle de Atocha
C. del Hospital
Calle de Santa Isabel
Ronda de Atocha
Po. Sta. Maria de la Cabeza
C. Sta. Maria de la Cabeza
Po. de la Delicias
C. Mendez Alvaro

Plaza de Murillo
Po. Rojas Clemente
Paseo del Prado
Paseo José Quer
Paseo Gomez Ortega
Paseo Paseo Mutis
Jardín Botánico
23
Calle de Alfonso
PARQUE DEL RETIRO
21
C. Claudio Moyano
58
Pta. del Angel Caído
Atocha ⓂM
Plaza del Emperador Carlos V
22
Paseo de la Infanta Isabel
Avenida Ciudad de Barcelona
ESTACIÓN DE ATOCHA
ⓂM Atocha Renfe
C. del Dr. Velasco
25
Alfonso XII
24
20

N

21

23

22 Shown in New York until 1981, *Guernica* returned to Spain after Franco's death in accordance with Picasso's wishes.

20

20

In the area

Some of the most animated scenes in Madrid are to be witnessed around Plaza de las Ventas on *corrida* (bullfight) days. Crowds of aficionados and devoted enthusiasts fill the streets after the fight.

■ Where to stay ➡ 26

What to see

Plaza Monumental de las Ventas (26)
Alcalá 237, 28028 ☎ 91 356 22 00

Ⓜ *Ventas* ◯ ***Corridas*** *Mar.–Oct. : Sun. 7pm* **Feria de San Isidro** *May–June: daily 7pm* ● *400 Ptas–15,000 Ptas; Victoria 3, 28012 ☎ 91 521 12 13 (tickets reserved in advance cost 20% more)*

This unusual building, erected in 1931, encloses one of the largest bullfighting arenas. Outside are monuments dedicated to two famous bullfighters, killed in the ring. The Feria of San Isidro (patron saint of Madrid) pits the most famous *toreros* and *novilleros* (novice bullfighters) against the most redoubtable fighting bulls or *novillos* (young bulls).

Museo Taurino (27)
Alcalá 237, 28028 ☎ 91 725 18 57

Ⓜ *Ventas* ◯ *Tue.–Fri., Sun. 9.30am–2.30pm* ● *free*

This collection comprises costumes and bullfighting memorabilia from the 17th century to the present day. These include lithographs by Goya, a costume worn by the legendary Manolete on the day he was gored by a bull named Islero, the Papal Bull of Pius V (1567) banning corridas, and posters signed by Miquel Barceló and Eduardo Arroyo.

The traditional *corrida* involves six bulls and six *toreros*. It opens with a fanfare of trumpets and cymbals, after which the *alguacilillos*, or mounted constables, gallop in at the head of the *toreros* and their *cuadrillas* (teams of assistants). Each of the six fights is divided into three 'acts'. In the first *tercio* (third), the *torero* uses his pink cape to attract the bull while testing his temperament, condition and charge. The *suerte de varas* (pic-ing of the bull) is where the picador, mounted on a padded horse, applies his pic to the bull, causing it to bleed and thus to lose strength. In the second *tercio*, known as that of the *banderilleras* (short barbed sticks decorated with ribbons and colored paper), the *banderilleros* must test the bull and correct any defects in its line of charge. In the final *tercio*, called the *faena*, the *torero* faces the bull alone. Using his *muleta* (scarlet cape), he calls the bull, sidesteps it and forces it to turn around him by a series of skilful passes – performed increasingly slowly – and by retreating or standing still close to the bull's horns. When the matador's preliminary work is complete, he must kill the bull, going in over the horns to administer a clean, fatal blow.

In the area

This huge landscape park in the English tradition was laid out in the early 1900s, and stretches from Plaza de España to the Ciudad Universitaria. It is fringed with museums and unusual monuments. The scene of repeated clashes during the Civil War, it is now overlooked by skyscrapers.

What to see

Museo de América (28)
Reyes Católicos 6, 28040 ☎ 91 543 94 37 ➡ 91 577 67 42

Ⓜ *Moncloa* 🕐 *Tue.–Sat. 10am–3pm; Sun., public holidays 10am–2.30pm*
● *500 Ptas; students 250 Ptas; over-65s, children, Sun. free* 🔲 🔲 🔲

The Museum of America documents the relationship between Spain and the American continent. Part of the collection comes from the *Real Gabinete de Historia Natural*, created in the 18th century. It is made up of objects brought back from scientific expeditions and from early excavations in Peru and the Mayan ruins of Palenque, and a selection of Mexican sacred objects, and subsequent acquisitions. The museum is organized into five sections: *Los Instrumentos del Conocimiento* examines myths and ideas about America from Columbus to the Enlightenment; *La Realidad de América* is devoted to the continent's geography and landscape, and its native peoples and populations; and *La Sociedad* looks at how the indigenous societies organized themselves. *La Religión* displays the Paracas Mummy and the Quimbayas Treasure, which is the most important pre-Hispanic collection of American gold objects. Finally, *La Comunicación* examines means of communication, and displays the jewel in the museum's crown – the Tro-Cortesian Codex, one of four Mayan manuscripts in existence, its hieroglyphs depicting scenes of daily life.

Ermita de San Antonio de la Florida (29)
Glorieta de San Antonio de la Florida 5, 28008
☎ 91 542 07 22 ➡ 91 588 86 79

Ⓜ *Príncipe Pío* 🕐 *Tue.–Fri. 10am–2pm, 4–8pm; Sat.–Sun. 10am–2pm* ● *300 Ptas; over-65s, students, children 150 Ptas; Wed., Sun. free* 🔲 🔲

Designed by Italian architect Felipe Fontana, the hermitage contains Francisco de Goya y Lucientes (1746–1828) largest cycle of frescos together with the artist's remains. The *Miracles of St Anthony*, which decorates the cupola, pendentives and transept, depicts Saint Anthony of Padua in Lisbon, where he brings a dead man back to life to testify to the innocence of his supposed assassin, the saint's father Don Martín de Bulloes. The church also houses the artist's remains. To preserve the frescos, a similar hermitage was built nearby in 1928 for church services.

Not forgetting

■ **Plaza de España (30)** *Two skyscrapers – a testament to Madrid's economic buoyancy during the early years of dictatorship.' Edificio España (1948–53) and the Torre de Madrid (1957) dominate the square. In the center of the plaza is a monument to Cervantes.*
■ **Templo de Debod (31)** Parque de la Montaña, 28008 *An Egyptian temple dating from the 4th century BC given to the city to thank its people for their contribution toward saving the temples of Nubia.*
■ **Museo Cerralbo (32)** Ventura Rodríguez 17, 28008 ☎ 91 547 36 46 🕐 Tue.–Sat. 9.30am–2.30pm; Sun. 10am–2pm
The residence and collection of Enrique de Aguilera y Gamboa, an aristocrat and respected archeologist. The museum provides an insight into the life of a late-19th-century nobleman.

■ Where to eat ➡ 38
■ After dark ➡ 86

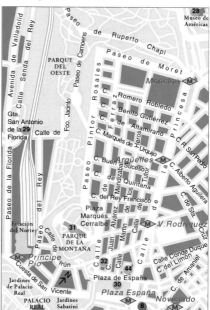

Cervantes looks down upon his two most famous creations: Don Quixote and Sancho Panza.

In the area

Here, in one of the liveliest districts in Madrid, you can take in a museum or simply mingle with the crowds in Plaza de Alonso Martínez.
■ Where to stay ➡ 22 ■ Where to eat ➡ 44 ■ After dark ➡ 68
➡ 78 ➡ 84 ■ Where to shop ➡ 130 ➡ 136 ➡ 138 ➡ 140

What to see

Biblioteca Nacional (33)
Paseo de Recoletos 20, 28001 ☎ 91 431 37 59 ➡ 91 577 56 34

🅼 Colón, Serrano 🅞 Mon.–Fri. 9am–9pm; Sat. 9am–2pm ● free, day pass for reading rooms available 🏗 🖵

The building housing the National Library and Archeological Museum (1866–92) was the most important structure built during the reign of Isabel II, and one of the first to use metal. The steps leading up to the library are decorated with 19th-century statues representing the fathers of the Castilian language. The pediment features an allegory of Arts and Letters with statues representing Study, Glory and Fame, and in the vestibule a statue by French sculptor Coullault Valeradu represents the polymath Don Marcelino Menéndez y Pelayo. The National Library has about 11 million volumes, one-third of which are housed in the main reading room. It also possesses a series of early printed books, manuscripts and prints, including engravings by Dürer.

Museo Arqueológico Nacional (34)
Serrano 13, 28001 ☎ 91 577 79 12 ➡ 91 431 68 40

🅼 Colón, Serrano 🅞 Tue.–Sat. 9.30am–8.30pm; Sun. 9.30am–2.30pm
● 500 Ptas; over-65s, students, children 250 Ptas; Sat. afternoon, Sun. morning free 🄴 🄶 ☎ 91 578 02 03 🄸

A vast collection of over 200,000 artifacts dating from prehistoric times to the 19th century. These include: a reproduction of the Altamira cave paintings, the gigantic bones of an elephant from Classical Antiquity, Iberian sculptures dating from the pre-Roman era, Roman mosaics from Las Estaciones, and the Treasure of Guarrázar – Visigothic votive crowns dating from the 7th century. Islamic culture is represented by lamps from the Alhambra in Grenada and by mosaics from the city of Medina Azahara in Córdoba. Finally, the Romanesque works of Maestro Mateo are among the jewels of the museum. Recent reorganization has transformed the museum into a first-rate institution with an educational slant.

Not forgetting

■ **Museo Municipal (35)** Fuencarral 78, 28004 ☎ 91 588 86 72
🅞 Tue.–Fri. 9.30am–8pm; Sat.–Sun. 10am–2pm *The finest Baroque portal in Madrid. The former hospice, now a Municipal Museum, houses a scale model of 1830s Madrid, the work of chronicler Ramón de Mesonero Romanos and of Ramón Gómez de la Serna, Madrid's most devoted poet.*
■ **Museo Romántico (36)** San Mateo 13, 28004 ☎ 91 448 10 71
🅞 Tue.–Sat. 9am–3pm; Sun. 10am–2pm *Spanish Romanticism, in the form of paintings, objects and documents displayed in a neoclassical building dating from the 18th century.*
■ **Plaza de Colón (37)**
A neo-Gothic statue of the legendary navigator and a rather unsuccessful sculptural group. The fountains represent Columbus' three ships.

MUSEO MUNICIPAL DE MADRID

Fast becoming a major hub, this square is surrounded by various ministries and administrative centers. It is an amalgam of architectural styles, including some exceptionally fine 19th-century buildings.

 # **What to see**

Museo Nacional de Ciencías Naturales (38)
José Gutiérrez Abascal 2, 28006
☎ 91 561 86 00 ➠ 91 564 50 78

Ⓜ Gregorio Marañon 🕓 Tue.–Fri. 10am–6pm; Sat. 10am–8pm; Sun. 10am–2.30pm ● **Museum** 400 Ptas, over-65s, students, children 300 Ptas **Exhibition** 200 Ptas; over-65s, students, children 100 Ptas ⊟ 🗑 ☎ (91) 564 61 69 ⊞

Madrid's Natural Science Museum has been elevated to the rank of a world-class educational institution by the renovation of these palaces, built for the 1881 National Exhibition of Industry and the Arts. It houses a public library and a collection of over 3,500,000 artifacts. The permanent exhibits are organized around three principal themes: The History of the Earth and Life; To the Rhythm of Nature; and The Museum of the Museum. The insect collection is remarkable for its wide variety of species; the dinosaur section has a complete skeleton of a megathere dating back over two million years; and the vertebrates section includes such exhibits as the African Elephant and the Marsupial Wolf of Tasmania. Invertebrates are represented by a vast collection of molluscs from the Philippines and Cuba.

Museo Lázaro Galdiano (39)
Serrano 122, 28006 ☎ 91 561 60 84 ➠ 91 561 77 93

Ⓜ Rubén Darío, República Argentina 🕓 Tue.–Sun. 10am–2pm ● 400 Ptas; students 200 Ptas; over-65s, children, free on Sat. ⊟

The private art collection of writer and editor José Lázaro Galdiano (1862–1947), is kept in the mansion he commissioned for his wealthy wife Doña Paula Florido. The collection includes Head of The Savior, attributed to Leonardo da Vinci, and works by Goya and other European artists, especially British painters. The museum also houses a collection of French 14th-century ivory sculptures; Spanish, Italian, Byzantine and Limoges enamels; religious gold and silverwork, and jewelry; Renaissance medals and bronzes. Textiles and fans complete this unusual collection.

Not forgetting
■ **Museo Sorolla (40)** Paseo General Martínez Blanco 37, 28010 ☎ 91 310 15 84 🕓 Tue.–Sat. 10am–3pm; Sun. 10am–2pm
The former home, with contents, of the painter Joaquín Sorolla y Bastida (1863–1923). A selection of works by the artist, generally considered to be Spain's best Impressionist painter. A delightful garden decorated with azulejos (ceramic tiles), fountains and pools.
■ **Museo de Escultura al Aire Libre (41)** Paseo de la Castellana 41, 28046 *A small open-air museum located under the flyover that links the calles of Juan Bravo and Eduardo Dato. A remarkable piece of civil engineering, the bridge was considered a model of urban design in the early 1970s. Displayed here are the works of 15 Spanish sculptors; notable among them are the Sirena Varada by Eduardo Chillida (comprising six tonnes of concrete suspended from the bridge), the mobile by Eusebio Sempere, Mère Ubu by Joan Miró, and Al otro lado del muro by José María Subirachs.*

■ Where to stay ➡ 26 ➡ 28
■ Where to eat ➡ 50 ➡ 52
■ After dark ➡ 68 ➡ 70
■ Where to shop ➡ 130

C.de Vitruvio
38
Museo de Ciencias Naturales
Paseo de la
Calle de Pedro
de
Serrano
Valdivia
42 43
Plaza Doctor Marañón
Calle de María de Molina
del Pinar
Hoyos
30
8
6
López de
39
Calle del
Miguel Ángel
Castellana
Calle de
39
Coello
22
del General Oráa
29
de
40
Glorieta de Emilio Castelar
León
26
C.Diego de León
C.de Rafael Calvo
Paseo de la Castellana
Calle de Claudio
32
45
1
41
Glorieta Rubén Darío
Paseo E. Dato
C. de Juan Bravo
M Rubén Darío
41
38
16 17
39
23
Calle Jenner
N ↑

41

Al otro lado del muro by José María Subirachs (1972).

MUSEO NACIONAL DE CIENCIAS NATURALES

40

MVSEO SOROLLA

MVSEO SOROLLA

40

40

41

The walk from Nuevos Ministerios to the Plaza de Castilla is like a journey through time, beginning with the architecture of the Franco dictatorship and finishing with the purest expressions of modernism. A curtain of stone, glass and metal stretches across these northern districts.

What to see

Azca (42)
Paseo de la Castellana 79, 28046

M *Nuevos Ministerios, Santiago Bernabéu*

A commercial center covering some 500 acres ➡ 142, the Azca complex sprang up during the final years of the Franco dictatorship. The building that best typifies the avant-garde architecture of the 1970s is the skyscraper designed by Javier Sáenz de Oiza, its smooth bronze-glass walls serving as a symbol of economic might over the people (and a nod to Frank Lloyd Wright). The Torre Europa and Torre Picasso are equipped with a fiber-optic network controlling light, temperature and communication systems, and the Torre Picasso, designed by Minoru Yamasaki (architect of the World Trade Center in New York), is the tallest skyscraper in Madrid. The Windsor tower by Genaro Alas and Pedro Casariego (Raimundo Fernández Villaverde, 65) is distinguishable by its cylindrical, smooth-surfaced structure. The most eye-catching Azca building is the Sollube, which has a 'chain-mail' structure of aluminium and white lacquer and a green-glass exterior.

Puerta de Europa (43)
Plaza de Castilla, 28046

M *Plaza de Castilla*

These two leaning towers rise to a height of over 370 feet, and tilt toward one another at an angle of 14.3°, forming a sort of *puerta* (door). Their green, smoked-glass surfaces reflect the surrounding buildings and the Madrid skyline. For architectural experts, the Puerta de Europa is the definitive skyscraper, arguably the most important architectural motif of the 20th century. The two towers seem to defy gravity, appearing locked in conflict. They are home to hundreds of offices.

Nuevos Ministerios (44)
Plaza de San Juan de la Cruz, 28003

M *Nuevos Ministerios*

The idea of bringing together the various government ministries within a single complex was the brainchild of the Spanish Republic. The project was completed under Franco at the end of the 1940s. This may explain the incongruous existence of a monument to the socialist Minister of Public Works, Indalecio Pieto, together with a monument to the dead dictator himself.

Not forgetting

■ **Palacio de Congresos y Exposiciones (45)** Paseo de la Castellana 99, 28046 ☎ 91 337 81 00 🕐 8am–8pm *A conference center and entertainment venue. The frieze by Joan Miró was added to the façade in 1980.*
■ **Estadio Santiago Bernabéu (46)** Paseo de la Castellana 104, 28046 ☎ 91 344 00 52 *Home of the Real Madrid football club. A model of 1940s 'sports architecture'.*

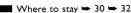

■ Where to stay ➡ 30 ➡ 32
■ Where to eat ➡ 60 ➡ 64 ■ After dark ➡ 68 ➡ 72 ➡ 80 ➡ 82 ■ Where to shop ➡ 142

Political figures of the 2nd Republic: I Pieto and F Largo Caballero.

43

42

42

45

Paradores de turismo
State-owned buildings, usually former castles, palaces
or monasteries, converted into luxury hotels. Book in
advance. *Requena 3, 28013 Madrid* ☎ *(91) 516 66 66*
➡ *(91) 516 66 57 or (91) 516 66 58*

Further afield

22
Days out

Sports and pastimes

Airships
Globos y dirigibles Boreal
☎ 91 561 39 68

Cycling
Federación Madrileña de Ciclismo
☎ 91 320 44 95

Golf
Federación de Golf
☎ 91 556 71 34

Paragliding
Hombre Pájaro
☎ 91 532 82 50

Hiking
Taller de naturaleza Las Acacias
☎ 91 465 45 99

Bungee jumping
Sport Adrenalin
☎ 91 365 19 23

Horseback-riding
Individual lessons, courses and rides.
Posta de Corpes
Cañada de "El Arenal" - Cadalsos de los Vidrios
(Par la C-501, carretera Plasencia)
☎ 91 861 14 16
● 2200 Ptas for 1 hour

Skiing
Navacerrada, Valcotos and Valdesqui are the three ski resorts closest to Madrid.
Information:
ATUDEM
(Asociación Turística de Estaciones de Esquí y Montaña)
☎ 91 359 15 57

Basic facts

San Lorenzo del Escorial, Aranjuez and Alcalá de Henares
are part of the Comunidad de Madrid, one of Spain's 15
autonomous local authorities. Segovia and Toledo belong
to Castilla y León and Castilla-La Mancha respectively.

➡ Further afield

Segovia (13–17)

56 miles
northwest of
Madrid
🚆 C-8b train,
from Atocha or
Chamartín Stations
journey time
1 hr 49 mins
● One-way ticket
750 Ptas
🚌 La Sepulvedana
from Patio de la
Florida 11, 28003
☎ 91 530 48 00
Journey time
1 hr 30 mins
● One-way ticket
765 Ptas
🚗 N–VI and
N–603
If you have time,
leave the N–VI
at Collado Villalba
and take the
C–601 across the
Sierra to Puerto
de Navacerrada
➡ 111, a busy
ski resort, and
down to Valsaín
and Granja de
San Ildefonso.
Tourist office
Plaza Mayor 10,
40001
☎ 921 46 03 34

San Lorenzo de El Escorial (5–8)

31 miles
northwest of
Madrid
🚆 C-8a train
from Atocha or
Chamartín Stations
Journey time 50
mins ● One-way
ticket 430 Ptas
🚌 Herranz from
La Moncloa
☎ (91) 890 41 00
Journey time 1 hr
● One-way ticket
380 Ptas 🚗 N–VI
and M–505
Tourist office
Florida Blanca 10,
28200
☎ 91 890 15 54

Toledo (18–22)

44 miles south of
Madrid
🚆 C-3 train from
Atocha Station
Journey time
1 hr 15 mins
● One-way ticket
615 Ptas
🚌 From Estación
Sur, Méndez
Álvaro, 28045
☎ 91 527 29 61
Journey time
1 hr 30 mins
● One-way ticket
570 Ptas
🚗 N–401 Park
by the city walls
Tourist office
Puerta Visagra,
45003
☎ 925 22 08 43

Alcalá de Henares (1–4)

20 miles northeast of Madrid

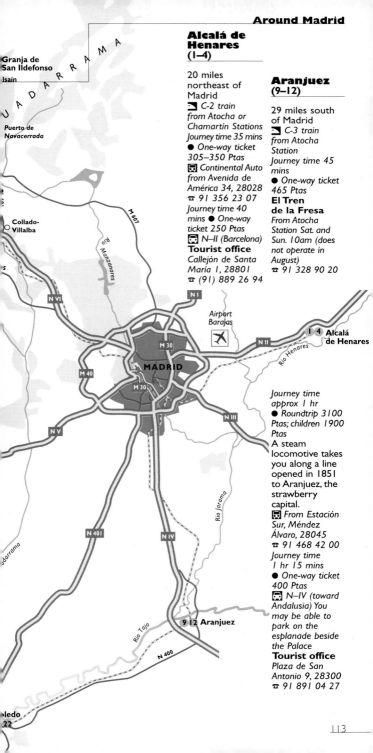 C-2 train from Atocha or Chamartín Stations Journey time 35 mins
● One-way ticket 305–350 Ptas
🚌 Continental Auto from Avenida de América 34, 28028 ☎ 91 356 23 07 Journey time 40 mins ● One-way ticket 250 Ptas
🚗 N–II (Barcelona)
Tourist office
Callejón de Santa María 1, 28801 ☎ (91) 889 26 94

Aranjuez (9–12)

29 miles south of Madrid
 C-3 train from Atocha Station Journey time 45 mins
● One-way ticket 465 Ptas
El Tren de la Fresa
From Atocha Station Sat. and Sun. 10am (does not operate in August)
☎ 91 328 90 20

Journey time approx 1 hr
● Roundtrip 3100 Ptas; children 1900 Ptas
A steam locomotive takes you along a line opened in 1851 to Aranjuez, the strawberry capital.
🚌 From Estación Sur, Méndez Álvaro, 28045 ☎ 91 468 42 00 Journey time 1 hr 15 mins
● One-way ticket 400 Ptas
🚗 N–IV (toward Andalusia) You may be able to park on the esplanade beside the Palace
Tourist office
Plaza de San Antonio 9, 28300 ☎ 91 891 04 27

Granja de San Ildefonso
Isaín

Puerto de Navacerrada

Collado-Villalba

Airport Barajas

MADRID

1 4 Alcalá de Henares

9 12 Aranjuez

•ledo
22

113

In the area

Once an important Roman city, in the Middle Ages, Alcalá became an Arab market town rivaling that of Toledo ➡ 122. The old streets and 14th-century walls remain, as does the Castilian-style Plaza Mayor. The medieval and Renaissance nucleus has been declared a historic monument.

Further afield

Universidad Complutense (1)

Founded by Cardinal Cisneros in 1495, the Universidad Complutense (*Complutum* was the Roman name of the city) formed the cultural hub of the town. The university consisted of 'major' and 'minor' colleges, together with numerous convents and churches. Among the students were humanists, politicians and great theologians such as Quevedo, Francisco Suárez and Saint Ignatius Loyola. Miguel de Cervantes – the famous author of *Don Quixote* – was born here in 1547. In 1561 Philip II transferred the capital to Madrid, though the town kept its university status until 1836, when the Complutense was moved to Madrid, causing Alcalá to slide into decline.

Colegio de San Ildefonso (2)
Plaza de Santo Domingo, 28801 ☎ 91 885 40 00

🕐 *daily 10am–6pm* ● *free* 🖼 ☎ *91 882 13 54 15* ● *300 Ptas* 🚻

Of the original building, only the Mudéjar amphitheater, with its fine coffered ceiling and plateresque rostrum, survives. The College façade is one of the purest examples of the plateresque style, so-called because its intricacy resembles worked silver (*platero* means silversmith). It was built in 1537 to a design by Rodrigo Gil de Hontañón, architect of the Cathedral of Segovia ➡ 120. Only two of the three great cloisters survive: the Baroque-style *Patio de Santo Tomás de Villanueva*, and the *Patio Trilingüe*, built in Italian Renaissance style.

Iglesia Magistral (3)
Plaza de los Santos Niños, 28801

🕐 *Mass 9.15am, 12.15pm, 6pm, 8pm*

The Iglesia Magistral was erected at the beginning of the 16th century in a style inspired by the Cathedral of Toledo ➡ 122. It contains the tomb of the great Baroque sculptor Gregorio Fernández and an altarpiece by Felipe Vigarny, dating from the early 16th century.

Convento de San Bernardo (4)
Plaza de las Bernardas, 28801 ☎ 91 888 11 22

🕐 *Church daily* 🖼 *daily ☎ 91 882 13 54 15* ● *Museum 300 Ptas;* *Church free* 🚻

Founded in 1618, this was the work of Juan Gómez de Mora. Oval-shaped in plan, it contains six chapels, the principal one housing an altarpiece in the form of an architectural canopy. This church, the Archbishop's Palace and the Madre de Dios convent are all part of the same complex.

Not forgetting

■ **Teatro Cervantes** Cervantes, 28801 ☎ 91 882 24 97 *One of the oldest classical theaters in Spain.* ■ **Convento de San Diego** Beatas 7, 28801 ☎ 91 888 03 05 *The famous garrapiñadas (caramelized almonds) are prepared by the nuns.* ■ **La Hostería del Estudiante** Colegios 3, 28801 ☎ 91 888 03 30 *Castilian cuisine. On public holidays, taste the famous migas con chocolate (fried bread dabbed with chocolate) – perfect with morning coffee.*

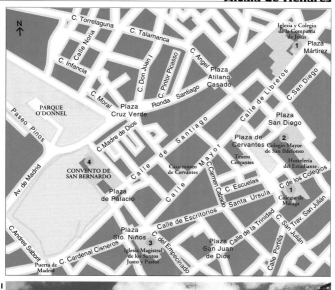

Iglesia y Colegio de la Compañía de Jesús **1** Plaza Mártirez

C. Torrelaguna

C. Talamanca

Calle Noria

C. Infancia

C. Don Juan I

C. Pintor Picasso

C. Angel

Plaza Atilano Casado

C. Moral

Ronda Santiago

Calle de Libreros

C. San Diego

PARQUE O'DONNEL

Paseo Pinos

Plaza Cruz Verde

C. Madre de Dios

Calle de Santiago

Plaza San Diego

Plaza de Cervantes

Colegio Mayor de San Ildefonso **2**

Teatro Cervantes

Hostelería del Estudiante

Av. de Madrid

4 CONVENTO DE SAN BERNARDO

Casa-museo de Cervantes

Calle Mayor

C. Carmen Calzado

C. Escuelas

Santa Úrsula

C de los Colegios

Plaza de Palacio

1 Colegio de Málaga

Calle de Escritorios

C. Andres Saborit

Plaza Sto. Niños

C. del Empecinado

C. Cardenal Cisneros

Iglesia Magistral de los Santos Justo y Pastor **3**

Puerta de Madrid

Plaza San Juan de Dios

Calle de la Trinidad

C San Julián

C San Trav. San Julián

Calle Portilla

Statue of Cervantes (left) and a square named after him.

In the area

The town here grew up around the monastery and palace complex commissioned by Philip II and completed in 1584. Set in the gardens of the park is the Casita del Príncipe, a tiny neoclassical palace designed by Juan de Villanueva, architect of the Prado Museum ➡ 96.

 **Further afield**

Monasterio de San Lorenzo (5)

Paseo Juan de Borbón, 28200
☎ **(91) 890 59 03**

🕐 *Summer:Tue.–Sun. 10am–7pm; winter / Tue.–Sun. 10am–6pm* ● *850 Ptas; over-65s, students 350 Ptas;Wed. children free* 🚻 🏛 🍴 💺 🏤

King Philip II had this monastery built to commemorate the Spanish victory over the French at the Battle of San Quintín in 1557. San Lorenzo was to serve also as a pantheon for the king's father, Charles I of Spain, and for future Spanish monarchs. In 1563 Philip II commissioned a design from Juan Bautista de Toledo, who had worked in Rome with Michelangelo. Work continued under Juan de Herrera, San Lorenzo's true creator, with the involvement of the king himself. The result was dubbed 'the eighth wonder of the world'. The structure is impressive and austere, reflecting the personality of the king, who was the supreme defender of Counter-Reformation ideas. The building forms an immense rectangle. Its long façade runs 680 feet, with four patios and represents the martyrdom of Saint Laurence (he was roasted to death on a gridiron). A Flemish-style pinnacle tower rises from each of its four corners. A statue of San Lorenzo and the Hapsburg coat of arms are the only ornamentation on its main face.

The library (6)

The library, clad in precious wood, is one of the highlights of the visit. The barrel-vaulted ceiling is decorated with allegorical figures representing the Seven Liberal Arts (Grammar, Rhetoric, Logic, Arithmetic, Music, Geometry and Astronomy). The bookshelves include fine reproductions of the first Castilian texts, a Mozarabic codex dating from the 10th century, the breviaries of the Catholic Monarchs and of Philip II, and numerous illuminated miniatures.

Basílica (7)

The basilica's 295-foot high cupola contains the Capilla Mayor (Great Chapel), which features a remarkable Renaissance altarpiece made of marble and porphyry. Note the sculptural groups, the work of Leone and Pompeyo Leoni, on either side of the presbytery, one representing the Emperor and his family at prayer, the other Philip II and his family at prayer.

Philip II's chambers (8)

These two simple rooms are surprisingly understated in comparison with the rest of the building. The bedroom has a balcony overlooking the Capilla Mayor, so that the king could hear Mass from his bed. The floor is covered with 16th-century Talavera tiles.

Not forgetting

■ **Fonda Genara** Plaza de San Lorenzo 2, 28200 ☎ 91 890 33 30 *Home cooking. Specialty:* puchero *(stew) de Luisa. Unusual décor.*

C. del Calvario
C. de San Antón
C. Juan de Toledo
C. del Infante
Calle del Rey
Carretera de la Estación

Fonda Genara
Comedia Nueva
Plaza Constitución
Plaza Virgen de Gracia

APTS. DE PHILIPPE II
LIBRARY
6
7
8
BASILICA
5
MONASTERY

PARQUE DE LA CASITA DEL PRÍNCIPE

Casita del Príncipe

N

6

5

5

In the area

A fine example of a royal town, now a historic monument. At the end of the 15th century the Catholic Monarchs made it their *Real Sitio* (royal site). In the 16th century, Philip II built a new palace here. Philip V made this the Court's summer residence at the start of the 18th century.

Further afield

The town (9)

The plans for the town were drawn up in 1747 by Ferdinand VI and Italian architect Bonavia. The streets were laid out in Baroque style, on a grid plan, with grand avenues converging on the palace. It was here that the Court witnessed some of the most momentous events in Spanish history, such as the *motín* (riot) of Aranjuez in 1808 – the conspiracy which paved the way for the Napoleonic invasion. The buildings are well preserved, and include a number of three- and four-storey houses dating from the 18th and 19th centuries with gardens and courtyards. The residences of the *oficios y caballeros* on Plaza de San Antonio, the palace of the Dukes of Medinaceli (now a restaurant), the hospital of San Carlos and the Convento de San Pascual are all worth seeing.

Palacio Real (10)
Avenida del Palacio Real ☎ 91 891 13 44

🕐 *June–Sep.: Tue.–Sun. 10am–6.30pm; / Oct.–May: Tue.–Sun. 10am–5.30pm* ● *500 Ptas; over-65s, students, children 250 Ptas, Wed. free* 🔲 🔲

The main body of the palace, in the fashionable Baroque style of the 18th century, was enlarged by the addition of two neoclassical wings, designed by Sabatini, which flank the Plaza Armería. ★ Do not miss the Porcelain Room.

Jardín de la Isla (11)
Behind the palace

🕐 *Tue.–Sun. 8am–8.30pm* ● *free*

A superb series of promenades modeled on Versailles. The paths and formal walks are punctuated by monumental fountains, arbors and magnificent trees, and cooled by the Tajo (Tagus) river.

Jardín del Príncipe (12)
Reina, toward la Casa del Labrador

🕐 *Gardens Tue.–Sun. 8am–8.30pm* ● *free Casa del Labrador 10am–6.15pm* ● *425 Ptas; over-65s, students, children 225 Ptas* 🔲 *Casa de Los Marinos 10am–6.15pm* ● *325 Ptas, over-65s, students, children 225 Ptas*

A garden laid out for the young Charles IV (1788–1808). Planted with a rich variety of trees, the garden covers almost 400 acres and is the perfect setting for a stroll. The Empire-style Casa del Labrador was formerly a Bourbon hunting lodge, and is well worth visiting for its collection of clocks. The Casa de Marinos is now a boating museum where Court barges are displayed.

Not forgetting

■ **Casa Pablo** Almíbar 42, 28300 ☎ 91 891 14 51 *Specialties: pheasant, suckling pig, lamb, seafood.* ■ **La Rana Verde** Reina 1, 28300 ☎ 91 891 32 38 *The dining rooms and terraces are worth a visit, but for the view over the Tajo rather than for the food.* ■ **El Bodegón** Gobernador 62, 28300 ☎ 91 892 51 73 *Occupies the old brick wine cellars and stables of the Medinaceli palace. Suckling pig and lamb roasted over a wood fire.*

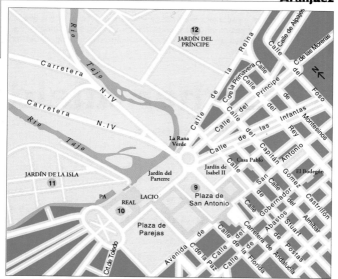

Río Tajo

Carretera N.IV

Carretera N.IV

Río Tajo

JARDÍN DE LA ISLA
11

PA
REAL
10

LACIO

Plaza de
Parejas

Jardín del
Parterre

Jardín de
Isabel II

9
Plaza de
San Antonio

La Rana
Verde

Casa Pablo

El Bodegón

12
JARDÍN DEL
PRÍNCIPE

Reina

Calle de la

C. de la Primavera

Calle del Príncipe

Calle del

Calle de las Infantas

Rey

Montesinos

Capitán Antonio

San Calle Gómez

Gobernador del

Castrillón

Abastos

Stuart

Almíbar

Carretera de Andalucía

de Postas

Crt. de Toledo

Avenida C. de la Paz

Calle del

Calle de la

de la Florida

Calle

Calle de la

Calle de

Calle

Calle

Calle

Foso

C. de las Moreras

Calle de Abapiés

N

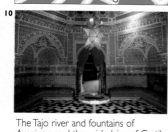

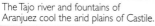

The Tajo river and fountains of
Aranjuez cool the arid plains of Castile.

In the area

This historic town, now a world heritage site, is perched on a granite rock between the Eresma and Clamores rivers. Originally a Roman settlement, it became a major center of textile and livestock production during the Middle Ages.

Further afield

The aqueduct (13)
Plaza del Azoguejo

The aqueduct is Segovia's most famous monument, and the best preserved building of the Western Roman Empire. Bringing water from 8 miles away to the Plaza del Azoguejo, where it reaches a height of 92 feet, it dates from the 2nd century AD, and is made of granite blocks joined together without the aid of mortar.

Plaza de San Martín (14)

🕐 *Keep* times vary **Church** Mass 11.30am, 12.30pm, 9pm

Site of the Romanesque church of San Martín. The Lozoya tower is a splendid example of a 14th-century fortified residence. A fine group is formed by the Renaissance-style Bornes Palace, the house known as the '15th-century house' and the Library.

The Cathedral (15)
Plaza Mayor, 40006 ☎ 921 46 22 05

🕐 *Museum and cloisters* daily 9.30am–7pm ● 250 Ptas 🔲

Begun in 1525, this is the last of the great Gothic cathedrals in Spain. Perched at the highest point of the town, the three naves above the altar rise to 108 feet. Between the cathedral and the Alcázar, do not miss one of the eighteen Romanesque churches of Segovia, San Esteban, with its elegant, tapering tower.

El Alcázar (16)
Plaza de la Reina Victoria Eugenia, 40003 ☎ 921 46 07 59

🕐 *Spring–summer: daily 10am–7pm; autumn–winter: daily 10am–6pm* ● *375 Ptas, children 175 Ptas* 🔲 🔲 🔲

In the 15th century Isabella the Catholic's father decided to erect a palace over a 12th-century tower. The Disney-style castle, all towers and turrets, now houses a military museum.

Iglesia de la Vera Cruz (17)
Carretera de Zamarramala ☎ 921 43 14 75

🕐 *Apr.–Sep.: Tue.–Sat. 10.30am–1.30pm, 3.30–7pm / Oct.–Mar.: Tue.–Sun. 10.30am–1.30pm, 3.30–6pm* ● *175 Ptas* 🔲 🔲

Built on a dodecagonal (twelve-sided) plan, this beautiful church belonging to the Knights Templar is well worth a visit. Its bell tower offers a breathtaking view over the town and the Alcázar.

Not forgetting

■ **Mesón Casa Cándido** Plaza del Azoguejo 5, 40001 ☎ 921 42 51 03
A renowned restaurant overlooking the aqueduct. Specialties include milk-fed lamb and pork.

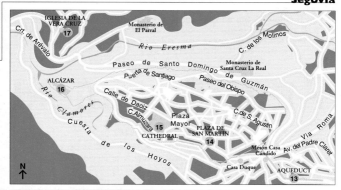

IGLESIA DE LA VERA CRUZ **17**

Monasterio de El Parral

Rio Eresma

Monasterio de Santa Cruz La Real

Paseo de Santo Domingo de Guzmán

Crt. de Arévalo

Puerta de Santiago

Paseo del Obispo

ALCÁZAR **16**

Rio Clamores

Calle de Daoiz

C.Almuzara

C.de S. Agustín

Via Roma

Plaza Mayor

PLAZA DE SAN MARTÍN

15 CATHEDRAL

14

Cuesta de los Hoyos

Mesón Casa Cándido

Av. del Padre Claret

Casa Duque

AQUEDUCT **13**

N

13

The 128 pillars and 163 arches of the Roman aqueduct carried water to Segovia up until 1988.

16

14

In the area

In 554 Toledo was the political and religious capital of Spain, and later became the seat of important councils. It was also a Moorish town. For some five centuries the three great cultures of the Iberian Peninsula – Muslim, Christian and Jewish – merged here.

Further afield

The Old Town (18)

Renowned for its damascenes (intricate, water-like inlays on steel) ➡ 134, Toledo has preserved its maze of medieval streets. The medieval Alcázar and Great Mosque were incorporated into a castle and cathedral, but the 16th-century Puerta de Bisagra and 12th–14th century Puerta del Sol at the entrance to the town can still be seen, as can the San Martín and Alcántara bridges, and the Moorish baths.

The cathedral (19)
Arco de Palacio 2, 45001 ☎ 925 22 22 41

🕐 *Oct 1–Apr. 30: Mon.–Sat. 10.30am–1pm, 3.30–6pm, Sun. 10.30am–1.30pm, 4–7pm / May 1–Sep. 30: Mon.–Sat. 10.30am–1pm, 3.30–7pm, Sun. 10.30am–1.30pm, 4–7pm* ● *500 Ptas* ▣ 🏛

The cathedral was begun in 1227 and completed in 1493. Its interior reveals various styles – note the Flamboyant Gothic high altar and the Renaissance choir and stalls. Worth seeing are the *Transparente* (screen) by Narciso Tomé, and the museum, which features works by El Greco and Van Dyck.

Santa María la Blanca (20)
Reyes Católicos 2, 45002 ☎ 925 22 72 57

🕐 *Oct. 1–Apr. 30: daily 10am–1.45pm, 3.30–6.45pm / May 1–Sep. 30: daily 10am–1.45pm, 3.30–5.45pm* ● *150 Ptas* ▣ 🏛

This stunning five-aisled Almohad – style synagogue dating from the 12th century was transformed into a church in the 15th century. The original horseshoe arches and interlaced decoration have been retained. Very pretty small garden at the entrance.

Iglesia de Santo Tomé (21)
Plaza del Conde 1, 45002 ☎ 925 25 60 98

🕐 *daily 10am–6.45pm* ● *150 Ptas*

A 14th-century church with a Mudéjar tower, and El Greco's *Burial of the Count of Orgaz* (1586), painted specifically for the church.

Mezquita del Cristo de la Luz (22)

🔲 *If you can find the person with the keys…*

A tiny mosque completed in 999, as testified by the Kufic inscription. The only entirely Moorish monument in the town, it was built in the Caliph style, with Visigothic columns and horseshoe arches.

Not forgetting

■ **Parador Nacional de Turismo Conde de Orgaz** Paseo los Cigarales, 45002 ☎ 925 22 18 50 *Splendid views over the town. Cuisine from La Mancha.* ■ **Casa Aurelio** Sinagoga 6, 45001 ☎ 925 22 20 97 *Castilian cuisine.* ■ **Asador Adolfo** Granada 5, 45001 ☎ 925 22 73 21 *Traditional cooking meets nouvelle cuisine.*

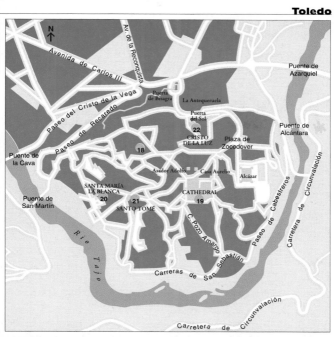

Where to shop

Where to shop
Look for luxury goods in the Salamanca distinct;
jewelry in Calle Serrano and Gran Vía; fashion in Calle
Almirante; traditional Spanish styles around the Puerta
del Sol; department stores on Calle Serrano, Goya and
Preciados.

Sales
Rebajas de temporada – seasonal sales
– are held twice a year: January–
February and July–August.

What to bring back

A torero's costume, a flamenco dress, castanets, a mantilla, a Spanish hairnet and a fan; a string of *Majorica* pearls and a piece of damascene work from Toledo; leather or a Real Madrid jersey; a fashionable handbag or shoes; olive oil, *jamón Serrano* and *turrón*.

60 Shops

THE INSIDER'S FAVORITES

In the area

The main reason for visiting this part of the city is its wonderful architecture, but don't miss the stores in the center of Madrid which overflow with souvenirs. ■ Where to stay ➡ 18 ■ Where to eat ➡ 36 ➡ 38 ■ After dark ➡ 76 ➡ 78 ➡ 82 ■ What to see ➡ 92

Where to shop

El Caballo Cojo (1)
Segovia 7, 28005 ☎ 91 366 43 90

Ⓜ *Sol, Ópera* **Handicrafts, ceramics** 🕐 *Mon.–Fri. 10am–2pm, 5–8.30pm; Sat. 10am–2pm; closed August* ▭

Behind a 19th-century shop front is a magnificent array of ceramics reproduced in period styles. Particularly impressive are the blown glass objects from Mallorca in their characteristic blue, writing desks, candelabra and a collection of holy-water basins priced between 1000 Ptas and 40,000 Ptas.

Monsy (2)
Plaza Mayor 20, 28012 ☎ 91 548 15 14

Ⓜ *Sol* **Souvenirs** 🕐 *Mon.–Sat. 9.30am–1.30pm, 4.30–8pm* ▭

Lovers of kitsch will be spoilt for choice among this feast of bric-à-brac: bottles of Tío Pepe made in Jerez, bullfighters' costumes, castanets, El Cid's sword, Real Madrid merchandise ➡ 108, and damascene objects from Toledo ➡ 122.

Justo Algaba (3)
Paz 4, 28012 ☎ 91 523 35 95 ➡ 91 523 37 17

Ⓜ *Sol* **Bullfighters' costumes, flamenco-style dresses** 🕐 *Mon.–Fri. 10am– 2pm, 5–8pm; Sat. 10am–2pm* ▭

This tailor serves some of the biggest names in bullfighting ➡ 100. Behind the window protected from the sun's rays, you can buy stockings, a *montera* (bullfighter's hat) and pumps to transform yourself into the perfect *torero*. From the workshop you can order an authentic made-to-measure *traje campero* (the suit worn by bullfighters for out-of-town practise sessions) or a flamenco-style dress with all the proper accessories. Prices depend on the number of hours of work involved and the quality of the materials and embroidery.

Seseña (4)
Cruz 23, 28012 ☎ 91 531 68 40

Ⓜ *Sol* **Capes** 🕐 *Mon.–Fri. 10am–3pm, 4.30–8pm; Sat. 10am–2pm* ▭

Picasso, Hemingway and Hillary Clinton are among the many who have been unable to resist Seseña's warm, dramatic Madrid-style capes. Seseña is now the only store specializing in this romantic garment. It is worth a visit just to admire the window display. Men's capes from 60,000 Ptas.

Not forgetting

■ **Casa Yustas (5)** Plaza Mayor 30, 28012 ☎ 91 366 58 34
Every kind of headgear from military caps to the famous Andalusian headdresses.
■ **El Riojano (6)** Mayor 10, 28003 ☎ 91 366 44 82
Living up to its reputation since 1855. Worth a visit as much for the décor as for the cakes.

■ Where
to shop
➡ 144

C.Santiago

Plaza
Cte.
Morenas

Mayor

6

C.Postas

59
Plaza
Mayor

5

C.Zaragoza

Calle de Carretas

3

26

C. de la Paz

Calle Espoz y Mina

Calle de la Cruz

4

Calle

Plaza
de la
Villa

5

2

4

Plaza
Provincia

Calle
Bolsa

Plaza
Jacinto
Benavente

Calle

C.de las Huertas

4

C.del Sacramento

C.Cuchilleros

5

C. Concepción

Jerónima

de

Atocha

Calle de Segovia

C. del Nuncio

Calle

de

Toledo

Calle

Colegiata

Tirso de
Molina

M

27

C.Doctor Cortezo

C. Relatores

Almendro

Baja

2

C. de la Magdalena

34

C. del

C.Cava

C.Cava Alta

Plaza Tirso
de Molina

24

Calle de la Cabeza

2

2

4

6

6

2

4

In the area

Steeped in Spanish tradition, this is the place to buy Spanish costumes, feminine finery and traditional sweets. ■ After dark ➥ 76 ■ What to see ➥ 92 ➥ 94 ■ Where to shop ➥ 130

Where to shop

Casa Jiménez (7)
Preciados 42, 28013 ☎ 91 548 05 26

Ⓜ Callao, Santo Domingo **Shawls, mantillas** 🕒 Mon.–Sat. 10.30am–1.30pm, 5–8pm ▭

Manila shawls imported from the Philippines and mantillas of silken lace are the specialties of this store which claims to be 'the best-stocked and oldest in Spain'. For almost a century it has been selling sumptuous, hand-embroidered shawls in brilliant colors with oriental motifs. Originally worn to keep out the cold, in the 18th century they came to be regarded as fashion accessories. Now part of Spanish tradition, shawls are still very popular and are worn for special occasions. Machine-made shawls start at 5000 Ptas, top-of-the-range 40,000 Ptas.

Casa Mira (8)
Carrera de San Jerónimo 30, 28014☎ 91 429 67 96 ➠ 91 429 82 21

Ⓜ Sol, Sevilla **Turrón** 🕒 Mon.–Sat. 9.30am–2pm, 6.30–9pm, Sun. 10.30am–2.30pm, 5.30–9pm ▭

Turrón (Spanish nougat) and *mazapán* (marzipan) are top of every Spaniard's list of Christmas goodies. If you happen to be passing by during the festive season, don't be surprised to find an endless queue of *Madrileños* waiting their turn to buy the turrón and other treats made here since 1885. Try turrones from Segovia ➥ 120 or Alicante, flavored with nuts, coconut, fruit or chocolate, or guirlache, another type of nougat. About 4000 Ptas a kilo.

Casa de Diego (9)
Plaza Puerta del Sol 12, 28013 Madrid
☎ 91 522 66 43 ➠ 91 531 02 23

Ⓜ Sol **Umbrellas, fans** 🕒 Mon.–Sat. 9.45am–1.30pm, 4.30–8pm
⟨⟩ Mesonero Romanos 4, 28013 ☎ 91 521 02 23

'Tomorrow it will rain' is the motto of this old store in the Puerta del Sol ➥ 94. Since 1858 they have been selling umbrellas made in their own workshops, as well as walking sticks, sunshades, shawls, mantillas, combs and a huge range of fans, made from paper, mother-of-pearl or gold. Fans start at 350 Ptas, but expect to pay 50,000 Ptas for hand-painted ones with mother-of-pearl blades.

Not forgetting

■ **M. Gil (10)** Carrera de San Jerónimo 2, 28014 ☎ 91 521 25 49 *Established 1880: mantillas, embroidered table linen from Lagartera (Toledo region ➥ 122), traditional hairnets, embroidered shawls and typical Madrileño costumes.*
■ **Carpincho (11)** Preciados 33, 28013 ☎ 91 521 13 60 *Range of high-quality ceramics from Seville, appointed agent for Majorica pearls and Lladró porcelain.*
■ **Manuel Herrero (12)** Preciados 7–16, 28013 ☎ 91 521 29 90 *Reasonably-priced leather fashions and shoes.*
■ **La Violeta (13)** Plaza de Canalejas 6, 28014 ☎ 91 522 55 22 *This store has been selling its famous sweets, colored, flavored and shaped like violets, since 1915.*

129

Basic facts

Madrid's shopping scene is dominated by El Corte Inglés where you will find everything from fashions to food all under one roof. More appealing are the smaller shopping malls incorporating small boutiques set in bright, stylish surroundings with plenty of bars and cafés; just the thing

➡ Where to shop

El Corte Inglés (14)
Preciados 1-2-3-4, 28013 ☎ 91 379 80 00 ➡ 91 521 56 57

M *Sol Fashions, records, tapes and CDs, videos, books, toys* ○ *Mon.–Sat. 10am–9.30pm* ⊞ ▢ ⚿ *Raimundo Fernández Villaverde 79, 28003 ☎ 91 556 33 00; Princesa 42, 28008 ☎ 91 542 48 00; Goya 76, 28009 ☎ 91 577 71 71; Goya 87, 28001 ☎ 91 577 71 71; Serrano 47, 28001 ☎ 91 432 93 00*

At the turn of the century, El Corte Inglés was just a tailor's workshop on Calle Preciados, specializing in gentlemen's outfits with a distinctly 'English' cut. As the years went by, their range of products and services increased enormously and Corte Inglés stores multiplied. Now the chain offers such services as coffee shops and restaurants, beauty and hairdressing salons, tobacconists, travel agencies and supermarkets. At present, Madrid has no fewer than sixteen shopping malls and stores under the banner of El Corte Inglés, all strategically situated and offering complementary services: the branch at Goya 76 sells fashions, leather goods, jewelry, perfumes and sportswear; along the street at Goya 87, the range includes household goods, books, photographic

130

14

for those who prefer relaxed, leisurely shopping.

equipment, CDs and videos. The huge selection of goods and brands, and the efficiency and quality of its services ensure the continued success of El Corte Inglés. It is now the only store in Madrid that can truly be called a 'department store'.

Not forgetting

El Jardín de Serrano
(15) Goya 6–8, 28001
☎ 91 577 00 12
Winner of the European Design Prize in the shopping mall category. Elegant and well situated, with boutiques on two levels, a large café and a shady garden.
ABC Serrano (16) Serrano 61, 28004 ☎ 91 577 50 31
Recently opened conversion of the old ABC and Blanco y Negro newspaper offices. Four levels of stores in a bright, congenial setting. Wonderful neo-plateresque façade on the Paseo de la Castellana side.
Multicentro Serrano 88 (17) Serrano 88, 28006 ☎ 91 547 50 01
One of Madrid's very first shopping malls, containing fashion boutiques and gift stores, and a pleasant café.

14

In the area

Elegant stores and cafés, theaters and state-of-the-art movie theaters, the Gran Vía is a must for visitors. ■ Where to stay ➡ 18 ➡ 20 ■ After dark ➡ 72 ➡ 74 ■ What to see ➡ 94

➡ Where to shop

Zara (18)
Gran Vía 32, 28013 ☎ 91 522 97 27 ➡ 91 532 95 31

Ⓜ *Callao* **Men's and women's ready-to-wear** 🕐 *Mon.–Sat. 10am–8.30pm* ▣ 🚻 *Princesa 63, 28008 ☎ 91 543 24 15; Bravo Murillo 104, 28039 ☎ 91 533 10 50*

Ever since it opened, Zara has been a fashion phenomenon with dozens of branches all over Spain and in big cities around the world (including New York). The secret of their success is simple: up-to-date styles at unbeatable prices. All over Madrid, their shop windows display the latest trends in men's, women's and children's clothes, as well as shoes, handbags and other accessories.

Casa del Libro (19)
Gran Vía 29, 28013 ☎ 91 521 21 13 ➡ 91 522 77 58

Ⓜ *Gran Vía, Callao* **Books** 🕐 *Mon.–Sat. 9am–9pm* ▣ 🚻 *Maestro Victoria 3, 28013 ☎ 91 521 48 98*

Books on every imaginable subject take up the five levels of this huge store. With a permanent stock of around 500,000 volumes, it is one of Europe's biggest bookstores. Despite its size it is still a friendly place and it is easy to while away a pleasant afternoon browsing through its shelves. Casa del Libro recently opened a large foreign language section.

Cortefiel (20)
Gran Vía 27-76, 28013 ☎ 91 522 00 93 ➡ 91 522 19 99

Ⓜ *Gran Vía, Callao* **Ready-to-wear** ▣ 🕐 *Mon.–Sat. 10am–8.30pm* 🚻 *Aguileras 62, 28015 ☎ 91 543 04 05; Paseo de la Castellana 146, 28046 ☎ 91 458 29 30*

With various branches scattered around the city, this chain store has, since the early 1930s, sold reasonably-priced casual fashions in fairly classic styles. A little further along the Gran Vía (at no. 59), Springfield caters for younger, sports-minded customers.

Grassy (21)
Gran Vía 1, 28013 ☎ 91 532 10 07 ➡ 91 575 48 67

Ⓜ *Banco de España, Gran Vía* **Jewelry** 🕐 *Mon.–Fri. 9.30am–1.30pm, 4.30–8pm, Sat. 9.30am–3.30pm* ▣ 🚻 *José Ortega y Gasset 17, 28006 ☎ 91 577 94 35*

One of Madrid's oldest and most prestigious jewelry stores, with the style and atmosphere of a bygone age.

Not forgetting
■ **Aldao (22)** Gran Vía 15, 28013 ☎ 91 522 11 56
A classic among Madrid jewellers.
■ **Madrid Rock (23)** Gran Vía 25, 28013 ☎ 91 523 26 52
Music store catering for every taste, with the accompaniment of very loud Spanish rock.

21

In the area

In the neighborhood west of the Gran Vía, traditional jewellers and ceramics stores stand side-by-side with modern fashion boutiques. All of them contribute to the buzz of this cosmopolitan thoroughfare.
■ Where to stay ➡ 20 ■ Where to eat ➡ 38 ■ After dark ➡ 80

Where to shop

Antigua Casa Talavera (24)
Isabel la Católica 2, 28013 ☎ 91 547 34 17

Ⓜ *Santo Domingo* **Ceramics** 🕙 *Mon.–Fri. 10am–1.30pm, 5–8pm; Sat. 10am–1.30pm* ▣

This turn-of-the-century store is an Aladdin's cave of traditional Spanish pottery, with reproductions of pieces dating from the 10th to the 18th century. These are manufactured in family-run workshops in Talavera (a little village in the Toledo region ➡ 122), Sevilla, Puente del Arzobispo, Granada and Manises. Baptismal fonts, candelabra, tiles (on which they will engrave a proverb of your choice), decorative plates and tureens are all sold here.

Hernández (25)
Gran Vía 56, 28013 ☎ 91 547 06 54

Ⓜ *Santo Domingo, Callao* **Handicrafts, jewelry, fans** 🕙 *Mon.–Sat. 10am–1.30pm, 4.30–8.30pm* ▬

The window of this traditional store looks like any other in the neighborhood, but go in and you will discover a wonderful array of feminine finery: fans, *Majorica* pearls, costume jewelry and damascene (steel with inlaid gold) knick-knacks from Toledo ➡ 122.

Zaraúz (26)
Gran Vía 45, 28013 ☎ 91 547 17 36

Ⓜ *Santo Domingo* **Men's and women's ready-to-wear** 🕙 *Mon.–Sat. 10am–2pm, 5–8.30pm* ▬ 🚇 *Goya 7–9, 28001 ☎ 91 435 49 48*

Locals love Zaraúz for the fine quality and discreet, elegant style of its suits and sportswear. Remarkable selection of neckties, prices up to 12,000 Ptas.

Regalos Ar (27)
Gran Vía 46, 28013 ☎ 91 522 68 69 ➡ 91 531 56 47

Ⓜ *Callao* **Handicrafts, porcelain, jewelry** 🕙 *Mon.–Sat. 10am–8pm* ▬

A modern store whose window displays an endless variety of gifts and attractive souvenirs, all 'made in Spain'. These include stunning porcelain, including a famous collection of figurines by Lladró for whom Regalos Ar is an appointed agent. Equally outstanding are the *Majorica* pearls, glassware and craft items.

Not forgetting

■ **Camper (28)** Gran Vía 54, 28013 ☎ 91 547 52 23
An internationally-famous Spanish firm whose first priority is comfort. Offers a huge range of designer shoes and boots, from the classic to the trendy, with some very witty touches.
■ **Bravo Java (29)** Gran Vía 54, 28013 ☎ 91 522 22 00
Renowned for the range and quality of its shoes.

Plaza de España
Plaza de España
C.R.León
Calle G. Molinas
Trv.Parada
Gran
Vía
Calle de San Bernardo
Calle Estrella
Calle de la Madera
C. Pizarro
C. de la Luna
N
C.del Río
Calle de Legañitos
C.Isabel La Católica
12
C.Flor Alta
C. Libreros
Silva
25
28
29
Calle de Tudescos
11
Sto. Domingo
26
Gran
Vía
27
C.del Reloj
Calle de Fomento
Calle de Torija
C.G. Rolland
Calle de la Bola
24
9
30
Plaza Santo Domingo
Calle
Sto. Domingo
C. de Jacometrezo
Vía
Callao

28

24

25

Majorica pearls, made on the island of Mallorca, are the nearest thing to real and cultured pearls. It's very hard to tell the difference.

28

135

In the area

Calle Almirante was the place to be in the heady days of 1980s fashion.
It turned out to be a flash in the pan, but some talent still survives.
■ Where to stay ➡ 22 ■ Where to eat ➡ 44 ■ After dark ➡ 68
➡ 76 ➡ 78 ➡ 84 ■ What to see ➡ 104

Where to shop

Ararat (30)
Almirante 10-11, 28004 ☎ 91 531 81 56 ➡ 91 532 10 47

Ⓜ *Colón, Banco de España* **Women's ready-to-wear** Ⓞ *Mon.–Sat.*
11pm–2pm, 5–8.30pm ▭

Although the neighborhood's golden age is over, Ararat continues to be
on the pulse with its designer boutiques, including Vértigo, VMR, Rosas
Rojas and A Menos Cuarto. Evening and town wear.

Piamonte (31)
Piamonte 16, 28004 ☎ 91 522 45 80 ➡ 91 521 82 25

Ⓜ *Colón, Banco de España* **Accessories, jewelry** Ⓞ *Mon.–Sat. 10.30am–2pm,*
5–8.30pm ▭ ⓘ *Marqués del Monasterio 5, 28004* ☎ 91 308 48 62

Since the 1980s, this store has gained a strong reputation and a large
clientele. Inside, accessories for every occasion are displayed in simple,
attractive surroundings: belts, purses, gloves and a small but interesting
collection of reasonably-priced jewelry. From Piamonte's own workshops
you can order top-quality bags in leather, canvas or other materials, in
the color of your choice. Orders take ten days. Around 15000 Ptas.

Joaquín Berao (32)
Conde de Xiquena 13, 28004 ☎ 91 310 16 20

Ⓜ *Colón, Banco de España* **Jewelry** Ⓞ *Mon.–Sat. 10.30am–2pm, 5–8.30pm* ▭
ⓘ *Conde de Aranda 7, 28001* ☎ (91) 576 73 50

In the mid-Eighties, Joaquín Berao left his experimental studio and set up
this little jewelry store to sell his own creations. Since then, he has
extended his collections of men's and women's jewelry and his fame has
spread beyond the borders of Spain. His most renowned creation is the
raspa (fishbone) a flexible necklet shaped like a fishbone. Specializing in
silver jewelry, Joaquín Berao also makes pieces in painted or gilded
bronze. The cheapest items are affordable: necklaces between 9000 Ptas
and 80000 Ptas.

Not forgetting

■ **Patrimonio Comunal Olivarero (33)** Meija Lequerica 1, 28004
☎ 91 308 0505 *All the olive oils sold here are from renowned producers.*
■ **Vime (34)** Augusto Figueroa 18, 28004 ☎ 91 532 0240
There are more than a dozen shoe stores concentrated in Calle Augusto Figueroa
and the surrounding streets. Ends of lines or models used for fashion exhibitions
are offered at bargain prices. This is one of Madrid's oldest stores, selling men's
and women's shoes.
■ **María José Navarro (35)** Conde de Xiquena 9, 28004
☎ 91 523 47 98 *Off-the-peg women's city wear with an international reputation for*
quality and elegance.
■ **Almirante 23 (36)** Almirante 23, 28004 ☎ 91 308 12 02
For the collector: postcards, cameras, tin boxes, bottles, spectacles, pictures,
puzzles, lead soldiers and many more curiosities.

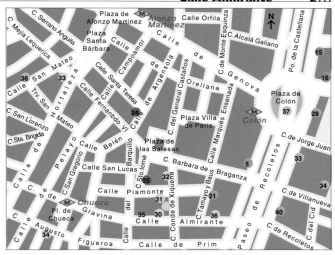

31

31

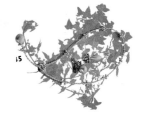

33

32

36

In the area

Some of Madrid's most stylish boutiques are in the neighborhood east of Paseo de Recoletos, behind the Biblioteca Nacional. ■ Where to stay ➡ 22 ■ Where to eat ➡ 42 ➡ 44 ➡ 46 ■ After dark ➡ 78 ➡ 84 ■ What to see ➡ 96 ➡ 104 ■ Where to shop ➡ 130 ➡ 144

Where to shop

Ispahan (37)
Serrano 5, 28001 ☎ 91 575 20 12 ➡ 91 577 76 41

Ⓜ *Retiro* **Carpets** 🕐 *Mon.–Sat. 10am–2pm, 4.30–8.30pm* ▣

This carpet store is worth a detour both for its stock and for the building, which underwent major renovations in order to provide space for an antiques center, designers and galleries. Ispahan has now taken over the entire space to display tapestries and Persian, Turkish, Chinese, Tibetan and Caucasian carpets, as well as reproductions of 15th- and 16th-century Spanish cartoons.

Farrutx (38)
Serrano 7, 28001 ☎ 91 576 94 93 ➡ 91 576 34 08

Ⓜ *Serrano, Retiro* **Shoes, handbags** 🕐 *Mon.–Sat. 10am–2pm, 5–8pm* ▣

This highly prestigious Spanish shoe manufacturer, famed for its original, elegant style, is a leader in its field for quality and design.

Adolfo Domínguez (39)
Serrano 18, 28001 ☎ 91 576 70 53

Ⓜ *Serrano Rubén Dario* **Ready-to-wear for men and women** 🕐 *Mon.–Sat. 10am–2pm, 5–8pm* ▣ 🏠 *Serrano 96 ☎ 91 576 80 51*

Simple lines, comfort and sophistication, harmonious colors and natural fabrics characterize the clothes created by this designer who became famous in the 1980s for his motto 'pleats are beautiful'. Adolfo Domínguez has since gained international renown and his beautiful sinuous creations appear in boutiques around the world.

Loewe (40)
Serrano 26, 28001 ☎ 91 577 60 56

Ⓜ *Serrano* **Accessories, ready-to-wear** 🕐 *Mon.–Sat. 9.30am–2pm, 4.30–8.30pm* ▣ 🏠 *Gran Via 8, 23013 ☎ 91 522 68 15*

Loewe specializes in leather, carefully selecting and treating the raw material to produce genuine works of art. As well as leather clothes, there are interesting silk scarves and neckties. Everything here is 'deluxe' – including the prices.

Not forgetting

■ **La Pajarita (41)** Villanueva 14, 28001 ☎ 91 435 74 54
Madrid's other famous traditional candy store ➡ 128. Candy in sixteen different flavors.
■ **Roberto Verino (42)** Claudio Coello 27, 28001 ☎ 91 577 73 81
Talented designer of women's ready-to-wear fashions who emerged in the 1980s.
■ **El Callejón de Jorge Juan (43)** Jorge Juan 14, 28001
Little cul-de-sac with charming boutiques, away from the hustle and bustle of the city. In 1994, the city fathers awarded the tiny street a special prize for its contribution to the environment.

150 ANIVERSARIO

LOEWE
Madrid 1846
150 ANIVERSARIO

40

40

ROBERTO VERINO

42

40

42

38

In the area

Salamanca is the place to go for luxury goods and modern Spanish and international fashion. Its style complements the neighborhood's majestic architecture. ■ Where to stay ➡ 22 ➡ 24 ■ Where to eat ➡ 44 ➡ 46 ➡ 50 ■ After dark ➡ 72 ➡ 78 ■ What to see ➡ 104

Where to shop

Artespaña (44)
Hermosilla 14, 28001 ☎ 91 435 02 21 ➡ 91 575 34 55

Ⓜ *Serrano* **Handicrafts** 🕒 *Mon.–Sat. 10.15am–2pm, 5–8.30pm* ▣

In this magnificent store, the national handicrafts organization offers a selection of furniture, accessories, fabrics and decorative items from Spain's finest craftspeople. Vases, tapestries and household linen are among the things that you can admire or buy here.

Del Pino (45)
Serrano 48, 28001 ☎ 91 435 26 70 ➡ 91 431 86 42

Ⓜ *Serrano* **Jewelry** 🕒 *Mon.–Sat. 10am–2pm, 5–8.30pm* ▣

A vast but well-chosen range of jewelry, in the latest shapes, colors and materials. The treasures displayed on the shelves and in the windows are hard to resist.

Elena Benarroch (46)
José Ortega y Gasset 14, 28006 ☎ 91 435 51 44 ➡ 91 431 49 60

Ⓜ *Núñez de Balboa* **Furs** 🕒 *Mon.–Sat. 10am–2pm, 4.30–8pm* ▣

After devoting seventeen years to revolutionizing fur design, Elena Benarroch turned her attentions to her firm's vast window, which she intended to be 'a place where people stop rather than simply pass by'. She achieved her objective. A spectacular Murano glass chandelier illuminates a space dedicated to sophisticated design. Luxury items carrying the best international labels are tastefully displayed. The selection extends from mink coats to sable rugs, through handmade Santa María Novella soaps, cashmere coats from Loro Plana, Philip Treacy hats, and shoes and bags from Bottega Veneta. Our advice: take time to soak up the atmosphere.

El Caballo (47)
Lagasca 55, 28001 ☎ 91 576 40 37 ➡ 91 578 08 80

Ⓜ *Serrano* **Saddlery and riding habits** 🕒 *Mon.–Fri. 10am–2pm, 5–8.30pm; Sat. 10.15am–2pm, 5–8pm* ▣

Bags, suitcases, belts, boots, walking shoes, saddles, riding accessories – the store offers an endless selection of leather goods of the highest quality, and a huge array of articles and clothes whose shape and motifs are inspired by Andalusian style. Everything on sale is manufactured in Seville, where the first El Caballo workshop was founded in 1892.

Not forgetting

■ **Santa (48)** Serrano 56, 28001 ☎ 91 576 86 46 *Luxurious Madrid chocolate manufacturer. A feast for the eyes as well as the taste buds.*
■ **¡ Oh ! Qué Luna (49)** Ayala 32, 28001 ☎ 91 431 37 25 *Nightwear for all the family. A lovely, original selection of lingerie and a new line in household linen..*

■ **Where to shop** ➡ 130 ➡ 144

Elena Benarroch's ventures demonstrate an intelligent and courageous creative talent.

In the area
This is the most modern part of Madrid, where you will find lots of
lively, practical shopping complexes. ■ Where to stay ➡ 30 ➡ 32
■ Where to eat ➡ 58 ■ After dark ➡ 68 ➡ 72 ➡ 74 ■ What to
see ➡ 108

Where to shop

Musgo (50)
Paseo de La Habana 34, 28036 ☎ / ➡ **91 562 86 24**

Ⓜ Santiago, Bernabéu **Gifts** 🕒 Mon.–Sat. 10.15am–2.15pm, 5–8.30pm
▨ 🚇 Hermosilla 34, 28001 ☎ 91 431 55 10 ; Serrano 18, 28001
☎ 91 575 33 50

What used to be a little gift store has become, twenty years later, a
mighty chain with outlets all around the city. The shop windows are
stunning at Christmas, when Musgo uses every trick in the book to
attract customers. This store specializes in clothes, leather accessories,
costume jewelry, watches, ornaments and practical household goods,
including small items of furniture. There is also a recently-opened
department selling children's and babies' clothes.

Massimo Dutti (51)
Paseo de La Habana 40, 28036 ☎ **91 563 93 22**

Ⓜ Santiago, Bernabéu **Men's and women's ready-to-wear** 🕒 Mon.–Sat.
10am–8.30pm ▨ 🚇 Velázquez 46, 28001 ☎ 91 431 77 90

In the early 1980s a young entrepreneur revolutionized menswear stores
by offering vast numbers of shirts in different styles but at the same price.
It was a complete success and the numerous stores in the chain now offer
even greater variety while sticking to the same principle. Today, Massimo
Dutti dresses men from head to toe in quality garments at reasonable
prices. Women, too, can now buy practical, comfortable clothes here for
every occasion.

Coronel Tapiocca (52)
Paseo de La Habana 52, 28036 ☎ **91 562 64 68** ➡ **91 563 37 40**

Ⓜ Santiago, Bernabéu, Concha Espina **Fashions, sportswear and outdoor gear**
🕒 Mon.–Sat. 10am–2pm, 5–8.30pm ▨ 🚇 Serrano 81, 28006 ☎ 91 563 22 21;
Genova 23, 28004 ☎ 91 308 29 08

Clothing and accessories for intrepid adventurers and urban explorers;
all-purpose boots, flasks, mountaineers' hats, rucksacks, compasses,
leather and linen bomber jackets, pocket flashlights and sweaters.
Coronel Tapioca also stocks comfortable and inexpensive casual styles
to wear around town.

Not forgetting
■ **Moda Shopping (53)** Avenida General Perón 40, 28020
☎ 91 581 15 25 *Large shopping mall with more than seventy stores under
one glass roof.*
■ **Todo Real Madrid (54)** La Esquina del Bernabéu, Avenida Concha
Espina 1, 28036 ☎ 91 458 69 25 *On the top floor of this shopping mall, a
boutique exclusively devoted to the wares of Real Madrid football club* ➡ 108.
■ **Antonio Parriego (55)** La Esquina del Bernabéu, 28036
☎ 91 344 17 06 *One of the five Parriego boutiques in Madrid. Fine quality leather
shoes and accessories at reasonable prices.*

54

MODA
CENTRO COMERCIAL

TU GUIA

52

53

A mingling of main roads and quiet streets around Santiago Bernabéu, the quarter dedicated to the round ball. The developments of the stadium date from 1992, the year when Spain hosted the World Cup.

143

Set aside at least a morning to mingle with the market crowds. Here, you will capture the authentic, or *castizo* atmosphere of the city. The Rastro, most famous of the flea markets, occupies what used to be the *barrios bajos* (working-class neighborhood). The markets specializing in

➤ Where to shop

El Rastro (56)
Ribera de Curtidores and surroundings, 28005

Ⓜ *Tirso de Molina, La Latina* **Flea market** 🕙 *Sun. and public holidays from 9am*

In the 16th century, makeshift stalls crowded this neighborhood's tanneries and abattoirs. The abattoirs have now gone, but the Rastro has become a Sunday institution. The market is a fascinating insight into Madrid life for the curious visitor and has become something of a ritual for the locals. Stop and take a look at some of the objects on offer. The stalls and stores with their idiosyncratic displays are irresistible: bric-à-brac, some antiques, handicrafts, clothes, plants, animals, books, furniture, household utensils… almost anything you can imagine could turn up here. You may be lucky enough to unearth some treasure, or you may find some curiosity you simply can't resist. Courteous bartering is acceptable in the street, but it's not so welcome in the stores. While strolling along the Ribera, the nearby river bank, don't forget to look in at some of the antique galleries: Nuevas Galerías (no. 12), Galerías Ribera (no. 15), Galerías Piquer (no. 29).

Mercado de la Paz (57)
Ayala 28, 28001 ☎ 91 435 07 43

Ⓜ *Serrano* **Food** 🕙 *Mon.–Sat. 9–3pm, 5–8.30pm* ▣

In this remarkably well-organized food market selling some exceptional quality produce, you can choose a tasty souvenir from among Spain's finest and best-known gourmet delights: serrano or jabugo ham, chorizo, *lomo*, rustic cheeses, olives, fresh vegetables and fruits, or just feast your eyes and senses on the riches of this prosperous agricultural land.

56

57

58

food and second-hand books are also worth a detour. An opportunity to pick up a bargain, or waste a few pesetas.

Cuesta de Moyano (58)
Cuesta de Claudio Moyano, 28014

Ⓜ Atocha **Second-hand books** 🕐 *nearly all the stalls are open during the week; on Sundays you have to get there between about 9.30am and 2pm*

The pretty wooden stalls along the Cuesta de Moyano have recently been renovated. Shaded by the awnings and the tall trees of the botanical gardens ➡ 98, you may find rare, second-hand books, as well as new ones at bargain prices. The book market marks the beginning of one the Madrileños' favorite walks, leading to Parque del Retiro ➡ 98.

Not forgetting

■ **Mercado de Sellos y Monedas (59)** Plaza Mayor, 28012
🕐 Sun., public holidays mornings
Stamp and coin market where collectors, dealers and curious onlookers gather under the arcades of Plaza Mayor ➡ 92.
■ **Centro de Anticuarios de Lagasca (60)** Lagasca 36, 28001
Antique dealers are scattered all over the Salamanca neighborhood. Some of the best ones, but also the most expensive, operate from this center.

Finding your way

Location of the city
Latitude N. 40° 24' - Longitude W. 3° 42'
Madrid is at the heart of the Iberian
Peninsula, 400 miles from Barcelona
and 350 miles from Seville. At 2120
feet above sea level, it is also Europe's
highest capital.

City layout
Madrid is divided into 21 *Distritos Municipales*,
numbered from the center outward: 01
(Centro), 02 (Arguanzela), 03 (Retiro) etc.
Prefixed by the figure 280, the number
determines the city code. Beware: this is not
the same as a zip code (also prefixed by 280).

7 Maps

Mini street glossary

Avenida: avenue
Calle: street
Callejón: alley, cul-de-sac
Camino: way
Carretera: road
Costanilla: sloping alley
Cuesta: sloping street

Glorieta: traffic circle
Pasaje: passage
Paseo: boulevard
Plaza: square
Puerta: gate
Ronda: ring road
Travesía: way, passage

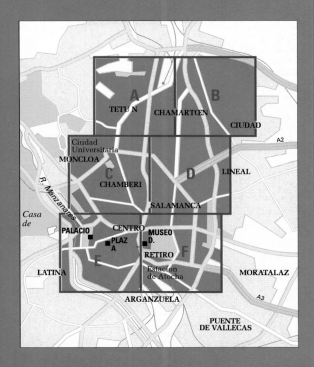

Street index

Each street name is followed by a bold letter indicating which map to refer to, and a grid reference.

Index

Luc–Ram

Abbreviations

Av.	=	Avenida	*Glr.*	=	Glorieta
C.	=	Calle	*M.*	=	Metro

Pl.	=	Plaza
Po.	=	Paseo

Subway map

◄ Metro ►

Opening hours from 6am to 1.30am

🔗 Connection to suburban trains

🔄 Connection to RENFE trains

🅿 Parking

9 Herrera Oria

Fuencar

Begoña

Barrio del Pilar

Chamart

Ventilla

Valdeacederas

1 Plaza de Castilla

Tetuán

Cuzco

Estrecho

Alvarado

Santiago Bernabéu

Guzman el Bueno

2 Cuatro Caminos

🔗 Nuevos Ministerios

Rep Arge

Metropolitano

6

Ríos Rosas

Ciudad Universitaria

Gregorio Marañón

7

Quevedo

Iglesia

Rubén Darío

3 Moncloa

San Bernardo

4 Argüelles

Ventura Rodríguez

Bilbao

Colón

Noviciado

Plaza de España

Tribunal

Alonso Martínez

🔗 R Príncipe Pío

Santo Domingo

GranVía

Chueca

de

Lago

Callao

Puerta del Angel

Sevilla

Banco de Esp

R Opera

Sol

Alto de Extremadura

La Latina

Tirso de Mo

Batán

Antón M

Puerta de Toledo

Lavapiés

At

Lucero

Acacias

Embajadores 🔗

Campamento

6

Pirámides

Palos de la Frontera

Laguna 🔗

Marqués de Vadillo

Empalme

Carpetana

Urgel

Delicias

Aluche

🅿 🔗 10 5

Oporto

Plaza Elíptica

Carabanchel

Vista Alegre

Opañel

6

Usera

Legazpi 3

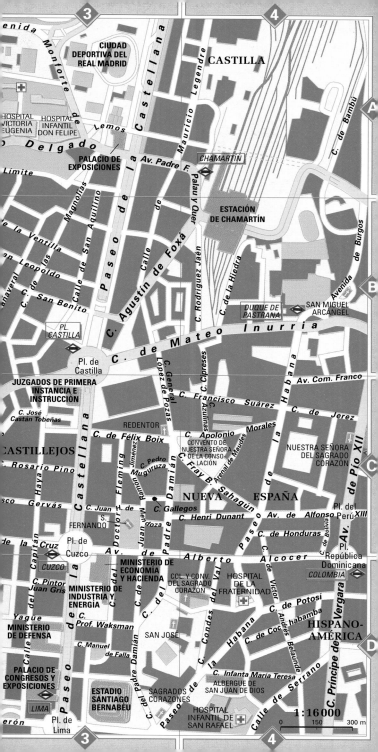

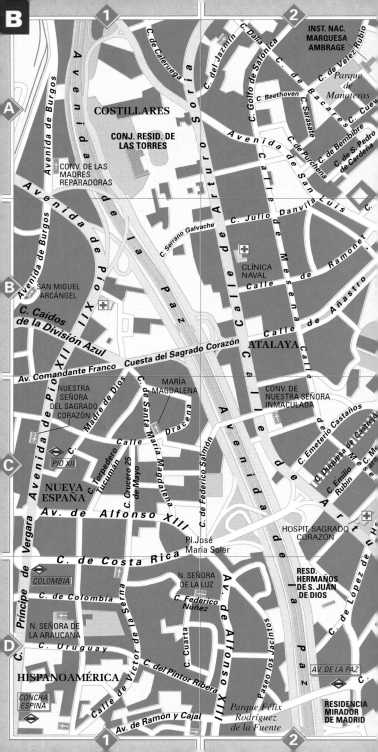

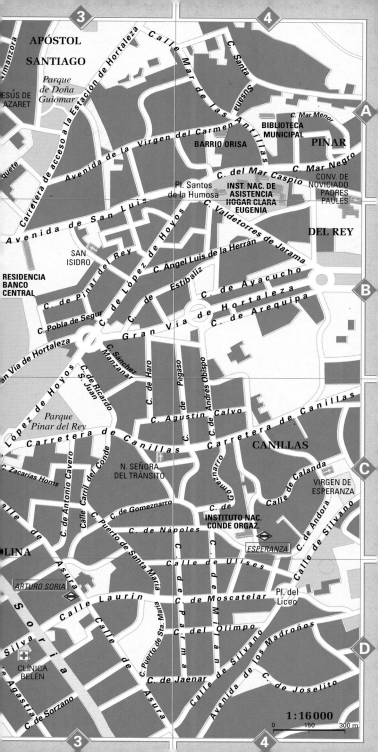

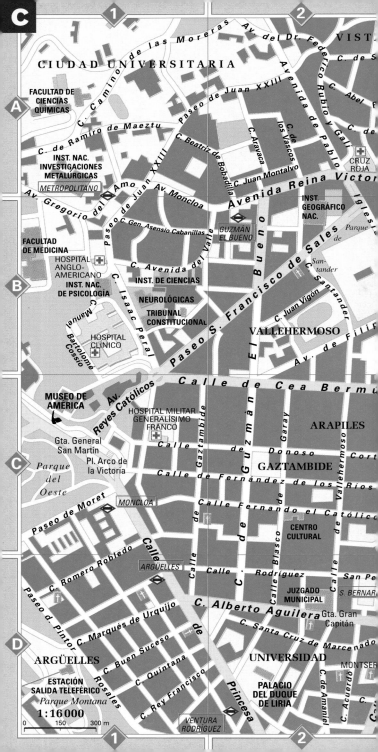

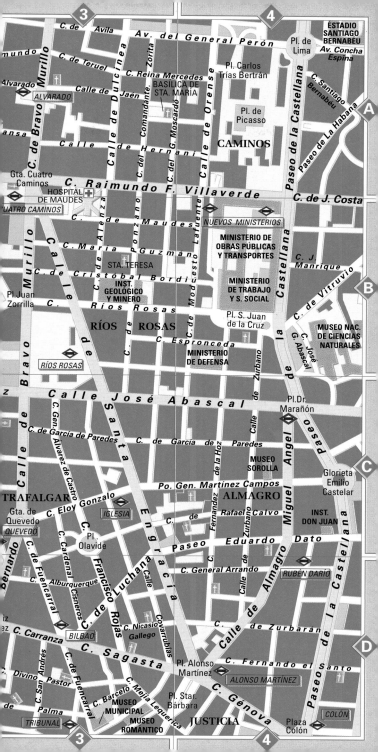

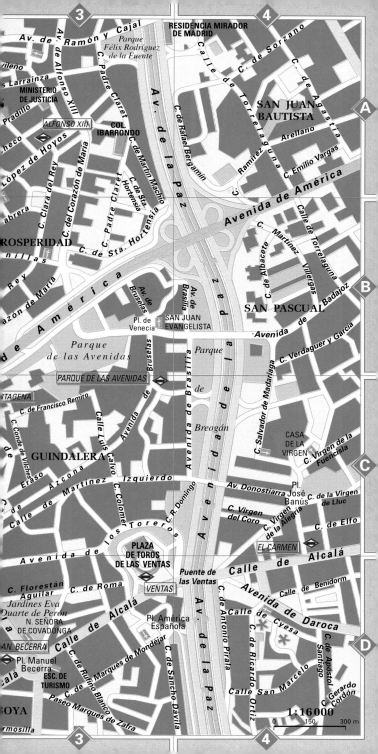

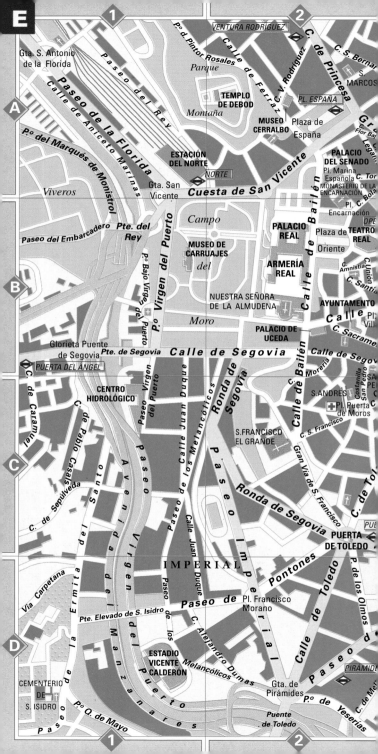

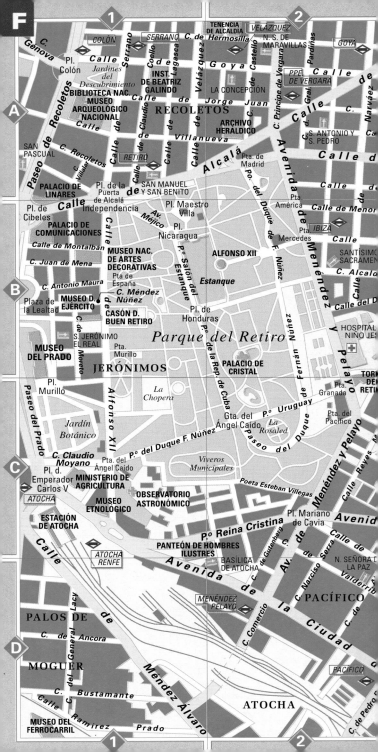

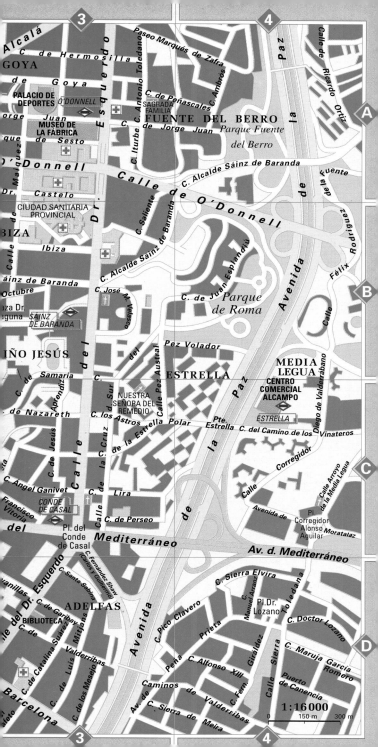

General index

See pages 6–15 for practical information about getting there, getting around, and getting by.

Index

We would like to thank the *Spanish Tourist Office* (OET), *Javier Calbet* of Acento Editorial, and all the organizations listed in the guide for their cooperation.

Picture

Credits

1 *and cover illustration Donald Grant*
6 *Vincent de Lapomarède*
8 *Kristof Chemineau (Airport map), Vincent de Lapomarède*
9 *Hotel Sofitel*
10 *RENFE (station exteriors, parking lot and trains), OET (station interior)*
12 *Vincent de Lapomarède (subway and bus), Gallimard-Éric Guillemot (subway tickets)*
14 *Gallimard-Éric Guillemot (money and newspapers)*
15 *Gallimard-Éric Guillemot (phonecards)*
16 *Vimagen Fotografos S.L.*
19 *1 Ritz,*
2 Palace,
4 Tryp Reina Victoria
21 *7 Arosa,*
8 Gaudí,
9 Imaginaria,
10 Tryp Ambassador
23
13 NH Santo Mauro,
14 NH Embajada,
15 Tryp Fenix,
16 NH Sanvy
25 *17 Villa Magna,*
18 Wellington
27
22 Guy Saint Clair,
24 Vimagen Fotografos S.L.,
25 NH Parque de las Avenidas,
27 NH Príncipe de Vergara
29 *29 Vincent de Lapomarède,*
30 Fernando Gordillo,
32 Style Escultor
31 *34 Meliá Castilla,*
37 Lola Heras,
39 Cuzco (doorman),
39 Vincent de Lapomarède (drawings)
33 *41 La Residencia de El Viso,*
42 Aristos
34 *Pedro Larumbe-Juan A. Sancho*

37 *1 Casa Lucio,*
2 Caroline Cuny,
4 De la Riva
39 *5 Botín,*
7 La Esquina del Real,
10 La Bola,
11 Cornucopia
41 *12 Viridiana,*
14 Errota -Zar,
16 Goya,
17 La Vaca Verónica
43 *18 San Carlo,*
19 Nicolás,
20 La Gamella
45 *24 Ciao Madrid,*
26 Al Mounia,
28 Pelotari
47 *29 El Amparo,*
30 La Paloma,
31 Teatriz,
32 La Trainera,
33 El Fogón
49 *35 Gargantuel,*
36 Castello 9,
37 El Pescador
51 *39 Pedro Larumbe-Juan A. Sancho,*
40 Berceo
53 *43 El Bodegón,*
44 Belagua,
45 Fdo. Sacristan
55 *47 Las Batuecas,*
49 Ana Fernandez
57 *50 O'Pazo*
51 Goizeko Kabi,
55 Alboran
59 *57 Casa Benigna,*
58 La Atalaya
61 *59 El Comité,*
60 La Tahona,
62 El Cenachero
63
64 Casa d'a Troya,
65 La Misión,
66 Nicomedes
65 *69 Aldaba,*
70 (exterior) and 72 Vincent de Lapomarède,
70 Cabo Mayor (interior),
71 Vimagen Fotografos S.L.
66 *Joy*
69 *3 Vincent de Lapomarède,*
4 Cafe de Oriente,
5 El Espejo
71 *7 Handicap,*
8 and badge Caroline Cuny,

9 Cerveceria Alemana,
10 La Daniela,
11 Las Cumbres, platter of tapas, Hotel Villa Magna
73 *12 Cock,*
13 Julio Moya,
16 Castellana 8
75 *17 Auditorio Nacional de Música,*
18 Fondation Juan March
77 *19 Teatro de Bellas Artes,*
21 Caroline Cuny,
22 Teatro Español,
23 Chicho (auditorium),
23 Vincent de Lapomarède (exterior),
23 Alberto Corazón (poster)
79 *25 Teatro de la Zarzuela,*
27 and 28 Vincent de Lapomarède
81 *29 Gallimard-Éric Guillemot (plate),*
29 Corral de la Morería (dancers),
30 Vincent de Lapomarède, castanets Hotel Villa Magna
83 *34 Gallimard-Éric Guillemot,*
35 Florida Park,
36 Vincent de Lapomarède,
37 Scala Melía
85 *39 Joy,*
41 Dusko Despotovic,
43 Palacio de Gaviria
86 *OET*
89 *OET*
91 *1 (door) and 3 Caroline Cuny,*
1 (façade, dining room) and 2 OET
93 *OET*
95 *9 (Baroque door) and 12 Caroline Cuny,*
9 OET (Metropolis building)
97
13 Museo del Prado,
14 Museo Thyssen-Bornemisza,
19 Museo del Ejército
99 *20 (building),*
21 (lake) and 22 OET,
20 Centro Cultural Reina Sofia (interior),
21 (Palacio de Cristal) and 23 Caroline Cuny
101 *26 Javier Calbet (façade),*
26 OET (bullring),
26 J. M. Navia (torero and picador)
103 *28 Museo de América,*
30 OET,
32 Caroline Cuny
105 *33 OET,*

34 Archivo Fotográfico Museo Arqueológico Nacional,
35 Museo Municipal,
37 Vincent de Lapomarède
107 *plaques,*
40 and 41 (panoramic view) Caroline Cuny,
41 Vincent de Lapomarède (sculpture)
109 *42 and 43 OET,*
44 Caroline Cuny,
45 Palacio de Congresos
110 *OET*
112 *OET*
115 *OET*
117 *OET*
121 *OET*
123 *OET*
124 *Gallimard-Javier Calbet*
127 *2 Monsy,*
4 Seseña,
6 Javier Sanz
129
7 Casa Jiménez,
8 and 10 Gallimard-Éric Guillemot,
9 and 11 Vincent de Lapomarède,
13 J. Jorge
131
14 El Corte Inglés,
16 Pedro Larumbe (façade),
16 (flags), 16 (street) and 17 Caroline Cuny
133
19 Casa del Libro,
21 Grassy
135 *24 Antigua Casa Talavera,*
25 Hernández,
28 Gallimard-Javier Calbet
137 *31 Piamonte,*
32 Joaquín Berao,
33 Patrimonio Comunal Olivarero,
36 Almirante 23
139 *38 Farrutx,*
40 Lœwe,
42 Roberto Verino
141
46 ABB Fotografos,
47 El Caballo,
48 Santa
143
52 Coronel Tapioca,
53 Moda Shopping,
54 Estudio San Simon,
145 *56 (bags),*
56 (birds), 57 and 58 Caroline Cuny,
56 Vincent de Lapomarède (umbrella and bric-à-brac)
146 *Alfonso Vargas García*